STATES OF EXCEPTION OR EXCEPTIONAL STATES

STATES OF EXCEPTION OR EXCEPTIONAL STATES

Law, Politics and Giorgio Agamben in the Middle East

Edited by
Simon Mabon, Sanaa Alsarghali and Adel Ruished

I.B. TAURIS
LONDON • NEW YORK • OXFORD • NEW DELHI • SYDNEY

I.B. TAURIS
Bloomsbury Publishing Plc
50 Bedford Square, London, WC1B 3DP, UK
1385 Broadway, New York, NY 10018, USA
29 Earlsfort Terrace, Dublin 2, Ireland

BLOOMSBURY, I.B. TAURIS and the I.B. Tauris logo are trademarks of Bloomsbury Publishing Plc

First published in Great Britain 2022
This paperback edition published 2024

Copyright © Simon Mabon, Sanaa Alsarghali, Adel Ruished and contributors 2022

Simon Mabon, Sanaa Alsarghali, Adel Ruished and contributors have asserted their right under the Copyright, Designs and Patents Act, 1988, to be identified as Editors and Authors of this work.

For legal purposes the Acknowledgements on p. xviii constitute an extension of this copyright page.

Series design by Adriana Brioso
Cover image: *Loss (Waiting Crowd)* by Sliman Mansour, 1986, oil on canvas.
Courtesy of the Artist.

All rights reserved. No part of this publication may be reproduced or transmitted in any form or by any means, electronic or mechanical, including photocopying, recording, or any information storage or retrieval system, without prior permission in writing from the publishers.

Bloomsbury Publishing Plc does not have any control over, or responsibility for, any third-party websites referred to or in this book. All internet addresses given in this book were correct at the time of going to press. The author and publisher regret any inconvenience caused if addresses have changed or sites have ceased to exist, but can accept no responsibility for any such changes.

A catalogue record for this book is available from the British Library.

A catalog record for this book is available from the Library of Congress.

ISBN: HB: 978-0-7556-2642-7
PB: 978-0-7556-4255-7
ePDF: 978-0-7556-2643-4
eBook: 978-0-7556-2644-1

Typeset by Deanta Global Publishing Services, Chennai, India

To find out more about our authors and books visit www.bloomsbury.com and sign up for our newsletters.

This book is dedicated to Mohammad, Tamer, Edward-Omi and future generations who continue to struggle against the excesses of sovereign power.

CONTENTS

List of Contributors ix
Foreword xii
Acknowledgements xviii

INTRODUCTION 1

Chapter 1
STATES OF EXCEPTION, BARE LIFE AND AGAMBEN IN THE MIDDLE EAST 5
   Simon Mabon

Chapter 2
THE GULF COOPERATION COUNCIL POLICE IMAGINED: THE STATE
OF EXCEPTION AND TRANSNATIONAL POLICING 27
   Staci Strobl and Simon Mabon

Chapter 3
CLAIMING AGENCY IN THE IRAQI STATE OF EXCEPTION 53
   Edith Szanto

Chapter 4
INSTITUTIONALIZING AUTHORITARIANISM: EGYPT, AL SISI AND THE
STATE OF EXCEPTION 75
   Lucia Ardovini

Chapter 5
A FORCED MARRIAGE? PALESTINE AND THE STATE OF EXCEPTION 95
   Sanaa Alsarghali

Chapter 6
SOVEREIGN POWER IN AN ICY CLIMATE: AN EXPLORATION OF
VIOLENCE, ENVIRONMENTAL CHALLENGES AND DISPLACEMENT IN
THE BEKAA VALLEY, LEBANON 119
   Ana Maria Kumarasamy

Chapter 7
PENAL PORTENTS, PENAL PRECEDENTS AND SPECTACLES OF
UNBEARABLE LIFE 143
    Madonna Kalousian

Chapter 8
THE POLITICS OF SECULAR CULTURAL PROPERTY IN EAST
JERUSALEM: THE CASE OF BIRKET HAMAM AL-BATRAK 167
    Adel Ruished

Chapter 9
BIOPOLITICS, DESTITUENT RESISTANCE AND POWER-SHARING IN
POST-WAR LEBANON 203
    John Nagle

CONCLUDING OBSERVATIONS 219

Index 222

CONTRIBUTORS

Professor Simon Mabon is Chair in International Politics at Lancaster University, where he directs the Richardson Institute. He holds a PhD in International Relations from the University of Leeds and is the director of the SEPAD project, funded by Carnegie Corporation, which looks at the position and contestation of sectarian identities within the contemporary Middle East (www.sepad.org.uk). Mabon is the author of a number of books on the contemporary Middle East including *Houses Built on Sand: Sectarianism, Revolution and Violence in the Middle East* (2020), *Saudi Arabia and Iran: Soft Power Rivalry in the Middle East* (2013) and *The Struggle for Supremacy: Saudi Arabia and Iran* (forthcoming). He has published in a range of Middle East and international relations journals including *Review of International Studies, Middle East Journal, Middle East Policy, British Journal of Middle East Studies, Politics, Religion and Ideology* and *Third World Quarterly*. He is the co-editor of a major new Middle Eastern book series.

In 2016–17 Mabon served as academic advisor to the House of Lords International Relations committee report into the UK's relations with the Middle East. He regularly consults with governmental agencies and for international news outlets including the BBC, CNN, CNBC, Sky, Al Jazeera, Al Arabiyya, France 24, Deutsche Welle and others. He tweets @profmabon.

Dr Staci Strobl is a professor of criminal justice at the University of Wisconsin-Platteville. She is the author of *Sectarian Order in Bahrain: The Social and Colonial Origins of Criminal Justice* (2018). In 2009, she won the Radzinowicz Memorial Prize for her work in the *British Journal of Criminology* on the criminalization of female domestic workers in Bahrain. Her main area of specialization is criminal justice as it relates to issues of gender, race, ethnicity and religious identity in the Arabian Gulf. In 2019, she and two colleagues won the paper of the year award for the Division of White Collar and Corporate Crime, American Society of Criminal Justice, for their research on coastal land loss and state-corporate crime in Louisiana (United States).

Dr Edith Szanto is an assistant professor at the University of Alabama in the Department of Religion. Formerly, she was an associate professor in the Department of Social Sciences at the American University of Iraq, Sulaimani. Dr Szanto received her PhD in Religious Studies from the University of Toronto in 2012. She is the author of 'Sayyida Zaynab in the State of Exception: Shi'i Sainthood as "Qualified Life" in Contemporary Syria', which was published in the *International Journal of Middle East Studies* in 2012. Since then, she has authored a number of articles and chapters on Islam, women and nationalism in Syria, Iraq and Iraqi Kurdistan.

Dr Lucia Ardovini is a Lecturer in International Relations at Lancaster University. Lucia's research has been focusing on current trajectories of Islamist movements across the MENA region, with a special focus on the Egyptian Muslim Brotherhood. In particular, she is tracing the organization's restructuring process following the 2013 coup, examining its repercussions on ideology, identity and organizational structures. She is the author of *Surviving Repression: the Egyptian Muslim Brotherhood after the 2013 coup* (Manchester University Press, 2022).

Dr Sanaa Al-Sarghali is an assistant professor of Constitutional Law at An-Najah National University. She is the First Palestinian female to obtain a PhD in constitutional law from UK, the UNESCO Chair holder on Human Rights, Democracy and Peace since 2020 and the director of the Constitutional Studies Center at An-Najah National University. In 2018, she was elected chairwoman of Women Media and Development "TAM" and in 2019, she was appointed by the Palestinian National Council as the 9th member of the Palestinian Constitutional Drafting Committee.

Al-Sarghali holds a Ph.D. in Constitutional Law from Lancaster University, an LLM in Law from Durham University in UK, and a BA in Law from An-Najah National University-Palestine. In 2018 She received the "Outstanding Alumni Award" from Lancaster University. Alsarghali has received various prestigious fellowships such as Kathleen Fitzpatrick Fellowship from the University of Melbourne. She is a fellow with SEPAD at Richardson Institute for Political Studies in the UK where her research focuses on constitutional identity, political sectarianism and power sharing in the Middle East and North Africa region. Her research in Palestine covers semi-presidential system's application and the future design of the Palestinian constitution.

Ana Maria Kumarasamy is a PhD candidate in Politics at Lancaster University. Her research interest centres around environmental insecurities, urban spaces and sovereignty in Lebanon. She is currently a PhD fellow at SEPAD (the Sectarianism, Proxies and De-sectarianisation) project and has previously worked as a coordinator at the Richardson Institute.

Dr Madonna Kalousian has recently received her PhD in English Literature and Creative Writing from Lancaster University. Her thesis is a study of Lebanese civil war and post-civil war literature, and her current research focuses on questions of violence, citizenship and surveillance in contemporary Syrian and Lebanese literature. She is the author of a number of articles and book chapters on literature, politics and the visual arts in the Levant.

Adel Ruished is a PhD postgraduate researcher in Politics and International Relations at PPR Department, Lancaster University, UK. His current research is concerned with Israeli–Palestinian political conflict with special focus on the City of East Jerusalem. More fundamentally, he is looking at the impact of contending political programmes on the daily life of Palestinian Jerusalemites post-Oslo peace accord. Currently he is conducting his filed work and data collection in East Jerusalem. He presented his research findings at CLT conference at Warwick University in Coventry in 2017, BRISMES conferences in London and Leeds in 2018 and 2019, as well as WOCMES conference in Seville, Spain, in 2018 and SEPAD workshop at Lancaster University in 2019. He also published several short articles at 'Ya Quds', al-Quds University Academic Newsletter of 2019, and the SEPAD report 'Urban Spaces and Sectarian Contestation' in 2020. Adel holds a Master's degree in Global Politics from the 'Government Department' at the LSE. He has served for twenty years as administrative director for Jerusalem Campus at al-Quds University.

Professor John Nagle is at School of Social Sciences, Education and Social Work at Queen's University Belfast. His research interests focus on social movements, divided cities, and conflict and peace building. He has published a number of books and articles in leading international journals.

FOREWORD

GIORGIO AGAMBEN WITH ARAB EYES

Sari Hnafi[1]

Giorgio Agamben (2015). *The State of Exception: The Permissible Man*
Translated by Nasser Ismail. Cairo: Orbits for Research and Publication, pp. 3–15

At the beginning of 2002, I was living in Ramallah in the West Bank and I was writing with my pen the daily violations of the Zionist entity in the Palestinian territories, and there was always a mystery that baffled me: Why is this entity keen to use the law to violate the law, while many dictatorial Arab countries have been characterized by violations of the rights of their citizens without even being concerned with the use of the legal framework? Perhaps my early acquaintance with Italian philosopher Giorgio Agamben's book (*homo sacer*) represented an important theoretical breakthrough to solve this mystery.

Inspired by the German philosopher Carl Schmitt, Giorgio Agamben deeply understood how the sovereign could declare the state of exception, to form a system that does not compromise the law that he has established through the constitution but by suspending this law. According to Agamben,

> The exception does not subtract itself from the rule; rather, the rule, suspending itself, gives rise to the exception and, maintaining itself in relation to the exception, first constitutes itself as a rule. The situation created in the exception has the peculiar characteristic that it cannot be defined either as a situation of fact or as a situation of right, but instead institutes a paradoxical threshold of indistinction between the two. (Agamben, 1998: 18)

Thus, the function of the law becomes fluctuating between exclusion and inclusion, because the authority does not operate only according to unilateral exclusion logic. Hence, what is inside or outside any group does not exclude one of the other, rather they overlap in an ambiguous manner. As such, according to Agamben, the state of exception has become the norm, forging a threshold between democracy and authoritarianism. Moreover, the state of exception not only content to increasingly appear as a method of rule or as an exceptional measure but also emerges as component paradigm of the judicial system. In developing the concepts of the "biopolitics" and 'bare life', Agamben demonstrates how sovereignty carries with it "power over life" through the rule of exception, wherein it is considered an authority above the law that constitutes it and the protector for implementing it.

I had the honour to be one of the pioneers who utilized Agamben's thought to dismantle the technology of Israeli control over Palestinian territories (Hanafi, 2004, 2009, 2012), as well as to disclose codes of Arab despotism (Hanafi, 2010), and subsequently some Arabic writings began to emerge using the Agambian theoretical framework. And in 2007, I proposed organizing a conference on the state of exception and the exception resistance in the Arab world (Hanafi, 2010), which was organized by the Arab Society for Sociology and the Center for Arab Unity Studies in Beirut, attempting to assess the amount of Arabic writings that have used Agamben's thought and to encourage similar studies. Perhaps what attracted many Arab and foreign researchers to Agamben was not only his thought, which revealed some flaws of modern democratic systems, but also the ethics of this philosopher. In fact, Agamben refused an offer to be visiting professor in the United States, because the government of this country had imposed the system of fingerprinting for foreigners, which Agamben considered this measure similar to human being's control over animals. And when I invited him to deliver the opening speech of the aforementioned conference, he also expressed his desire to visit Palestine through Jordan, whereupon he asked me many questions, among them was how is it possible not to meet any Israeli on his way to Palestine.

Why is the state of exception thought considered a basic theoretical framework for understanding authority mechanisms in the Arab region?

There are four forms (repertoires) of the state of exception as authority mechanism in the Arab region:

The first form, which is the most clear and common, is the state of emergency. In countries such as Syria, Jordan, Algeria and Egypt, the emergency law was still, for a long time, a hanging sword over people's necks there, through which people are treated differently according to the degree of their loyalty to the ruling elite.

The second form of the state of exception is when a ruler not only suspends laws and regulations but also regularly creates new classifications. According to such new classifications, the government becomes exempted from some obligations and duties, and/or abstract undesirable groups some of their rights. Agamben's vision of sovereignty is based on strategic and situational exercise of power, wherein it responds to crises and challenges through invoking normative political exceptions, since the entire law is situational and discretionary. For instance, in Egypt and Jordan the election law is often amended after each election, to block way for specific political and social forces to power, while enable other forces to gain access.

The third form of the state of exception occurs when a law is issued involving a rule for its suspension without determining the context. It is important to mention that suspending the rule does not mean its cancellation, since established ambiguous zone is not separate from judicial system (at least, this is the allegation).

The fourth and last form of the state of exception is when bureaucracy governs society more than laws and regulations. In this case, rational rules often disappear from the bureaucracy and instead its decisions become unpredictable.

Accordingly, some of these forms of the state of exception made young Tunisians, Egyptians, Syrians, Bahrainis and Yemenis feel transformed into permissible beings, that are, starved and isolated bodies. Indeed, such forms stripped them of the political subjectivity and the right to belong to political currents or parties which the regime included in forbidden circle. Arguably, when the ruler became the sole decision-maker in implementing or suspending the law, and in granting or depriving Arab human being decent and just life, his apparatuses violated this human being through economic plundering and police bullying and detention, torture and liquidation, without fair accountability. In this context, Mohsen Bouazizi, the Tunisian sociologist, wrote about Tunisian youth's silent expressions to confirm indifference to public affairs, departure from politics and complete drowning in private affair (Bouazizi, 2010).

However, what Bouazizi did not see was that the son of his city, Sidi Bouzid (Mohamed Bouazizi), had transcended mere indifference, as he separated from social structures to become the engine for social movement. In effect, his body, similar to bodies of many Tunisian youth, was target for oppressive regime of disciplinary power and biopower that aimed at radically erase any abstract form of political activism. With his suicide, Mohamed became actor for resisting this regime where potency is achieved in the moment the body destroys itself. We are in a moment, as Palestinian researcher May al-Jayyousi described it, that resembles the state of Palestinian resistance fighters in occupied Palestinian territories who challenged sovereign authority – this authority who wanted for them to be permissible people where they can be killed without sacrificing them (it is death that has no value) (al-Jayyousi, 2010). Hence, Mohamed Bouazizi and his companions who suicidally died turned into self-sacrificing actors, thereby reversing relationship with the sovereign power.

Perhaps what makes the state of exception most obvious is the refugee issue. As Agamben points out, refugees "represent worrying element in modern nation-state system, and the main reason is that when refugees break line of communication between man and citizen, between nativity and nationality, they place the original story of contemporary sovereignty in face of crisis" (Agamben, 1998:131). The irony that what Palestinians in Lebanon are currently experiencing is that they are excluded from rights, but they are included when making laws. They can acquire neither rights of Lebanese who live on their land nor rights of foreigners in Lebanon. By returning to Weber, Lebanon is a sovereign state because its government alone monopolizes within its borders, the right to the legitimate use of force. Yet, refugee camps represent an exception. Despite Lebanese claims to the contrary, the Lebanese law was suspended for practical purposes, wherein it is randomly applied and in rare cases within the camp's borders. In this sense, camps became "spaces of exception", since residents live "in a zone of indistinction between inside and outside, between exception and rule, between banned and permitted, wherein concepts of personal right and legal protection no longer carry any meaning" (Agamben, 1998: 70).

It may be the case that Agamben has not noticed that in order to understand the state of exception somewhere, it is not sufficient to study the ruler or the sovereign in his capacity as one (prime minister, for example). In fact, the sovereign could be multiple. For instance, within the refugee camps in Lebanon there exists a variety of partial sovereignties that constitute actual rulers such as the Lebanese government and semi-fictitious rulers such as Popular Committees, Palestine Liberation Organization including other factions, the United Nations Relief and Works Agency (UNRWA) and some humanitarian agencies. Paradoxically, all of these sovereignties contribute to consecrating the state of exception and participate in suspending the law, wherein they consented full suspension of sovereign power in the camp for substituting it with "temporary" or 'emergency' sovereignties in its place. More importantly, these emergency sovereignties exist in mutual contradiction which instead of establishing order in the camp, they leave it in a state of vacuum, chaos and social emptiness. In effect, each sovereign or ruler, party or agency, enters into competition not for wining loyalty of every Palestinian but to achieve hegemony and gain control over every refugee. In this context, Agamben adds that 'contrary to modern code which depicts portray political sphere in terms of citizens' rights, free will and social contracts, it appeared that only bare life truly represents the politician from the sovereignty point of view" (Agamben, 1998: 106). Here, refugees turn into individuals of "bare life' instead of being political subjectivities participating in managing their society.

It is important to mention that when Agamben used the term 'bare life' to describe refugees, he was referring to the life of *homo sacer* (the permissible man), the ambiguous personality that lived in ancient Rome. This permissible man is a cursed or exiled man stripped of his citizenship (thus became "consecrated" to gods) where anyone can kill him without punishment but by virtue of his consecration cannot be sacrificed in religious ritual. Therefore, the life of the permissible man bears no significance to the ruler, he only exists in his biological capacity or in bare life (zoé) as something below the degree of humanity. Hence, this permissible man should be supported with most primitive requirements (i.e with food, water and shelter), and excluded from human natural existence in political life 'bio' through deportation or detention.

In line with this, Agamben and his students in the field of refugee and forced migration studies say that refugees could be considered living the bare life of the permissible man – as, for example, a Palestinian refugee in Lebanon lives on the margins of the law and is uninvolved in establishing or implementing the law. The Palestinian refugee also has voice neither in the legal formulation of his situation nor in political processes, whether Palestinian or Lebanese, that affect his life. In addition, the Lebanese government refused to assume responsibility for the refugees and assigned management of their lives to the UNRWA agency, knowing that mandate of this agency is limited to providing bare life for the refugees without defending their interests or even intervening to protect them. Adding to this, concrete walls, barbed wires and military checkpoints encircling each camp identify legal and physical boundaries of the Lebanese state concerning the provision of Palestinian refugees welfare, happiness and even their lives. As such, there is no meaningful evidence of the status of the "permissible man" living in chaotic urban conditions which resemble imprisonment better than the refugee life inside the camp. And Agamben was right when he said that

> 'the camp, to the extent that it deprives its inhabitants political status and reduces their entire existence to bare life, becomes an absolute biopolitical space that has been achieved wherein the sovereign is faced only with pure life, without any mediation. And this is what makes from the camp the accurate paradigm of political space, and that's when politics turns into bio-politics and when citizen is actually confused to the permissible man. (Agamben, 1998: 171)

I am very pleased that this book is introducing the thought of Agamben and the state of exception to the Arab reader, and I am also honoured to foreword it. In conclusion, I would like to raise two points of criticism.

The first criticism is concerned with how scholars used Agamben's thought. Agamben is a philosopher concerned with clarifying possible mechanisms that a ruler utilizes for achieving control. He is neither sociologist nor anthropologist, and his thought does not express sociological fact. To begin with, some scholars twisted the neck of reality to suit Agamben's theory. The various forms of the state of exception do not mean that a ruler can resort to it at any time or place. The fact that Agamben considered the camp as the paradigm for exercising power over people does not mean that it is the only paradigm.

As for the second criticism, it is concerned with Agamben's theory. In fact, Agamben has not paid enough attention to the subjectivity of social actor (agency). While it is true that the sociopolitical action is affected by existing structure, but the social actor also impacts this structure and obliges it to undergo constant restructuring. In fact, Agamben views the camp as a collective detention centre and the actors in it as mere 'victims-survivors', similar to his famous book *Auschwitz: The Witness and the Archives* (Agamben, 1999). Yet, despite ferocity and corruption of the Ben Ali regime in Tunisia and its use of permanent state of exception and emergency, he was unable to establish a total authoritarian regime. Similarly, the Egyptian state with its million and a half security men and policemen, in addition to 350,000 soldiers and its torture prisons (under its control and international intelligence services), failed in confronting revolutionary youth in Tahrir Square and demonstrations in other cities. It is interesting to note that oppression in Tunisia was the factor of weakness rather than strength, wherein 'stubborn and strong" Ben Ali regime failed in pushing the Tunisian army to crack down demonstrations similar to what the Tunisian police did. On the contrary, the army played important role in forcing Ben Ali to flee. Another manifestation of the regime's weakness was exemplified when deported educated opponents outside Tunisia turned into spokesmen and theorists for the revolution. As for the Egyptian regime, policy of privatization transformed the state into a special state for inheritance and for a coterie of businessmen linked to the ruling party and its supporters. This resulted in dissolving class, social or sectarian rules, making it vulnerable in face of masses of young people associated with large, middle and working classes.

Note

1 Professor of Sociology at the American University of Beirut (Department of Social Sciences and Media Studies) and Chief Editor of the Arab Journal of Sociology – *Idafat*. He is Vice President of the International Society of Sociology and member of the Board of Trustees of the Arab Council for Social Sciences. Hanafi's Forward has been translated from Arabic into English by Adel Ruished.

References

Agamben, Giorgio. *Homo Sacer, Sovereign Power and Bare Life*. Stanford, CA: Stanford University Press, 1998.

Agamben, Giorgio. *Remnants of Auschwitz*. New York: Zone Books, 1999.

Hanafi, Sari. 'Targeting Space by the Bio-Politics: The Israeli Colonial Project'. Palestine Report, 2004.

Ophir, Audi, Michal Givonj, and Sari Hanafi. *The Power of Inclusive Exclusion: Anatomy of Israeli Rule in the Occupied Palestinian Territories*. New York: Zone, 2009.

الجيوسي، مي. ' تشكل الذات وحالة الاستثناء: الجسد كموقع للمقاومة '. في حالة الاستثناء والمقاومة في الوطن العربي . بيروت: مركز دراسات الوحدة العربية, (2010).

بوعزيز، محسن. 'سيسيولوجية اللامبالاة: دراسة في التعبيرات الصامتة لدى الشباب التونسي'. في حالة الاستثناء والمقاومة في الوطن العربي. بيروت: مركز دراسات الوحدة العربية, (2010).

حنفي، ساري. 'التطهير المكاني: محاولة جديدة لفهم استراتيجيات المشروع الكولونيالي الاسرائيلي'. في المستقبل العربي، رقم 360، صفحة 84-76, (2009).

حنفي، ساري. ed.'حالة الاستثناء والمقاومة في الوطن العربي'. بيروت: مركز دراسات الوحدة العربية, (2010).

حنفي، ساري. 'سلطة الاقصاء الشامل: تشريح الحكم الاسرائيلي في الاراضي الفلسطينية المحتلة'. بيروت: مركز دراسات الوحدة العربية, (2012).

ACKNOWLEDGEMENTS

The editors would like to express their deepest gratitude to the iconic artist Sliman Mansour. It is an honour to have Mansour's painting *The Waiting Crowd* as the book cover. This artwork is one of a series of four paintings that reflect the psychological and political situation of the Palestinian people shortly before the First Intifada in 1987. Indeed, this painting, like the rest of Mansour's artwork, seeks to reflect the hopes and realities of a people who have been living under occupation for the better part of a century, and is a telling representation of the continuing Palestinian resistance against Israeli occupation.

The editors would also like to thank Professor Sari Hanafi, whose kind words offer a fitting intellectual introduction to this book. Professor Hanafi has also served as a source of intellectual inspiration through his writings on Agamben and the wider Middle East.

The editors would like to extend their gratitude to the remaining outstanding scholars, who participated in the two conferences of "Middle East in Danger" that took place in Lancaster in 2017 and 2018. This book is a result of those stimulating and enriching conversations which offered a depth that could fill many more books.

INTRODUCTION

In the opening page of Giorgio Agamben's seminal text *State of Exception*, the Italian philosopher observes a fundamental problem of engaging with the concept of a state of exception, a concept contiguous with sovereign power and thus at the very heart of contemporary life. Agamben observes that the concept is elusive as a consequence of its position at the limit between law and politics:

> If exceptional measures are the result of periods of political crisis and, as such, must be understood on political and not juridico-constitutional grounds then they find themselves in the paradoxical position of being juridical measures that cannot be understood in legal terms, and the state of exception appears as the legal form of what cannot have legal form. On the other hand, if the law employs the exception that is the suspension of the law itself as its original means of referring to and encompassing life, then a theory of the state of exception is the preliminary condition for any definition of the relation that binds and, at the same time, abandons the living being to law. (p. 1)

For Agamben, it is only through interrogation of the ambitious zone between law and politics that greater understanding of the stakes involved in the difference between the political and juridical emerge. Here, Agamben nods not only to what follows in *State of Exception*, but to his broader intellectual project *homo sacer*, which sets out to interrogate what it means to act politically.

In the years since its publication (2003), *State of Exception* has taken place within the pantheon of great tomes on sovereignty, providing a rich and challenging exposition through which the contemporary understanding of sovereign power can be interrogated. In *State of Exception*, Agamben presents a departure from Carl Schmitt's approach to sovereign power, predicated on the ability to decide the exception, through engaging with the work of other luminaries of twentieth-century social theory including Hannah Arendt, Michel Foucault and Walter Benjamin. In undertaking this task, Agamben situates the state of exception and sovereign power in a zone of anomie. Agamben's work has facilitated critical scholarship on a range of topics including the US response to the War on Terror, urban life across the world, refugees, borders, fisheries and countless examples.

Although the merits of using Agamben's work in the Middle East are many, there are a number of issues, discussed in more detail in the opening chapter.

Of these issues, one requires a brief note of response, concerning the application of 'travelling' theory. As Edward Said observes, when theory travels, the movement across time and space is not unimpeded, with both mode of representation and pattern of institutionalization shaped by the contingencies and peculiarities of time and space (1981). Thus, while ideas of the state of exception and bare life are typically identifiable across time and space, these are shaped by context-specific contingencies. What we seek to do in this collection of essays is to explore the ways in which these context-specific contingencies operate. Moreover, we seek to demonstrate the plurality of ways in which Agamben's thought can help to interrogate life across the Middle East.

This book investigates the emergence of the state of exception concept as paradigm for government and exerting political power in a number of Arab countries in the Middle East. In the following chapters, authors bring attention to intensified implementation of this concept in the period of post 'Arab Spring' revolutions in many of these countries. In the opening chapter, **Simon Mabon** shows the ways in which Giorgio Agamben's ideas can help to understand the regulation and performance of political life in the Middle East. Here, the manipulation of legal structures – seen in the deployment of a state of exception – is undertaken to ensure the survival of regimes. This deployment regulates the daily life of individuals, creating conditions of bare life wherein individuals are reduced to the figure of hominy's sacrifice, a figure cast aside from the polis yet bound by its laws. This explanation offers powerful tools to understand the relationships between rulers and ruled across the region.

In this context, **Staci Strobl** explains that many ruling regimes in the Gulf have excluded entire Shia' communities and placed them in a zone of indistinction (state of exception). Under the pretext of their disloyalty to the regime and acting as agents to Iran, these regimes not only suspended legal status of the entire population as citizens and stripped them legal protection but also policed them by hiring internal and regional security forces for retaining political power and ensure regime survival.

Edith Szanto reviews the permanent states of exception that the Kurdish population has suffered in northern Iraq. She highlights how under this exception many examples of agency have been overlooked, simply because the forms of agency expressed are often religious in nature and thus seen as 'unpalatable' from a Western gaze. Szanto unpacks this bias, suggesting that the difference between Agamben's notions of 'bare life' and a 'qualified life' needs to be more nuanced and go beyond preconceived conceptions.

Away from the Persian Gulf, **Lucia Ardovini** traces the suspension of functioning normal laws and the perpetual extension of the state of emergency in Egypt before, during and after the rise of Muslim Brotherhood to power. More importantly, she shows how the SCAF utilized emergency regulations for retaining control over hinges of authority amid the so-called Arab Spring revolution, and circumventing calls of Egyptians for acquiring civil liberties and human rights.

Sanaa Alsarghali provides us with constitutional analysis regarding the Palestinian Basic Law and the role it plays during the 2007 FatahHamas clash.

She indicates that while the concept of the state of exception can shed light on the mechanisms of sovereign power, the Basic Law raises questions about the difference between states of exception, emergency and necessity. She argues that Agamben's theory does not always apply and that state of exception can occur in exceptional states like Palestine. Alsarghali's analysis relies on the power struggle and internal Palestinian politics without forgetting the role played by Israel as an occupying force and the international community in denying pure Palestinian decision in democratic life in 2006. She uses 'nested' sovereignty to describe the internal power struggle that keeps state of exception until today.

Ana Kumarasamy takes us to the Bekaa Valley on the Lebanese-Syrian borders and shows how the Lebanese government reordered this valley into space of exception. Such reordering enabled the Lebanese government to suspend legal status of fleeing Syrians and implement techniques to regulate their daily life, including exploitation of environmental insecure conditions, hoping to accelerate their return to Syria.

Madonna Kalousian resembles Syrian political imprisonment experience with the 'camp' paradigm and argues that modern state implements this paradigm to govern not only inside prison but also beyond. In this sense, sovereign not only maintains specter of power and erasure of prisoners' human rights inside prison but also merges what lies outside it into a zone of indistinction. Thereby, whole population subject to the same specter of power can induce inclusion and exclusion at the sovereign's own will. She concludes that this state of indistinction (exception) discloses that production of bare life represents major function of sovereign power.

Adel Ruished shows how the Israeli–Palestinian political contest to entrench control in East Jerusalem situated the Patriarch's Pool in a double state of exception. Such exception suspended legal status and turned the pool into space of exception, wherein both governments circumvented Palestinian Jerusalemites' socio-economic rights and regulated their conservation plans of the pool. Albeit unsuccessful, the author alludes to local strategies employed to neutralize this exception, in an attempt to retrieve the right to safeguards and revitalize the pool.

Despite grim evisceration of qualified political life and minimal contestation which the state of exception concept permits, **John Nagle** offers a glimpse of hope for exiting the emerging paradigm of government in the region. In this context, John brings attention to Agamben's destituent power mechanisms which enabled families of civil war victims in Lebanon to challenge attempts of the Lebanese political elites to exclude them as security threats to power-sharing in the country. Through reliance on professional legal challenge, these groups evaded the regulatory grasp of authority, deactivated government institutions and rendered inoperative practices and techniques of sovereign power.

Chapter 1

STATES OF EXCEPTION, BARE LIFE AND AGAMBEN IN THE MIDDLE EAST[1]

Simon Mabon

On 23 December 2016, Eman Salehi, a Shi'a Bahraini sports journalist, was shot dead in front of her young son by a member of Bahrain's ruling family, the Al Khalifa. Salehi's murder took place within the broader political struggle across the island that emerged following the Arab Uprisings of 2011. A 34-year-old man turned himself into the police whereupon military authorities launched an investigation; there was later no charge.

In the early months of the 2011 protests, a three-month-long state of emergency was declared by King Hamad, seemingly giving security personal the ability to address the protesters without recourse to the rule of law. Although the state of emergency ended in June 2011, many of the features that helped define and regulate political life at this time remain in operation, helping maintain sovereign power. Thus, what was previously considered to be an exception to the *norm*, deemed necessary because of the political environment, now becomes the *norm*.

Events in Bahrain reveal a great deal about what political theorists such as Giorgio Agamben have termed the 'state of exception'. The idea of the *state of exception* concerns derogation from the rule of law in times of crisis, when the sovereign defines the exceptional circumstances that require such moves. Within such conditions, regimes are free to act with impunity, unlimited by the rule of law and unbound by the laws of the state. One such consequence is the ability to create *bare life*, where individuals may be stripped of their political meaning and left as the ancient figure of *homo sacer*, the individual who can be killed with impunity. When looking at the case of Eman Salehi, it is easy to see parallels between Salehi and the *homo sacer*, the individual who can be killed with impunity. The creation of *bare life* is an increasingly common feature of Middle Eastern politics, emerging from derogation from the rule of law and imposition of emergency powers in times of crisis. Amid the turmoil of regional politics, a number of regimes across the Middle East had embraced emergency laws as a means of ensuring their survival, creating conditions where individuals can be cast as the figure of *homo sacer* within bare life.

In the years after the Arab Uprisings, political life across the Middle East has become contested along myriad lines, creating conditions of instability and uncertainty that have cast doubt on the ability of the sovereign to exert absolute power. This inability undermines the very essence of sovereign power, leading to declarations of emergency legislation and states of exception. The great Arab intellectual Ibn Khaldun argued that politics is essentially about the survival of the species. In *The Muqadimah*, a magnum opus of Arab history and intellectual thought, Ibn Khaldun articulates how societies form out of a collective sense of *asabiyyah*, or kinship, which transcends other identities. For Ibn Khaldun, solidarity achieved through the cultivation of *asabiyyah* was an essential part of the survival of a dynasty and essential when morphing from a nomadic to sedentary way of life. Around 700 years after Ibn Khaldun, an Italian philosopher also set out to explore the nature of political life and the essence of political structures. While Agamben's work differs greatly to that of Ibn Khaldun, offering a rich theoretical discussion of the contradictions within political systems, it shares a number of foundational parallels, as both seek to understand the regulation of life.

With the onset of the Arab Uprisings in late 2010, states across the Middle East faced a number of serious challenges in their efforts to regulate life, increasing tensions between regime and society, while also seeking to ensure their survival amid rising regional pressures. The onset of violent protests in Syria, Iraq, Bahrain and Yemen would also have broader ramifications within those states not hit by protests. Within this climate, regimes attempted to retain power through a range of different ways, including by framing events as security challenges and by using political and legal channels to prevent the emergence of protest movements. One such mechanism was to declare a state of emergency, which, when placed within political debates about the nature of statehood, is understood as a state of exception.

In this chapter I seek to show the ways in which Giorgio Agamben's ideas can help to understand political life in the Middle East with a focus upon the ideas of *state of exception* and *bare life*. Taken together, these aspects present a political, legal and spatial mapping of sovereign power which has the potential to reduce individuals to the figure of *homines sacri*, a figure cast aside from the *polis* yet bound by its laws. Such concepts, I argue, offer powerful tools to understand the relationships between rulers and ruled across the region.

I begin by providing an overview of the concept of the state of exception and its application in the Middle East. While a great deal of work has been done on the concept of the state of exception and the creation of *bare life* that follows, there is very little consideration of the consequences of the state of exception in the Middle East, which poses a number of theoretical and empirical questions. I then seek to bring in a more normative or informal dimension to considerations of the state of exception. Although formal structures (found in law and institutions) play a prominent role within the creation of the exception, the complexity of political organization across the Middle East suggests that we must also consider the role played by informal structures – such as religion and tribalism – to gain a more nuanced understanding of the concept, along with the construction of *the camp* and how people then reside in *bare life*. While a comprehensive overview of Agamben's thought is not possible, this opening chapter seeks to provide an introduction to key ideas and to demonstrate the plethora of ways in which Agamben's ideas can be applied to the contemporary Middle East. It also, however, seeks to point to a number of ways in which the application of his ideas to the Middle East can help aid broader engagement with Agamben's work.

A 'new paradigm of government'

Constitutional documents typically possess clauses that provide rulers with the capacity to suspend the law in times of crisis. Derogation from the rule of law and declaration of emergency powers – a state of emergency or *exception* – are seen to be *necessary* features to ensure the survival of the *polis*. Discussions about the exception are typically related to debates about sovereign power, questions about who possesses the right to determine when the rule of law should be suspended. The origins of the idea of the *exception* are found in ancient Greece, yet our exploration begins in earnest with the German jurist Carl Schmitt, whose work sought to articulate the political flaws with the Weimar Republic in Germany. In one of the more quoted opening lines of a book on political theory, Schmitt identifies the sovereign as 'he who defines the exception', where the exception is neither external nor internal to the juridical order but serves as a means of derogating from the normal situation to the extraordinary. This Schmittian view of sovereignty relates to *the decision* to determine the suspension of the law. From this point, Schmitt continues to reveal the contradictions inherent within ideas of sovereignty, seemingly predicated upon a threshold of indifference, where external and internal blur with one another. The suspension of the norm and movement to the state of emergency, for Walter Benjamin, is the new norm.[2]

It does not lead to the abolition of the norm or of the juridical order itself. Instead, for Agamben, this order is

> the structure in which the state of exception [. . .] is realized *normally*. The sovereign no longer limits himself [. . .] to deciding on the exception on the basis of recognizing a given factual situation (danger to public safety): laying bare the inner structure of the ban that characterizes his power, he now de facto produces the situation as a consequence of his decision on the exception.[3]

It is this decision that is central to understandings of sovereignty, not only for Schmitt but also for Giorgio Agamben, who takes these ideas and develops them as part of his *homo sacer* project which locates sovereign power in the regulation of life through exception.

In pursuit of his task, Agamben builds on Foucault, in particular his vision of biopolitics, which is articulated as what 'brought life and its mechanisms into the realm of explicit calculations and made knowledge-power an agent of transformation of human life'.[4] For Foucault, the emergence of biopolitics denotes the threshold of modernity, placing life at the centre of political order. This ability to 'let life live' is a key component of this. In contrast, Agamben rejects Foucault's assertion that biopolitics was the threshold of modernity and instead traces it back to Greek antiquity.

Agamben's work on sovereignty is predominantly found across his *homo sacer* project, which offers a multifaceted understanding and engagement with sovereign power and the relationship between rulers and ruled. As the scholar of Islamic law and Islamic intellectual history Wael B. Hallaq acknowledges, the concept of sovereignty 'gives birth to law'[5] but for Agamben, it is the state of exception that is central to understanding sovereign power. Here, the sovereign prerogative – the ability to decide upon the exception – is a key component of emergency legislation and sovereign power more broadly.

Much like Schmitt, the sovereign decision remains integral, determining the arena over which law applies and, conversely, where it does not. Here, as Agamben notes, 'the rule, suspending itself, gives rise to the exception and, maintaining itself in relation to the exception, first constitutes itself as a rule'.[6] As a consequence, drawing on Schmitt, Agamben argues that

> The sovereign, who can decide on the state of exception, guarantees its anchorage to the juridical order. But precisely because the decision here concerns the very annulment of the norm, that is, because the state of exception represents the inclusion and capture of a space that is neither outside nor inside (the space that corresponds to the annulled and suspended norm), 'the sovereign stands outside [*steht außerhalb*] of the normally valid juridical order, and yet belongs [*gerhort*] to it for it is he who is responsible for deciding whether the constitution can be suspended in toto'.[7]

The location of the exception is key feature of the opening of *State of Exception*, where Agamben suggests that two main positions are held: the first locates the exception as an 'integral part of positive law because the necessity that grounds it is an autonomous source of law'[8] but the second suggests that the exception is 'essentially extrajuridical'. For Agamben, both approaches are problematic. Instead, the exception

> is neither external nor internal to the juridical order, and the problem of defining it concerns precisely a threshold, or a zone of indifference, where inside and outside do not exclude each other but rather blur with each other. The suspension of the norm does not mean its abolition, and the zone of anomie that it establishes is not (or at least claims not to be) unrelated to the juridical order.[9]

The state of exception manifests as the legal form of what Agamben argues cannot have legal form, a type of no-man's land – a paradox, the type of which features across Agamben's work. Put another way, the exception suspends constitutional norms and grants the sovereign power to take any decision in a way that makes legal that which cannot be legal. In this, Agamben builds on Benjamin's claim that the exception is now the norm.

From this, Agamben articulates a view that the state of exception is a *state of emergency* predicated upon the sovereign decision from which the state is able to render the lives of those under its rule into what he terms *bare life*. It is the perennial condition of exception that is referred to as 'the dominant paradigm of government in contemporary politics'.[10] The state of exception is then, for Agamben, 'the preliminary condition for any definition of the relation that binds and at the same time abandons the living being to the law', where the law survives its suspension in the form of the force of law. Ultimately, Agamben's project seeks to facilitate inclusion through exclusion – put another way, a closing off against an outside.

The state of exception is understood as a 'zone of anomie', a space that is devoid of law following the deactivation of legal norms and the collapse of the normal order.[11] It is a concept fundamental to sovereign power, serving as 'the preliminary condition for any definition of the relation that binds and at the same time abandons the living being to the law'.[12] This state of exception is 'illegal' but perfectly 'juridical and constitutional', a measure that is realized through the production of new norms.[13] Here, the law suspending itself produces a new set of norms – a new juridical order – to shape and reshape the relationship between rulers and ruled. Within this, new laws provide the sovereign with the ability to *abandon* the living being to the law.[14] Here, 'the sovereign no longer limits himself [. . .] to deciding on the exception (. . .) laying bare the inner structure of the ban that characterizes his power, he now de facto produces the situation as a consequence of his decision on the exception.'[15]

This 'paradigm of government' allows the law to encompass life 'by means of its own suspension', regulating life by placing *bare life* at the vanguard of politics.[16] Such a view is predicated on the assumption that 'the state of exception is the preliminary condition for any definition of the relation that binds and at the same time abandons the living being to the law'.[17] Fundamental to this position is the concept of necessity, viewed as the original source of political action and as an objective given, 'releasing a particular case from the literal application of the norm'. Of course, such an interpretation of necessity is subjective and, for Agamben, is 'undecidable in fact and law'.[18] Such a view is supported by referring to the work of Balladore-Pallieri, who argues that necessity is 'relative to the aim that one wants to achieve'.[19]

It is the inclusive exclusion that is central to Agamben's work, a zone of indistinction that reveals the structure of political relations – the site within which meaning and political life is stripped from individuals, reducing them to bare life. While some suggest that this project is an attempt to 'correct' or 'complete' Foucault's approach to biopolitics, perhaps a more appropriate position is that it builds on Walter Benjamin's critique of Schmitt, demonstrating that the exception has indeed become the rule.

A fundamental part of Agamben's project is a vision of the political which draws a distinction between *bare life* and the 'good life', evoking ideas of the

Aristotelean political life. Or, as Thomas Lemke suggests, a distinction between 'the natural existence and the legal status of a human being'.[20] This distinction differentiates between those acknowledged as *fully human* as a consequence of their participation in political life and those who have political meaning stripped from them. In pursuit of this, the sovereign produces a *biopolitical body*, building on – although in some ways deviating from – Foucault's idea of 'letting life live'.

Central to Agamben's work is the idea of the ban, the idea of inscribing exclusion through inclusion[21] which is predicated upon the historical figure of the *wolfman*, a figure who appears to occupy the roles of both man and beast while transgressing beyond the law and society. In order to understand sovereign power 'we must learn to recognise this structure of the ban in the political relations and public spaces in which we still live'. It is here that we can understand the distinction between the political life and the bare life and the way in which sovereign power regulates life.

As Agamben notes,

> The life of the bandit . . . is not a piece of animal nature without any relation to law and the city. It is, rather, a threshold of indistinction and of passage between animal and man, physis and nomos, exclusion and inclusion: the life of the bandit is the life of the loup garou, the werewolf, who is precisely neither man nor beast, and who dwells paradoxically within both while belonging to neither.

Here, contradiction and a zone of indistinction are once again central in Agamben's political project as the distinction between realms and concepts blurs.

The fundamental practice of sovereign power is the creation of bare life, the stripping of political meaning from life, reducing it to its *natural* form but remaining exposed to sovereign power, abandoning individuals to the force of law. This idea of *bare life* is positioned as central to contemporary politics by Agamben, and it is a common feature of the modern *polis*, where 'bare life has the peculiar privilege of being that whose exclusions found the city of men'.[22] Once political meaning is removed – yet remaining bound by sovereign power – one can be reduced to the figure of *homines sacri*, the eponymous figure from Agamben's project, named after the individual from ancient Rome who can be killed with impunity outside of religious rituals due to their abandonment.

Through this,

> the realm of bare life – which is originally situated at the margins of the political order – gradually begins to coincide with the political realm, and exclusion and inclusion, outside and inside, *bios* and *zoe*, right and fact, enter into a zone of irreducible indistinction. At once excluding bare life from and capturing it within the political order, the state of exception actually constituted, in its very separateness, the hidden foundation on which the entire political system rested.[23]

The importance of the ban is perhaps surpassed only by the permanent possibility of the ban, creating conditions where everyone can become *homines sacri*, an idea which is central to the regulation of life within the sovereign order. Through the exception becoming the norm, or the central feature of contemporary political life, abandonment and bare life no longer only apply to particular subjects, but rather 'we are all virtually *homines sacri*'.[24] This emerges from 'a biopolitics that technologizes, administers, and depoliticizes and thereby renders the political and power relations irrelevant'.[25] Within the state of exception, bare life moves from particular spaces and definitive categories to dwell 'in the biological body of every living being'.[26]

While grounded in the interaction of political and legal theory, Agamben's approach contributes to debate in a range of other disciplines. As geographers such as Claudio Minca and Rory Rowan will attest, there is a strong spatial core running through Agamben's work, an attempt to map 'socio-geographical phenomena within which the exception operates'.[27] In such sites, the ban exists as the manifestation of sovereign power, creating *homines sacri* as a consequence of stripping political meaning from life.[28] It is with the idea of the ban that an outside is taken – along with an inside – and through this constitutive act, the sphere of the political is born, along with the 'paradox of sovereignty'.[29] For Agamben, the paradox emerges from the idea that the sovereign is the preliminary condition of the relation that simultaneously binds and abandons individuals to the law.

These ideas – and their spatial components – are brought to the fore through the concept of *the camp*, 'the hidden paradigm of the political space of modernity', a site of possibility as well as a specific area within which life is stripped of meaning.[30] It is here where sovereign power operates without limits, a zone of indistinction where the sovereign possesses a 'natural right to do anything to anyone'.[31] Put another way, the camp is the site that emerges when the state of exception becomes the rule. As Agamben himself notes, the camp '*is the space that is opened when the state of exception begins to become the rule*'[32] (emphasis in original). It is the space where law, fact, fear, rule and exception coalesce, colliding with one another. Those living in the camps are found in a 'zone of indistinction between outside and inside, exception and rule, licit and illicit, in which the very concepts of subjective right and juridical protection no longer make any sense'.[33]

Camps are perhaps the most obvious examples of spaces of exception, the arena where the sovereign decision to suspend the rights of the citizens and impose long-term regulatory powers on inhabitants, creating a space that is simultaneously inside and outside the sphere of sovereign power.[34] Here,

> Insofar as its inhabitants were stripped of every political status and wholly reduced to bare life, the camp was also the most absolute biopolitical space ever to have been realized in which power confronts nothing but pure life, without any mediation. This is why the camp is the very paradigm of political space at the point at which politics becomes biopolitics and *homo sacer* is virtually confused with the citizen.[35]

While the idea of a camp is often associated with fences and material borderlines, as Lemke articulates, Agamben's project is less interested in the physical entity (although this should not be entirely ignored). Instead, it is a thing that 'symbolizes and fixes the border between bare life and political existence'.[36] Such a view goes beyond physical sites such as the Nazi concentration camps, refugee camps or urban ghettos to include 'every single space that systematically produces bare life'. Thus, we should view *the camp* as a metaphysical entity, a site of possibility, a space that can reduce life to its barest form. Indeed in such a view, sovereignty is at the nucleus of biopolitics, articulating how the sovereign order eviscerates political meaning from the lives of people within the *polis*, leaving them in a zone of indistinction: simultaneously bound by the law but abandoned by it.

Travelling with Agamben

In recent years, a number of scholars have applied Agamben's work to the Middle East from a range of different disciplines, looking at a number of contrasting case studies. From the refugee camps of Lebanon and Jordan to the plight facing migrant workers in the Gulf, Agamben's ideas provide valuable insight into interrogating contemporary politics across the Middle East. As with all theoretical positions, Agamben's work provides a lens through which to view the world, a means through which to explore relations between rulers and ruled and to interrogate the ways in which power operates.

Within this body of work, Sari Hanafi, John Nagle, Sara Fregonese, Adam Ramadan, Ronit Lentin and others have used Agamben's work to highlight a range of different facets of sovereign power, political life and the precarious nature of life for those caught in bare life, not only interrogating the lived experience but also exploring spatial arenas that help to perpetuate the existence of an expendable life.[37] Such projects aid exploration of how a distinction can be drawn between urban environments where life can operate. As Hanafi and Long acknowledge, while the state of exception refers to the suspension of the law by the sovereign state, in the Lebanese camps, 'a tapestry of multiple, partial sovereignties' operate that facilitate, challenge and interact with the suspension of the law.[38]

This simultaneously applies both to those Palestinians expelled from their homes in the 1948 *nakba*, many of whose descendants continue to live in the Palestinian territories and to those not expelled and who remained in Israel as 'Israeli Arabs', living under military rule justified through British Mandate Emergency Regulations of 1945. Ensuing laws continue this exclusionary inclusion, restricting the capacity of both groups for political, social and economic activity. During the Israeli occupation of southern Lebanon, the Al-Ansar detention camp – controlled by the Israeli Defence Forces (IDF) – was home to around 15,000 Lebanese and Palestinian prisoners, detained with little evidence of wrongdoing. Here, as Laleh Khalili argues, was 'a specific legal and political setting for "war prisons" that stripped persons of their juridical rights, gave function to extraterritoriality, and allowed differing definitions of sovereignty'[39] serving as an example of the competing sovereignties in operation.

The interaction of these emergency powers with 'partial sovereignties' leaves the camp in a state of void and anomie. Inhabitants of the camps thus become *homo sacer*, residing in bare life as individuals with no political significance to the sovereign, excluded from the law yet included by its very inclusion. As Silverman suggests, Palestinians in camps across Lebanon are 'excluded from rights while being included in law-making'.[40] They are afforded the rights neither of the Lebanese – whose land they reside in – nor of foreigners and in the aftermath of war in Syria, the number of people living in camps across Lebanon rose dramatically.

As we have seen, camps have the capacity to become spaces of exception. As Sari Hanafi and Taylor Long suggest, in spite of claims to the contrary, Lebanese law is rarely enforced, 'has been suspended within the confines of the camp. In this sense, the camps have become 'spaces of exception'', yet we must not dismiss agency from those residing within, in spite of Agamben's assertion that once in bare life, one must accept the condition of 'being thus'. This is a central criticism of Agamben when applied to the camp. While it may hold for the concentration camps of Nazi Germany, camps in Lebanon and Jordan are replete with expressions of agency, in spite of the myriad claims to sovereign power. Edith Szanto makes similar points when discussing the Shi'a shrine town of Sayyida Zaynab, which was transformed from a refugee camp to an area of 'qualified life'.[41]

Deploying a broader definition of the camp, Ronit Lentin documents how Agamben's approach can shed light on the plight of the Palestinian peoples living under what she terms a 'racial exception'. Using Agamben's ideas, Lentin argues that the Israeli state should be viewed as a settler colonial society, or an ethnocracy, a racial state that instituted the state of exception and zones of abandonment from its establishment.[42] Sharing both a similar approach and line of inquiry, Sari Hanafi refers to this project as 'spacio-cide', a deliberate ideology targeting the space upon which Palestinians live.[43]

Building on this view, we should perhaps employ a more fluid understanding of the camp, not restricting our analysis of it to particular spaces or sites of exception but viewing the camp as a space where all can be potentially reduced to bare life. Indeed, across the Middle East, rulers created states of exception, rendering people into (potential) conditions of bare life as a means of biopolitical regulation and control.[44] In pursuit of this, an account of context-specific sovereign power is required which locates the biopolitics – and sovereign power more broadly – within the peculiarities and contingencies of life in the Middle East.[45]

Here, two additional points are worth further elaboration. The first concerns the regulation of the biopolitical body. Across the Middle East, the provision of welfare services and public goods – or lack thereof – serves to place limits on life that is deemed politically useful. Yet in a number of cases, notably across Palestine, Lebanon, Syria, Egypt and elsewhere, the provision of these services and, ultimately, the control over life are often undertaken by non-state actors, or actors who occupy hybrid roles, which can have serious implications for both sovereign power and the designation and creation of bare life.

This leads to a second point concerning sovereignty itself. Across the Middle East, a wide range of forms of sovereign power are in operation, beyond what is typically accepted in the Weberian–Westphalian tradition. From the authoritarian and ethnocratic regimes found across the Gulf to the sites of fragmentation such as Libya, Syria and Yemen where power over life is spread across a range of state and non-state actors, questions over the operational source of sovereign power are prominent. In a number of cases, notably Lebanon and Palestine, power is devolved – directly or indirectly – to local state and non-state actors, revealing a form of hybrid sovereignty. In the Lebanese case, some have even suggested that the Ta'if power-sharing agreement is the source of sovereign power. What is of note here, and perhaps of interest to Agamben scholars not working on the Middle East, is the way in which sovereign power and the regulation of life operate when sovereign power itself is pluralized across different state and non-state actors.

Critical reflection

Although Agamben's work is undeniably persuasive, a number of serious issues remain and are worth articulating for our study and indeed work on the Middle East more broadly.[46] First, as a number of scholars have argued, Agamben paints his subjects as 'fundamentally passive', lacking agency against sovereign violence.[47] For Agamben, once an individual is stripped of political meaning, they are cast into conditions of bare life and forced to accept conditions of 'being thus'. Yet this appears unrealistic. Agency can be expressed in myriad ways, even when political meaning has been stripped from life, from the refugee who stitched their lips together to the self-immolation of Mohamed Bouazizi. Moreover, as Szanto has argued, the case of the Syrian shrine town of Sayyida Zaynab constitutes both a space of exception, beginning its existence as a refugee camp, and a site of possibility where those who express devotion to Sayyida Zaynab continue to express aspects of a 'qualified life', escaping bare life in the process.[48] Szanto's suggestion points to some of Agamben's later ideas, discussed in more detail by John Nagle, notably of *destituent power*, the ability to deactivate and transform elements of sovereign power.

In response to charges of denying or dismissing agency, Agamben speaks of the possibility of destituent power, positioned in contrast to acts of constitutive power and resistance. For Agamben, expressions of resistance seek to oppose and replace the sovereign and its regulation of life with a 'constitutive order'. This, in turn, along with forms of constitutive power, reinforces the sovereign's logic of power, feeding into the intensification of the exception. In contrast, destituent power and resistance are not necessarily aimed at overthrowing and replacing existing governance structures, but rather operates as 'a force that, in its very constitution, deactivates the governmental machine' (2014: 65). Such an approach seeks to render powerless technologies and techniques of sovereign power, ensuring their ineffectiveness, evading their initial purpose and placing techniques of government beyond regulatory power. While a reactive process, for Agamben 'the capacity to deactivate something and render it inoperative – a power, a function, a human operation – without simply destroying it but by liberating the potentials that have remained inactive in it in order to allow a different use of them' (1998, 1274). Such ideas are explored in more detail by John Nagle in this volume.

An additional tension emerges when considering the application of Agamben's ideas beyond the Western philosophical tradition from where they emerged, moving beyond the assumption of Western-centric ideas about political life, state–society relations and sovereignty more broadly. As Wael Hallaq suggests, there are five form properties possessed by modern states that are imperative for political organization to be considered as a state. For Hallaq these are its constitution as a historical experience, its sovereignty and ensuing metaphysics, its legislative monopoly, its bureaucratic machinery and its cultural hegemonic engagement with the social order.[49] The acceptance of such a position provides an entry point for engagement with Agamben's ideas in the Muslim world, although it is in the metaphysical experience and cultural hegemonic engagement with the social order that the state differs from those considered by Agamben.

Within the context of these five characteristics, two are of particular importance in our exploration, helping provide greater awareness of the conditions that can give rise to the state of exception. First, the metaphysics of state serves as both empirical and ideological grounding for exploration, facilitating awareness of institutional organization and also the ideology at the heart of the construction of such institutions. Such a metaphysical position is then encapsulated within the concept of sovereignty that is both internal and external, a zone of indistinction itself. Identifying this empirically and ideologically helps to articulate the conditions that give rise to both the sovereign, which 'gives birth to law',[50] and the state of exception itself. From this, it appears that Hallaq's definition of a state contains within it the very notion of the state of exception, the ability to suspend the law to preserve the law.

The second concept is cultural engagement, which provides the conditions through which ideas and the state of exception can thrive. The journey from colonialism to independence – and having overthrown the yoke of oppression – is a prominent feature of the state of exception, helping to establish the state and with it, the embodiment of law. Building upon this, exploration with the conditions and cultural relations that manifest in the state helps to shape the nature of its legal and political systems and, ultimately, the state of exception.

One of the other issues for exploration when deploying Agamben's ideas builds on questions of application in a non-Western context, relating to concerns about the structure and operation of sovereign power within the *polis*. Indeed, as I have argued in more detail elsewhere,[51] the nature of political projects across the Middle East – and in other non-Western and post-colonial contexts – may be dramatically different to that to which Agamben initially envisaged his operating.

While Western democracies may be characterized by a particular form of institutional ordering, civil society and set of norms, the Middle Eastern context is characterized by a different set of norms, histories, cultures and contexts that result in a particular type of interplay between states, regimes, society, people, institutions, civil society and other attributes of political life. As Joel Migdal observes, the state in the Middle East – and non-Western world more generally –

can be viewed as an 'organisation, composed of numerous agencies led and coordinated by the state's leadership (executive authority) that has the ability or authority to make and implement the binding rules for all the people as well as the parameters of rule making for other social organisations in a given territory'.[52]

Additionally, a further distinction must be made between terms that are often lazily used in an almost interchangeable manner. Indeed, ideas of state, sovereign, government and regime are often conflated which prohibits analytical clarity and also obfuscates efforts to understand the ways in which sovereign power operates. Regimes are defined as more permanent ways of representations of political organization than leaders or governments, yet less permanent than states. Regimes are central to the development of political projects, typically with roots pre-dating the state and acting within political projects in pursuit of their own survival. From this, states are a 'more permanent structure of domination and coordination including a coercive apparatus and the means to administer a society and extract resources from it'.[53] Within this definition, sovereignty is then 'the ability to regulate life based upon the context-specific relationship between ruler and ruled that is shaped by a range of contingent factors'.[54]

Within these contingencies and possibilities are a range of issues, ideational and material, local and global, which all condition the nature of sovereign power and the ways in which agency operates.

A normative renaissance

When exploring Agamben's work in the contemporary Middle East, one of the areas that require engagement concerns the role of religion and normative values within the workings of sovereign power. Supplementing formal state structures that regulate life are the informal, normative structures that may support legal structures or may supplement them, much like those which featured in the tale of Antigone. As we have seen, Agamben's work on the exception is couched in ideas of necessity, holding that it is preferable not to perform mass than to partake in inappropriate places unless this is because of a supreme necessity, as 'necessity has no law'. The Western, Christian roots of such a position may pose issues when applying Agamben's ideas beyond the West into Islamic contexts. Yet as we saw earlier, we can circumvent such claims through identifying similar characteristics in different contexts. In Islam, for example, we can see similar ideas of necessity and transgression that can give the exception is fundamental essence.

The following verses from the Quran illustrate this point: 'Forbidden to you for food are carrion, blood, swine-flesh, and that which has been dedicated to any other than Allah; (. . .) That is corruption. (. . .) Whomever is forced by hunger, not by will, to sin, for him Allah is Forgiving, Compassionate.'[55] Moreover, if this act of transgression 'is driven by necessity, neither craving nor transgressing, it is no sin for him. For Allah is Forgiving, Compassionate'.[56] Acknowledging this helps us to move beyond this initial criticism to consider the way in which Islam can regulate life and interact with sovereign power.

For Joseph Schacht, one of the most prominent Islamic scholars, Islam is a biopolitical way of ordering life:

> The central feature that makes Islamic religious law what it is, that guarantees its unity in all its diversity, is the assessing of all human acts and relationship, including those which we call legal, from the point of view of the concepts 'obligatory/recommended/indifferent/reprehensible/forbidden.'[57]

Yet as Shahab Ahmed argues, we should not talk of a *singular Islam* with the capacity to regulate the lives of all Muslims. Instead, myriad interpretations exist, ranging from the individual to the communal.[58] Moreover, as Shadi Hamid stresses, faith must be placed in context, which means that ideas interact with a range of contingent factors that shape time and space, leading to a range of different understandings of political life and the way in which sovereign power regulates life.[59]

The Quran details the nature of such guidelines, in accordance with Schacht's assertion that Islam is a biopolitical religion: 'We have revealed to you the scripture with the truth that you may judge between people by what God has taught you.'[60] Such a vision is universal: 'the Word of your Lord has been fulfilled in truth and in justice. None can change His Words.'[61] Yet transgression from Islamic teachings is possible, as the Surah of Al Mai'dah articulates which goes some way to revealing the possibility found in religion. It also supports ideas found in Agamben about potentiality.

Leaving people in place and space – interpreting divine law from such positions

> As far as civil and social governance is concerned, Islam laid down its foundation and principles, and prescribed for the umma that it employ judgment and discretion in this area, because it changes along with time and place and it advances along with civilization and knowledge. Among its basic principles is that authority over and command of the umma belongs to it itself [*sultat al-umma laha*] and that its affairs are a matter of consultation within it. Its government is a type of republic within which the successor of the Prophet [*khalifat al-rasul*] is not superior under its rules to the weakest individuals from amongst the governed, but is only the executor of the revealed law and the opinion of the *umma*, preserving religion and worldly interests, joining ethical virtues and material benefits, and thus leading to the universalization of human brotherhood by unifying the basic moral principles of nations.[62]

Perhaps the most obvious point of tension emerges when considering the source of sovereign power and tensions between rulers and religion.

Traditionally, rulers have sought to defer to Sharia and not to legislate, often co-opting members of the *ulemma* as a means of ensuring religious compliance and deriving legitimacy for their actions.[63] Yet a point of tension quickly emerges between what appear to be competing sources of sovereign power. As we have seen, both Schmitt and Agamben argue that sovereign power is found in the decision to suspend the law. Yet consideration of a number of constitutions raises questions about the fundamental source of sovereignty. Indeed, a contradiction arises between the source of sovereignty – and authority – and the sovereign decision to suspend the law. In Saudi Arabia, take the following articles of the Basic Law denoting the sources of sovereign power:

> Article 1: The Kingdom of Saudi Arabia is a sovereign Arab Islamic State. Its religion is Islam. Its constitution is Almighty God's Book, The Holy Qur'an, and the Sunna (Traditions) of the Prophet (PBUH). Arabic is the language of the Kingdom. The City of Riyadh is the capital.
>
> Article 7: Government in the Kingdom of Saudi Arabia derives its authority from the Book of God and the Sunna of the Prophet (PBUH), which are the ultimate sources of reference for this Law and the other laws of the State.

Here, a void emerges where contesting claims to power and authority render other sovereign assertions vacuous. Yet Articles 61, 62 and 82 stress that emergency powers – and the suspension of the rule of law – are deployed by the king:

> Article 61: The King shall announce any state of emergency or general mobilization and shall declare war. The Law shall specify rules for this purpose.
>
> Article 62: If an imminent danger is threatening the safety of the Kingdom, the integrity of its territories or the security and interests of its people, or is impeding the functions of official organizations, the King may take urgent measures to deal with such a danger. When he considers that these measures should continue, necessary arrangements shall be made in accordance with the Law.
>
> Article 82: No provision of this Law whatsoever may be suspended except on a temporary basis, such as in wartime or during the declaration of a state of emergency. Such a suspension shall be in accordance with the terms of the Law and may not violate Article 7.

Thus, a fundamental tension emerges, a *zone of indistinction*, between sources of sovereign power much like that seen in Antigone. It is clear from the articles set out in the Saudi Basic Law that sovereign authority is derived from the Quran, yet for the likes of Schmitt and Agamben, the roots of sovereignty are found in the *decision* about the exception.

Indeed, as Joseph Nevo and others have noted, Islam serves as a 'double-edged sword', both legitimizing and de-legitimizing action through recourse to Islamic rhetoric.[64] Here, sovereign power has been contested by groups rejecting the Islamic legitimacy of the sovereign, holding that their rule is against the true tenets of Islam. Similar views can be seen in Judaism, where the idea of the State of Israel is seen to be against the vision of Eretz Yisrael,[65] while disengagement from Gaza and the West Bank was met with vocal criticism from a range of rabbis.[66] From such a position, a zone of indistinction emerges, a void where sovereign power is contested by religious leaders.

Accepting the importance of the normative leads to an additional serious challenge concerning the potential repercussions for sovereignty, as such norms transcend territorial borders, resulting in transgression in a number of different contexts.

> Dar al-Islam is not ... inherently a territorial concept. Rather, it is a legal construct that has a territorial dimension: a territorial expression of the *umma* [...] which itself has a political component. Thus, the dar al-Islam can be considered a political-territorial expression of that community in which the Islamic religion is practiced and where it is protected by a Muslim ruler. Similarly, the dar al-sulh can be described as an area in which the practice of Islam is permitted but not under the protection of a Muslim ruler. In the dar al-harb, though Islam may be practiced, it does not enjoy the protection of the non-Muslim ruler. [67]

Such ideas are not limited to particular delineated territorial communities. As Dale Eikelman and James Piscatori argue, politics can possess an Islamic dimension through 'the invocation of ideas and symbols, which Muslims in different contexts identify as "Islamic," in support of ... organized claims and counterclaims', which find meaning across different communities and state borders.[68] The plurality of ideas and symbols within Islam which can then be used in different ways, creating a range of different interpretations, leads us to myriad understandings of Islam.

Yet it is not just religion that has the power to regulate life. Local customs and traditions also possess a strong regulatory power, both in harness and in defiance of state structures as we saw in the case of Antigone. Ideas of culture and tradition serve as a mechanism for self-recognition, allowing parallels to be drawn with the past alongside an image of the future. Those who do not act in accordance with such visions are then cast aside.[69] One only has to consider the tribal dress routinely worn by leaders across the Gulf to see how important tribal values continue to be as a means of legitimation.[70]

As I have argued elsewhere, it is imperative to recognize the importance of normative values in analysis of the Middle East. Indeed, in a time when states have fragmented and face a range of competing claims to sovereign power, ideational reserves offer a means of demonstrating legitimacy and vitality. Moreover, amid the emergence of divisions taking place along sect-based lines, fundamental claims to ordering based on religion – a *nomos* – can run contrary to a form of domestic and/or regional politics predicated on Westphalian assumptions about the *polis*.[71] With this in mind, to present a thesis of sovereign power that ignores the importance of normative and ideational factors poses serious problems when seeking to understand the contemporary Middle East.

Deploying Agamben

This chapter closes with some brief remarks and points of reflection for those intending to use Agamben in their exploration of Middle Eastern politics. There are a number of good reasons to do so, given that his ideas help to interrogate contemporary understandings of sovereign power and how sovereign power is deployed. Glancing at the history of political life across the Middle East, one easily observes the level of contestation and struggle between rulers and ruled. From the struggle against colonial rulers to the tensions between nationalist, religious, tribal, ethnic, sectarian and economic groupings, political power was contested in a plethora of ways, resulting in the creation of a range of mechanisms designed to eviscerate political meaning from individuals and, ultimately, to regulate life. Understanding the way in which such moves occur is a complex phenomenon and requires the identification of – and potential engagement with – a number of areas which span different disciplines.

1. The state of exception as a paradigm of government

Agamben's approach allows for a rigorous structural examination of the way in which sovereign power regulates political life. His assertion that the state of exception exists as a paradigm of government within the context of a 'global civil war' has a sizeable impact on constitutional forms which, in turn, shapes the mechanisms of sovereign power. This 'civil war' allows the state to address challenges from political adversaries *and* categories of (non)citizens, eliminating those it chooses to. Here, we must look at the way in which political structures operate prior to derogation and the typology of biopolitical system that operates and the way in which biopolitical structures that regulate life are embedded within the fabric of political projects. This engagement is a necessary component when seeking to apply Agamben's ideas beyond the Western world, where democracy and the rule of law are not always common features of political life.

2. Contextualizing the sovereign decision

The second stage requires consideration of the emergence of the sovereign decision within the contingency of local and regional contexts. It necessitates an exploration of the issues that shape and indeed prompt the decision on the exception. Inquiry into such factors allows for understanding the nature of the political and the conditions that give rise to the decision. Once again, such contextualization is necessary to allow for engagement with Agamben's ideas of sovereign power in the Middle East.

3. Understanding and tracing derogation

The third stage traces the legal aspects of derogation from the rule of law and the way in which emergency legislation is deployed. It requires a consideration of the mechanisms through which the sovereign decision can be implemented along with exploration of juridical oversight. Fundamentally, this is an exploration of constitutional law, requiring an understanding of legal clauses and the way in which juridical processes work.

4. The camp and agency

The final stage requires consideration of *the camp* in all of its myriad forms. It necessitates differentiation of the physical spaces of the camp and the metaphysical sites of possibility within which all can be reduced to *homines sacri*. Exploration of the physical site requires consideration of the way in which life is included by its very exclusion and the way in which the physical environment serves as a way of reinforcing sovereign power.

In this context, we must consider agency, the way in which individuals express and perform their identities. While Agamben's position appears to dismiss the very possibility of agency, as Edith Szanto and Patricia Owens powerfully assert, agency can be expressed in myriad ways, with powerful consequences, which requires further careful examination. As John Nagle argues in this volume, ideas of *destituent power* offer powerful approaches to deactivating processes of sovereign power. This approach allows for an analysis of the ways in which Agamben's thought can aid our analysis of contemporary politics. Yet the deployment of Agamben's ideas can also prompt deeper reflection into particular aspects of regional affairs, as this volume attests. Indeed, this can range from analysis of constitutional clauses and the state of exception to rumination about the nature of destituent power and resistance.

Taken together, this four-stage framework facilitates the deployment of Agamben's ideas in the Middle East. While it is clear that Agamben's work has a number of serious flaws, such an approach helps to understand the manifestation of sovereign power beyond the Western world and, with it, allows for a critical reflection on the nature of political life and the relationship between rulers and ruled. In an increasingly precarious time across the region, drawing on Agamben's ideas can provide rich scope for reflecting on the ways in which sovereign power operates and the conditions that regulate life.

Notes

1. My thanks to John Nagle and my co-editors for comments on earlier drafts of this chapter.
2. Walter Benjamin, *On the Concept of History*, VIII.
3. Giorgio Agamben, *Homo Sacer, Sovereign Power and Bare Life* (Stanford, CA: Stanford University Press, 1995), 140.
4. Michel Foucault, *The History of Sexuality: Volume I: An Introduction* (New York: Vintage Books, 1990), 143.
5. Wael Hallaq, *The Impossible State* (New York: Columbia University Press, 2013), 29.
6. Agamben, *Homo Sacer*, 18.
7. Giorgio Agamben, *State of Exception* (Chicago: University of Chicago Press, 2005), 35.
8. Ibid., 23.
9. Ibid.

10 Ibid., 2.
11 Agamben, *Homo Sacer*, 50.
12 Agamben, *State of Exception*, 23.
13 Ibid., 28.
14 Ibid.
15 Ibid., 170.
16 Ibid., 3.
17 Ibid., 23.
18 Ibid., 24–31.
19 G. Balladore-Pallieri, *Diritto Costituzionale* (Milan: Giuffrè, 1965), 168.
20 Thomas Lemke, '"A Zone of Indistinction": Critique of Giorgio Agamben's Concept of Biopolitics', *Outlines: Critical Practice Studies* 7, no. 1 (2005): 5.
21 Derek Gregory, *The Colonial Present: Afghanistan, Palestine, Iraq* (Oxford: Blackwell, 2004), 258.
22 Agamben, *Homo Sacer*, 7.
23 Ibid., 9.
24 Ibid., 115.
25 Jenny Edkins, and Veronika Pin-Fat, 'Introduction: Life, Power, Resistance', in *Sovereign Lives: Power in Global Politics*, ed. Jenny Edkins, Michael J. Shapiro and Veronika Pin-Fat (New York: Routledge, 2004), 9.
26 Agamben, *Homo Sacer*, 140.
27 Oliver Belcher, Lauren Martin, Anna Secor, Stephanie Simon and Tommy Wilson, 'Everywhere and Nowhere: The Exception and the Topological Challenge to Geography', *Antipode* 40 (2008).
28 Richard Ek, 'Giorgio Agamben and the Spatialities of the Camp', *Geografiska Annaler Series B: Human Geography* 88B (2006): 363–86; Derek Gregory, 'The Black Flag: Guantanamo Bay and the Space of Exception', *Geografiska Annaler: Series B, Human Geography* 88, no. 4 (2006): 405–27; Claudio Minca, 'The Return of the Camp', *Progress in Human Geography* 29 (2005): 405–12; Claudio Minca, 'Giorgio Agamben and the New Biopolitical Nomos', *Geografiska Annaler: Series B, Human Geography* 88, no. 4 (2006): 387–403; S. Reid-Henry, 'Exceptional Sovereignty? Guantanamo Bay and the Re-colonial Present', *Antipode* 39 (2007): 627–48.
29 Belcher et al., 2008 and Minca 2006.
30 Agamben, *Homo Sacer*, 123.
31 Agamben, *State of Exception*, 109.
32 Agamben, *Homo Sacer*, 168–9.
33 Ibid., 170.
34 Nasser Hussein, 'Beyond Norm and Exception: Guantanamo', *Critical Inquiry* 33 (2007): 735–41.
35 Agamben, *Homo Sacer*, 171.
36 Lemke, 'Zone of Indistinction', 6.
37 Sari Hanafi and Taylor Long, 'Governance, Governmentalities, and the State of Exception in the Palestinian Refugee Camps of Lebanon', *Journal of Refugee Studies* 23, no. 2 (1 June 2010): 134–59; Sari Hanafi, 'Governing the Palestinian Refugee Camps in Lebanon and Syria. The Cases of Nahr el-Bared and Yarmouk Camps', in *Palestinian Refugees: Identity, Space and Place in the Levant*, ed. Are Knudsen and S. Hanafi (Routledge, 2011); A. Ramadan, 'In the Ruins of Nahr al-Barid: Understanding the Meaning of the Camp', *Journal of Palestine Studies* 40, no. 1 (2010): 49–62; A. Ramadan, 'Destroying Nahr el-Bared: Sovereignty and Urbicide in the

Space of Exception', *Political Geography* 28, no. 3 (2009): 153–63; A. Ramadan and S. Fregonese, 'Hybrid Sovereignty and the State of Exception in the Palestinian Refugee Camps in Lebanon', *Annals of the American Association of Geographers* 107, no. 4 (2017): 949–63.

38 Hanafi, 'Governing the Palestinian Refugee Camps', 30.
39 Laleh Khalili, 'Incarceration and the State of Exception: Al-Ansar Mass Detention Camp in Lebanon', in *Thinking Palestine*, ed. Ronit Lentin (London: Zed, 2008), 101–16.
40 Silverman, 'Redrawing the Lines of Control: Political Interventions by Refugees and the Sovereign State System', Paper presented at Dead/Lines: Contemporary Issues in Legal and Political Theory, University of Edinburgh, 28 April 2008. Cited in Hanafi and Long, *Governance, Governmentalities*.
41 Edith Szanto, 'Sayyida Zaynab in the State of Exception: Shi'I Sainthood as "Qualified Life" in Contemporary Syria', *International Journal of Middle East Studies* 44 (2012): 285–99.
42 See Ronit Lentin, *Traces of Racial Exception: Racializing Israeli Settler Colonialism* (London: Bloomsbury, 2018) and R. Lentin (ed.), *Thinking Palestine* (London: Zed Books, 2008); Ronit Lentin, 'Palestine/Israel and State Criminality: Exception, Settler Colonialism and Racialization', *State Crime Journal* 5, no. 1 (2016): 32–50.
43 S. Hanafi, 'Explaining Spacio-Cide in the Palestinian Territory: Colonization, Separation, and State of Exception', *Current Sociology* 61, no. 2 (2013): 190–205.
44 Simon Mabon, *Houses Built on Sand: Violence, Sectarianism and Revolution in the Middle East* (Manchester: Manchester University Press, 2020).
45 Ibid., see also Mabon, 'The World Is a Garden: *Nomos*, Sovereignty and the (Contested) Ordering of Life', *Review of International Studies* 45, no. 5 (2019): 870–90.
46 See Mabon, *Sovereignty, Arab Uprisings and Bare Life*. Available online: https://pomed.org/wp-content/uploads/2017/08/Lust_FINAL.pdf.
47 Michael Hardt and Antonio Negri, *Empire* (Cambridge, MA: Harvard UP, 2000).
48 Szanto, 'Sayyida Zaynab'.
49 Hallaq, *Impossible State*, 23.
50 Ibid., 29.
51 Mabon, *Houses*.
52 Joel Migdal, *Strong Societies, Weak States* (Princeton, NJ: Princeton University Press, 1988), 19.
53 Robert M. Fishman, 'Rethinking State and Regime: Southern Europe's Transition to Democracy', *World Politics* 42, no. 3 (1990): 428.
54 Mabon, *Houses*, 11.
55 Quran, verse 5:3, 'Surah of Al Mai'dah'.
56 Quran, verse 2:173.
57 Ibid.
58 Shahab Ahmed, *What Is Islam? The Importance of Being Islamic* (Princeton, NJ: Princeton University Press, 2007).
59 Shadi Hamid, *Islamic Exceptionalism: How the Struggle over Islam Is Shaping the World* (New York: St Martin's Press, 2016).
60 Quran, verse 4:105.
61 Quran, verse 6:115.
62 Muhammad Rashid Rida, *Al- Khilafa aw al-Imama al-ʿUzma* (Cairo: al-Zahra' li'l-iʿlam al-ʿarabi, 1988 [1922]).
63 Seen in the case of Saudi Arabia and Egypt, albeit in contrasting ways.

64 Joseph Nevo, 'Religion and National Identity in Saudi Arabia', *Middle Eastern Studies* 34, no. 3 (1998). See also the seizure of the Grand Mosque of Mecca in 1979 by an Islamist who rejected the Islamic credentials of the House of Saud. See T. Hegghammer, and S. Lacroix, 'Rejectionist Islamism in Saudi Arabia: The Story of Juhayman Al-'Utaybi Revisited', *International Journal of Middle East Studies* 39, no. 1 (2007): 103–22.
65 Rabbi Y. Ginsburgh, *On the Way to a Jewish State: Israeli Politics according to Kabbalah* (United States of America and Israel: Gal Einai, 2014).
66 Elisha Efrat, *The West Bank and Gaza Strip: A Geography of Occupation and Disengagement* (Oxon: Routledge, 2006).
67 M. Parvin and M. Sommer, 'Dar Al-Islam: The Evolution of Muslim Territoriality and Its Implications for Conflict Resolution', *International Journal of Middle East Studies* 11 (1980): 4–5.
68 Dale F. Eickelman and James Piscatori, *Muslim Politics* (Princeton, NJ: Princeton University Press, 1996), 4.
69 Hamid Rabi, *Suluk al-malik fi tadbir al-mamalik: ta'lif al-'allamma shihab al-Din ibn Abi al-Rubayyi'* (Cairo: Dar al-Sha'b, 1980), 218.
70 Philip S. Khoury and Joseph Kostiner (eds), *Tribes and State Formation in the Middle East* (Berkeley: University of California Press, 1990).
71 Mabon, 'The World Is a Garden'.

References

Agamben, Giorgio. *Homo Sacer, Sovereign Power and Bare Life*. Stanford, CA: Stanford University Press, 1995.
Agamben, Giorgio. *State of Exception*. Chicago: University of Chicago Press, 2005.
Ahmed, Shahab. *What Is Islam? The Importance of Being Islamic*. Princeton, NJ: Princeton University Press, 2007.
Balladore-Pallieri, G. *Diritto Costituzionale*. Milan: Giuffrè, 1965.
Belcher, Oliver, Lauren Martin, Anna Secor, Stephanie Simon, and Tommy Wilson. 'Everywhere and Nowhere: The Exception and the Topological Challenge to Geography'. *Antipode* 40 (2008): 499–503.
Benjamin, Walter. *On the Concept of History VIII*. London and New York: Continuum, 2005.
Edkins, Jenny and Veronika Pin-Fat. 'Introduction: Life, Power, Resistance'. In *Sovereign Lives: Power in Global Politics*, edited by Jenny Edkins, Michael J. Shapiro and Veronika Pin-Fat. New York: Routledge, (2004): 1–21.
Efrat, Elisha. *The West Bank and Gaza Strip: A Geography of Occupation and Disengagement*. Oxon: Routledge, 2006.
Eickelman, Dale F. and James Piscatori. *Muslim Politics*. Princeton, NJ: Princeton University Press, 1996.
Ek, Richard. 'Giorgio Agamben and the Spatialities of the Camp'. *Geografiska Annaler Series B: Human Geography* 88B (2006): 363–86.
Fishman, Robert M. 'Rethinking State and Regime: Southern Europe's Transition to Democracy'. *World Politics* 42, no. 3 (1990): 422–40.
Foucault, Michel. *The History of Sexuality: Volume I: An Introduction*. New York: Vintage Books, 1990.
Ginsburgh, Rabbi Y. *On the Way to a Jewish State: Israeli Politics according to Kabbalah*. United States of America and Israel: Gal Einai, 2014.

Gregory, Derek. *The Colonial Present: Afghanistan, Palestine, Iraq*. Oxford: Blackwell, 2004.
Gregory, Derek. 'The Black Flag: Guantanamo Bay and the Space of Exception'. *Geografiska Annaler: Series B, Human Geography* 88, no. 4 (2006): 405–27.
Hallaq, Wael. *The Impossible State*. New York: Columbia University Press, 2013.
Hamid, Shadi. *Islamic Exceptionalism: How the Struggle over Islam Is Shaping the World*. New York: St Martin's Press, 2016.
Hanafi, Sari. 'Governing the Palestinian Refugee Camps in Lebanon and Syria. The Cases of Nahr el-Bared and Yarmouk Camps'. In *Palestinian Refugees: Identity, Space and Place in the Levant*, edited by Are Knudsen and S. Hanafi, 29–49. Oxon: Routledge, 2011.
Hanafi, Sari. 'Explaining Spacio-Cide in the Palestinian Territory: Colonization, Separation, and State of Exception'. *Current Sociology* 61, no. 2 (2013): 190–205.
Hanafi, Sari and Taylor Long. 'Governance, Governmentalities, and the State of Exception in the Palestinian Refugee Camps of Lebanon'. *Journal of Refugee Studies* 23, no. 2 (2010): 134–59.
Hardt, Michael and Antonio Negri. *Empire*. Cambridge, MA: Harvard University Press, 2000.
Hegghammer, Thomas and Stephan Lacroix. 'Rejectionist Islamism in Saudi Arabia: The Story of Juhayman Al-'Utaybi Revisited'. *International Journal of Middle East Studies* 39, no. 1 (2007): 103–22.
Hussein, Nasser. 'Beyond Norm and Exception: Guantanamo'. *Critical Inquiry* 33 (2007): 735–41.
Khalili, Laleh 'Incarceration and the State of Exception: Al-Ansar Mass Detention Camp in Lebanon'. In *Thinking Palestine*, edited by Ronit Lentin, 101–16. London: Zed, 2008.
Khoury, Philip S. and Joseph Kostiner, eds. *Tribes and State Formation in the Middle East*. Berkeley: University of California Press, 1990.
Lemke, Thomas. "'A Zone of Indistinction": Critique of Giorgio Agamben's Concept of Biopolitics'. *Outlines: Critical Practice Studies* 7, no. 1 (2005).
Lentin, Ronit. *Traces of Racial Exception: Racializing Israeli Settler Colonialism*. London: Bloomsbury, 2018.
Lentin, Ronit, ed. *Thinking Palestine*. London: Zed Books, 2008.
Lentin, Ronit. 'Palestine/Israel and State Criminality: Exception, Settler Colonialism and Racialization'. *State Crime Journal* 5, no. 1 (2016): 32–50.
Mabon, Simon *Houses Built on Sand: Violence, Sectarianism and Revolution in the Middle East*. Manchester: Manchester University Press, 2020.
Mabon, Simon. 'The World Is a Garden: *Nomos*, Sovereignty and the (Contested) Ordering of Life'. *Review of International Studies* 45, no. 5 (2019): 870–90.
Migdal, Joel. *Strong Societies, Weak States*. Princeton, NJ: Princeton University Press, 1988.
Minca, Claudio. 'The Return of the Camp'. *Progress in Human Geography* 29 (2005): 405–12.
Minca, Claudio. 'Giorgio Agamben and the New Biopolitical Nomos'. *Geografiska Annaler: Series B, Human Geography* 88, no. 4 (2006): 387–403.
Nevo, Joseph. 'Religion and National Identity in Saudi Arabia'. *Middle Eastern Studies* 34, no. 3 (1998).
Parvin, M. and M. Sommer. 'Dar Al-Islam: The Evolution of Muslim Territoriality and Its Implications for Conflict Resolution'. *International Journal of Middle East Studies* 11 (1980).
Qur'an. Translated by Abdullah Yusuf Ali. Ware, Hertfordshire: Wordsworth Editions Limited, 2013.

Rabi, Hamid. *Suluk al-malik fi tadbir al-mamalik: taʾlif al-ʿallamma shihab al-Din ibn Abi al-Rubayyiʿ*. Cairo: Dar al-Shaʾb, 1980.
Ramadan, Adam. 'Destroying Nahr el-Bared: Sovereignty and Urbicide in the Space of Exception'. *Political Geography* 28, no. 3 (2009): 153–63.
Ramadan, Adam 'In the Ruins of Nahr al-Barid: Understanding the Meaning of the Camp'. *Journal of Palestine Studies* 40, no. 1 (2010): 49–62.
Ramadan, Adam and Sara Fregonese. 'Hybrid Sovereignty and the State of Exception in the Palestinian Refugee Camps in Lebanon'. *Annals of the American Association of Geographers* 107, no. 4 (2017): 949–63.
Rida, Muhammad Rashid. *Al–Khilafa aw al-Imama al-ʿUzma*. Cairo: al-Zahraʾ liʾl-iʿlam al-ʿarabi, 1988 [1922].
Reid- Henry, S. 'Exceptional Sovereignty? Guantanamo Bay and the Re-colonial Present'. *Antipode* 39 (2007): 627–48.
Schacht, Joseph. *An Introduction to Islamic Law*. Oxford: Clarendon Press,1964.
Szanto, Edith 'Sayyida Zaynab in the State of Exception: Shiʾi Sainthood as "Qualified Life" in Contemporary Syria'. *International Journal of Middle East Studies* 44 (2012): 285–99.

Chapter 2

THE GULF COOPERATION COUNCIL POLICE IMAGINED

THE STATE OF EXCEPTION AND TRANSNATIONAL POLICING

Staci Strobl and Simon Mabon

Introduction

In response to the events known as the 'Arab Spring', the Gulf Cooperation Council (GCC) countries formed a regional police agency (GCC Police) as a mechanism of ensuring the survival of monarchical rule across member states. The agreement for the agency, signed in 2014, is unique among transnational security organizations. Most regional security organizations, such as EUROPOL and INTERPOL, primarily share information, intelligence, training and tactics among their national police, rather than having their own standing police force. However, according to press releases at the time of its inception, the GCC Police reportedly plans to have a standing police force that would be at the ready for use by regional and member state authorities in the face of challenges to their rule.

This chapter focuses on the nature of post-Arab Spring policing in the Gulf in the context of identity-based order maintenance[1] and authoritarian regimes in the modern era. It uses Agamben's notion of *states of exception* and *bare life* as a theoretical explanation for understanding the GCC Police as a response to the Arab Spring, and contextualizes the decisions of Gulf states to start policing transnationally (Area 2 among the list of ways to employ Agamben within this volume). An externally aligned regional police force builds on the historical use of outside mercenaries and military forces to control marginalized people within Gulf states, and the GCC effectively casts entire communities of identity-based activists and other civil society actors as internal threats. By looking at other examples of regional policing around the world, it becomes apparent that the GCC Police are slated to have significantly more powers than comparative institutions, in particular, INTERPOL, EUROPOL and the United Nations (UN) Police (formerly UN Civil Police), showing a unique use of transnational policing as a technology of government and *bare life* in the Gulf milieu.

In what follows, we argue that the creation of the GCC Police serves to reinforce sovereign power within – and between – member states of the Gulf Cooperation Council. Using the work of Giorgio Agamben, we suggest that the GCC Police serves as a tool of sovereign power, re-enforcing a *state of exception* and zones of indistinction *within* and *between* states that allows for the abandonment of individuals into bare life.

GCCPOL

The GCC Police is a relatively new force attempting to 'strength[en] the security cooperation among the [member states] in the field of combatting crime' (GCC 2019a), and, as aforementioned, augments and enhances past sovereign projects in the Gulf to regulate the political life of perceived internal enemies. It has a specific focus on counterterrorism and civil defence (GCC no date). It is important to note that counterterrorism efforts in the Gulf countries often entail rooting out alleged Iranian-backed insurgency plots that critics of this characterization would simply call 'pro-democracy advocacy', revealing processes of sectarianization that ground local dissent within broader geopolitical currents;[2] ultimately, ruling regimes perceive these activities as threatening national security.[3] The term 'civil defence' in the GCC Police Mission also appears to refer to threats to sovereignty and national security, as opposed to typical police goals of public safety.

Since its inception, the institution has taken on the appellation 'GCCPOL', discursively linking it to the other worldwide -POLs, despite its differences in the level of governance behind its operations (see next section) and its intended use of a standing force. The difference is deliberate. It was at the 35th GCC Summit in 2014 that Gulf leaders announced the creation of a regional police force based in Abu Dhabi. Qatari foreign minister Sheikh Khalid Bin Mohammed Al-Attiyah told reporters that the new police would 'be an Interpol-like force *but inside* GCC countries' (authors' emphasis).[4] In other words, it would be more 'inside' the countries than INTERPOL, a not insignificant remark in terms of understanding how the force will be distinct from typical models of transnational policing, discussed further. It also provides a prime example of language revealing the sovereign project. When Al-Attiyah declares the GCC Police are INTERPOL-like 'but inside' the countries themselves, he is describing the new institution as a deliberate in their boundary-blurring, betraying that the GCC governments desire more policing power than typical -POLs, operating inside GCC states but positioned outside while deriving power from within. The parallels with Agamben's discussion of sovereign power here are easily drawn, identifying a zone of indistinction in which both sovereign and GCC force appear to operate.

Reading further into Al-Attiyah's sentiment, the policy of INTERPOL to explicitly hold back from state-level political entanglements represents a model that was seen by Gulf rulers as falling short of what they needed in their region. Linking this again to Agamben, we see that the logic of sovereign projects consistently finds itself cut through with prejudicial or partisan political power that undermines the inclusivity of the state apparatuses. In this case, the GCC Police firmly become a threshold space between the outside and the inside, legitimizing a policing project that is structured to be hard on political opposition within, while being advantageously allied with political friends abroad.

Contextual background

By way of background, the Gulf Cooperation Council has six members in the Arabian Gulf region: Saudi Arabia, Kuwait, Bahrain, Qatar, Oman and the United Arab Emirates (UAE). In addition, Yemen, Jordan and Morocco each have cooperation agreements with the GCC although they are not full member states. Broadly speaking, the GCC mission is to effect cooperation between member states in the areas of security, economics, education, culture, technological advancement, business development, resource extraction and agriculture, to name a few areas.[5] The new GCC Police's mission includes 'strengthening the security cooperation among the [member states] in the field of combatting crime'[6] with a specific focus on counterterrorism and civil defence.[7] The GCC monarchies are Sunni and connect to each other through historic tribal alliances and shared culture, in addition to having linkages related to geographic proximity and shared economic and security interests. However, some populations within these countries belong to other sects or ideologies within Islam (notably Shi'ism or Salafi movements).

The Arab Spring Uprisings, the most robust being in Bahrain, drew in part from Shi'a opposition groups and pointed to historical patterns of Sunni subjugation of Shi'a people throughout the Gulf. The protest movement in Bahrain challenged the capacity of a Sunni royal family to hold onto power in the wake of widespread social disillusionment with the lack of democracy and social and economic equality, with strong participation by the Shi'a majority underclass. In March of 2011, military forces from the GCC's Peninsula Shield Force (PSF) put down the non-violent protests in Bahrain[8] and destroyed the Pearl Monument (standing at the place where protesters first gathered in large numbers) in a clear demonstration of sovereign power, viewed by some as a form of urbicide, or violence against socioculturally diverse city residents. During and after the Arab Spring, crimes related to political speech, such as insulting rulers and disparaging leaders, have been increasingly prosecuted throughout the region, in violation of Articles 19 and 20 of the United Nations' Universal Declaration of Human Rights.[9] The use of such strategies in Bahrain – and elsewhere – is not new, but rather represents the broad regulation of life in an effort to assert sovereign power.[10]

The GCC Police is allegedly preparing to act as a standing force at the ready to stifle future protests like the Arab Spring Uprisings should they arise. Likely, its creation is a tactic to avoid repeating criticisms that military forces were inappropriately used against Bahraini protesters in 2012 while permitting internal civil society to be targeted by regional forces.[11] It also points to a broader cultivation of conditions that may prevent such protests from emerging at all. The timing of the GCC Police Mission, envisioned as the enforcement arm of a regionally aligned strategy to uphold individual Sunni state sovereignty, has been questioned by democratic movements and minority Shi'a groups.[12] It appears to be a strategy for politically fragile states to bulk up their staying power, though of course this strategy is not explicitly stated in the founding documents for the force. Human Rights Watch in particular has raised the concern that 'the [envisioned GCC Police] gives gulf governments another legal pretext to stamp out dissent. . . . Citizens and residents of the [G]ulf should note that their governments have agreed to share personal information [internationally] at the whim of an interior minister', based on the initiative's provisions allowing for the suppression of 'interference in the domestic affairs' of other GCC countries.[13]

Deploying Agamben to understand the GCC Police

According to Agamben, a feature of the law in sovereign states is that it contains the simultaneous capacity for the suspension of that law.[14] The inherent existence of the exception to the law, whether normative or within the law itself, is the means by which a sovereign controls political life and, in particular, can cast some people outside of it.[15] The unravelling of what is prescribed as law from the very authoritative source (the sovereign) of the law itself is a particularly useful framework in spaces like the Middle East, where the formal rule of law is not necessarily the most robust feature of political life and normative practices routinely usurp it.[16] Known as the *state of exception*, this reality of the source of law undoing the law is 'neither external nor internal to the juridical order . . . inside and outside do not exclude each other but rather blur with each other'.[17] In the Gulf context, Sunni, tribal-based sovereignties show overt signs of managing the inside from the outside and the outside from the inside. The interconnected nature of regional, transnational communities, whether based on ethnic, sect, tribal or other commonalities, serves as a means of uniting people within and outside national contexts. As Mabon describes for the Middle East in general, political projects within particular states often clash with other loyalties operating transnationally, leading to 'existential challenges'[18] seemingly originating within the state's territory itself but not contained by it. The state seeks to 'close off an inside against and outside' and in doing so creates the conditions of Agamben's notion of *bare life*, or the quality of existence for groups whose full political participation is suppressed or cut off; the state in essence is unable to forefront its own legitimacy without excluding many within its domain and individuals become displaced from the inside.[19]

The recent formation of a GCC Police shows the *state of exception* logic operating in state decision-making which compels states towards transnational cooperation. Under new security agreements, the order maintenance functions of ordinary policing, constitutionally a matter of the Gulf states' ministers of the interiors, ironically drift into the purview of GCC foreign ministries and the transnational joint security agreement for policing. As such, policing in the region begins to operate more collectively and externally (yet also to the benefit of each countries' internal political order, operating as a *state of exception*). Although on one hand, transnational agreements limit sovereignty, on the other, a perceived shared existential threat may make some loss of sovereignty palpable and provide for the continuation of that sovereignty in the face of legitimacy questions within. This, for Agamben, results in the cultivation of two simultaneous zones of indistinction: *within states* stemming from the ability of the GCC force *and* national governments to impose *states of exception* in states and also *between states*, due to the formation of the GCC force and its transnational powers.

For example, Shi'a identities cross borders and are perceived as threatening to individual state legitimacy. Shi'a have historically been perceived by Sunni monarchies as cooperating with their co-religionists across borders, in terms of both loyalty and their quest for the realization of civil rights within their countries. As a response, Sunni monarchies mirror their perception of the threat with cooperation across borders, as both a 'technique of government' and the revealing indicator of the *state of exception* logic of sovereignty itself.[20] Uniting under a new police institution that potentially force-multiplies the responses to any one country's internal unrest, and providing external support to internal police order maintenance functions, the Sunni monarchies aim to manage the existential political threat posed by divergent identity groups. Yet while Shi'a groups have been a focus of much concern among GCC states – perhaps with the slight caveat of Kuwait – in recent years focus has also turned to Islamist movements and pro-democracy activists.

The GCC countries manifest this show of sovereignty in a distinct way when compared to other transnational police organizations globally, as will become apparent later. In engaging the contextual factors that surround the *state of exception* in the Gulf, the Shi'a and civil society uprising in Bahrain in 2012 is an important moment. However, smaller but no less palpable movements sprung up in Oman, Saudi Arabia and UAE (these also giving rise to perceived existential threats from not just Shi'a but also Salafi/Muslim Brotherhood groups). The resulting law enforcement-based technologies of government, especially the GCC Police, find themselves in a distinct space when considering the global trend towards transnational police organizations. Gulf monarchies appear to be capitalizing on this trend while also expanding and extrapolating on existing models of international policing in pursuit of regime survival.

Continuity and change in Gulf policing: A history of blurring

To explore how Gulf policing operates, facilitated by a *state of exception*, it is important to show how these conditions are both persistent and lead to innovations, such as the GCC Police, as states adapt their technologies of government to perceived threats. As Agamben has articulated, the manifestations of *bare life* change and renew themselves[21] but are fundamentally still tied to the original paradox of sovereignty being based on both juridical practices and its capacity to forego those practices as a permanent *state of exception*. The *state of exception* then can be seen and felt precisely where the contradictions blur into one reality creating a zone of indistinction in the process, and, broadly speaking,

Agamben encourages a reading of political reality that is not merely inside–outside but could also be the blurring of police–military (the inside and outside of the use of force) and high–low (the big and small projects within police functions), as will be discussed further. Perhaps where there is blurring, there is also a *state of exception* and in the history of Gulf policing and the GCC Police, blurring is rampant.

As Marc Owen Jones documents, there is a long history of this blurring in Bahrain, through the use of foreign mercenaries, colonial advisors and the balancing of both sectarian and demographic interests within the security apparatus and regulation of life across the state.[22] Yet this is not limited to history. One contemporary instance of blurring is the use of outside mercenaries to police Emirati opposition in the Arab Spring. Activists in the United Arab Emirates joined the Arab Spring Uprisings in March 2011 when they drafted and posted an online petition calling on the UAE president to hold direct elections to parliament and to reconstitute the body with legislative powers. A total of 133 Emiratis signed the petition, using the now-defunct UAEHewar website, and hailing from all the emirates in the federation. In response, police arrested five of the main activists behind the petition, Nasser bin Ghaith, Ahmed Mansoor, Fahad Salim Dalk, Hassan Ali al-Khamis and Ahmed Abdul Khaleq. Subsequently, the state-controlled media painted these activists as agents of Iran and religious extremists while the UN Working Group on Arbitrary Detention expressed concern and ordered their release. Known as the 'UAE Five', they were tried for publicly insulting the UAE leadership and ultimately sentenced to three years imprisonment each, but then pardoned twenty-four hours later, ostensibly to show magnanimity.[23] A later 'UAE Seven' were arrested after calling for reform as part of the Islamist group Reform and Social Guidance Association. Meanwhile, the crown prince of Abu Dhabi hired the mercenary firm Blackwater to install several hundred undercover police, posing as foreign construction workers, whose mission in part was to put down protests. By the end of July 2012, fifty-four political prisoners languished in the UAE, including a young 'stateless' (*bidoun*) Emirati whose crime was tweeting about the Arab Spring.[24]

In particular, the use of external security forces to police internal civil society dissidents had gained quick traction in the region, seemingly suspending constitutional provisions to the contrary, blending legal and illegal behaviour – operating with impunity, beyond the law – in service to sovereign interest. Events in Bahrain also embodied this notion when the PSF, built of Saudi Arabian and Emirati military, quashed the public protests in March of 2011 and destroyed the Pearl Monument. During the Bahrain uprising, over a hundred protesters and several police lost their lives during the first two years of the ongoing unrest. In February and April of 2019, citizenship revocation was handed down to dozens of people, mostly Shi'a, simultaneously through the use of mass trials.[25] Although King Hamad bin Isa Al Khalifah reversed the revocations in about 500 cases, several hundred Bahrainis continue to be newly stateless, requesting asylum in other countries. And, those who received restored citizenship tended to not be the most prominent figures, such as Sheikh Isa Qasim.[26] Speaking up about rights violations unleashes the criminal justice apparatus of anti-Shi'a discrimination and the machineries of sovereign power deployed by the state.

Despite being formally envisioned as public safety agency for burgeoning nation states in the late colonial era, the UAE police cast people within their territories as outsiders – often into conditions of *bare life* – from the beginning, revealing that the blurring characteristic emblematic of a *state of exception* is linked to the earliest national law enforcement. To explain, modern policing, as institutions belonging to the nation state and allegedly focused on public safety in multicultural communities, has a very recent history in the region, particularly in the UAE. Up until the 1950s, most emirates had tribal law enforcement in the form of armed retainers loyal only to the individual rulers, and drawn from sheikhs within the rulers' tribes and hired hands from allied Sunni tribes or countries. Throughout the nineteenth and early twentieth centuries, the British attempted to install uniformed police forces as part of their development project, aiming to enhance general public safety in the Trucial States (as the UAE was known in the colonial period). The British desired forces that purportedly would police in a broad way, over the more narrow goals of its rulers who focused mainly on maintaining tribal political order and subject loyalty. The British, in line with European notions of policing, were interested in suppressing crime, undertaking criminal investigations, executing warrants and operating police stations and prisons, in addition to maintaining political order. Of course, in line with Agamben, these imperial forms of policing are not outside the project of political order and sovereignty itself and, in fact, are fundamental to the form the *state of exception* takes in a colonial state. Through the bureaucratic machinations of crime control and policing, the British shifted power at the local level into their imperial domain while at the same time seeking to maintain rulers' sovereignty in a new way. In other words, the imperial project, though cloaked in the rule of law, ultimately re-enforced the insider–outside zones of distinction within the emirates, eventually creating hybridized forms of imperial-tribal control.

This negotiation between colonial and local forms of law and order is exemplified by the early failures of modern policing in the region and a resulting concession to a hybridized form. One of the earliest attempts to establish a police wing of the Trucial Oman Levies (whose jurisdiction included present-day UAE and Oman) failed in the early 1960s because rulers were reluctant to support it in their budgets, still preferring their customary tribal enforcement of loyal tribal and Sunni retainers. Likewise, the first police force belonging to the city of Abu Dhabi failed for the same reason, royal reluctance to support it financially even though the rulers had acquiesced to the Political Residency (British colonial administration in the region) demands for it. Eventually, more local, tribal control was fused with the colonial bureaucratic forms for a hybrid model. For example, the first commander of the viable Abu Dhabi force was Sheikh Sultan bin Shakbut al Nahyan, the son of Emir Sheikh Shakhbut II bin Sultan Al Nahyan; therefore, even the new modern force could not be more closely connected to the ruler himself, bringing in customary notions of order maintenance into an institution that would be the cornerstone of law and order in the eventual nation state. As such, the main tasks of the new force were to escort the royal family, guard the emirates emerging oil extraction operations and to man checkpoints at Abu Dhabi Island and al-Ain, places where non-Abu Dhabians potentially entered the emirate,[27] all tasks that focused on protecting the interests of the ruling families, with the imperial forms of crime control (criminal investigations, executing warrants and operating police stations and prisons) as secondary tasks.

This history of reluctant modern policing is important because it highlights the stickiness of customary notions of order maintenance in the UAE and the Gulf region as a whole which can run contrary to more formal institutions of power. It is also important because the exception to the force is built in from the beginning; where it is bureaucratically structured to focus on broad goals of public safety, it ultimately retains its primary mission of protecting emirs, blurring and sometimes substituting the functions of public safety and regime protection. Although the British were successful in establishing modern policing, the political context for policing was that it was acceptable to rulers only if its implicit mission involved protecting the rulers and maintaining tribal order, thereby baking into the foundations of policing, in the UAE and other Gulf countries, an identity and power-differential in the very operation of police services. As tribal retainers were replaced by police, the socially desired (at least by the rulers) function they served transferred, albeit in a modified way, to the modern police force, making it a hybrid of British notions of police as a public safety entity and the Emirati notion of policing as a maintenance of tribal social order, contradictory functions that place it firmly in the blurred realm of the state of exception.

Although post-independent forms of policing continued to evolve, the persistence of policing as a means of maintaining tribal sovereignties remains a feature of current Emirati policing. As one scholar described the contemporary security forces, they remain 'fragmented and shot through with informal patronage, and senior ranks include many members of the ruling families'.[28] Further, suspicion of the Shi'a community and its lack of loyalty to the ruling families are palpable, a thread that continues from earlier decades. Today, although the Shi'a community is relatively small (15 per cent), suspicion of these communities as having loyalty to Iran and being second-class citizens is present in unofficial discourse among tribal elites. Further, the large amount of expatriate residents of the country in financial, service and construction industries represents another public that stands outside the tribal order and can be construed as less deserving of police services and protection.

Similarly, in Bahrain, a majority Shi'a country, the same process of Sunni tribal retainers being replaced by a modern police force consisting overwhelmingly of Sunni and tribal loyalists occurred earlier and with a heavier hand by the British than in the UAE. In *Sectarian Order in Bahrain: The Social and Colonial Origins of Criminal Justice*,[29] Strobl describes the deep administrative takeover of Bahrain by way of the Orders-in-Council of 1919 and the forced abdication of Sheikh Isa bin Ali al Khalifah. These events provided an entre for a British-inspired and largely British-controlled development of a Levy Corps for internal order maintenance. Later this morphed into the formation of the Bahrain State Police in the late 1920s under the command of Sir Charles Belgrave. Like in the Emirates, the foundations of modern policing in Bahrain involved regime loyalty, so much so that Shi'a recruits began to be selected against as early as the 1930s amid concerns about divided loyalties. Instead, the force relied in the colonial era on officers from other parts of the British Empire such as India and Sudan. Policing in Bahrain comes of age while discursively the Shi'a, and in particular Shi'a of Persian ethnic origin, were being constructed as a criminal class and the target of police scrutiny for their perceived ties to Iran (which at the time had claims to Bahrain pending in the League of Nations). This social construction dovetailed with long-standing al Khalifah exploitation of indigenous Shi'a populations who they had conquered, and imposed a feudal system on, in the late eighteenth century. As in other parts of the Gulf, customary policing in the country was originally the purview of the royal family's armed retainers who were known for their 'repeated excess earn[ing] them the animosity of the people'.[30]

It seems the British intervention in Emirati and Bahraini policing created a compromise between public safety overtures and sovereign protection that even today cannot be easily disentangled and de-blurred, at times resulting in conditions of bare life for citizens and residents of Gulf states, abandoned by the law and subjected to the whim of the sovereign. Theoretically, the situation hangs together when considered as an Agambenian undoing of the promises of modern law enforcement within that law enforcement itself. Initially, the early forces in Abu Dhabi and Dubai were heavily engineered and supplied by colonial administrators, and British contract officers served in the top leadership and as a percentage of the force itself. Though not officially a part of the British colonial police service, the Abu Dhabi and Dubai forces drew heavily from these ranks, with top commanders and consultants having extensive experience in colonial outposts like India, Sudan and Palestine. Moreover, they sent their recruits to British military and policing training institutes in Kuwait.[31] As such, the imperial and police occupational networks were complicit in setting up the politicized and identity-based style of policing, implicitly accepting the heavy-handed role of rulers and royal families in the operations of the police. The small world of functionaries willing to strike the balance between the forces of modernization and the customs of ruling families rotated among the Gulf countries at least through the 1990s. As Paul Rich describes, 'often a British official has [expatriate] family links with the Gulf', for example, a Foreign Office official who grew up in the Emirates and later worked in Qatar or an ambassador to the UAE who had previously served as a junior political agent in another Gulf country.[32] Further, the persistence of police institutions that would include regime-loyal groups – and excluding those deemed to be hostile to the regime – while simultaneously criminalizing political opposition also represents the persistence of Agambenian *bare life*. The nature of these institutions shows how the institution of policing is a critical component of maintaining the *state of exception* over time.

Similar trends in police history are found throughout the Gulf among British colonial possessions (all the GCC member states except Saudi Arabia), albeit with slightly different time frames and institutional trajectories. The transition took place earliest in Bahrain, which had the first modern police forces in the late 1920s.[33] The importance of recognizing this transitional history rests in acknowledging the foundational identity-based orientation of policing in the Gulf from its modern inception. There is no separation between the development of uniformed officers cloaked in the Western-style notions of public safety in modernizing societies without the simultaneous strong underlying orientation towards protecting and privileging Sunni citizens and those citizens who are loyal to Sunni-identified monarchies. This deeply conservative and identity-oriented foundation of the police function is a constant refrain in the last few decades that subsequent events have influenced, though not fundamentally altered.

In Agambenian terms, those identity-based groups perceived as disloyal are the human victims of the sovereign's activities in being cast as outsiders from within, abandoned into *bare life* through the cultivation of a *state of exception*. In the case of Bahrain, this was formally declared through the State Security Decree of 1974, which was in force until the formative months of Hamad's rule in 2001. During this period, the mechanisms for the exception to become the norm – even if the formal state of emergency had ended – were implanted across the state, becoming embedded in the fabric of the state and its means of maintaining order. As Marc Owen Jones explains, 'The broad nature of the law, and its lack of clear definition of the acts it sought to criminalize, led to it being used to target the long-term detention of political criminals for the non-violent expression of their opinions . . . a repress first, asks questions later approach.'[34] After only about a decade outside an official state of emergency, another one was declared in 2011 after the Bahrain Spring protests. It lasted for three months, perhaps solely to justify the presence of the GCC military force on Bahrain, imposing order and once again abandoning individuals into *bare life*, as evidenced by the criminalization of political dissent, documented in the Bahrain Independent Commission of Inquiry (BICI).[35] It is telling that after the emergence of the coronavirus pandemic in early 2020, Bahrain chose not to declare a state of emergency, instead using the tools of sovereign power that had been built into the state over the preceding decades.

The activity of Gulf police, in creating outsiders from within by way of its policing, has been actively supported by Western allies whose geopolitical concerns privilege other interests, such as regional security and the energy industry. Despite having authoritarian governments blurring legal and extra-legal law enforcement, police from the UAE and Bahrain continue to be educated and trained by the British, and a steady stream of Western police consultants, often American, are hired by the Gulf monarchies for various logistical and technical projects. In 2017, the *Guardian* newspaper reported on the millions of dollars the UK government had earned since millions in training the police for 'repressive' regimes, including the UAE, Saudi Arabia, Bahrain, Oman and Kuwait at the College of Policing (now located in Coventry) in the previous year. In 2016–17, the UK earned $2.5 million in educational and training fees from these countries.[36] As one human rights organization representative contextualized:

The College of Policing appears to have made a substantial profit from a massive crackdown on dissent in the Gulf since the Arab spring. Ministers say this training will improve Gulf policing but, in reality, things have gotten worse as UK-trained bodies in Bahrain and Saudi Arabia have increased their use of torture and the death penalty for juveniles and protesters.[37]

In the spring of 2012, one of the authors (Staci Strobl) was on a research fellowship at the College of Policing and personally observed that Bahraini mid-level officers were participating and passing a human rights course. Meanwhile, in their off-hours on campus, these same officers attempted to convince this author that Shi'a protesters in their country were 'animals' who on a whole systematically abused their children, forced them to protest against the regime and were 'horrible people'. They implied that this inherently Shi'a behaviour of child abuse and disloyalty to the regime, which they linked together, necessitated a justifiable cloud of suspicion over Shi'a communities for the good of national security (personal communications, April 2012). Although this is only one anecdote, the experience suggests that human rights courses were acting as a box-checking exercise for participants without having the deeper effects of orienting police behaviour and policy towards individual-level, reasonable suspicion generally suitable for criminal justice organizations that are respectful of human rights. From a critical perspective, it also shows the power of the popular, discursive framing in the capacity of individual police actors to rationalize their role in repressive state power by absorbing and reproducing anxieties perpetrated by the state. In the Agamben framework, much of the insider–outsider social groupings important to sovereign control also manifest in language, including the way people talk about their social and political world, serving to dehumanize and facilitate the abandonment into bare life.

As Elizabeth Monier points out, anxieties around identity-politics heavily characterized the Arab Spring in the Gulf and the unrest that came before.[38] The events exacerbated an already identity-differential police service, and in the eyes of the rulers, the police appeared to fall short of sovereign expectations for the maintenance of the political order in the federated states. As aforementioned, the rulers viewed the Arab Spring as a coordinated transnational movement that necessitated a cooperative regional response, yet the UAE petition-signers, for instance, framed their purposes as national in scope albeit inspired by events in other countries collectively known as the Arab Spring or inspired by transnational Islamist movements. For Augustus Norton the events led to a deepening of existing sectarian cleavages as the Gulf monarchies teamed up in their resolve to quash the civil and democratic aspirations,[39] often of Shi'a communities or those of the *bidoun* (stateless people) and their allies. For example, throughout the uprisings in the spring of 2011, riot police – typically comprised of foreign nationals offered Bahraini passports in return for service – were deployed and visible throughout Manama as a part of everyday life[40] and police raided homes in Shi'a villages at night to round up anti-regime activists.

The sectarian nature of the uprisings in Saudi Arabia is also particularly stark and involved the largest street protests in the country's history.[41] The execution of Sheikh Nimr Baqr al-Nimr in January of 2017, along with forty-seven other alleged terrorists,[42] represented possibly the most aggressive criminal justice response to post-Arab Spring in the region. Sheikh Nimr, a Shi'a cleric, was a major leader of protests in the Eastern Province of the country that criticized the Saudi government's long-standing discrimination against the Shi'a minority groups, citing over the years such injustices as Shi'a being portrayed in Saudi textbooks as unbelievers and the government's failure to share the economic largess of the oil industry profits, among many other concerns. During the unrest in 2012, al-Nimr was shot in the leg by police and arrested for sedition. Before being executed for his anti-government activities, he staged a hunger strike from jail. Activists claim that he was tortured while in custody.

Scaling up the capacity of national and local police agencies in the Gulf in the form of a transnational force like the GCC Police suggests that the means for continued discriminatory, regime-backing order maintenance will be force-multiplied through transnational engagement. It is this ramping up of capacity that represents the variation on the persistence of the state of exception in general. Rather than local police and military force responding to internal civil unrest of a perceived internal enemy, the new force is planned as a standing one that is ready and has the resources and cooperation of several countries behind it, operating in conditions of perceived necessity and circumventing the rule of law, with potentially serious repercussions for those perceived to challenge ruling elites. In addition, the force replaces the PSF military forces in intervening in individual GCC states' civil unrest, thus potentially avoiding the perception of external military interference in internal affairs. Police, as the globally recognizable force for internal public safety, will likely appear more suitable in responding to public protests. However, the nature of the use of force by uniformed officers, whether police or military, is likely to involve similar strategies and tactics, blurring the line between police and military in the region, and blending internal policing with military functions like civil defence, and simultaneously blurring the survival of sovereignty with the degradation of that sovereignty. Of course, questions also remain as to the ultimate source of sovereign power for such a force which gains its mandate from the GCC collective.

Innovation within the state of exception

The invention of the GCC Police is envisioned with a joint police command, making the policing organization North Atlantic Treaty Organization (NATO)-like in its readiness and reach. This would be distinct from the existing PSF which is not under a joint command but relies on the coming together of national military forces to respond to a specific circumstance, as was the case in Bahrain in 2011. One defence expert has opined that the current weakness in such a response is the lack of being able to work together cohesively when the crisis hits. The new force, however, would strive for common training, standards, procedures, technology and deployments thus improving joint operations; the force would be able to cooperatively strike the perceived Iranian-backed terrorist threat within the Gulf states' populations.⁴³

Common operational worthiness is also a rationale for the recent push by the United States to encourage an additional joint-military command in the greater region as well. As US general Anthony Zinni (retired) stated, the proposed Middle Eastern Strategic Alliance (MESA) would help shore up strategic interests in the Gulf, such as trade routes and energy interests while also overcoming the various bilateral agreements, and the lack of cohesive military structures, technology and administration, which shapes the regional security apparatuses today. MESA has been slow to get going, according to General Zinni, due to concerns about the possibility of a too-outsize role for Saudi Arabia and the perceived detraction from existing bilateral relations with the United States.⁴⁴ Unlike MESA, however, the GCC Police initiative appears to have originated within the GCC countries' leadership. In fact Abdel Aziz Aluwaisheg, assistant secretary-general for Political Affairs and Negotiation, cited the local grounded-ness of the GCC Police, among other existing regional security initiatives as a reason that a US-led MESA was unneeded and would be redundant.⁴⁵

The standing force has not yet been implemented but remains in the planning stages; very little information has been released about the status of its development. It is not clear whether the idea has been quietly shelved or is being discretely assembled, the latter of which is the best assumption based on limited transparency. At the same time, internal differences across the GCC countries, exacerbated by the Qatar crisis, may be slowing down the most cohesive part of the imagine force, having a standing capacity. For example, initially Kuwait and Oman had reservations about additional external meddling in their sovereign affairs as a result of policing collectively, though these concerns were overcome in completing security agreements.

So far, the GCC Police have implemented the sharing of security data, information and strategies, seen in the number of people (academics, human rights defenders and others) refused entry from particular states in spite of a lack of connection. Moreover, in Abu Dhabi in February of 2019, the Joint Operation to Combat Crimes workshop was continued from a previous session, consisting of high-level representatives from the UAE, Saudi Arabia and Kuwait. The goal of the sessions is to operationalize the strategic objectives of strengthening the security cooperation among the GCC Police forces in the field of combatting crime. In pictures posed on the GCC website, every attendee was evidently male, even though the UAE and Kuwait have hundreds of female police officers in their forces.⁴⁶ The workshop came on the heels of a consultative visit with INTERPOL in Lyon, France, during which a GCC delegation conferred with experts in counterterrorism, organized crime and maritime security. They discussed best practices from the INTERPOL perspective and unspecified, future cooperative efforts between the GCC Police and the INTERPOL.⁴⁷ This activity appears to be the fruit of an earlier memorandum of understanding signed between the GCC and INTERPOL to foster cooperation in combatting crimes that cross borders within the GCC region.⁴⁸

INTERPOL and other police professional networks appear willing to accept the GCC Police uncritically. This may allow it to quietly blur the lines between outside–inside and continue to create the boundaries of *bare life*, without significant international outcry. Most significantly in January of 2020, the International Association of Chiefs of Police (IACP), the most prestigious international police professional organization, has signed a memorandum of understanding with the GCC Police, something of an implicit endorsement by the IACP for what the GCC Police hope to become. Abdullatif bin Rashid Al Zayani, secretary-general of the GCC, and Vincent Talucci, executive director of the IACP, agreed to cooperative activities consisting of exchanging strategic information, combatting crimes of all types and organizing specialized training courses in security affairs. Although details of the agreement are vague, the development means that the GCC Police will have access to the top police leaders globally. According to its website, the IACP is a 'progressive' police professional organization of 30,000 members from 160 countries, committed to 'advancing safer communities through thoughtful, progressive police leadership'. Financial backers for the IACP in general include organizations that typically do not enter into any kind of relationship with non-democratic regimes, such as the MacArthur Foundation, the Joyce Foundation, the Laura and John Arnold Foundation and Michael Jordan (although to be clear, it is not necessarily the case that these particular charitable funds will be directly used by the IACP in support of their cooperation with the GCC Police).[49]

Dovetailing the rise of the GCC Police is the apparent renaissance of security studies at the Naif Arab University for Security Sciences (NAUSS) in Riyadh, originally founded in 1978. Although not explicitly linked, it appears that GCC ministers of the interior and foreign ministers are further cooperating in bolstering a region-wide training platform that would augment or replace the typical post-colonial training education networks with the UK noted earlier. Certainly, having training significantly shift from Europe to the Gulf region means that it can be more easily shielded from media scrutiny while also helping condition particular visions of security and order that facilitate the reproduction of the status quo. The timing of the reinvigoration of NAUSS to train the region's police after the *Guardian* broke the story about repressive regimes being trained and educated in the United States, as noted earlier, is suspicious. Although one cannot be sure, it might be a strategic move on the part of the Gulf governments to maintain their style of policing freer from challenge or criticism by locating it in their own region and in the least transparent state within it.

In 24 May 2019, this author attended a side event of the 28th Session of United Nations Office of Drugs and Crime (UNODC) Commission on Crime Prevention and Criminal Justice in Vienna entitled 'Law Enforcement Capacity-Building in the Gulf Region and Networking at the Interregional Level'. The event was sponsored by the UNODC, the GCC and NAUSS. During the presentation, representatives of NAUSS, flanked by several ministers and deputy ministers of the interior of various Gulf states, detailed a new police education curricular plan centring on police leadership, police operations and crime-fighting strategies as learning objectives. It appeared to be missing typical police education modules on human rights, police ethics and multicultural policing. When asked about whether the curriculum featured best practices in multicultural policing in diverse societies, given the unrest being policed in Bahrain for instance, the representative from the school essentially dodged the question, indicating those topics were both within the curriculum and being developed. The representative also offered that he planned to recruit curriculum consultants at a future American Society of Criminology (ASC) conference, a premier professional event for criminologists and criminal justice scholars, the following fall in San Francisco. Meanwhile, the academic job postings on the *Chronicle of Higher Education* website throughout 2020 also reveal that NAUSS is actively recruiting criminal justice academics from the West, in particular the United States, to teach the curriculum, more so than in the past. It will be important to monitor whether the involvement of prestigious professional organizations and academics trained in the wider criminology and criminal justice fields from the West contribute to building a robust, liberal education for Gulf police officers or whether these efforts are window dressing to legitimize illiberal training modules primarily in support of politicized state interests, effectively normalizing practices used to regulate life and create bare life in *states of exception*.

Transnational policing: Not often 'standing'

Although transnational policing is in itself a blurring of the inside and outside, examples of it have developed ways of operating to limit the melding of policing into other state functions or operating too militarily (externally). Police scholars have not agreed on a standard definition of what truly constitutes transnational policing, but for our purposes here, we consider a starting point to be that it is the product of multilateral police agency agreements (as opposed to bilateral police cooperation). In their review of the literature on transnational policing, John McDaniel et al. note:

> Transnational policing as a concept represents only a disparate and disjointed assortment of structures, relationships, networks, and organizations, which shift and change over time, often with remarkable speed.... New methods and relationships have been established as older ones died out, normally without an overarching ethos, strategy, or sense of orderliness.[50]

They further surmise that the politicization of policing objectives can threaten the legitimacy of such forces and that stable fixtures of this form of policing have measures to prevent this, as described further.

For example, INTERPOL (originally the International Criminal Police Commission organization) is the original transnational police agency commissioned in 1923. Revived in 1956 after a hiatus during the Second World War, the organization today has 190 member states, operating through a variety of formal treaties and professional contracts, and acts as the world's third-largest intergovernmental institution. INTERPOL aims to foster international cooperation between and among its 190 members through its function as a repository for crime data and intelligence. It also assists in the coordination of joint investigatory operations and exchange of consultants and experts.[51] In order to prevent the organization from becoming overtly politicized, the INTERPOL constitution prohibits work on crimes or police operations that do not relate to the wishes of several member countries. It also forbids involving itself in political, military, religious or racial crimes. Stated areas of concern for INTERPOL are organized crime, piracy, environmental crime, financial crime, terrorism, human trafficking, transnational vehicle theft, art theft, drug trafficking and cybercrime, to name several. INTERPOL has no standing police or direct investigatory force of its own, but rather relies on member country for all on-the-ground policing activities. Its approximately 500 employees act as contact points and data and intelligence collators for member state police agencies.[52]

Another example is EUROPOL which draws from the police forces within twenty-eight EU nations, for activities including joint operation and investigatory teams, coordination of specific transnational investigations, cooperation between investigators and prosecutors across borders, and the development of expertise and intelligence relevant to combatting European organized crime.[53] Since the late 1990s, the organization has focused on terrorism, illegal migration, nuclear smuggling, transnational vehicle theft and counterfeiting. Like INTERPOL, the organization does not have its own uniformed police officers or detectives, but instead relies on nation states to devote parts of their forces to the transnational efforts.

Even more recently than EUROPOL has been the proliferation of other -POLs. In 2017 the advent of AFRIPOL, the 'African Union Mechanism for Police Cooperation', joined the growing collection of police regional cooperative organizations such as ASEANPOL (based in the Association of Southeast Asian Nations) and AMERIPOL (the Police Community of the Americas). AFRIPOL, for instance, involves the member states of the African Union (AU); this new transnational policing institution established a framework for police cooperation in African member states. According to its website, its main objectives are to foster strategic, operational and tactical linkages among national police agencies. It asserts that it follows the principles of respect for democratic rule, human rights and the rule of law (AFRIPOL n.d.). Cooperative efforts have included a cross-border crime risk analysis workshop in 2019 in conjunction with EUROPOL.[54] Like the other transnational police organizations, AFRIPOL does not have a standing police force but relies on the forces of member states.

Meanwhile, the UN Police also function as a transnational policing organization with its peacekeeping mission rooted in the overall framework of international law and universal human rights. Unlike the earlier described transnational police organizations, the UN Police has a standing police force of approximately 11,000 officers who provide operational support to UN member states' police agencies as part of 16 different operational missions. Their primary duties include such as activities as protecting civilians, securing elections, investigating sexual and gender-based violence, and responding to and preventing organized crime.[55] They also assist in reforming and restructuring national and local law enforcement agencies in conflict and post-conflict countries.

Most UN peacekeeping operations operate under the administration of the United Nations Department of Peacekeeping Operations (DPKO) which can only take on a UN Police deployment if ordered to do so by a resolution of the UN Security Council, which will set out the operation's scope and size. The General Assembly of the UN, in turn, determines the operating budget.[56] As such, the use of this unique intergovernmental standing force has a significant governance apparatus guiding its deployments, seeking significant review and approval from member states.[57]

Taken all together, with the exception of the UN Police, transnational police organizations do not consist of standing forces, but rather operate through the cooperative use of various national forces, often to combat specific crimes or conduct particular cross-border investigations. Further, the organizations have governance provisions that prevent their use for overt political order maintenance by individual member countries. This, these two basic facets, can be considered cornerstones of transnational policing, at least before the GCCPOL.

The GCC Police: Standing 'high' and 'low'

Planning to have a standing police (not military) force at the ready to be deployed within Gulf states for the purpose of internal order maintenance is relatively unique; the only intergovernmental standing police force currently operating is the UN Police. Other intergovernmental standing forces are military, not police. If implemented as originally imagined, the GCC Police would be a new experiment in transnational policing, surpassing the scope of existing regional models. As argued here, the inventiveness of it is underscored by GCC monarchies' commitment to being ready to strike at internal enemies, those in the spaces of *bare life*, in a force-multiplied way. Again, the logic of the conditions of a *state of exception* is operating here: at the creation of a force that is ostensibly modelled after non-discriminatory and highly regulated examples of transnational policing, there is instead embedded discriminatory and relatively unregulated manifestations of sovereign power. Moreover, this is reinforced through the creation of a transnational standing force with *internal* powers, positioned outside the state yet with the power to operate domestically, with the capacity to abandon individuals into a transnational form of bare life. The situation represents both a major police innovation and a consequential widening of the scale of scope of bare life.

Major police innovations, like the proliferation of -POLs in general, have almost exclusively been attributable to the industrialized, developed world. Among other examples of major innovations, 'community oriented policing' which has been an umbrella strategy that has transformed police deployment and police–public relations, was first imagined through Japan's *koban* system of decentralized neighborhood-level police, or in Finland, or in the United States, or a return to Peelian Principles,[58] depending on the telling. Practised wholeheartedly in the United States and the United Kingdom starting in the late 1980s and early 1990s, the innovation spread throughout the world through such police professional networks as the International Association of Police Chiefs (IACP), coming to the Gulf in the early 2000s and leading to community policing units in Bahrain, Oman, Kuwait and the UAE. More recently, 'hot spots' policing, or the use of geo-spatial mapping to analyse and respond to crime, has been trending among police professional organizations. Given that modern policing around the world is a European, imperial overlay and a direct result of colonial regimes, perhaps it is not surprising that the centre of the policing world remains discursively centred on the metropoles. Yet, the GCC is adapting the -POL trend, and its unique approach may go unnoticed on the world stage. It appears on the surface to be like all the other -POLs modelled on the West, and yet its adaptation acts as a major police innovation in itself.

As aptly acknowledged in the burgeoning criminological perspective known as Southern Criminology, innovations from the adaptations of these European-style systems in non-Western or developing countries are often overlooked to the detriment of academic understanding. In a project they call 'global cognitive justice', breaking from the hegemony of Western thinking means interrupting the habit of seeing the North as normative and the South as catching up to the progression of that normativity.[59] Here the Global South is a construct for non-European spaces often at the losing end of global capitalist regimes; however, the Gulf is slightly outside this frame as an economically successful example of a non-Western space. Nonetheless, the notion that histories of policing and crime control in seemingly peripheral spaces are more complex, and even innovative, is important for going beyond the mere observation that policing in the Gulf is post-colonial. Whereas the entanglement of the British, and later the American, police professional apparatus with the Gulf countries is certainly an important facet, the GCC Police stands to surpass those influences by improvising a new mode of policing that blends the juridical with the non-juridical, acting in a manner both overarching and regional while also nimbly responding to perceived local public order threats from those designated as internal enemies.

It remains to be seen whether this innovation catches and inspires the raising of other transnational police forces. It also will be important to notice whether the history of Western complicity in discriminatory policing in the region will continue through the transnational sphere, allowing the style of policing to force-multiply (from the point of view of each individual state vis-à-vis the capacity of the larger force to scale up policing in locales region-wide).

In looking at policing across time and space, Jean-Paul Brodeur makes a distinction between 'high' and 'low' policing. In 'high' policing, the primary methodology is intelligence sharing and coordinated operational efforts. 'High' policing is very susceptible to being used to protect state interests over those of the public or individual, as Brodeur put forth in earlier scholarship. Secret police operate using 'high' policing methods, but these same methods, if grounded in a rule of law, are used in democratic frameworks. INTERPOL, EUROPOL and other regional forces like AFRIPOL are almost exclusively operating in the realm of 'high policing' with their focus on data, intelligence and cooperative networking among agencies. Meanwhile 'low' policing refers to the everyday phenomenon of policing in local areas aimed at criminal investigations to maintain public safety and order in particular communities or societies. 'Low' policing is the purview of local and national police forces in nearly every corner of the globe where modern policing occurs. However, 'low' policing in its corrupt form can lead to abuse of power, discrimination and cronyism.[60]

The GCC Police, however, in aspiring to a standing police force that strikes locally, appears to be merging 'high' and 'low' functions in a new way, hoping to manoeuvre deftly between the two realms at will, much as Agamben points to the *state of exception* as blending the inside and the outside, the juridical with the non-juridical or the law with what is outside the law. The repercussions for individuals, of course, remain at the low realm, yet cut across state borders, creating a transnational form of bare life. This is particularly true in the Bahraini case. Many have been cast into bare life in the form of statelessness through the increased use of citizenship revocations as punishment for political opposition. With policing potentially politicized at the transnational level through the GCCPOL, it follows that these stateless individuals may face the prospect of being unwelcome by the authorities in other Gulf countries where they may have familial connections and to which they might seek to relocate. Individuals may potentially become region-less as well as stateless.

Therefore, being able to both coordinate regionally and strike locally – empowered by a region-wide *state of exception* – is potentially the Gulf monarchies' contradictory solution to their perceived state of emergency brought on by the Arab Spring and post-Arab Spring unrest. The amount of governance behind this solution rests with the six-member states of the GCC, much less governance than associated with the only other standing intergovernmental police force which operates at the behest of the UN General Security Council and the administrative control of the UN General Assembly. All other examples of regional police forces have stopped short of creating standing forces instead aspiring to the positive hallmarks of 'high' policing to augment existing state criminal justice functions. Yet the establishment of a standing force speaks to region-wide concerns about challenges to the status quo and, ultimately, regime survival.

Conclusions: Policing within states of exception

Agamben's notion of the camp, or the site in which *bare life* occurs, is potentially reinforced when envisioned as the community – comprised of member state communities – targeted by the GCC Police. As a site of metaphysical possibility (as Mabon observes in this volume), the camp exists as a space where individuals can be abandoned into bare life at the whim of the sovereign. The establishment of the GCC Police, operating transnationally and nationally while engaging in both high and low policing, serves as a means of regulating this space, reinforcing the status quo at the cost of political expression and dissent against ruling elites.

The Gulf states have Shi'a and Salafi communities which are policed differentially based on their perceived disloyalty to mainstream Sunni hegemonic rule, while civil society organizations, academics and human rights organizations have also been identified as threats to regime survival. Political life, such as political expression and dissent that threatens the reputation of the nation's rulers, is increasingly criminalized and simultaneously backed up by transnational, regional blocks oriented towards consolidating their use of force powers. The targets of the new police force have essentially already been perceived as guilty of the crime of regime disloyalty before the criminal justice process even begins – many of whom did so within the confines of domestic laws – based on structures of exclusion already operating in the region from the inception of modern policing and now being expanded. Therefore, it does not matter on some level whether the targeted population follows the law or not, as the stripping of their full humanity (the death penalty in Saudi Arabia and citizen revocation in Bahrain) has attached to entire communities by association and shared identity. As the government institutions authorized in using force, the GCC Police stands to perpetuate a state-sponsored anomie that locks individuals into cycles of criminalization and punishment, extracted from typical legal notions of individual culpability and ultimately into bare life. In support of this, the GCC Police capitalizes on transregional framing of security threats, intelligence sharing and the identification of domestic dissent as that which may also possess regional characteristics. While the Qatar crisis has certainly posed a challenge to the organization of the GCC as a six-member organization, there is little doubt that the force stands to operate across the five other member states.

Future research into transnational policing should continue to engage with Agamben's 'state of exception' as a theoretically important avenue to explore the relationships between politics, global governance, sovereignty and policing, positioned against the rule of law, derogation and protection of the individual. As a transnational policing institution, the GCC Police have deliberately weakened the bonds of policing to their underlying governance and communities in order to strengthen each regime's power through regional alliance. This development challenges a major normative standard generally accepted by police scholars and best articulated by David Bayley: a minimally acceptable police force anywhere on the globe should be connected to a rule of law, exhibit transparency, be oriented towards public safety and respect human rights.[61] As this chapter has shown, the new GCC Police appear poised to hit none of those norms, as sovereigns maintain *bare life* in their states through innovative, transnational means in hopes of reinforcing a sovereignty status quo.

Notes

1 Here order maintenance refers to the criminal justice function of preventing or reacting to disturbances of the public peace (James Q. Wilson, 'Dilemmas of Police Administration', *Public Administration Review* 28 (1968): 407–17.

2   Simon Mabon, *Houses Built on Sand: Violence, Sectarianism and Revolution in the Middle East* (Manchester: Manchester University Press, 2020).
3   Toby Mattheisen, *Sectarian Gulf: Bahrain, Saudi Arabia, and the Arab Spring that Wasn't* (Stanford: Stanford Briefs/Stanford University Press, 2013); Sossie Kasbarian and Simon Mabon, 'Contested Spaces and Sectarian Narratives in Post-Uprising Bahrain', *Global Discourse* 6, no. 4 (2016): 677–96.
4   *Al Arabiya News*, 'GCC States to Create Regional Police, Navy', 14 December 2019. Available online: https://english.alarabiya.net/en/News/middle-jeast/2014/12/09/Regional-stability-on-table-as-GCC-summit-kicks-off-.html (accessed 8 January 2020).
5   Gulf Cooperation Council (GCC), 'The Charter', 1981. Available online: https://www.gcc-sg.org/en-us/AboutGCC/Pages/Primarylaw.aspx (accessed 18 January 2020).
6   Gulf Cooperation Council (GCC), 'Security Cooperation: Achievements, Overall Security Strategy', No date. Available online: https://www.gccsg.org/enus/CooperationAndAchievements/Achievements/SecurityCooperation/Achievements/Pages/Firsttheoverallsecuritystrateg.asp (accessed 18 January 2020).
7   Gulf Cooperation Council (GCC), 'Security Cooperation: Achievements, Overall Security Strategy', No date. Available online: https://www.gccsg.org/enus/CooperationAndAchievements/Achievements/SecurityCooperation/Achievements/Pages/Firstheoverallsecuritystrateg.aspx (accessed 18 January 2020).
8   Rolin G. Mainuddin, 'Arab Spring and Democratic Transition in the GCC: Continuity Amidst Change', *Asian Journal of Peacebuilding* 4, no. 2 (2016): 161–86; Sally Khalifa Isaac, 'A Resurgence in Arab Regional Institutions? The Cases of the Arab League and the Gulf Cooperation Council Post-2011', in *Regional Insecurity after the Arab Uprisings: Narratives of Security and Threat*, ed. Elizabeth Monier (New York: Palgrave Macmillan, 2015), 151–67.
9   Human Rights Watch (HRW), 'Arab Gulf States', 2017. Available online: https://www.hrw.org/news/2017/07/12/arab-gulf-states-assault-online-activists (accessed 2 January 2020).
10 Mabon, *Houses Built on Sand*; Marc Owen Jones, *Political Repression in Bahrain* (Cambridge: Cambridge University Press, 2020).
11 Mainuddin, Arab Spring and democratic transition in the GCC, 2016, 175.
12 Staci Strobl, 'The Roots of Sectarian Law and Order in the Gulf', in *Beyond Sunni and Shi'a*, ed. F. Wehrey (London: Hurst & Co, 2017), 205–35, 232.
13 Human Rights Watch (HRW), 'GCC: Joint Security Agreement Imperils Rights', 24 April 2014. Available online: https://www.hrw.org/news/2014/04/26/gcc-joint-security-agreement-imperils-rights# (accessed 2 June 2020).
14 Giorgio Agamben, *State of Exception* (Chicago: University of Chicago Press, 2005), 28.
15 Mabon, *Houses Built on Sand*, 13.
16 Ibid.
17 Agamben, *State of Exception*, 23.
18 Mabon, *Houses Built on Sand*, 20.
19 Ibid., 21.
20 Agamben, *State of Exception*, 6–7.
21 Alex Murray, *Giorgio Agamben* (London: Routledge, 2010), 71.
22 Jones, *Political Repression in Bahrain*.
23 Christopher Davidson, 'Fear and Loathing in the Emirates' (blog post). *Sada*, 18 December 2012. Carnegie Endowment for International Peace. Washington, DC;

Ingo Forstenlechner, Emilie Rutledge, and Rashed Salem Alnuaim, 'The UAE, the "Arab Spring" and Different Types of Dissent', *Middle East Policy* 19, no. 4 (2012, Winter): 54–67.
24 Davidson, Christopher, *After the Sheikhs: The Coming Collapse of the Gulf Monarchies* (Oxford: Hurst, 2013).
25 Amnesty International (AI), 'Bahrain Mass Trial Revoking Citizenship of 138 People a Mockery of Justice', *Amnesty.org*, 21 April 2019. Available online: https://www.amnesty.org/en/latest/news/2019/04/bahrain-mass-trial-revoking-citizenship-of-138-people-a-mockery-of-justice/ (accessed 6 October 2019).
26 *Reuters*, 'Major Opposition Figures Not among Those Given Back Bahraini Citizenship', *Reuters.com*, 29 April 2019. Available online: https://www.reuters.com/article/us-bahrain-security-idUSKCN1S50PC (accessed 6 October 2019).
27 Cliff Lord and Athol Yates, *The Military and Police Forces of the Gulf States (Volume 1): Trucial States and the United Arab Emirates, 1951–1980* (Warwick: Helion & Company, 2019).
28 Steffen Hertog, 'Rentier Militaries in the Gulf States: The Price of Coup-Proofing', *International Journal of Middle Eastern Studies* 43, no. 3 (2011): 402.
29 Staci Strobl, *Sectarian Order in Bahrain: The Social and Colonial Origins of Criminal Justice* (Lanham, MD: Lexington Books, 2018).
30 Mahdi Abdulla Al-Tajir, *Bahrain: 1920–1945: Britain, the Shaikh and the Administration* (London: Croom Helm, 1987), 2.
31 Lord and Yates, *The Military and Police Forces of the Gulf States*.
32 Paul Rich, *Creating the Arabian Gulf: The British Raj and the Invasion of the Gulf* (Lanham, MD: Lexington Book, 2009), 17.
33 Strobl, *Sectarian Order in Bahrain*.
34 Jones, *Political Repression in Bahrain*, 208–9.
35 Bahrain Independent Commission of Inquiry, *Report of the Bahrain Independent Commission of Inquiry*, 2011.
36 Lucas Amin, 'UK Police Earned Millions Training Officers in Repressive Regimes', The *Guardian*, 15 September 2017. Available online: https://www.theguardian.com/law/2017/sep/15/uk-police-earned-millions-training-officers-in-repressive-regimes (accessed 23 April 2020).
37 Amin, 'UK Police Earned Millions' (quoting a human rights organizer), no page number.
38 Elizabeth Monier, 'Introduction: Narratives of (In)security and (In)stability in the Middle East', in *Regional Insecurity after the Arab Uprisings: Narratives of Security and Threat*, ed. Elizabeth Monier (New York: Palgrave Macmillan, 2015), 1018.
39 Augustus R. Norton, 'The Geo-Politics of the Sunni-Shia Rift', in *Regional Insecurity after the Arab Uprisings: Narratives of Security and Threat*, ed. Elizabeth Monier (New York: Palgrave Macmillan, 2015), 129–50.
40 Simon Mabon, 'Sects and the City: Reflections from Manama', in *Urban Spaces and Sectarian Contestation*, ed. C. Mabon and J. Nagle (Lancaster: Sectarian Proxies and De-sectarianisation (SEPAD), Lancaster University, 2020), 25, 22–7.
41 Toby Mattheisen, *Sectarian Gulf*, 73.
42 BBC, 'Sheikh Nimr al-Nimr: Saudi Arabia Executes Top Shia Cleric', *BBC*, 2 January 2016. Available online: https://www.bbc.com/news/world-middle-east-35213244 (accessed 23 April 2020).
43 Justin Vela, 'GCC to Set Up Regional Police Force Based in Abu Dhabi', *The National* (UAE), 9 December 2014. Available online: https://www.thenational.ae/world/gcc

-to-set-up-regional-police-force-based-in-abu-dhabi-1.284863 (accessed 25 April 2020).
44 Anthony C. Zinni, 'Why Has the Gulf Failed to form a Sustainable Defense Structure? A Special Conversation with General Anthony C. Zinni (presentation via Zoom)', 20 May 2020. Washington, DC: Gulf International Forum.
45 Abdel Aziz Hamad Aluwaisheg, 'Abbreviated Remarks Delivered to the National Council at U.S.-Arab Relations', 28th Arab-U.S. Policymakers Conference on 23 October 2019, Washington, DC. Available online: https://ncusar.org/aa/2019/10/gulf-security-architectures/ (accessed 2 June 2020).
46 Gulf Cooperation Council (GCC), 'The GCCPOL Launches the First Phase of the GCC First Joint Operation to Combat Crimes' (press release), 17 February 2019. Available online: https://www.gcc-sg.org/en-us/MediaCenter/NewsCooperation/News/Pages/news2019-2-17-1.aspx (accessed 25 April 2020).
47 Gulf Cooperation Council (GCC), 'The GCCPOL Visits the International Criminal Police Organization (INTERPOL)', 8 January 2019. Available online: https://www.gcc-sg.org/enus/MediaCenter/NewsCooperation/News/Pages/news2019-1-8-5.aspx.
48 Al Defaiya, 'Gulf Cooperation Council, Interpol to Boost Cooperation', *Al Defaiya*, 2 June 2017. Available online: https://www.defaiya.com/news/Security/Security/2017/02/06/gulf-cooperation-council-interpol-to-boost-cooperation (accessed 2 June 2020).
49 International Association of Chiefs of Police (IACP), 'About Us', *IACP.org*. No date. Available online: https://www.theiacp.org/about-iacp (accessed 25 April 2020).
50 John L. McDaniel, Karlie E. Stonard, and David J. Cox (eds), *The Development of Transnational Policing: Past, Present and Future* (New York: Routledge, 2019), 1–13.
51 Maria (Maki) Haberfeld, William McDonald and Agostino von Hassell, 'International Cooperation in Policing: A Partial Answer to the Query?' in *Comparative Policing: The Struggle for Democratization*, ed. M. Haberfeld and I. Cerrah (Thousand Oaks: Sage Publications, 2008).
52 John Peter Casey, Michael J. Jenkins and Harry R. Dammer, *Policing the World: The Practice of International and Transnational Policing*, 2nd edn (Durham: Carolina Academic Press, 2018).
53 Ibid.
54 Frontex, 'Frontex and AFRIPOL Hold Risk Analysis Workshop in Algeria', *Frontex: European Border and Coast Guard Agency*, 13 September 2019. Available online: https://frontex.europa.eu/media-centre/news-release/frontex-and-afripol-hold-risk-analysis-workshop-in-algeria-20H3pq (accessed 24 April 2020).
55 United Nations Peacekeeping, 'UN Police', No date. Available online: https://peacekeeping.un.org/en/un-police (accessed 24 April 2020).
56 Casey et al., *Policing the World*.
57 Anna K. Jarstad, and Timothy D. Sisk, *From War to Democracy: Dilemmas of Peacebuilding* (Cambridge: Cambridge University Press, 2008).
58 These nine principles were articulated by Sir Robert Peele in 1829 to guide ethical policing and include the famous adage 'the police are the public and the public are the police'.
59 Kerry Carrington, Russell Hogg, John Scott, Máximo Sozzo and R. Walters, *Southern Criminology* (New York: Routledge, 2019).
60 Jean-Paul Brodeur, *The Policing Web* (Oxford: Oxford University Press, 2010).
61 David Bayley, *Changing the Guard: Developing Democratic Policing Abroad* (Oxford: Oxford University Press, 2006); David Bayley, 'Democratizing the Police Abroad: What to Do and How to Do It', *Issues in International Crime* (Washington, DC: National Institute of Justice, 2001).

References

Agamben, Giorgio. *State of Exception*. Chicago: University of Chicago Press, 2005.
Al Arabiya News. 'GCC States to Create Regional Police, Navy'. *Al Arabiya News*, 14 December 2019. Available online: https://english.alarabiya.net/en/News/middle-jeast/2014/12/09/Regional-stability-on-table-as-GCC-summit-kicks-off.html (accessed 8 January 2020).
Al Defaiya. 'Gulf Cooperation Council, Interpol to Boost Cooperation'. *Al Defaiya*, 2 June 2017. Available online: https://www.defaiya.com/news/Security/Security/2017/02/06/gulf-cooperation-council-interpol-to-boost-cooperation (accessed 2 June 2020).
Al-Tajir, Mahdi Abdulla. *Bahrain: 1920–1945: Britain, the Shaikh and the Administration*. London: Croom Helm, 1987.
Aluwaisheg, Abdel Aziz Hamad. 'Abbreviated Remarks Delivered to the National Council at U.S.-Arab Relations, 28th Arab-U.S'. Policymakers Conference on 23 October 2019, Washington, DC. Available online: https://ncusar.org/aa/2019/10/gulf-security-architectures/ (accessed 2 June 2020).
Amin, Lucas. 'UK Police Earned Millions Training Officers in Repressive Regimes'. *The Guardian*, 15 September 2017. Available online: https://www.theguardian.com/law/2017/sep/15/uk-police-earned-millions-training-officers-in-repressive-regimes (accessed 23 April 2020).
Amnesty International (AI). 'Bahrain Mass Trial Revoking Citizenship of 138 People a Mockery of Justice'. *Amnesty.org*, 21 April 2019. Available online: https://www.amnesty.org/en/latest/news/2019/04/bahrain-mass-trial-revoking-citizenship-of-138-people-a-mockery-of-justice/ (accessed 6 October 2019).
Bahrain Independent Commission of Inquiry. *Report of the Bahrain Independent Commission of Inquiry*, 2011.
Bayley, David. *Changing the Guard: Developing Democratic Policing Abroad*. Oxford: Oxford University Press, 2006.
Bayley, David. 'Democratizing the Police Abroad: What to Do and How to Do It'. In *Issues in International Crime*. National Institute of Justice, US Department of Justice. Washington, DC: National Institute of Justice, 2001. Available online: https://www.ojp.gov/ncjrs/virtual-library/abstracts/democratizing-police-abroad-what-do-and-how-do-it
Bayley, David. 'Foreword'. In *The Development of Transnational Policing: Past, Present and Future*, edited by J. L. M. McDaniel, K. Stonard, and D. J. Cox, xvii–xviii. New York: Routledge, 2019.
BBC. 'Sheikh Nimr al-Nimr: Saudi Arabia Executes Top Shia Cleric'. *BBC*, 2 January 2016. Available online: https://www.bbc.com/news/world-middle-east-35213244 (accessed 23 April 2020).
Brodeur, Jean-Paul. *The Policing Web*. Oxford: Oxford University Press, 2010.
Carrington, Kerry, Russell Hogg, John Scott, Máximo Sozzo and R. Walters. *Southern Criminology*. New York: Routledge, 2019.
Casey, John Peter, Michael J. Jenkins, and Harry R. Dammer. *Policing the World: The Practice of International and Transnational Policing*, 2nd edn. Durham: Carolina Academic Press, 2018.
Davidson, Christopher. *After the Sheikhs: The Coming Collapse of the Gulf Monarchies*. Oxford: Hurst, 2013.
Davidson, Christopher. 'Fear and Loathing in the Emirates' (blog post). *Sada*, 18 December 2012. Carnegie Endowment for International Peace, Washington, DC.

European Union. 'European Arrest Warrant'. *European Justice*. Available online: https://e-justice.europa.eu/content_european_arrest_warrant-90-en.do (accessed 24 April 2020).
Forstenlechner, Ingo, Emilie Rutledge, and Rashed Salem Alnuaim. 'The UAE, the "Arab Spring" and Different Types of Dissent'. *Middle East Policy* 19, no. 4 (2012, Winter): 54–67.
Frontex. 'Frontex and AFRIPOL Hold Risk Analysis Workshop in Algeria'. *Frontex: European Border and Coast Guard Agency*, 13 September 2019. Available online: https://frontex.europa.eu/media-centre/news-release/frontex-and-afripol-hold-risk-analysis-workshop-in-algeria-20H3pq (accessed on 24 April 2020).
Gulf Cooperation Council (GCC). 'The Charter'. 1981. Available online: https://www.gcc-sg.org/en-us/AboutGCC/Pages/Primarylaw.aspx (accessed 18 January 2020).
Gulf Cooperation Council (GCC). 'The GCCPOL Launches the First Phase of the GCC First Joint Operation to Combat Crimes' (press release), 17 February 2019. Available online: https://www.gcc-sg.org/en-us/MediaCenter/NewsCooperation/News/Pages/news2019-2-17-1.aspx (accessed 25 April 2020).
Gulf Cooperation Council (GCC). 'The GCCPOL Visits the International Criminal Police Organization (INTERPOL)'. Available online: https://www.gcc-sg.org/en-us/MediaCenter/NewsCooperation/News/Pages/news2019-1-8-5.aspx (accessed 8 January 2019).
Gulf Cooperation Council (GCC). 'Security Cooperation: Achievements, Overall Security Strategy'. No date. Available online: https://www.gccsg.org/enus/CooperationAndAchievements/Achievements/SecurityCooperation/Achievements/Pages/Firsttheoverallsecuritystrateg.aspx (accessed 18 January 2020).
Haberfeld, Maria, William McDonald and Agostino von Hassell. 'International Cooperation in Policing: A Partial Answer to the Query?' In *Comparative Policing: The Struggle for Democratization*, edited by M. Haberfeld and I. Cerrah, 341–71. Thousand Oaks: Sage Publications, 2008.
Hertog, Steffen. 'Rentier Militaries in the Gulf States: The Price of Coup-Proofing'. *International Journal of Middle Eastern Studies* 43, no. 3 (2011): 400–2.
Human Rights Watch (HRW). 'Arab Gulf States'. 2017. Available online: https://www.hrw.org/news/2017/07/12/arab-gulf-states-assault-online-activists (accessed 2 January 2020).
Human Rights Watch (HRW). 'GCC: Joint Security Agreement Imperils Rights'. 24 April 2014. Available online: https://www.hrw.org/news/2014/04/26/gcc-joint-security-agreement-imperils-rights# (accessed 2 June 2020).
International Association of Chiefs of Police (IACP). 'About Us'. *IACP.org*, No date. Available online: https://www.theiacp.org/about-iacp (accessed 25 April 2020).
Jarstad, Anna K., and Timothy D. Sisk. *From War to Democracy: Dilemmas of Peacebuilding*. Cambridge: Cambridge University Press, 2008.
Jones, Marc Owen. *Political Repression in Bahrain*. Cambridge: Cambridge University Press, 2020.
Kasbarian, Sossie and Simon Mabon. 'Contested Spaces and Sectarian Narratives in Post-Uprising Bahrain'. *Global Discourse* 6, no. 4 (2016): 677–96.
Khalifa Isaac, Sally. 'A Resurgence in Arab Regional Institutions? The Cases of the Arab League and the Gulf Cooperation Council Post-2011'. In *Regional Insecurity after the Arab Uprisings: Narratives of Security and Threat*, edited by Elizabeth Monier, 151–67. New York: Palgrave Macmillan, 2015.
Lord, Cliff and Athol Yates. *The Military and Police Forces of the Gulf States (Volume 1): Trucial States and the United Arab Emirates, 1951–1980*. Warwick: Helion & Company, 2019.

Mabon, Simon. *Houses Built on Sand: Violence, Sectarianism and Revolution in the Middle East*. Manchester: Manchester University Press, 2020.

Mabon, Simon. 'Sects and the City: Reflections from Manama'. In *Urban Spaces and Sectarian Contestation*, edited by C. Mabon and J. Nagle, 22–7. Lancaster: Sectarian Proxies and De-sectarianisation (SEPAD), Lancaster University, 2020.

Mainuddin, Rolin G. 'Arab Spring and Democratic Transition in the GCC: Continuity Amidst Change'. *Asian Journal of Peacebuilding* 4, no. 2 (2016): 161–86.

Mattheisen, Toby. *Sectarian Gulf: Bahrain, Saudi Arabia, and the Arab Spring that Wasn't*. Stanford: Stanford Briefs/Stanford University Press, 2013.

McDaniel, John L. M., Karlie E. Stonard, and David J. Cox, eds. *The Development of Transnational Policing: Past, Present and Future*, 1–13. New York: Routledge, 2019.

Monier, Elizabeth. 'Introduction: Narratives of (In)security and (In)stability in the Middle East'. In *Regional Insecurity after the Arab Uprisings: Narratives of Security and Threat*, edited by Elizabeth Monier, 1018. New York: Palgrave Macmillan, 2015.

Murray, Alex. *Giorgio Agamben*. London: Routledge, 2010.

Norton, Augustus R. 'The Geo-Politics of the Sunni-Shia Rift'. In *Regional Insecurity after the Arab Uprisings: Narratives of Security and Threat*, edited by Elizabeth Monier, 129–50. New York: Palgrave Macmillan, 2015.

Reuters. 'Major Opposition Figures Not among Those Given Back Bahraini Citizenship'. *Reuters.com*, 29 April 2019. Available online: https://www.reuters.com/article/us-bahrain-security-idUSKCN1S50PC (accessed 6 October 2019).

Rich, Paul. *Creating the Arabian Gulf: The British Raj and the Invasion of the Gulf*. Lanham, MD: Lexington Book, 2009.

Strobl, Staci. *Sectarian Order in Bahrain: The Social and Colonial Origins of Criminal Justice*. Lanham, MD: Lexington Books, 2018.

Strobl, Staci. 'The Roots of Sectarian Law and Order in the Gulf'. In *Beyond Sunni and Shi'a*, edited by F. Wehrey, 205–35. London: Hurst & Co, 2017.

United Nations. 'Peacekeeping'. *UN Police*, No date. Available online: https://peacekeeping.un.org/en/un-police (accessed 24 April 2020).

United Nations. 'Universal Declaration of Human Rights'. 1948. Available online: https://www.un.org/en/universal-declaration-human-rights/ (accessed 22 April 2020).

Vela, Justin. 'GCC to Set Up Regional Police Force Based in Abu Dhabi'. *The National (UAE)*, 9 December 2014. Available online: https://www.thenational.ae/world/gcc-to-set-up-regional-police-force-based-in-abu-dhabi-1.284863 (accessed 25 April 2020).

Wilson, James Q. 'Dilemmas of Police Administration'. *Public Administration Review* 28 (1968): 407–17.

Zinni, Anthony C. 'Why Has the Gulf Failed to Form a Sustainable Defense Structure? A Special Conversation with General Anthony C. Zinni (Presentation Via Zoom)'. 20 May 2020. Washington, DC: Gulf International Forum.

Chapter 3

CLAIMING AGENCY IN THE IRAQI STATE OF EXCEPTION

Edith Szanto

Iraq has been categorized by political scientists and politicians as a 'failed state'. This assessment served those who sought Kurdish independence, for instance, after the catastrophic rise of ISIS, also known as the Islamic State of Iraq and Syria or Da'ish in Arabic, in the summer of 2014. The argument started with the statement that Iraq was a 'failed state' and continued to reason that, therefore, there was no point in maintaining unity. Given the lack of a unified functioning state, the reasoning closed with the recommendation that Kurds ought to declare independence. This line of reasoning became particularly popular in 2017 when the Kurds held a vote on the question of independence. At the time, the discourse focused on Da'ish as proof of Iraq's status as a 'failed state'. It did not answer the question of whether Iraq had always been a 'failed state' or since when it had become such a state.

Iraq and Iraqi Kurdistan have not exactly constituted models for a functioning state for much of their recent history. Writing about Iraq and Iraqi Kurdistan since the 1980s, which featured the Iran–Iraq War including the Anfal Campaign against the Kurds, some scholars have drawn on Giorgio Agamben's work and have even taken Agamben's work in new directions. These scholars include Simon Mabon, Ana Maria Kumarasamy and Fazil Moradi, all of whom have analysed life in Iraq through the lens of Agamben's 'state of exception'.[1] Fazil Moradi, in particular, also drew on Achilles Mbembe's 'necropolitics',[2] which was in turn influenced by Agamben's work. Mbembe, fittingly for Kurdistan during the Anfal Campaign, writes about the politics of death inverting Foucault's biopower to the power over death.

Though attention to the workings of power has produced wonderful insights, it tends to draw consideration away from agency. For this reason, Simon Mabon has elsewhere called for scholars to examine forms of agency amid war and 'states of exception'.[3] This chapter heads that call. Based on the premise that Iraq constitutes a 'state of exception' or at least has constituted a 'state of exception' at some point or points in recent history, the question of agency arises. Agency is often posited as a kind of civil liberty. Common versions of the question of agency ask: Where do we see colonized peoples acting in their own interests? Where do we see women acting in their own interests? A meta-analysis might ask, and this is indeed one of the main points of this chapter: What do scholars even count as forms of agency? In other words, who decides whether 'they' are acting 'in their own self-interest'?

So what counts as agency and when? Yours truly, for instance, has implicitly argued elsewhere that conversion from Islam to a liberal interpretation of Zoroastrianism has constituted an urban, educated middle- to upper-class form of agency on the part of Iraqi Kurds following the 2014 fall of Mosul to Daʻish.[4] Matt Agorist has claimed that Shiʻa participation in the annual Arbaeen pilgrimage to Karbala comprises agency and protest against Daʻish in 2014 and the following years.[5] The focus on such acts of resistance to ISIS as religious agency reveals an implicit bias. By identifying resistance as agency, scholars are claiming that resistance makes possible 'qualified life' or *bíos* in the state of exception.

Steven Ramey has pointed out that scholars have favourite examples they like to draw on, while they neglect examples that might not fit so neatly or are not as palatable.[6] Specifically, by looking at religious performances and identities in Iraq, this chapter argues that Iraqis enacted forms of agency that have not, hereto, been recognized as forms of agency because they are 'unpalatable' to many North American and European audiences that only recognize acceptable, liberatory acts of resistance as agency.[7] Good Muslims, who according to Mahmood Mamdani are liberal, secular, American-loving and in this case include 'open-minded Muslims who nominally convert to Zoroastrianism', are used to exemplify heroic agents in the face of necropolitics in states of exception.[8] Bad Muslims, according to Mamdani, are described as terrorists. Bad Muslims are the ones engaged in activities or thoughts that do not involve loving America. Bad Muslims are seldom recognized for having agency and as desirous of a 'qualified life'. According to Giorgio Agamben, in the 'state of exception' life or at least some lives are reduced to *zoon* or 'bare life'. The opposite of 'bare life' is *bíos* or 'qualified life'. To live a qualified life is to live a political life, to matter. What this chapter draws attention to are religious acts that are not usually recognized as forms of agency, not because they don't enact forms of resistance but because their acts are labelled as unacceptable in European and North American public discourses.

This chapter first briefly recounts Iraqi history from 1920 to 2014, in order to provide a background to the rise of Daʻish. Next, it examines a recognized form of religious agency, an acceptable way to resist Daʻish: conversion to Yezidism and Zoroastrianism. Then the chapter looks at religious agents who are not always recognized as enacting resistance: Kurdish Sufis and in the following section, Shiʻa who joined militias to fight against Daʻish. Finally, it turns to the Kurdish Referendum in 2017 and its aftermath. The referendum ultimately failed in producing an independent Kurdish state. While it constituted an act of resistance, it was not followed up by the kind of violence that is necessary for the establishment of unquestionable sovereignty. Instead, leaders compromised. In the longer term, the paradoxical effect is that the 'regard for human life', as Kurdish politicians later framed their actions, prolonged a state of exception where the rules remain opaque and multiple regimes of laws govern but also exclude certain populations.

The Iraqi state and the history of its exception

Iraq has popularly been seen as a failed state, but this was not always the case. The area of Mesopotamia, the land between the rivers, has witnessed flourishing empires as well as wars. Though such an assertion risks essentializing a land with shifting borders and peoples with changing dividing lines, it merely restates Michel Foucault's 'inversion of Clausewitz's aphorism – politics is the continuation of war by other means'.[9]

Scholars such as Fazil Moradi and others have previously described all or parts of Iraq at different moments in history as an Agambian 'state of exception'. In this state, the difference between peace and war collapses. The sovereign acts outside of the rule of law. In Moradi's example, Saddam Hussein was the sovereign who implicitly declared the state of exception when he gassed his own citizens, Kurdish residents in and around Halabja and in other areas in 1988.[10] Thinking about a different time and place within Iraq, Simon Mabon and Ana Maria Kumarasamy have argued that Sunni Arabs post the fall of Saddam Hussein in 2003 in the Anbar Province especially, but also elsewhere, were reduced to 'bare life' as they were living in a 'state of exception'.[11] This, Mabon and Kumarasamy explain, is the reason that the call to arms by Da'ish found resonance among some Sunni Arabs. Moreover, they warn that the defeat of Da'ish does not necessarily lead to the cessation of violence, especially if the 'state of exception' in the Anbar Province remains resolved. Turning their attention to Kurds, Kamal Soleimani and Ahmad Mohammadpour describe Iranian Kurdish workers who cross the border to the autonomous Kurdish region of Iraq as living in a 'state of exception'.[12]

Historically speaking, Iraq has been conquered and divided often. When it was united, it was often united under strong, dictatorial rulers who governed through ruthlessness. One might argue, of course, that the entire question of whether a modern nation state is united has an underlying prescriptive moralizing tone. The British combination of three Ottoman provinces, Mosul, Baghdad and Basra in 1920, forced together groups that had inhabited different environmental zones, practised very different kinds of agriculture, belonged to different linguistic and cultural communities.[13] Within a month following the San Remo Conference in April 1920, when Mesopotamia was allotted to the British as a Mandate, the Iraqi revolt broke out.[14] During this revolt, Shi'a in the South, Kurds under the leadership of Sheikh Mahmud Barzinji and some Arab Sunnis fought against British forces. To mend together the three unrelated provinces that had become Iraq, the British installed Prince Faysal, the son of the Sharif of Mecca.[15]

This externally imposed Hashemite dynasty in Iraq had lasted for thirty-seven years when it was overthrown in 1958 when socialist, communist and Ba'th ideas spread throughout the Middle East. The Ba'th and the communists fought over Iraq for a decade until the Ba'th finally emerged victorious. Saddam Hussein quickly rose to positions of power, largely because of his willingness to kill even his allies and well-wishers, because they could pose a threat one day. Himself a Sunni, Saddam actively repressed Shi'ism following 1974, when Muharram processions in Karbala turned into anti-government demonstration. During the 1980s war with Iran, Iraq underwent a purge of Shi'a suspected to be of Iranian descent.[16] In the 1990s, as Fanar Haddad explains, the first Gulf War of 1991 and years of sanction led to increased sectarianism.[17]

The Kurds had been led to believe they would be granted an independent Kurdistan by the 1920 Treatise of Sevres, but were deprived of it when Attatürk's chief negotiator İsmet İnönü was able to have much of Ottoman Kurdistan allotted to Turkey and the rest was divided up by Syria and Iraq.[18] In 1931 young Mullah Mustafa Barzani, whose elder brother was a tribal chief who was fighting against an increasingly centralized Baghdad that aimed to gain better control over the country by breaking up the power of tribal leaders, joined the fighting. The fighting lasted two years. Then Mustafa Barzani surrendered and was placed in detention. During the chaos of the Second World War, he was able to escape and finally help found the Kurdish Republic of Mahabad in Iranian Kurdish territory in 1945 with Soviet help.[19] Masoud Barzani, Mustafa Barzani's son and the president of Iraqi Kurdistan from 2005 to 2017, was born there that year. The republic was dissolved in 1946. Two years later, Masoud Barzani went into exile to Russia, where he remained for a decade.

When Abdul Karim Qasim deposed King Ghazi II in 1958, he invited Mustafa Barzani to return to Iraq and chose to negotiate with him on behalf of the Kurds.[20] However, when Barzani was not granted Kurdish independence three years later, he revolted. Skilled at manipulating tribal rivalries, Qasim was able to defeat and marginalize Barzani. This victory was made easier due to internal Kurdish rivalries that divided and incapacitated the Kurdish movement. In 1975 Jalal Talabani split from Barzani's KDP (Kurdish Democratic Party) and founded the PUK (Patriotic Union of Kurdistan).[21] Kurdish tribal and religious leaders who had become politicians continued their internal struggle for power while also receiving support from interested and competing neighbouring countries that manipulated these divisions for their own benefit.

During the Iran–Iraq War, the Kurdish borders were porous as Iran supplied the Kurds with weapons in order to weaken the Iraqi central government. In response to their 'treason', Saddam gassed the Kurds in a drawn-out act of genocide in 1988 wherein he killed up to 180,000 Kurds, mostly civilians.[22] Drawing on Achilles Mbembe, Saddam's strategy can be described as *necropolitics*.[23]

When George Bush Sr encouraged Iraqis to rise up against Saddam in 1990 following the first Gulf War after the Iraqi invasion and annexation of Kuwait, he backed the Kurds by establishing a no-fly zone. However, no such backing was extended to others and more than 100,000 Arab Shi'a were killed for daring to revolt in the Shi'a-majority provinces of the South in 1991.[24] Having gained autonomy, the power vacuum in the autonomous Kurdish region led to the Kurdish Civil War between Barzani's KDP and Talabani's PUK which lasted from 1994 to 1997.[25] After American mediation, the two parties finally came to an agreement and divided up their territory. The Kurds greatly benefited from the American War on Iraq in 2003 and the new Iraqi government that rose up after it. In 2006, Jalal Talabani became the president of Iraq and stayed in office until 2014, though he was incapacitated for the last two years of his term, having suffered a debilitating stroke in 2012.

When the Arab Spring broke out in Tunisia in 2010/2011, few expected it to affect Iraq. There had been protests against government corruption and people had been killed in the Kurdish cities of Sulaimani and Duhok the year before. The concurrent American departure had gone relatively smoothly and without incident. The oil price was high, and this meant that both Baghdad and Erbil had money. Both the central Iraqi and the Kurdish regional government (KRG) spent money on social services and citizens were optimistic. Erbil, the capital of the Kurdish autonomous region, was expected to become the next Dubai. The rest of Iraq was not doing as well as the Kurdish area, but it was recovering as well. The general assumption was that Iraq had seen enough change. Although Saddam Hussein and the wars he dragged the country into were still remembered, that phase of Iraq's history was increasingly becoming distant. A general feeling of exhaustion was universal within the population. By 2011, it was assumed that Iraqis would resist the tide of protests that spread across the Middle East.

Everything seemed stable until 18 December 2012, when the Kurdish president of Iraq, Jalal Talabani, had a stroke, which left him unable to participate in politics. Iraq had adopted Lebanon's confessional political model. The Iraqi president would be Kurdish, the prime minister Shi'a and the Speaker of the House Sunni. Politically savvy, Talabani made the presidency, which is largely symbolic, a peace broker and helped prevent Sunni and Shi'a factions from clashing with each other. With him out of the way, Prime Minister Nouri al-Maliki rose to power. Immediately, Maliki ordered a raid on the home of Rafi al-Issawi, the Sunni finance minister, and arrested ten of al-Issawi's bodyguards. On 21 December, anti-government protests broke out in Fallujah.[26] Massive protests in the Anbar Province soon spread to other Sunni areas. Sunnis were disconcerted about their political and economic marginalization after the departure of the American troops. The protests received financial support from wealthy Sunni businessmen and politicians in Iraq and the Gulf. Soon, the demonstrations were met with state violence, which only perpetuated them.

The Islamic State of Iraq and Syria (ISIS or Da'ish) had already existed for a number of years prior to their takeover of Mosul, operating mainly in northeastern Syria, along the Iraqi border hugging the Kurdish areas. Their capital was Raqqah. In early June 2014, Da'ish took over Mosul and executed 1,700 soldiers of the Iraqi army, most of whom were Shi'a. To the Islamic State, these Shi'a were not Muslim and, as such, were killable.

Mosul itself is a predominantly Sunni Arab city with grievances against the central government. When Mosul fell, a popular assumption was that the residents of Mosul wanted to join Da'ish, not necessarily because they agreed with Da'ish's interpretation of Islam, though some did, but because they shared a common dislike of the Iraqi government. By the end of June, Da'ish declared an Islamic caliphate with Abu Bakr al-Baghdadi as the caliph. Non-Muslims would have to pay 'protection' fees from now onwards, as they did supposedly in the early Islamic period. In July a mass exodus of Christians from Da'ish territories depopulated a string of small but historic Christian villages around Mosul.

In August of that year, 2014, Da'ish took over the Sinjar district, which was home to hundreds of thousands of Yezidis. Yezidism is a syncretic religion with

Zoroastrian and Sufi elements. They worship the peacock angel and practise endogamy.[27] For many Muslims, Yezidis are not considered to be a 'people of the book', which means they are not a *protected people*. Some Muslims even consider them to be devil worshippers.[28] According to Da'ish, Yezidis are polytheists and must be converted, killed or enslaved. In fact, no attempt to convert them took place. When Da'ish conquered Sinjar, they killed the men and boys and enslaved the women and girls. These female slaves were then sold in Da'ish-held areas as sex-slaves. Aside from killing minorities, Da'ish also killed, beheaded and burned Muslims who did not agree with them or fought against them. They considered Sunni Muslims who did not pledge loyalty to their caliph to be apostates and, hence, deserving of death. Shi'a Muslims, wherever found, were to be given the same treatment as the Yezidis. Those Muslims who did pledge their allegiance were now subjected to the harshest interpretations and enforcement of Islamic law. For example, women had to not only cover their hair but also wear the face-veil. Women were no longer allowed to practice professions, where they might come in contact with men. Religious censorship was now enforced at universities and the curriculum was rewritten. While the Sunni areas occupied by Da'ish have always been conservative, the restrictions Da'ish imposed were unprecedented, especially in their violent discrimination against minorities and intolerance of Shi'ism.

What is important to note here is that Da'ish not only instituted a system for controlling bodies within their jurisdiction; they exercised power over life, but also over death. With regard to life, Da'ish routinely ordered many civilian young women living in Raqqah and Mosul whom to marry. Da'ish widows were quickly remarried to other fighters. Children and orphans of the caliphate's soldiers were indoctrinated into a macabre version of boy scouts, where they were taught how to properly behead people. As to death: Da'ish ordered fighters to the front and even to commit suicide operations, thereby controlling, managing and calculating death. This type of bureaucratic death administration is reminiscent of the fascist regimes of mid-twentieth-century Europe. In spite of its claim to be the reincarnation of the universal caliphate of early Islamic times, for all intents and purposes the Islamic caliphate is a modern state par excellence.[29] Moreover, especially after the fall of Mosul in 2014, parts, if not all of it, could be classified as an Agambian 'state of exception'. In this state of exception, Christians, Shi'a and even Sunnis who did not fully agree with Abu Bakr al-Baghdadi were reduced to *zoon*, bare life.

Religion and the romance of resistance

There was an emphasis on Da'ish's brutality in the Iraqi areas under its control and that had far-reaching consequences in terms of sectarianism and religious pluralization. First, it divided Muslims in the Middle East in general and Iraq in particular. While some ultra-religious Muslims sympathized with Da'ish, many others disagreed and turned towards quietist forms of Salafism or towards Sufism. Many others – especially those belonging to the upper classes and urban intellectuals – became secular in their political outlook and among the Kurds some even converted to other religions, especially Zoroastrianism.

Kurds in particular converted in noticeable numbers to Zoroastrianism and, at least during the summer of 2014, Kurds converted 'symbolically' to Yezidism, despite the fact that technically neither Zoroastrianism nor Yezidism accept converts.[30] One must be born a Zoroastrian or a Yezidi. In any case, the founders of the two new Zoroastrian centres in Sulaimani claim that Zoroastrianism was the 'original' religion of the Kurds. Therefore, Kurds are simply reclaiming their original identity by converting and (re)creating their own version of the religion.[31]

The turn towards neo-Zoroastrianism in Iraqi Kurdistan is predominantly an urban phenomenon among self-proclaimed intellectuals, which includes returnees as well as local artists, broadly defined.[32] Returnees are Kurds who left Kurdistan starting in the 1970s and particularly during the 1990s, when the PUK and the KDP engaged in the Kurdish Civil War, and immigrated to Europe, especially Sweden and England, often acquiring a second citizenship. Many of these returned to Iraqi Kurdistan between 2009 and 2014, the 'golden years' in Kurdistan, when the national budget, given the rising price of oil and relative political stability, promised citizens better economic prospects. While abroad, they adopted particular 'modern Western ideals' including secularism, rationalism, women's rights and legitimacy based on historicity. It is not so much that these notions were not known previously but given the view of Middle Easterners in Europe as unskilled and uneducated and hence lower class, these returnees will often cling to 'modern values' in order to defend themselves against stereotypes. Neo-Zoroastrianism hence becomes the carrier not only of a romantic nationalist ideology but also of Euro-American notions of progress and its accompanied values. The idea that Zoroastrianism was the 'original' religion of the Kurds goes back to the 1920s;[33] however, it became especially salient in 2014 when many Kurds wanted to turn away from Islam because they identified the latter with Da'ish. The hype around Zoroastrianism wore off rather quickly after internal disputes over financial transactions and personal differences tore rifts into the small community after 2016.[34] However, while it lasted, the neo-Zoroastrian movement in Kurdistan, which remained largely independent from Zoroastrian communities and organizations elsewhere around the globe, displayed a tangible example of agency in the face of *necropolitics* as practised by Da'ish.[35]

Other religious groups that were affected by the rise of Da'ish in 2014 include the Sufis. Anti-Sufi Salafism became prominent and widespread in Kurdistan following the Iran–Iraq War and the subsequent no-fly zone in certain Kurdish areas. Before that Kurdistan – especially the countryside – used to be overwhelmingly Sufi.

Until at least the 1970s and perhaps into the 1980s, Sufism was the dominant religious force in Iraqi Kurdistan. Sufi Kurds were mainly divided into Naqshbandis and Qadiris, which in turn were subdivided into a variety of sub-branches.[36] Particularly after the Tanzimat in the 1850s and the fall of the Kurdish emirates, Sufi sheikhs provided rural Kurds with local authority figures and functioned as judges, arbitrators and military leaders. Moreover, many gained wealth and influence after the 1850s, because they often registered *awqaf* lands in their own names.³⁷ Some of these Sufi sheikhs later became active in Kurdish nationalist movements. For example, Sheikh Ubeydullah, as Kamal Soleimani explains, was both a Naqshbandi sheikh and a proto-nationalist leader.³⁸ The Barzani family, which have been at the forefront of the battle for Kurdish independence, have produced influential Naqshbandi sheikhs.³⁹ Jalal Talabani's family has been one of two families that have produced prominent Qadiri sheikhs. The other family is the Barzinji family. While the Talibanis' lands centred around Kirkuk, Barzinji lands were located in and around Sulaimani. Sheikh Mahmud, who led a Kurdish revolt against the British in 1920, was also a Barzinji and the great-grandson of the Qadiri sheikh and famous miracle worker, Kak Ahmed.⁴⁰ In short, Kurdish Sufi sheikhs have often been deeply concerned with and involved in politics. Unlike Sufi sheikhs elsewhere, Kurdish sheikhs were mainly admired for their heroism, their masculinity and their leadership abilities.⁴¹ These ascribed qualities enabled many sheikhs to become politicians.

While Sufi sheikhs retained power either as sheikhs of Sufi orders or as politicians, as in the case of Masoud Barzani, Sufism as a religious movement weakened following the early 1990s and gave way to the rise of Salafism. Salafism was able to spread due to Saudi-funded mosques which were built in Kurdish villages in the early 1990s after large parts or even entire villages and their attendant Sufi shrines were destroyed during the decade-long Iran–Iraq War.⁴² More recently, the spread of Gülenist schools, private schools that adhere to the dogma of the Turkish preacher Fethullah Gülen and teach a form of anti-Shiʻa Sufism that idealizes Ottoman history and religiosity, has further weakened indigenous forms of Sufism.

When traditional Naqshbandi and Qadiri Sufism still reigned over the countryside, Kurds were on better terms with Iraqi Shiʻa. In the 1920s, Sheikh Mahmud Barzinji of Sulaimani rose up against the British mandate authorities at the same time as the Shiʻa in southern Iraq rebelled.⁴³ According to Hayder al-Khoei Kurdish Sufis greatly sympathized with the Shiʻa and he holds that this sympathy might further have resulted from doctrinal overlaps.⁴⁴ Qadiri Kasnazani Sufis, for instance, promote devotion to the family of the Prophet, which includes the Shiʻa Imams. Moreover, the fact that Arab Sunnis marginalized both Kurdish Sunnis and Arab Shiʻa politically for decades may have played a role too. Today, middle-class Kurdish Sunnism has become coloured by Saudi influences, Gülenism and various schools of neo-traditionalism.

What are the factors that led to the decline of Sufism in Kurdistan and also to the increasing hostility among Kurds vis-à-vis Arab Shiʻa? First, the Kurds still feel marginalized and because Shiʻa were able to constitute the majority in parliament post-2003, Kurds blamed the Shiʻa for the alienation of Sunni Arabs and the rise of Daʻish in 2014. Second, after Saddam's Anfal Campaign forced hundreds of thousands of Kurds to flee from their homes, the countries of the Arabian Peninsula contributed to rebuilding efforts in the early 1990s. They especially supported the construction of mosques and the education of sheikhs. Thus, Salafism heavily influenced the countryside. Many others left their villages and came to the cities for better opportunities. There, in the cities, they no longer felt tied to the same community-based Sufi orders. Instead, they now searched for new religious groups.

One kind of Sufism that has been thriving in Kurdish cities is the Gülen Movement. Their Sufism is anti-Shi'a, anti-PKK and pro-Turkish. The Gülen spread their ideology through schools, kindergartens, universities and informal networks. Together with the Salafists, the Gülen have radically altered the religious landscape of urban Iraqi Kurdistan. While once the Kurds harboured great sympathy for the Shi'a, as a Sunni urban elite oppressed them both, many Kurds blamed Shi'a for the country's woes. However, this does not mean that they have been siding with Arab Sunnis. In fact, after the summer of 2014 Sunni Arabs who were fleeing to Kurdistan, those who had already been living there previously and those who simply visited, all were seen with great suspicion. There were even protests in Sulaimani in the fall of 2014 that demanded that all Arabs be thrown out of the city and that no internally displaced persons (IDPs) be allowed in. In short, these facts point to great religious and ideological divisions within Kurdish society. Notably, the conservative Sunni segment of Kurdish society, which does not necessarily agree with Da'ish, tends to be friendlier towards their co-religionists regardless of their ethnic background.

In the centre and south of Iraq, even more so than in Kurdistan, religious affiliation continues to define people's identity. Sunnis faced difficulties as a minority after the fall of Saddam in 2003, because they are generally identified with the Ba'th regime. Meanwhile, Shi'ism, which is the religion of the Arab majority, continues to lay claim to the emotional loyalty and revolutionary fervour of the masses.[45] After Da'ish murdered 1,700 Iraqi soldiers, who were mainly poor Shi'a, annual Muharram rituals became ways for Iraqi Shi'a to 'fight' against Da'ish and its ideology through emphasizing their Shi'a identity. The Arbaeen march, which occurs forty days after the tenth of Muharram, when Imam al-Husayn was martyred in 680 CE and leads from the Iraqi city of Najaf to Karbala, 80 kilometres to the north, turned into a protest against Da'ish.[46] Religion thus once again became a way for the masses to claim agency in the face of *necropolitics*.

Being religious, according to Karl Marx, signifies passiveness. Marxism is also prevalent among nationalist Kurdish circles, especially those following Abdullah Öcalan, the founder and ideologue of the People's Worker Party, seen as a 'Kurdish terrorist organization' by the Turkish government and hailed as freedom fighters by nationalist Kurds. Öcalan argues that Islam is reactionary and that it must be cast aside in order to be able to embrace modernity, progress and, ultimately, independence.[47] Ideological views of religion aside, religion in Kurdistan can and often does function as a political force which at least to some extent allows peasants, for example, access to social and political elites by joining a Sufi order. Others, such as intellectuals and returnees, have expressed their distaste for Islam by converting to Zoroastrianism. Far from the notion that apostasy and conversion are impossible taboos in the Middle East, religious manoeuvring is a form of popular agency.

In addition to Zoroastrianism, Salafism and Gülenism, new forms of spirituality have also spread in Iraqi Kurdistan, as attested by the ubiquitous presence of self-help manuals and translations of Osho's books, and Deepak Chopra's bestsellers, Steven Covey's *7 Habits of Highly Successful People* and most recently, Sheryl Sandberg's *Lean In*. What does this mean? It underscores that piety constitutes a kind of response, a form of agency in *states of exception*, giving people control over their own lives not usually anticipated.[48]

In Iraq and in Iraqi Kurdistan, religion constitutes a major site for locating and studying agency in the face of *necropolitics*, because *necropolitics* itself has been exercised along religious lines and standards by Da'ish, Saddam's government in the post-1991 Gulf War period and the various Islamist political parties that came to dominate post-2003 Iraq.[49]

The rise of militias

Iraq, Syria, Libya and Egypt, among many other Middle Eastern countries, were all known for their military strength in the 1950s. They had received independence in the previous decade and now used their military for internal struggles of power. A new elite group of young men, many of who came from humble backgrounds and who had been educated in military schools, deposed monarchs and led their nations towards progress. At least that is how these elites portrayed themselves.

In the case of Syria and Iraq, communists and Ba'th struggled for power until the 1960s, when the Ba'th won. In both countries, the Ba'th government over-represented a minority that proceeded to rule with the help of a powerful military and police apparatus. After the fall of Saddam in 2003, the Americans and their allies disbanded the Iraqi army. Conscription was abandoned and as such the new Iraqi government could only call upon a relatively small army of trained soldiers, 1,700 of whom were massacred by Da'ish in Mosul in 2014. The central government had, in a sense, no choice but to rely upon militias, especially the *Hashd al-Sha'bi* but also the Kurdish Peshmerga and others to fight Da'ish. In the United States, abandoning conscription and low enlistment numbers has led to the hiring of private contractors who are not always subject to federal US regulations in times of war. In Iraq, the same goes for the religious militia.

On 13 June 2014, the arguably highest-ranking Shi'a scholar in Iraq, Ayatollah 'Ali al-Sistani called upon all Iraqis to defend Iraq against Da'ish. Some Sunnis interpreted this as a call for Shi'a to kill Sunnis, while others believed he was only calling for more Iraqis to volunteer to the Iraqi army. Regardless of his intentions, Sistani's fatwa gave birth to the independent Popular Mobilization Units or the *Hashd al-Sha'bi*, which have been fighting Da'ish since. At first, they functioned as a paramilitary movement that was independent of the Iraqi state apparatus. Within less than a year, Prime Minister al-'Abadi sought to include them under the umbrella of the Iraqi state. Yet, the *Hashd al-Sha'bi* remain loyal to their own chain of commands. Theoretically, they coordinate with the federal Iraqi military and the Kurdish Peshmerga forces. Yet, they also occasionally commit rogue actions and get into skirmishes with their allies and with Sunnis who are not part of Da'ish.

Joining Shi'a militias is not what 'Good Muslims,' the way Mahmoud Mamdani describes them, do. Mamdani explains that Good Muslims are liberal and their politics are pro-American.[50] It is Americans, in other words, who decide on who is a 'Good' versus a 'Bad Muslim' and the criteria is their utility. The militias were at first welcomed and celebrated, but their relationship with the United States was rather ambivalent and unstable. Nevertheless, the militias were founded as forces of resistance. They represented popular agency.

In the meanwhile, other religious and ethnic minorities have established their own militias. The Feyli Shi'a Kurds,[51] Christians, Kakais and Yezidis have their own brigades that operate under the Ministry of the Peshmerga. While these groups fought Da'ish, they occasionally also fought each other in competition over land and resources in the name of nationalism.

Encouraged by Iran, the PUK cooperated with the *Hashd al-Sha'bi* in the town of Tuz Khurmato, in the disputed territories between Baghdad and Erbil in 2015 and 2016. But because of tensions that emerged, the other Kurdish parties, especially the KDP, criticized the PUK for cooperating with Shi'a militias. On 17 February 2015, Masoud Barzani during his visit to Kirkuk said that the Kurds do not need Shi'a militias in their fight against Da'ish.[52] Barzani's comments followed remarks by Iraqi prime minister Haider al-'Abadi who stated that the *Hashd al-Sha'bi* represents all of Iraq and that anyone who protects the principles of the country is a member of the force. In 2016, the United States helped organize a concerted and common effort to retake Mosul from Da'ish. While many Iraqis, including Kurds, Sunnis and Shi'a, were grateful and viewed the continued fight against Da'ish as important, they were also worried that Kurds and Shi'a forces would turn on each other once Da'ish would be defeated.

These forces can be described as militias because they are outside of the state. They exist separately from the real army, which was defeated by Da'ish in June 2014. These are ordinary young men. They are not necessarily trained fighters. They are not even regularly paid by the state. Yet, for many of these fighters, it is not their material circumstances or their political participation that made them able to attain a 'qualified life'. Young fighters lead a qualified life that derives meaning from religion and/or nationalism. The fight songs of the *Hashd al-Sha'bi* are Shi'a religious chants, *latmiyyat hussayniyyah*. And the use of Shi'a symbols and rituals for political or revolutionary purposes is neither new nor unusual.[53]

Arguing that religion can make a 'bare life' into a 'qualified life' is to paraphrase Karl Marx. It is to say the working people in Iraq – be they Kurds, Arabs, Sunnis, Shi'is – constitute the masses, who are oppressed by global exploitative capitalism, as well as corrupt politicians. And religion, whatever its form, is their only available crutch. And as such, religion makes it possible to attain a 'qualified life'.

The media has taken an active part in making sense of this particular state of exception. However, the case of the Arab world after the Arab Spring has been a particular challenge. Classically, as Mahmood Mamdani explained, the West has called one group the 'good' Muslims and the other group the 'bad' Muslims.[54] The ethical epithet is of course meaningless and tells us more about Western economic and political interests than about the content of Muslim theology.

As of 2017, the United States supports both the Kurds and the Shi'a in Iraq. The Islamic State of Iraq and Syria has come to personify absolute evil. Abu Bakr al-Baghdadi and his followers have been equated with Hitler and the Nazis, who according to Hollywood are the other personification of evil. As a consequence, civilian casualties in Raqqah, Mosul and the Anbar Province have been under-reported. The dead there have become what Judith Butler calls 'unmournable'.[55]

Managing Kurdish states of exception

From 2014 to 2017, while Da'ish fought for and controlled areas around Mosul, Kirkuk and other disputed territories rich in oil, the autonomous Kurdish government had to deal with the war against Da'ish, restricted funds allotted by Baghdad and limited cash flow due to low oil prices and hundreds of thousands of refugees. There were multiple states of exception, layers of laws and temporary bans. Militias arose, elections were suspended, checkpoints instructed not to let certain populations pass into other cities and provinces.

During this time, the KRG under the leadership of Masoud Barzani gained sympathy from Europe and the United States. Assuming that their cooperation in fighting against Da'ish meant they had become loyal friends who could count on one another, Barzani called for a referendum on Kurdish independence in northern Iraq on 27 September 2017. It was a gamble, but in the best-case scenario, he would become the ruler of a sovereign Kurdistan. In the worst case, he'd go down in history as a national hero, rather than a corrupt politician who had used a state of exception to amass power and resources. In either case, the wider family could only win.

In the weeks and months leading up to the referendum, European and North American expatriates, especially those working in the industry, were advised to leave. There was a festive mood throughout Iraqi Kurdistan. In both Barzani-controlled territory, or the territory under the auspices of the KDP (Kurdistan Democratic Party), and the areas controlled by the PUK (Patriotic Union of Kurdistan, formerly led by the late Iraqi president, Jalal Talabani), this was the only issue that was assured to unite everyone: the question of independence. Those who quietly dissented would explain that they had not given up on the dream of independence but thought this was not an appropriate time.[56] The majority was celebrating. For example, the malls in Sulaimani were decorated with banners and hosted live music in order to foster this atmosphere. The fact that the Trump administration had already announced that it would not be supporting the Kurds in their bid for independence did little to hamper the party.

The vote went ahead, and the vast majority of Kurds voted 'yes' for independence. Acting quickly, the Shi'a prime minister al-'Abadi took control over the borders, called upon Iran and Turkey to close their borders and for international airlines to stop flying to Erbil and Sulaimani. Armed forces accrued on both sides of Kirkuk as tensions built. Less than three weeks later, Iraqi forces took Kirkuk with minor resistance from the Kurds. The Iranians had brokered a truce via Soleimani, who was later assassinated by US agents in January 2020. As KDP Peshmerga withdrew, they destroyed a bridge between Kirkuk and Erbil behind themselves. The reconstruction of this bridge took months. The shortest route between Sulaimani and Erbil, two of three provincial capitals in the autonomous Kurdish region, led over Kirkuk and this bridge. The traffic of people and things was redirected towards the north, where a new road opened up. The destruction of the bridge symbolized the severing of Kurdistan from Iraq. Immediately, there was mudslinging between the PUK and the KDP. Each side accused the other of cowardice and of betraying the 'Kurdish cause'.[57] At the same time, politicians defended their decision not to engage militarily by citing their belief in the value of human life. What kind of life they meant, 'qualified life' or 'bare life', remained uncertain.

What is of particular interest to the analysis of the 'state of exception' and the question of agency are the public discourses that accompanied the referendum and the Shi'a takeover of Kirkuk. These discourses focus on 'rights' and 'suffering'. A common argument revolved around the idea that the Kurds deserved certain rights because of all they had suffered. In Agamben's terms, the Kurds deserved to live a 'qualified life' with political rights because they had been reduced to *zoon*, the bare life of an animal within complex 'states of exception'.

The centrality of suffering and its moral weight have been a defining feature of the Kurdish discourse surrounding their quest for independence since the genocidal Anfal Campaign which Saddam Hussein unleashed upon the Kurds in 1988 and 1989.[58] In this they resemble both Jewish Israeli narratives and Palestinian accounts. The Kurdish narrative is a tragic romance, wherein the people suffer unjustly but continue to place their hopes in their leaders to save them. Because Kurds are innocent and suffer unfairly, they deserve their own nation based on a moral claim. Practical issues were generally brushed off with the trust that everything would be resolved once sovereignty was achieved. Once they had independence, they would no longer live in a state of exception, they would be able to live 'qualified lives' and they would no longer be trapped in 'states of exception'.

The central government focused on another issue: land. Baghdad accused the Kurds of wanting to keep the lands they had won from Da'ish but which were disputed territories. Through the referendum, the Kurds allegedly wanted to legitimate their claim on not only the Kurdish autonomous region of Iraq but also adjacent areas including Yezidi areas and Kirkuk. Minorities in the disputed territories worried. Many Arabs and Turkmen boycotted the referendum in disputed Kirkuk.[59] These disputed territories are not only inhabited by multiple religious and ethnic groups, they are also often blessed with natural oil reserves. In wake of the referendum, the Kurds militarily held many of these key strategic areas, including Kirkuk, having taken these while fighting Da'ish. The Kurds not only claimed that they had a right to these lands because they were won through battle, but because they, the Kurds, were supposedly the superior administrators of these areas. In an article published by the *Jerusalem Post*, Mohamed Bakr further argues that Kirkuk experienced less violence under Kurdish administration from 2015 to 2017 than it had previously.[60] The focus on Kurdish 'rights' and their 'suffering' further served to distract Iraqi Kurds and foreclosed the possibility of a realistic assessment of the KDP's increasing authoritarianism, corruption and mismanagement, the crippling rivalry between the Kurdish parties and their reliance on oil revenues. It engendered blind faith among the masses.

The central government immediately denounced the referendum and called for punitive measures, which were within the central government's constitutional rights. The Kurds were shocked. Many were disappointed, especially by the lack of American support.[61] Among other measures, the central government retook oil-rich Kirkuk, which according to the central government does not belong to the territory administered by the KRG. By the end of the first week in October, troops were amassing near Kirkuk. There were earlier, unofficial skirmishes, but on 16 the tension had built to such levels that fighting broke out in several areas. Just as everyone feared the beginning of a civil war between Arabs and Kurds, the PUK ordered their Peshmerga, their fighters, to stop and retreat. Consequently, the Iraqi army (read: mostly Arab Shi'a forces) quickly conquered the city with relatively little blood loss.

The KDP accused the PUK of being traitors and of having betrayed the Kurdish dream.[62] Meanwhile the PUK claimed that it had done so after coming to the decision that they were not willing to sacrifice the lives of their men.[63] Declining to fight thus came to constitute a moral high ground. Drawing on Agamben, one could say that the PUK decided that the violence and sacrifice necessary for the founding of a sovereign state was not worth it, at least the particular state which would have arisen from the violence was not going to be worth the price. The PUK's discourse, which emphasized their desire to save Kurdish lives, depicted the PUK as tragic heroes who were already suffering undeservedly while morally remaining innocent and hence undeserving of and immune to any criticism. The PUK's argument implies that the Kurds cannot live 'qualified lives' in a sovereign state founded by Barzani.

In the aftermath of the referendum, Masoud Barzani officially stepped down as the president of the Kurdish regional government.[64] He had remained in office unelected since 2013 when his term expired. At first, he received a two-year extension by the Kurdish parliament but remained in office even after his extension expired in 2015 until 2017. During this time, he was accused of amassing power and money.

Some Kurds hoped that the central government would now come to their rescue and pay their salaries, which the Kurdish government, largely because of corruption and financial mismanagement, had been unable to pay in full since 2014. However, the central government did not turn out to be a hero that saves its citizens from difficulties. It took Baghdad another six months to send money for salaries.[65] The establishment of normalcy, the reassertion of central authority over the far reaches of the country and the end of the 'state of exception' under Da'ish and under an autonomy that exceeded the constitution did not lead to the kind of 'qualified life' many had hoped for. However, the re-establishment of elections for the office of the KRG's presidency did signal Michel Foucault's 'inversion of Clausewitz's aphorism – politics is the continuation of war by other means'.[66]

In summer 2018, Barham Salih became the president of Iraq. Salih presented himself as the right-hand man of the late president Jalal Talabani and thereby symbolically invoked the peace and prosperity which Talabani was now known for. To what extent Salih recreated or ameliorated the conditions that gave rise to Da'ish in the first place will be seen in the years to come.

In sum, this chapter examines a variety of religious forms of agency in contemporary Iraq. It draws on Giorgio Agamben but also speaks back to Agamben by pointing out how Iraqis, Sunnis and Shi'a Arabs, Kurds and others rise above 'bare life' and claim agency in Iraqi 'states of exception'. By doing so, it heeds Simon Mabon's call for scholars to examine forms of agency in the midst of war, a 'state of exception'.[67]

Religious forms of agency are interesting because they reveal what Lila Abu-Lughod has called politics of the 'the romance of resistance'.[68] Abu-Lughod asks social scientists to think about why and in what forms of resistance they are interested in. For the most part, scholars and journalists have written about Kurdish conversion as a form of agency and about Shi'a mourning processions as protest against Da'ish. As Mabon and Kumarasamy have also acknowledged, heading the call of Abu Bakr al-Baghdadi was a form of agency among Sunni Arabs, especially in the Anbar Province.[69] The rise of Shi'a militias similarly exemplified religious agency, as did the rise of other armed groups. These groups clearly had agency but have not usually been examined as such. These groups did not ultimately bring an end to the Iraqi 'state of exception'. The next larger attempt at attaining sovereignty, the referendum in September 2017, failed in achieving Kurdish independence and instead perpetuated the state of exception with additional legal bans and restrictions. Why is it important to examine these instances of agency? Instances of resistance point to possible developments. And if we look carefully, we can see possibilities we don't want to see.

Notes

1 Simon Mabon and Ana Maria Kumarasamy, 'Da'ish, Stasis and Bare Life in Iraq', in *Iraq after ISIS: The Challenges of Post-War Recovery*, ed. Jacob Eriksson and Ahmed Khaleel (London: Palgrave Macmillan, 2019), 9–28; Fazil Moradi, 'The Ba'th State of Exception: Configuration of Authority, Violence and Life', Presentation at the 2nd Annual American University of Iraq Conference on the Middle East, Sulaimani, Kurdistan Region of Iraq, 27 June 2012.
2 Moradi, 'The Ba'th State of Exception'.
3 Simon Mabon, 'Sovereignty, Bare Life and the Arab Uprisings', *Third World Quarterly* 38, no. 8 (2017): 1782–99.
4 Edith Szanto, '"Zoroaster Was a Kurd!": Neo-Zoroastrianism among Iraqi Kurds', *Iran and the Caucasus* 22, no. 1 (2018): 96–110.
5 Matt Agorist, 'Millions of Muslims March against ISIS during Pilgrimage and Mainstream Media Completely Ignores It', *The Free Thought Project*, 28 November 2016. Available online: https://thefreethoughtproject.com/20-million-muslims-march-against-isis/ (accessed 5 May 2018).

6   Steven Ramey, 'Accidental Favorites: The Implicit in the Study of Religion', in *Claiming Identity in the Study of Religion – Social and Rhetorical Techniques Examined*, ed. Monica Miller (Sheffield, UK: Equinox, 2015), 223–38.
7   See a similar point being made by yours truly with regard to women in the Syrian uprising and civil war. Cf. Edith Szanto, 'Depicting Victims, Heroines, and Pawns in the Syrian Uprising', *Journal of Middle East Women's Studies* 12, no. 3 (2016): 306–22.
8   Mahmood Mamdani, 'Good Muslim, Bad Muslim: A Political Perspective on Culture and Terrorism', *American Anthropologist, New Series* 104, no. 3 (2002): 766–75.
9   Michel Foucault, *Society Must Be Defended: Lectures at the Collège de France*, ed. Mauro Bertani and Alessandro Fontana, trans. David Macey (New York: Picador, 2003), 15–16.
10 Moradi, 'The Ba'th State of Exception'.
11 Mabon and Kumarasamy, 'Da'ish, Stasis and Bare Life in Iraq', 9–28.
12 Kamal Soleimani and Ahmad Mohammadpour, 'Life and Labor on the Internal Colonial Edge: Political Economy of kolberi in Rojhelat', *British Journal of Sociology* 71, no. 4 (March 2020): 741–60.
13 William L. Cleveland and Martin Bunton, *A History of the Modern Middle East*, 4th edn (Boulder, CO: Westview Press, 2009), 204.
14 Ibid., 164.
15 Ibid., 207.
16 Marion Farouk-Sluglett and Peter Sluglett, *Iraq since 1958: From Revolution to Dictatorship* (London: IB Tauris, 2001), 158.
17 Fanar Haddad, *Sectarianism in Iraq: Antagonistic Visions of Unity* (New York: Columbia University Press, 2011).
18 Cleveland and Bunton, *A History of the Modern Middle East*, 178.
19 Farouk-Sluglett and Sluglett, *Iraq since 1958*, 27–30.
20 Cleveland and Bunton, *A History of the Modern Middle East*, 329–30.
21 Farouk-Sluglett and Sluglett, *Iraq since 1958*, 189.
22 'Halabja Genocide', *Kurdish Regional Government – Iraq: Representation in the United States*. Available online: http://new.krg.us/aboutkurdistan/halabja-genocide/ (accessed 27 June 2017).
23 Achilles Mbembe, 'Necropolitics', translated by Libby Meintjes, *Public Culture* 15, no. 1 (2003): 11–40.
24 Charles Tripp, *A History of Iraq* (Cambridge: Cambridge University Press, 2000), 244–50.
25 Farouk-Sluglett and Sluglett, *Iraq since 1958*, 298–99.
26 Sam Wyer, 'Political Update: Mapping the Iraq Protests', *Institute for the Study of War*, 11 January 2013. Available online: http://www.understandingwar.org/backgrounder/political-update-mapping-iraq-protests (accessed 4 May 2018).
27 Garnik Asatrian and Victoria Arakelova, 'Malak-Tāwūs: The Peacock Angel of the Yezidis', *Iran & the Caucasus* 7, no. 1/2 (2003): 1–36.
28 Zaim Khenchelaoui, 'The Yezidis, People of the Spoken Word in the Midst of People of the Book', *Diogenes* 47 (1999): 20–37.
29 Cf. Olivier Roy, *Globalized Islam* (New York: Columbia University Press, 2004), 61–5.
30 'Head of Zoroastrian Temple Says People Are Returning to Their Roots', *Rudaw*, 1 February 2016. Available online: http://rudaw.net/english/kurdistan/310120162 (accessed 1 December 2016); 'Iraqi Kurds Abandon Their Religion to Zoroastrianism to Escape Islamic Extremism', *EKurd*, 3 May 2015. Available online: http://ekurd.net/kurds-abandon-their-religion-to-zoroastrianism-to-escape-islamic-extremism

-2015-05-03 (accessed 1 December 2016); Mayada Kordy Khalil, 'Kurds Go Back to Zoroastrianism: Interview with Pir Luqman', *SBS*, 3 April 2016. Available online: http://www.sbs.com.au/yourlanguage/kurdish/en/content/kurds-go-back-zoroastrianism (accessed 1 December 16); Alaa Latif, 'Fed Up with Islam and Sectarianism, Some Iraqis Embrace Zoroastrianism', *The Daily Beast*, 31 May 2015. Available online: http://www.thedailybeast.com/articles/2015/05/31/fed-up-with-islam-and-sectarianism-some-iraqis-embrace-zoroastrianism.html (accessed 1 December 2016).
31 Szanto, 'Zoroaster Was a Kurd!', 100–9.
32 Ibid., 96–100.
33 Christine Allison, 'Representations of Yezidism and Zoroastrianism in the Kurdish Newspapers Hawar and Roja Nû', in *From Daēnā to Dîn: Religion, Kultur und Sprache in der iranischen Welt: Festschrift für Philip Kreyenbroek zum 60. Geburtstag*, ed. Christine Allison, Anke Joisten-Pruschke and Antje Wendtland (Wiesbaden: Harrassowitz, 2009), 285–91.
34 Szanto, 'Zoroaster Was a Kurd!', 108–9.
35 Cf. Edith Szanto, 'Islam in Kurdistan: Religious Communities and Their Practices in Contemporary Northern Iraq', in *Handbook of Contemporary Islam and Muslim Lives*, ed. Mark Woodward and Ronald Lukens-Bull (New York: Springer, 2020).
36 Martin van Bruinessen, *Mullas, Sufis and Heretics: The Role of Religion in Kurdish Society* (Istanbul: Isis Press, 2000); Martin van Bruinessen, 'The Qadiriyya and the Lineages of Qadiri Shaykhs in Kurdistan', *Journal of the History of Sufism*, special issue: The Qadiriyya Order, ed. Thierry Zarcone, Ekrem Işın and Arthur Buehler 1–2 (2000): 131–49; Martin van Bruinessen, 'The Naqshbandi Order in Seventeenth-Century Kurdistan', in *Naqshbandis: cheminements et situation actuelle d'un ordre mystique musulman*, ed. Marc Gaborieau, Alexandre Popovic and Thierry Zarcone (Istanbul-Paris: Editions Isis, 1990), 337–60.
37 Othman Ali, 'Southern Kurdistan during the Last Phase of Ottoman Control: 1839–1914', *Journal of Muslim Minority Affairs* 17, no. 2 (1997): 287.
38 Kamal Soleimani, 'Islamic Revivalism and Kurdish Nationalism in Sheikh Ubeydullah's Poetic Oeuvre', *Kurdish Studies* 4, no. 1 (2016): 5–24.
39 Bruinessen, 'The Naqshbandi Order in Seventeenth-Century Kurdistan', 337–60.
40 Bruinessen, 'The Qadiriyya and the Lineages of Qadiri Shaykhs in Kurdistan', 131–49.
41 Frederick Barth, *Principles of Social Organization in Southern Kurdistan* (Oslo: Brødrene Jørgensen boktr, 1953), 82–6.
42 Camilla Insom, 'Evolving Sacred Landscape: Sufi Saint Cult in Kurdistan Village Shrines', Presentation at the 8th Conference of Iranian Studies of the Societas Iranologica Europaea (Saint Petersburg, Russia, 2015).
43 David McDowall, *A Modern History of the Kurds*, 3rd edn (London: I.B. Tauris, 2007), 154–9.
44 Hayder al-Khoei, 'Natural Alliance', *Kurdish Herald* 1, no. 2 (June 2009). Available online: http://www.kurdishherald.com/issue/002/article06.php (accessed 1 December 2016).
45 Shi'ism has often been interpreted to function in two binary modes: as either revolutionary and politically active or salvific and politically passive. See, for example, Kamran Scot Aghaie, *The Martyrs of Karbala: Shi'i Symbols and Rituals in Modern Iran* (Seattle, WA: University of Washington Press, 2004) and Lara Deeb, *An Enchanted Modern: Gender and Public Piety in Shi'i Lebanon* (Princeton, NJ: Princeton University Press, 2006).

However, these modes do not need to be mutually exclusive and even salvific modes of piety can have political consequences and significance. See Edith Szanto, 'Beyond the Karbala Paradigm: Rethinking Revolution and Redemption in Twelver Shi'a Mourning Rituals', *Journal of Shi'a Islamic Studies* 6, no. 1 (2013): 75–91.
46 Agorist, 'Millions of Muslims March against ISIS during Pilgrimage and Mainstream Media Completely Ignores It', Cf. Edith Szanto, 'The Largest Contemporary Muslim Pilgrimage Isn't the Hajj to Mecca, It's the Shiite Pilgrimage to Karbala in Iraq', *The Conversation News Source*, September 2020. Available online: https://theconversation.com/the-largest-contemporary-muslim-pilgrimage-isnt-the-hajj-to-mecca-its-the-shiite-pilgrimage-to-karbala-in-iraq-144542 (accessed 1 November 2020).
47 Cf. Matthew Barber, 'Sunni Kurdish Converts to Zoroastrianism in Iraqi Kurdistan: Kurdish Nationalism and the Contemporary Attraction for an Ancient Faith', Master's Thesis, University of Chicago, 2015.
48 Other forms of agency can include the introduction of Syrian cuisine by Syrian Kurdish refugees living in Iraqi Kurdistan. See Sherwan Hindreen Ali, 'The Levantine–Kurdish Synthesis: How Syrian Refugees Revolutionized the Kurdish Restaurant Scene', *Syrian Studies Association Bulletin* 22, no. 1 (2017): 7–10.
49 Cf. Moradi, 'The Ba'th State of Exception'.
50 Mamdani, 'Good Muslim, Bad Muslim', 767–78.
51 Michael Knights, 'Iran's Expanding Militia Army in Iraq: The New Special Groups', *CTC Sentinel* 12, no. 7 (August 2019): 5.
52 Global Security, 'Hashd al-Shaabi', Available online: http://www.globalsecurity.org/military/world/para/hashd-al-shaabi.htm (accessed 1 December 2016).
53 See Aghaie, *The Martyrs of Karbala*.
54 Mamdani, 'Good Muslim, Bad Muslim', 766–74.
55 Judith Butler, *Precarious Life: The Powers of Mourning and Violence* (New York: Verso, 2004).
56 Cf. David Zucchino, 'After the Vote, Does the Kurdish Dream of Independence Have a Chance?', *New York Times*, 30 September 2017. Available online: https://www.nytimes.com/2017/09/30/world/middleeast/kurds-iraq-independence.html (accessed 20 November 2020).
57 Mohsen Milani, 'The Turbulent History Shaping Iran's Opposition to an Independent Iraqi Kurdistan', *World Politics Review*, 14 November 2017. Available online: https://www.worldpoliticsreview.com/articles/23610/the-turbulent-history-shaping-iran-s-opposition-to-an-independent-iraqi-kurdistan (accessed 20 November 2020).
58 Cf. Edith Szanto, 'Mourning Halabja on Screen: Or Reading Kurdish Politics through Anfal Films', *Review of Middle East Studies* 52, no. 1 (2018): 135–46; and Andrea Fischer-Tahir, 'Gendered Memories and Masculinities: Kurdish Peshmerga on the Anfal Campaign in Iraq', *Journal of Middle East Women's Studies* 8, no. 1 (2012): 92–114.
59 'Kirkuk Votes to Take Part in Kurdish Independence Poll', *Al-Jazeera*, 27 August 2017. Available online: https://www.aljazeera.com/news/2017/08/kirkuk-votes-part-kurdish-independence-poll-170829134834287.html (accessed 4 May 2018).
60 Mohamed 'Mera' Bakr, 'The Kurds and Kirkuk, before and after October 16', *Jerusalem Post*, 21 November 2017. Available online: https://www.jpost.com/Opinion/The-Kurds-and-Kirkuk-before-and-after-October-16-514864 (accessed 4 May 2018).
61 Joost Hiltermann, 'What Did the Kurds Get Out of the Referendum?', *The Atlantic*, 27 September 2017. Available online: https://www.theatlantic.com/international/archive/2017/09/kurds-iraq-barzani-isis-referendum/541260/ (accessed 4 May 2018).

62	Denise Natali, 'Iraqi Kurdistan Was Never Ready for Statehood', *Foreign Policy*, 31 October 2017. Available online: https://foreignpolicy.com/2017/10/31/iraqi-kurdistan-was-never-ready-for-statehood/ (accessed 4 May 2018).
63	'Bafel Talabani: PUK Chose "Tactical Withdrawal" from Kirkuk after Casualties', *Rudaw*, 21 October 2017. Available online: http://www.rudaw.net/english/kurdistan/211020179 (accessed 4 May 2018).
64	'Masoud Barzani to Step Down as KRG President', *Al-Jazeera*, 29 October 2017. Available online: https://www.aljazeera.com/news/2017/10/masoud-barzani-step-krg-president-171029161347180.html (accessed 4 May 2018).
65	Margaret Coker, 'After Months of Acrimony, Baghdad Strikes Deal with Kurds', *New York Times*, 22 March 2018. Available online: https://www.nytimes.com/2018/03/22/world/middleeast/iraq-kurds-agreement.html (accessed 4 May 2018).
66	Foucault, *Society Must Be Defended*, 15–16.
67	Mabon, 'Sovereignty, Bare Life and the Arab Uprisings', 1782–99.
68	Lila Abu-Lughod, 'The Romance of Resistance: Tracing Transformations of Power through Bedouin Women', *American Ethnologist* 17, no. 1 (1990): 41–55.
69	Mabon and Kumarasamy, 'Da'ish, Stasis and Bare Life in Iraq', 9–28.

References

Abu-Lughod, L. 'The Romance of Resistance: Tracing Transformations of Power through Bedouin Women'. *American Ethnologist* 17, no. 1 (1990): 41–55.

Aghaie, K. S. *The Martyrs of Karbala: Shi'i Symbols and Rituals in Modern Iran*. Seattle, WA: University of Washington Press, 2004.

Agorist, M. 'Millions of Muslims March against ISIS during Pilgrimage and Mainstream Media Completely Ignores It'. *The Free Thought Project*, 28 November 2016. Available online: https://thefreethoughtproject.com/20-million-muslims-march-against-isis/ (accessed 5 May 2018).

Ali, O. 'Southern Kurdistan during the Last Phase of Ottoman Control: 1839–1914'. *Journal of Muslim Minority Affairs* 17, no. 2 (1997): 283–91.

Ali, S. H. 'The Levantine–Kurdish Synthesis: How Syrian Refugees Revolutionized the Kurdish Restaurant Scene'. *Syrian Studies Association Bulletin* 22, no. 1 (2017): 7–10.

Allison, C. 'Representations of Yezidism and Zoroastrianism in the Kurdish Newspapers Hawar and Roja Nû'. In *From Daēnā to Dîn: Religion, Kultur und Sprache in der iranischen Welt: Festschrift für Philip Kreyenbroek zum 60. Geburtstag*, edited by C. Allison, A. Joisten-Pruschke, and A. Wendtland, 295–1. Wiesbaden: Harrassowitz, 2009.

Asatrian, G. and V. Arakelova. 'Malak-Tāwūs: The Peacock Angel of the Yezidis'. *Iran & the Caucasus* 7, no. ½ (2003): 1–36.

'Bafel Talabani: PUK Chose "Tactical Withdrawal" from Kirkuk after Casualties'. *Rudaw*, 21 October 2017. Available online: http://www.rudaw.net/english/kurdistan/211020179 (accessed 4 May 2018).

Bakr, M. 'The Kurds and Kirkuk, before and after October 16'. *Jerusalem Post*, 21 November 2017. Available online: https://www.jpost.com/Opinion/The-Kurds-and-Kirkuk-before-and-after-October-16-514864 (accessed 4 May 2018).

Barber, M. 'Sunni Kurdish Converts to Zoroastrianism in Iraqi Kurdistan: Kurdish Nationalism and the Contemporary Attraction for an Ancient Faith'. M.A. Thesis, The University of Chicago, 2015.

Barth, F. *Principles of Social Organization in Southern Kurdistan*. Oslo: Brødrene Jørgensen boktr, 1953.
Bruinessen, M. van. *Mullas, Sufis and Heretics: The Role of Religion in Kurdish Society*. Istanbul: Isis Press, 2000.
Bruinessen, M. van. 'The Qadiriyya and the Lineages of Qadiri Shaykhs in Kurdistan'. *Journal of the History of Sufism*, special issue, T. Zarcone, E. Işın and A. Buehler (eds.), *The Qadiriyya Order*, vols. 1–2 (2000): 131–49.
Bruinessen, M. van. 'The Naqshbandi Order in Seventeenth-Century Kurdistan'. In *Naqshbandis: cheminements et situation actuelle d'un ordre mystique musulman*, edited by M. Gaborieau, A. Popovic and T. Zarcone, 337–60. Istanbul-Paris: Editions Isis, 1990.
Butler, J. *Precarious Life: The Powers of Mourning and Violence*. New York: Verso, 2004.
Cleveland, W. L. and M. Bunton. *A History of the Modern Middle East*, 4th edn. Boulder, CO: Westview Press, 2009.
Coker, M. 'After Months of Acrimony, Baghdad Strikes Deal with Kurds'. *New York Times*, 22 March 2018. Available online: https://www.nytimes.com/2018/03/22/world/middleeast/iraq-kurds-agreement.html (accessed 4 May 2018).
Deeb, L. *An Enchanted Modern: Gender and Public Piety in Shi'i Lebanon*. Princeton: Princeton University Press, 2006.
Farouk-Sluglett, M. and P. Sluglett. *Iraq since 1958: From Revolution to Dictatorship*. London: IB Tauris, 2001.
Fischer-Tahir, A. 'Gendered Memories and Masculinities: Kurdish Peshmerga on the Anfal Campaign in Iraq'. *Journal of Middle East Women's Studies* 8, no. 1 (2012): 92–114.
Foucault, M. *Society Must Be Defended: Lectures at the Collège de France*. Edited by M. Bertani and A. Fontana, translated by. D. Macey. New York: Picador, 2003.
Haddad, F. *Sectarianism in Iraq: Antagonistic Visions of Unity*. New York: Columbia University Press, 2011.
'Halabja Genocide'. *Kurdish Regional Government – Iraq: Representation in the United States*. Available online: http://new.krg.us/aboutkurdistan/halabja-genocide/ (accessed 27 June 2017).
'Hashd al-Shaabi'. *Global Security*. Available online: http://www.globalsecurity.org/military/world/para/hashd-al-shaabi.htm (accessed 1 December 2016).
'Head of Zoroastrian Temple Says People Are Returning to Their Roots'. *Rudaw*, 1 February 2016. Available online: http://rudaw.net/english/kurdistan/310120162 (accessed 1 December 2016).
Hiltermann, J. 'What Did the Kurds Get Out of the Referendum?'. *The Atlantic*, 27 September 2017. Available online: https://www.theatlantic.com/international/archive/2017/09/kurds-iraq-barzani-isis-referendum/541260/ (accessed 4 May 2018).
Insom, C. 'Evolving Sacred Landscape: Sufi Saint Cult in Kurdistan Village Shrines'. Presentation at the 8th Conference of Iranian Studies of the Societas Iranologica Europaea 2015, Saint Petersburg, Russia.
'Iraqi Kurds Abandon Their Religion to Zoroastrianism to Escape Islamic Extremism'. *EKurd*, 3 May 2015. Available online: http://ekurd.net/kurds-abandon-their-religion-to-zoroastrianism-to-escape-islamic-extremism-2015-05-03 (accessed 1 December 2016).
Khalil, M. K. 'Kurds Go Back to Zoroastrianism: Interview with Pir Luqman'. *SBS*, 3 April 2016. Available online: http://www.sbs.com.au/yourlanguage/kurdish/en/content/kurds-go-back-zoroastrianism (accessed 1 December 2016).

Khenchelaoui, Z. 'The Yezidis, People of the Spoken Word in the Midst of People of the Book'. *Diogenes* 47 (1999): 20–37.

al-Khoei, H. 'Natural Alliance'. *Kurdish Herald* 1, no. 2 (2009). Available online: http://www.kurdishherald.com/issue/002/article06.php (accessed 1 December 2016).

'Kirkuk Votes to Take Part in Kurdish Independence Poll'. *Al-Jazeera*, 27 August 2017. Available online: https://www.aljazeera.com/news/2017/08/kirkuk-votes-part-kurdish-independence-poll-170829134834287.html (accessed 4 May 2018).

Knights, M. 'Iran's Expanding Militia Army in Iraq: The New Special Groups'. *CTC Sentinel* 12, no. 7 (2019): 1–12.

Latif, A. 'Fed Up with Islam and Sectarianism, Some Iraqis Embrace Zoroastrianism'. *The Daily Beast*, 31 May 2015. Available online: http://www.thedailybeast.com/articles/2015/05/31/fed-up-with-islam-and-sectarianism-some-iraqis-embrace-zoroastrianism.html (accessed 1 December 2016).

Mabon, S. and A. M. Kumarasamy. 'Daʻish, Stasis and Bare Life in Iraq'. In *Iraq after ISIS: The Challenges of Post-War Recovery*, edited by J. Eriksson and A. Khaleel, 9–28. London: Palgrave Macmillan, 2019.

Mabon, S. 'Sovereignty, Bare Life and the Arab Uprisings'. *Third World Quarterly* 38, no. 8 (2017): 1782–99.

Mamdani, M. 'Good Muslim, Bad Muslim: A Political Perspective on Culture and Terrorism'. *American Anthropologist* 104, no. 3 (2002): 766–75.

'Masoud Barzani to Step Down as KRG President'. *Al-Jazeera*, 29 October 2017. Available online: https://www.aljazeera.com/news/2017/10/masoud-barzani-step-krg-president-171029161347180.html (accessed 4 May 2018).

Mbembe, A. 'Necropolitics'. trans. L. Meintjes, *Public Culture* 15, no. 1 (2003): 11–40.

McDowall, D. *A Modern History of the Kurds*, 3rd edn. London: I.B. Tauris, 2007.

Milani, M. 'The Turbulent History Shaping Iran's Opposition to an Independent Iraqi Kurdistan'. *World Politics Review*, 14 November 2017. Available online: https://www.worldpoliticsreview.com/articles/23610/the-turbulent-history-shaping-iran-s-opposition-to-an-independent-iraqi-kurdistan (accessed 20 November 2020).

Moradi, F. 'The Baʻth State of Exception: Configuration of Authority, Violence and Life'. Presentation at the 2nd Annual American University of Iraq Conference on the Middle East. Sulaimani, Kurdistan Region of Iraq, 27 June 2012.

Natali, D. 'Iraqi Kurdistan Was Never Ready for Statehood'. *Foreign Policy*, 31 October 2017. Available online: https://foreignpolicy.com/2017/10/31/iraqi-kurdistan-was-never-ready-for-statehood/ (accessed 4 May 2018).

Ramey, S. 'Accidental Favorites: The Implicit in the Study of Religion'. In *Claiming Identity in the Study of Religion – Social and Rhetorical Techniques Examined*, edited by M. Miller, 223–38. Sheffield: Equinox, 2015.

Roy, O. *Globalized Islam*. New York: Columbia University Press, 2004.

Soleimani, K. 'Islamic Revivalism and Kurdish Nationalism in Sheikh Ubeydullah's Poetic Oeuvre'. *Kurdish Studies* 4, no. 1 (2016): 5–24.

Soleimani, K. and A. Mohammadpour. 'Life and Labor on the Internal Colonial Edge: Political Economy of Kolberi in Rojhelat'. *British Journal of Sociology* 71, no. 4 (2020): 741–60.

Szanto, E. 'Islam in Kurdistan: Religious Communities and Their Practices in Contemporary Northern Iraq'. In *Handbook of Contemporary Islam and Muslim Lives*, edited by M. Woodward and R. Lukens-Bull, 1–16. New York: Springer, 2020.

Szanto, E. 'The Largest Contemporary Muslim Pilgrimage Isn't the Hajj to Mecca, It's the Shiite Pilgrimage to Karbala in Iraq'. *The Conversation News Source*, September 2020.

Available online: https://theconversation.com/the-largest-contemporary-muslim-pilgrimage-isnt-the-hajj-to-mecca-its-the-shiite-pilgrimage-to-karbala-in-iraq-144542 (accessed 1 November 2020).

Szanto, E. 'Mourning Halabja on Screen: Or Reading Kurdish Politics through Anfal Films'. *Review of Middle East Studies* 52, no. 1 (2018): 135–46.

Szanto, E. '"Zoroaster Was a Kurd!": Neo-Zoroastrianism among Iraqi Kurds'. *Iran and the Caucasus* 22, no. 1 (2018): 96–110.

Szanto, E. 'Depicting Victims, Heroines, and Pawns in the Syrian Uprising'. *Journal of Middle East Women's Studies* 12, no. 3 (2016): 306–22.

Szanto, E. 'Beyond the Karbala Paradigm: Rethinking Revolution and Redemption in Twelver Shi'a Mourning Rituals'. *Journal of Shi'a Islamic Studies* 6, no. 1 (2013): 75–91.

Tripp, C. *A History of Iraq*. Cambridge: Cambridge University Press, 2000.

Wyer, S. 'Political Update: Mapping the Iraq Protests'. *Institute for the Study of War*, 11 January 2013. Available online: http://www.understandingwar.org/backgrounder/political-update-mapping-iraq-protests (accessed 4 May 2018).

Zucchino, D. 'After the Vote, Does the Kurdish Dream of Independence Have a Chance?'. *New York Times*, 30 September 2017. Available online: https://www.nytimes.com/2017/09/30/world/middleeast/kurds-iraq-independence.html (accessed 20 November 2020).

Chapter 4

INSTITUTIONALIZING AUTHORITARIANISM

EGYPT, AL SISI AND THE STATE OF EXCEPTION

Lucia Ardovini

On 25 January 2011, chants asking for 'bread, freedom and human dignity' resonated across Egypt, marking the beginning of the popular uprisings that would lead to the deposition of long-standing dictator Hosni Mubarak. Together with the calls for basic human rights, one of the main grievances behind the popular protests was centred around the increasing restriction of the political space, upheld by a state of emergency that had been ruling over the country almost uninterrupted since the 1967 Six Days' War. Over the course of almost fifty-three years, Egypt's state of emergency had been routinely used to suspend the rule of law and to grant the presidency extraconstitutional powers, drastically reducing political agency and compromising the very notion of citizenship.

While this state of emergency was temporarily lifted following Mubarak's removal, the current military regime reissued it a few weeks after seizing power through the July 2013 coup d'etat. Since then Egypt has fallen into the most repressive period of its troubled history so far, characterized by unprecedented breaches of human rights, while citizens exist in a state of limbo as all political agency has been taken away from them. This chapter argues that Egypt's perpetual state of emergency can be analysed through the lens of Agamben's state of exception, as constitutional powers have been repeatedly abused in order to maintain and normalize the rule of political elites. To do this, the chapter unpacks the historical relationship between the state of emergency and Egyptian politics, with a special focus on the post-Arab Uprisings period, as a way to identify the factors that allowed for authoritarian rule to become the norm.

Introduction

On 14 January 2020, President Abdel Fattah al Sisi extended a nationwide state of emergency for a further three months, for the eleventh consecutive time since the aftermath of the Alexandria and Tanta church bombings in 2017.[1] While deeply divisive, al Sisi's decision is far from being unexpected, as Egypt has existed under a de facto and de jure state of emergency for most of its modern history as an independent nation state.[2] To put things into perspective, a state of emergency ruled over Egypt for a staggering total of sixty-one years between 1956 and 2017, with brief periods of its suspension being an exception and lasting only three years under Gamal Abdel Nasser and eighteen months under Anwar Sadat. It was not until after the Supreme Council of the Armed Forces (SCAF) lifted it in 2012 that Egypt experience the longest period in its history without a national state of emergency – with the exception of a few months in the beginning of 2013.[3] Unsurprisingly, the almost permanent suspension of civil and political rights that came with almost thirty years of uninterrupted emergency status under the presidency of Hosni Mubarak was one of the main grievances fuelling the popular protests of January 2011, and had been part of the country's secular and religious activism long before the outbreak of the so-called Arab Uprisings. Discontent over the lack of political space, the heavy policing of agency and the perpetual state of 'bare life' Egyptians are forced to live under continue to drive protests across the country. Indeed, this routine renewal of emergency laws by virtually all Egyptian presidents to date reveals a deeply entrenched 'regime of rule'[4] by extraordinary powers, which is therefore fundamental to contextualize the almost normalized permanence of authoritarianism over the country.

The normalization of extra-constitutional rule also speaks directly to Giorgio Agamben's 'state of exception', through which the Italian philosopher investigates how the supposedly temporary suspension of laws within a state of emergency or crisis ends up becoming a prolonged state of being. From this, the convergence of the juridico-political 'state of exception' with the biopolitical reduction of life leads the citizens to be fully stripped of their political status and agency, living in a state of 'bare life'.[5] Therefore, this chapter will apply Agamben's concept to the study of the resilience of Egyptian authoritarianism and of the ever-escalating restriction of political space. In recent years a growing number of scholars have sought to engage with questions about political transition across Egypt. In particular, Tarek Osman, Carrie Wickham and Mona el-Ghobashy[6] have provided their own explanations for the continuing lack of stability and resilient authoritarianism that have come to characterize the country. In a different piece, I have also engaged in a preliminary discussion of the historical and structural factors that allow for a state of exception to take over Egyptian political life.[7] This chapter contributes to these debates by further unpacking Egypt's historical relationship between resilient authoritarian rule and the cyclical imposition of states of exception/emergency, with a special focus on the al Sisi's regime.

The contributions to this volume make it clear that Egypt is not alone in experiencing such phenomena, as emergency powers have routinely been used as mechanisms of state control and repression in times of instability and uncertainty. Authoritarian and oppressive regimes in the region and elsewhere are known for regularly recurring to the imposition of states of exception and of emergency as a way to strengthen their fading legitimacy and prevent popular unrest. However, Egypt's long history of existing under repeated states of exception makes its case rather unique, as the suspension of civil rights and of the political space has become inherently tied to the notion of governance and the lack of political agency. This chapter therefore critically analyses this relationship, beginning with a short but comprehensive evaluation of Agamben's state of exception, unpacking the roots and applications of the concept in order to set up a clear analytical framework. It then moves onto the study of different states of exception throughout Egypt's modern history, providing a detailed analysis of the historical relationship between the suspension of the rule of law and political power in the country. It starts with the imposition of Martial Law No. 15/1922 in 1914, before moving onto the examination of how this phenomenon allows al Sisi's contested authoritarian regime to maintain power today.

Following from this, throughout the chapter Agamben's thought is applied to the Egyptian case with the aim of highlighting three significant contributions that come with this approach. First of all, throughout this volume Agamben's conceptualization of the state of exception is used to propose a new lens through which to look at the proliferation and longevity of different forms of authoritarianism in the Middle East and North Africa (MENA) region. Consequently, this also demonstrates that while Agamben's thought was indeed developed in a Western, Christian and Liberal Democratic context, it is in no way bound by these criteria and can therefore be applied to the study of other regional and cultural systems. Most importantly, using the state of exception as an analytical tool allows for the examination of authoritarianism in Egypt as a phenomenon that is not inextricably associated to military rule, but it is rather characteristic of different presidencies and modes of governance.

Giorgio Agamben's 'state of exception' and the MENA region

Agamben's state of exception is theorized and explored in the third of a series of books that unpack the concept of sovereignty from an interdisciplinary and critical perspective.[8] Here, Agamben's inquiry is driven by the question of how law copes when inevitably faced by the irreducibly non-legal: life itself. It is starting from this question that he proposes an understanding of the state of exception as 'the preliminary condition for any definition of the relation that binds and at the same time abandons the living being to the law'.[9] It generally occurs when constitutional rights are suspended or restricted by a sovereign who seizes an extension of their power to face an alleged crisis or emergency. Throughout the book, Agamben investigates the outcomes of supposed times of crisis during which governments legally seize increased powers. Accordingly, the exception comes in when the suspension of law during an emergency status becomes a prolonged state of being – the norm – depriving citizens of their civil and political rights in the long term. Here a clear parallel with Egypt can already be drawn as political space in the country has been heavily restricted since the 1950s and has now all but disappeared, with heavy restrictions being imposed on freedoms of assembly and of speech, resulting in the almost complete disappearance of political agency.

Agamben's state of exception grants a sovereign or government the authority to operate outside of the law, as its emergence is linked to the contradictory nature of sovereignty and of the juridical sphere, especially where the law is allowed to suspend itself in order to protect it. It is important to note here that he bases this concept on a Western, Christian and Liberal Democratic context, as he identifies the state of exception as a modern institution with roots in the French Revolution, ascendancy during the First World War and dominance by the mid-twentieth century as the 'paradigmatic form of government'.[10] Moreover, he further clarifies that 'the modern State of Exception is a creation of the democratic-revolutionary tradition and not the absolutist one',[11] as he cites examples such as the Third Reich – '[it]can be considered a State of Exception that lasted 12 years'[12] – and President Lincoln's abolition of slavery in 1862.[13] Quotes like this are often used by critics to argue against the applicability of Agamben's thought outside of a Western context, but the case study of this chapter shows that this is not the case. This is especially true when it comes to applying the state of exception to the study of prolonged authoritarianism in the MENA. Constitutionalism and a rule of law based on the European liberal democratic model is widespread in the region, a legacy of colonial control and interference that comes with the imposition of Westphalian sovereignty.[14] Without generalizing, while Middle Eastern states have developed their own governance structures over time, it is undeniable that the conditions that allow for the law to suspend itself are deeply embedded in their systems of governance. Recent works by Simon Mabon, Khaled Furani, Adam Ramadan and Edith Szanto also support this approach and have begun to successfully apply an Agambian lens to the study of state–society relations in the region.[15]

Another example of the state of exception's applicability beyond a European context lies in Agamben's understanding of 'necessity' as the original source of law, justifying the need for political action if there is no time for recourse to a higher authority.[16] A state of exception is therefore also a state of emergency, allowing for the law to be suspended to protect itself. Necessity is also fundamental for the emergence of the exception, as it embodies the justification for action, making the exception an '"illegal" but perfectly "juridical and constitutional" measure that is realized in the production of new norms'.[17] While Agamben's idea of necessity is directly inspired by the work of Grotius,[18] and therefore has an inherently Christian connotation, it can be also found within other religious traditions and is indeed present within Islam. The concept of necessity provides scope for suspension from the norm across different normative contexts – for example, *Darurah* (necessity) as a concept is widely featured in Shari'a Law and often provides a context for transgression.[19] Transgression derived from necessity is also found elsewhere within Islam, with the Qu'ran even suggesting that 'whom is driven by necessity, neither craving nor transgressing, it is no sin for him. For Allah is Forgiving, Compassionate'.[20]

The emergence of the state of exception is therefore linked to the contradictory nature of sovereignty and of the juridical sphere, especially where the law is allowed to suspend itself in order to protect it. Another example of its applicability outside of a Western context is found within Agamben's work itself, especially when it comes to the inspiration he draws from Carl Schmitt. Schmitt renowned definition of a sovereign is 'he who decides on the exception', which also directly leads to the equation of the state of exception to a dictatorship whereby 'the dictator/sovereign unites the legal and the non-legal by means of an extra-legal decision "having the force of law"'.[21] According to Schmitt, this allows for the juridical order to remain preserved even when the law itself is suspended. However, Agamben distances himself from such a position and rather argues that the state of exception is not to be compared to a dictatorship, where 'laws continue to be made and applied (albeit non-democratically), but one in which law is rather entirely emptied of content'.[22] Once again, Agamben's own definition is fit to apply to the study of prolonged authoritarianism in Egypt that, as this chapter shows, it is not necessarily linked to military dictatorship but rather is engrained in the country's constitutional and juridical structures and, as a result, in the 'bare life' of its citizens.

The state of exception and modern Egyptian history

Since the institution of the British protectorate in Egypt in 1882, the necessity to maintain legitimacy, sovereignty and territorial and social control has been a distinct characteristic of the state, leading to the cyclical imposition of states of emergency and martial laws aimed at responding to these very issues. As said earlier, this is not necessarily a new phenomenon, as states and authoritarian regimes have historically relied on different kinds of exception rule to consolidate and reinforce their authority – essentially since the stipulation of constitutions that allow for the seizing of emergency powers. This kind of repressive regimes rely on a routine imposition of states of exception for reasons that go beyond engaging with crises, but are rather aimed at deterring protests and unrest, persecuting opposition groups and strengthening political authority when popular legitimacy starts being eroded. Most of all, the seizing of emergency powers allows for the total disregard and circumvention of civil and human rights obligations, often leading to the complete suspension of political agency and to the citizens living a life that is 'bare' – 'stripped of all (political) meaning'.[23] Within these practices, what makes the case of Egypt rather unique is the historical permanence of this condition and the extent to which, given its longevity throughout most of the country's modern history, the severe lack of political space and civil rights has become almost normalized. Under al Sisi's iron fist this pattern is arguably being taken to a new level, where what we are witnessing is a clear institutionalization of authoritarian rule – in other words, the exception has now become the norm.

Despite this, almost no work has been undertaken applying Agamben's thought to Egypt. As I have argued elsewhere,[24] the existing literature on state formation and sovereignty in Egypt is divided between two main strands: historical approaches, such as of Roger Owen, Nazih Ayubi and Simon Bromley,[25] who have explored the particular experiences of modern state-building as a result of colonial imposition and their implications for post-colonial state-building and politics; and orthodox comparative politics approaches, such as of Maye Kassem, Joshua Stacher and Jason Brownlee,[26] which examine how political institutions are crafted in ways that reproduce authoritarianism. More recently, Samera Esmair has identified the existence of different states of exception leading up to the 2011 Uprisings, drawing attention to the unique relationship between this phenomenon and the Egyptian nation state. Following from this, this examination goes even further and aims at demonstrating that the state of exception is no longer solely the exception in Egypt but has rather become the norm within political life.

From here onwards the state of exception is used to refer to Egypt's long-standing state of emergency that is inherently tied to the country's modern political history. Because of this, its analysis is fundamental when trying to contextualize the thriving and normalization of authoritarian rule in Egypt. In line with Agamben's own understanding, the state of emergency is a legal construct that originates from a myriad of laws, constitutional articles, amendments, decrees and legislations that collectively grant the executive extensive discretionary powers.[27] These allow for the restriction of civil liberties, sanctioned censorship, the expansion of police and military jurisdiction, and most importantly blur the lines between civilian and military legal processes.[28] Because of the encompassing and escalating nature of the heavy restrictions that such an emergency status imposes on society, resistance against it has historically been a key part of the country's secular and religious opposition, and has therefore long been inherently tied to Egyptians' political consciousness. Long before the Arab Uprisings this sentiment was fuelling the demand for greater political freedoms that is central to the long legacy of dissent, protest and activism in the country. Kira Allmann notes that while this was somewhat obscured by the global attention paid to media activism in 2011, it is undeniable that opposition to emergency rule has been a core vessel of anti-regime sentiment and mobilization in the lead-up to the popular protests. Furthermore, she emphasizes that 'protesting the emergency became an important vehicle and training opportunity for activism in spaces where political participation was strictly curtailed', and emergency laws were targeted by religious and secular forces alike as the primary impediment to political participation.[29]

This is the case as the Egyptian security landscape has been shaped by the recurrent imposition of emergency statuses by different regimes throughout the twentieth century, to the extent of emergency regulations becoming deeply intertwined with both political institutions and the citizens' psyche. This is a trend that began under the British occupation during the First World War, where Martial Law No. 15/1922 was imposed for the first time in 1914.[30] During the course of the following decades and up until the coming of Gamal Abdel Nasser, various emergency and martial laws would be routinely imposed and suspended, usually in line with decreasing patterns of the state's legitimacy, in a prelude of what was to characterize Egypt up until today. Nasser's era consolidated the ostensibly mutually dependent relationship between the suspension of law under emergency status and governance, and first included the conditions for the state of exception to arise in the Egyptian constitution. In particular, Law No. 162 of 1958 is widely considered the blueprint for subsequent legislations allowing for an emergency status to rule undisturbed over the country throughout the following decades. Enforced for the first time in 1967 during the Six Days' War, it has arguably kept Egypt under an almost uninterrupted state of exception ever since. Composed by twenty articles, Law No. 162/1958 authorizes the executive to 'restrict freedom of assembly, detain suspects for up to six months without a hearing, and conduct searches without a warrant during a state of emergency',[31] essentially granting undisputed powers to the president. Used by Nasser to keep at bay the political opponents that actively threatened his legitimacy, the Muslim Brotherhood being the main one, the law would go on to be included in every subsequent constitution up until the current one, making intractable emergency rule – and bare life – a new normality for Egyptians.

Anwar Sadat followed in his predecessor's steps by not only recurring to the imposition of several emergency statuses himself but also adding to the juridical bases for the state of exception to become almost impossible to challenge. Law No. 162/1958 was included in the 1971 Constitution and complemented by the addition of Art. 148, which allows for the exception to de facto rule the country undisturbed, giving the president power to declare a state of emergency whenever they see fit.[32] This was further strengthened by the addition of other articles that grant the presidency further extraordinary powers when faced by a crisis, even if such is not deemed imminent enough to require the official declaration of a state of emergency. In particular, Art. 74/1971 authorizes the president to enact extraordinary measures 'should there emerge an instant and brave risk that threatens national unity or safety of the motherland or obstructs the performance by State institutions of their constitutional role', while Art. 48/1971 allows for state censorship to be imposed on all forms of expression 'in case of a declared state of emergency'.[33] By 1971 it had become clear that the state of exception was no longer solely the exception in Egypt but had rather long become the norm governing political life and spaces.

All together, these articles and laws have been crucial in maintaining Egypt under an almost uninterrupted state of exception since 1967. This timeline is important to underline since the institution of a state of exception presenting authoritarianism as the norm is usually associated to Hosni Mubarak's presidency, but instead has older roots that made his thirty years rule possible. This being said, however, Mubarak's era definitely witnessed the almost permanent suspension of the rule of law and of civil/political rights that allowed for various forms of activism to develop, inflating popular grievances that would eventually escalate into the 2011 popular uprisings. His thirty years rule would be characterized by the very relationship between the exception and sovereignty that would make for it to become the norm and was once again engrained deeply within the juridical and constitutional system, as well as sociopolitical life. Aside from re-imposing Law No. 162 of 1958 soon after his appointment, Mubarak adopted an exceptionally broad definition of terrorism – now included in the 2014 Constitution – that not only allowed for the gross breach of human rights but slowly eroded the very concept of citizenship and civil/political rights. Articles 54 to 56, concerning freedom of assembly, stated 'Citizens shall have the right to association as defined in the law. It is prohibited to establish societies whose activities are hostile to the social system, clandestine or have a military character' and 'Public meetings, processions and gatherings are allowed within the limits of the law',[34] heavily restricting the already narrow political space and leaving little to no room for non-governmental political activities. They also allowed for the indefinite detention without trial of civilians in military courts,[35] something that also happened during Nasser's era and is now the norm under al Sisi.

The Human Rights Association for the Assistance of Prisoners (HRAAP) reported in 2007 that under the terrorism law approximately 15,000–20,000 were being held without trial, in some cases for as long as two decades.[36] Similarly, Amnesty International reported that in 2010 alone between 5,000 and 10,000 people were being held in long-term detention without any charge, while roughly 17,000 more were being detained, and the average estimate of political prisoners was as high as 30,000.[37] Therefore, when looking at the outbreak of the 2011 Uprisings, the fact that the abolition of emergency law was one of the revolutionaries' main demand should not come as a surprise. Nor the fact that upon seizing power after Mubarak's removal the SCAF vowed 'to end the State of Emergency as soon as the current circumstances are over' but left it untouched until it expired in March 2012.[38] Unsurprisingly, SCAF also refrained from removing the articles that made it possible from the constitution, but rather added a series of amendments to the penal code that made for its re-imposition on 13 June 2012, just two weeks before the pledged handover of power to an elected government.[39] As well as revealing SCAF's unwillingness to relinquish powers, Decree 499/2012 further expanded the military's judicial power of arrest and detention of civilians, therefore granting them extraordinary powers not supported by general law, once again suspending it in order to allegedly protect the law itself.[40]

Soon after being sworn Egypt's first democratically elected president on 30 June 2012, Mohammed Morsi suspended the SCAF-imposed state of emergency, annulled the recent controversial constitutional amendments and began meticulously enforcing decrees aimed at restricting the power of the military.[41] Being the first president with no affiliations to the military establishment, during the first few months of his presidency it seemed like the sword of Damocles hanging over the revolutionary process – the return of a state of emergency – had been fought off for good. However, on 22 November 2012, as Egypt entered the eighteenth month without an operating constitution, Morsi released a constitutional decree expanding the presidency's legislative and juridical powers, with Art. VI stating that 'The President may take the necessary actions and measures to protect the country and the goals of the revolution', in a clear parallel with Art. 148/1971.[42] The Brotherhood government declared that the decree was the only way to achieve 'revolutionary demands and rooting out remnants of the old regime', in an attempt to overcome the country's political deadlock but had effectively already moved towards the re-imposition of an emergency status.[43] The popular discounted caused by this decree and by the subsequent protests against the declaration of the 2012 Constitution violently escalated in the so-called battle of Ittihadiya, and kept intensifying until 27 January 2013 when Morsi declared a return to the state of emergency. Despite him claiming that 'I am against any emergency measures, but I have said that if I must stop bloodshed and protect the people then I will act',[44] such an extreme measure only further fuelled the popular unrest that eventually led to the July 2013 *coup*, in a manner that much resembled the lead-up to Mubarak's ousting only two years prior.

Therefore, it can be seen that even before al Sisi's ever-escalating authoritarianism, Egypt had already been characterized by a steady erosion of civil rights and political space. Much like in Agamben's account of the state of exception, the routine imposition of emergency statuses had become engrained within the own concept of sovereignty in the country and indeed indispensable to maintain power despite the historical lack of governmental legitimacy. Similarly, the emergence of the state of exception in the case of Egypt is not solely limited to the regimes that relied on military power, as the case of Mohammed Morsi demonstrates, but rather is common to different 'styles' of governance, therefore contesting the immediate association of military rule to the longevity of authoritarianism. That being said, the historical processes that allowed for the state of exception to become engrained in Egypt's juridical and constitutional systems have deep roots in Egyptian history and are also engrained in within activist discourses, meaning that their presence and permanence has become almost normalized.

Al Sisi and the state of exception

Since coming to power in 2014, al Sisi has deployed an overt and systematic counter-revolution. Almost seven years after the coup d'etat that violently removed Mohammed Morsi from power, it seems that Egypt has come full circle again and that its citizens' fight for 'bread, freedom and human dignity' is back at square one. This should not come as a complete surprise, as the Raba'a and Nad'ha massacres that killed more than 1,000 Brotherhood supporters in August 2013 were just the prelude to al Sisi's iron fist. Yet, the military's seizure of power was initially supported and welcomed by a significant part of the Egyptian population, which was left dissatisfied and alienated by the Brotherhood's government. While the return of the military deep state was not something that protesters and activists campaigned for during the months that led to Morsi's toppling, its re-establishment was perceived by many as the return of 'the devil we know' and therefore also learnt how to fight, in opposition to the novelty of an Islamist-led government. However, seven years on, Egypt is in the midst of such a brutal counter-revolution that has all but wiped out the goals of the 2011 Uprisings and what little gains were made after, political space has disappeared and its citizens are once again living under a state of exception.

Throughout most of this, general law has been suspended under the justification of a crisis so big that 'normal' measures would not apply anymore. Ironically, factors contributing to the restriction of the political space under Morsi, such as the issuing of the controversial Brotherhood's Constitution and the group's tendency to monopolize political power and ostracize the opposition, were the main reasons behind the protests that supported his removal. Not only these conditions have worsened under al Sisi, together with the massive escalation of police brutality and human rights abuses, but the now overt persecution of freedoms of assembly and expression have arguably erased what little gains were made after the 2011 Uprisings. As it is reported by Human Rights Watch: 'Instead of addressing the urgent need for reforms, Egyptian authorities have spent the last years engaging in repression on a scale unprecedented in Egypt's modern history.'[45] It almost seems that, together with returning to the 'devil they know', Egyptians have also returned to the suspension of laws that is typical of Agamben's state of exception and goes hand in hand with authoritarian measures in the country.

Institutionalizing authoritarianism

Al Sisi's resort to the suspension of law and the seizing of extra-constitutional powers came even before his election as president and found its ground in the country's legal framework that throughout the decades had allowed for such an occurrence to become the norm. An emergency status was declared less than a month after Morsi's removal, following the Raba'a and Nad'ha massacres during which police and military forces slaughtered over a thousand Brotherhood supporters.[46] This was made possible by the July 2013 Constitutional Declaration, issued by interim president Adly Mansour, according to which the president not only held legislative authority but also could declare a state of emergency whenever he sees fit.[47] Unsurprisingly, the appointment of extrajudicial powers to the president was later codified in the January 2014 Constitution, which includes both Art. 162/1958 and Art. 148/1971 and heavily borrows from Mubarak's 'war against terrorism'.[48] The very broad definition of terrorism included in the constitution refers to any 'act that might obstruct the work of public officials, institutions and so on', allows for the military trial of civilians and prescribes a prison sentence of up to ten years for anyone who is part of a group that 'harms national unity or social peace'.[49] Furthermore, mirroring emergency measures employed by both Nasser and Mubarak, Law 107/2013 on 'the Right to Public Meetings, Processions and Peaceful Demonstrations' goes against international standards by granting authorities the power of dispersing any public meeting of more than ten people and sets heavy prison sentences for vague offences such as 'attempting to influence the course of justice'.[50]

What makes these measures even more worrying is the fact that they might apply to anyone who took part in the January 2011 Uprisings and even in the popular protests that led to al Sisi's rise to power in the summer of 2013. While exact numbers are hard to achieve, especially considering the levels of state propaganda in Egypt, it is estimated that under these laws 41,163 Egyptians were arrested in the period between July 2013 and May 2014 alone, including 36,478 detained during political events and a further 3,048 arrested as MB's members.[51] These numbers have arguably not decreased with time, further adding to a worsening of living conditions that under the state of exception have set Egypt back to those that contributed to the rage leading to the events of January 2011. Even more worryingly, Human Rights Watch has reported that since 2014 Egyptian courts have issued over 2,500 death sentences, often without a proper trial. For the sake of comparison, it is worth noting that during the last ten years of Mubarak's rule, which was also marked by repression and authoritarianism, only 530 death sentences were issued.[52]

Along with the deprivation of civil and political rights, Egyptians are also suffering from the daily challenges posed by the worsening economy and security. As I have argued elsewhere, the ever-worsening state of the economy means that daily hardships are now being not only faced by Egypt's poorest but have become a reality even for those who under Mubarak belonged to the working/middle class.[53] It is easy to draw a correlation between military rule and the drastic drop in economic and living conditions, with Egypt's external debt under Sisi jumping from $38 billion to more than $80 billion, while taxes on hundreds of products and services have skyrocketed even further.[54] Similarly, so far counterterrorism legislations have only succeeded in heavily restricting the rights of the average citizens, while achieving very little in terms of containing or preventing the rise of violent rebel groups that are taking control of Egypt's unpatrolled territories.[55] This is particularly significant when considering that the provision of security is core to the armed forces' image and legitimacy, and a failure in doing so could lead to a further escalation of repressive measures to shield the regime's faltering legitimacy.

This is why, under the guise of fighting terrorism, Egyptian authorities have shown an increasing disregard for the rule of law. With their powers unchecked under the ongoing state of emergency, torture and forced disappearances are targeting dissidents of all backgrounds and even apply to internationally known figures, such as the recent case of the arrest of activist and student Patrick Zaki.[56] Mohammed Morsi's death after five years in prison was also a clear indicator of the overcrowding and neglect that characterizes Egyptian prisons but failed to generate an international outcry. So far, however, it seems like Donald Trump's 'favourite dictator' feels untouchable and knows that his actions will not be accounted for.

Going back to Agamben, this escalation of authoritarian rule and the complete erasure of political space are made possible by the regime's seizing of extrajudicial powers in a time of perceived crisis and to the normalization of the 'exception' and of the 'bare life' that ensues. This became evident once again in the lead-up to the March 2018 presidential elections, which took place during the state of emergency.[57] The obvious restrictions on freedoms of expression characteristic of emergency law are further aggravated by the December 2016 Law creating a Supreme Council for the Administration of the Media, which grants the executive power over the media outlets and contributed to making Egypt into one of the world's most dangerous countries for journalists.[58] It was therefore not a surprise when al Sisi won the elections with, allegedly, 97 per cent of the vote,[59] nor when repressive measures escalated further shortly afterwards. Since securing another four years in power, al Sisi has overseen the passing of a law that excludes military officers from being investigated for their role in the August 2013 Raba'a Massacre,[60] and another one that makes it possible to treat personal social media accounts with more than 5,000 followers as media outlets.[61] Not only are both these laws unconstitutional, but they also grant the executive the power to further crack down on dissent. The extent to which this is being implemented, with the clear aim of wiping out every possible expression of dissent, was the raiding of Mada Masr's offices in November 2019 by plain-clothed military personnel. Mada Masr is the last independent news outlet in the country, and the intimidation and arrest of its editors and staff are clear indication of what would follow if they do not shut down or relocate elsewhere.[62]

Since then, Sisi has further escalated his reliance of extra-constitutional powers and has effectively institutionalized authoritarian rule. This is yet another nod to Agamben, as in today's Egypt the exception has most definitely become the norm. In fact, while al Sisi's rule is undeniably reminiscent of the country's military past, his repressive policies have so far failed to generate the loyalty that his predecessors could rely on. As a result, despite the erasure of political space and the complete crackdown on dissent, the president still appears vulnerable and is constantly trying to solidify his faltering legitimacy. In a bid to further secure his rule and tackle the authority crisis, a constitutional referendum in April 2019 has approved amendments that lengthen the presidential term to six years and allow him to stand for one more, meaning that Sisi could indeed rule until at least 2030. Further, amendments to Artis. 185, 189 and 193 allow the president to oversee the judiciary and to appoint the heads of key courts, while Art. 190 now grants him the power to revise legislation before it becomes law.[63] Therefore, though there is an undeniable element of historical continuity, it is fair to argue that Sisi is bringing this to new levels and essentially trialling new experimental practices of power building, as the regime circumvents the rule of law to institutionalize authoritarian rule.[64]

It is important to note once again that most of these extrajudicial measures are only made possible by the almost uninterrupted permanence of a state of emergency, while also not being new to Egyptians or unique to al Sisi's regime. On the contrary, this goes back to the argument that there is a clear pattern in Egypt's modern history that sees the presidents routinely recurring to the imposition of emergency laws as a way of seizing and maintaining powers. This also further strengthens the link between the scope of this chapter and Agamben's theory by showing the extent to which the permanence of a state of exception has come to be normalized in an Egyptian context, as it is embedded in both bureaucratic and juridical practices. Consequently, while it is undeniable that human rights abuses and the suspension of civil and political rights have reached an unprecedented peak under al Sisi, it is important to keep in mind that this is made possible by the historical permanence of an emergency status over the country that has made for it to become the norm, rather than the exception.

Conclusion

This chapter sought to apply Agamben's state of exception to the case of Egypt's resilient authoritarianism, with the aim of highlighting three main contributions.

First, proposing a new lens through which to look at the proliferation and longevity of different forms of authoritarianism in the MENA region. Second, demonstrating the applicability of Agamben's thought to non-democratic, non-Western contexts; and lastly, applying the state of exception to the study of authoritarianism in Egypt as something that is not inextricably associated to military rule, but it is rather characteristic of different presidencies and modes of governance. It has shown that a state of exception can indeed occur in an authoritarian context and that it is not solely restricted by and contained within Christian/democratic traditions. In turn, this also means that Agamben's thought can be applied to the non-Western world and, in the case of the permanence of emergency legislations, it can be used as a theoretical approach that allows for the examination of emergency legislations as a mechanism of control in the MENA region.

Throughout the chapter it has been shown that Agamben's state of exception makes for an original lens for the investigation of the permanence and steady escalation of authoritarianism and extrajudicial rule in Egypt. A genealogical analysis of the now seemingly unbreakable relationship between emergency legislation and executive power in the country has shown that the bases for the embedding of the state of exception within Egypt's constitutional and juridical structures have been present since 1914. The routine imposition of states of emergency and exception has in fact characterized political rule in the country for most of its modern history, as the seizing of powers beyond the scope of those outlined in the constitution has become synonymous with the presidency. This fits with Agamben's notion of the state of exception and particularly with the argument that such state arises when the suspension of law during an emergency status becomes a prolonged state of being – the norm – depriving citizens of their civil and political rights in the long term, forcing them to exist in a space of 'bare life'. In this particular case, it has been shown that the normalization of a state of exception can be considered one of the defining characteristics of modern Egyptian regimes, regardless of whether they have a military connotation or not, with its routine imposition being embedded in both democratic and legal structures. When saying that the ever-worsening restriction of the political space in Egypt has become normalized, this chapter is not arguing that it has been fully accepted and is therefore left unchallenged. Rather, the normalization of a state of emergency is one of the grievances that has been fuelling activism and dissent since the 1950s. Therefore, what is meant here by the 'normalization' of emergency measures is that very often it is them, rather than a political figure of authoritarianism in itself, which become the focus of political activism and of revolutionary demands. Because of this, what has become apparent in the Egyptian case is that the law has historically been used as a tool of the powerful, to serve the purpose of regime survival, whatever the price.

Nevertheless, despite the escalation of extra-constitutional powers, police brutality and the over violations of human rights, it is worth noting that things seem far from stable in al Sisi's Egypt. Despite ruling with an iron fist, the complete erasure of political space and the increasingly harsher crackdowns on dissent across the board have seemingly not totally discouraged Egyptians. The recent wave of protests that briefly took over the country in September 2019 demonstrates that Egypt is on the verge of collapse and that its citizens are being driven to new extremes by the worsening economic situation, unemployment rates and the escalating costs of necessary goods. This is a clear nod to the structural issues and grievances that fuelled the outbreak of the 2011 Uprisings and, what is even more telling is the regime's reactions to what were peaceful and relatively contained popular demonstrations. While indiscriminate arrests and brutality are sadly familiar by now, they also reveal the extent to which the regime is worrying over any sort of manifestation of discontent against it. While al Sisi's strongman façade is starting to reveal deep cracks, and there are allegations of an internal *coup* being in the making, it remains to be seen how these new tensions will play out within a social and political system where the exception has long become the norm.

Notes

1 Middle East Monitor, 'Egypt Extends State of Emergency for the 11th Time since 2017', January 2020. Available online: https://www.middleeastmonitor.com/20200115-egypt-extends-state-of-emergency-for-11th-time-since-2017/.
2 K. Allman, 'Revolution and Counter-Revolution in Egypt's Emergency State', in *Oxford Human Rights Hub*, March 2018. Available online: http://ohrh.law.ox.ac.uk/revolution-and-counter-revolution-in-egypts-emergency-state/.
3 S. Eldeen, 'Egypt Back under Emergency Law', *Carnegie Endowment for International Peace*, May 2017. Available online: http://carnegieendowment.org/sada/69886.
4 Allman, 'Revolution and Counter-Revolution in Egypt's Emergency State'.
5 S. Weber, 'Bare Life and Life in General', *Grey Room* 46 (2012): 8.
6 T. Osman, *Egypt on the Brink* (London: Yale University Press, 2010); M. El-Ghobashy, 'The Metamorphosis of the Egyptian Muslim Brothers', *International Journal of Middle East Studies* 37, no. 3 (August 2005): 373–95; C. Wickham, *The Muslim Brotherhood: The Evolution of an Islamist Movement* (Princeton: Princeton University Press, 2013).
7 L. Ardovini and S. Mabon, 'Egypt's Unbreakable Curse: Tracing the State of Exception from Mubarak to Al Sisi', *Mediterranean Politics*, February 2019. Available online: https://doi.org/10.1080/13629395.2019.1582170.
8 Preceded by *Homo Sacer* (1998) and *Remnants of Auschwitz* (1995).
9 S. Humphreys, 'Legalizing Lawlessness: On Giorgio Agamben's State of Exception', *The European Journal of International Law* 17, no. 3 (2006): 680.
10 G. Agamben, *State of Exception* (Chicago: University of Chicago Press, 2005), 5.
11 Ibid.
12 Ibid., 2.
13 Ibid., 21–2.
14 L. Fawcett, 'States and Sovereignty in the Middle East: Myths and Realities', *International Affairs* 93, no. 4 (2017): 803.
15 See, for example, S. Mabon, 'Sovereignty, Bare Life and the Arab Uprisings', *Third World Quarterly* 38, no. 8 (2017): 1782–99; K. Furani, 'States of Exception, Ethics and New Beginnings in Middle East Politics', in *International Journal of Postcolonial Studies* 16, no. 3 (2014): 346–64; A. Ramadan and S. Fregonese, 'Hybrid Sovereignty

and the State of Exception in the Palestinian Refugee Camps in Lebanon', *Annals of the International Association of Geographers* 17, no. 4 (2017): 949–63; E. Zsanto, 'Sayyida Zaynab in the State of Exception: Shi'i Sainthood as "Qualified Life" in Contemporary Syria', *International Journal of Middle East Studies* 44, no. 2 (2012): 285–99.

16   Agamben, *State of Exception*, 24–7.
17   Ibid., 28.
18   Ibid., 24–5.
19   Al-Qur'an [5:3], 'Surah of Al Mai'dah'.
20   Ardovini and Mabon, 'Egypt's Unbreakable Curse: Tracing the State of Exception from Mubarak to Al Sisi'.
21   Humphreys, 'Legalizing Lawlessness: On Giorgio Agamben's State of Exception', 680.
22   Ibid., 681.
23   Weber, 'Bare Life', 8.
24   Ardovini and Mabon, 'Egypt's Unbreakable Curse: Tracing the State of Exception from Mubarak to Al Sisi'.
25   R. Owen, *State, Power and Politics in the Making of the Modern Middle East* (Abingdon: Routledge, 2004); N. Ayubi, *Over-stating the Arab State: Politics and Society in the Middle East* (London: I.B. Tauris, 1995); S. Bromley, *Rethinking Middle East Politics* (Austin: University of Texas Press, 1994).
26   J. Brownlee, 'Unrequited Moderation: Credible Commitments and State Repression in Egypt', *Studies in Comparative International Development* 45, no. 4 (December 2010): 468–89; M. Kassem, *In the Guise of Democracy: Governance in Contemporary Egypt* (London: Garnet & Ithaca Press, 1999); J. Stacher, *Adaptable Autocrats: Regime Power in Egypt and Syria* (Stanford: Stanford University Press, 2012).
27   Allman, 'Revolution and Counter-Revolution in Egypt's Emergency State'.
28   Egyptian Organization for Human Rights, 'EOHR Issues Report on Impact of Emergency Law', *IFEX*, February 2003. Available online: https://www.ifex.org/egypt/2003/02/28/eohr_issues_report_on_impact_of/.
29   Ibid.
30   Egyptian Organization for Human Rights, 'Egypt and the Impact of 27 Years of Emergency on Human Rights', May 2008. Available online: http://en.eohr.org/2008/05/28/%E2%80%9Cegypt-and-the-impact-of-27-years-of-emergency-on-human-%20rights%E2%80%9D/#more-22.
31   International Center for Not-for-Profit Law, 'Law No. (162) of the Year 1958'. Available online: http://www.icnl.org/research/library/files/Egypt/162-1958-en.pdf.
32   Constitution of the Arab Republic of Egypt, 1971. Available online: http://www.palataurascentrostudi.eu/doc/EGY_Constitution_1971_EN.pdf.
33   Ibid.
34   Constitution of the Arab Republic of Egypt, 1971. Available online: http://www.palataurascentrostudi.eu/doc/EGY_Constitution_1971_EN.pdf.
35   D. Williams, 'Egypt Expands 25 Years Old Emergency Law', *The Washington Post*, May 2006. Available online: http://www.washingtonpost.com/wp-dyn/content/article/2006/04/30/AR2006043001039.htm.
36   Human Rights Association for the Assistance of Prisoners, 'Detention and Detainees in Egypt 2003', Cairo, 2003, 18.
37   Amnesty International Public Statement, 'Egypt: Keep Promise to Free Detainees by End of June', June 2010. Available online: https://www.amnesty.org/en/documents/MDE12/027/2010/en/.

38 'Statement from the Supreme Council of the Egyptian Armed Forces', *The New York Times*, February 2011. Available online: http://www.nytimes.com/2011/02/11/world/middleeast/11egypt-military-statement.html?_r=0.
39 A. Zwitter, 'The Arab Uprising: State of Emergency and Constitutional Reform', *ASPJ Africa & Francophonie* 2 (2014): 51.
40 Cairo Institute for Human Rights Studies, 'Welcome to the Military State of Egypt: Minister of Justice Decree More Repressive than State of Emergency, Grants Military Police and Military Intelligence Judicial Authority to Arrest Civilians', *Statements and Position Papers*, June 2012. Available online: http://www.cihrs.org/?p=2846&lang=en.
41 K. Fahim, 'In Upheaval for Egypt, Morsi Forces Out Military Chiefs', *The New York Times*, August 2012. Available online: http://www.nytimes.com/2012/08/13/world/middleeast/egyptian-leader-ousts-military-chiefs.html?hp.
42 Ahram Online, 'English Text of Morsi's Constitutional Declaration', *Ahram Online*, November 2012. Available online: http://english.ahram.org.eg/News/58947.aspx.
43 M. Revkin, 'Egypt's Untouchable President', *POMEPS Briefings: The Battle for Egypt's Constitution*, January 2013, 13.
44 'Egypt's Morsi Declares "State of Emergency"', *Al Jazeera*, January 2013. Available online: http://www.aljazeera.com/news/middleeast/2013/01/2013127195926600436.html.
45 'Egypt: New Leader Faces Rights Crisis', *Human Rights Watch*, June 2014. Available online: http://www.hrw.org/news/2014/06/09/egypt-new-leader-faces-rights-crisis.
46 'Egypt Declares State of Emergency', *Al Jazeera*, August 2013. Available online: http://www.aljazeera.com/news/middleeast/2013/08/201381413509551214.html.
47 See Art. 154 of the July 2013 Constitutional Declaration, as found in 'July 2013 Egyptian Constitutional Declaration', *Carnegie Endowment for International Peace*. Available online: http://egyptelections.carnegieendowment.org/2013/07/15/full-text-of-the-july-2013-egyptian-constitutional-declaration.
48 J. Stork, 'Egypt: Painting "Terrorism" with a Very Broad Brush', *Human Rights Watch*, May 2014. Available online: http://www.hrw.org/news/2014/05/05/egypt-painting-terrorism-very-broad-brush.
49 Ibid.
50 Ardovini and Mabon, 'Egypt's Unbreakable Curse: Tracing the State of Exception from Mubarak to Al Sisi'.
51 C. Aiena, 'The Never-ending Story of Egypt: Al Sisi and the Military Legacy', *Islamic Human Rights Commission*, July 2014. Available online: http://www.ihrc.org.uk/publications/briefings/11123-the-never-ending-story-of-egypt-al-sisi-and-the-military-legacy.
52 A. Magdi, 'Why Executions in Egypt Are Skyrocketing and Why They Should End', *Human Rights Watch*, March 2019. Available online: https://www.hrw.org/news/2019/03/25/why-executions-egypt-are-skyrocketing-and-why-they-should-end.
53 L. Ardovini, 'Egypt's Faltering Legitimacy: Sisi's Contested Victory and Pressing Challenges', *Foreign Policy Centre*, April 2018. Available online: https://fpc.org.uk/sisi/.
54 T. Ozhan, 'What Sisi's "Victory" Means for Egypt's Future', *Middle East Eye*, April 2018. Available online: https://www.middleeasteye.net/columns/what-sisis-victory-means-egypts-future-1166881278.
55 L. Ardovini, 'Egypt's Faltering Legitimacy: Sisi's Contested Victory and Pressing Challenges'.

56 'An Egyptian Human Rights Defender Disappeared and Tortured', *Egyptian Initiative for Personal Rights*, February 2020. Available online: https://eipr.org/en/press/2020/02/egyptian-human-rights-defender-disappeared-and-tortured-eipr-gender-rights-0.
57 Hosni, 'Egyptians Divided as Sisi Continues to Extend State of Emergency'.
58 K. Chick, 'The Most Dangerous Job in Journalism Is Just Being a Reporter in Egypt', *Foreign Policy*, January 2017. Available online: https://foreignpolicy.com/2017/01/16/the-most-dangerous-job-in-journalism-is-just-being-a-reporter-in-egypt-sisi-muslim-brotherhood/.
59 H. Hendawi, 'Egypt's President Wins Re-election with 97 Percent of Vote', *AP*, April 2018. Available online: https://apnews.com/16adfce98b7d4f6b8441f52d0b2156e0.
60 'Egypt Passes Law that Could Shield Top Military Brass from Prosecution', *Reuters*, July 2018. Available online: https://www.reuters.com/article/us-egypt-parliament-military/egypt-passes-law-shielding-senior-military-officers-from-prosecution-idUSKBN1K61L7.
61 'Egypt Targets Social Media with New Law', *Reuters*, July 2018. Available online: https://www.reuters.com/article/us-egypt-politics/egypt-targets-social-media-with-new-law-idUSKBN1K722C.
62 'Mada Masr: Egypt Independent News Outlet's Office "Raided"', *BBC News*, November 2019. Available online: https://www.bbc.com/news/world-middle-east-50537578.
63 'Egypt Constitutional Changes Could Mean Sisi Rule Until 2030', *BBC News*, April 2019. Available online: https://www.bbc.com/news/world-middle-east-47947035.
64 L. Ardovini, 'Institutionalising Authoritarianism: Al Sisi's Struggle for Power', *ISPI*, January 2019. Available online: https://www.ispionline.it/en/pubblicazione/institutionalizing-authoritarianism-egypt-al-sisis-struggle-power-22087.

References

Agamben, G. *State of Exception*. Chicago: University of Chicago Press, 2005.
Aiena, C. 'The Never-Ending Story of Egypt: Al Sisi and the Military Legacy'. *Islamic Human Rights Commission*, July 2014. Available online: http://www.ihrc.org.uk/publications/briefings/11123-the-never-ending-story-of-egypt-al-sisi-and-the-military-legacy.
Allman, K. 'Revolution and Counter-Revolution in Egypt's Emergency State'. *Oxford Human Rights Hub*, March 2018. Available online: http://ohrh.law.ox.ac.uk/revolution-and-counter-revolution-in-egypts-emergency-state/.
Amnesty International Public Statement. 'Egypt: Keep Promise to Free Detainees by End of June'. June 2010. Available online: https://www.amnesty.org/en/documents/MDE12/027/2010/en/.
'An Egyptian Human Rights Defender Disappeared and Tortured'. *Egyptian Initiative for Personal Rights*, February 2020. Available online: https://eipr.org/en/press/2020/02/egyptian-human-rights-defender-disappeared-and-tortured-eipr-gender-rights-0.
Ardovini, L. 'Egypt's Faltering Legitimacy: Sisi's Contested Victory and Pressing Challenges'. *Foreign Policy Centre*, April 2018. Available online: https://fpc.org.uk/sisi/.
Ardovini, L. 'Institutionalising Authoritarianism: Al Sisi's Struggle for Power'. *ISPI*, January 2019. Available online: https://www.ispionline.it/en/pubblicazione/institutionalizing-authoritarianism-egypt-al-sisis-struggle-power-22087.

Ardovini, L. and S. Mabon. 'Egypt's Unbreakable Curse: Tracing the State of Exception from Mubarak to Al Sisi'. *Mediterranean Politics*, February 2019. Available online: https://doi.org/10.1080/13629395.2019.1582170.

Ayubi, N. *Over-stating the Arab State: Politics and Society in the Middle East*. London: I.B. Tauris, 1995.

Bromley, S. *Rethinking Middle East Politics*. Austin: University of Texas Press, 1994.

Brownlee, J. 'Unrequited Moderation: Credible Commitments and State Repression in Egypt'. *Studies in Comparative International Development* 45, no. 4 (December 2010): 468–89.

Cairo Institute for Human Rights Studies. 'Welcome to the Military State of Egypt: Minister of Justice Decree More Repressive than State of Emergency, Grants Military Police and Military Intelligence Judicial Authority to Arrest Civilians'. *Statements and Position Papers*, June 2012. Available online: http://www.cihrs.org/?p=2846&lang=en.

Chick, K. 'The Most Dangerous Job in Journalism Is Just Being a Reporter in Egypt'. *Foreign Policy*, January 2017. Available online: https://foreignpolicy.com/2017/01/16/the-most-dangerous-job-in-journalism-is-just-being-a-reporter-in-egypt-sisi-muslim-brotherhood/.

Constitution of the Arab Republic of Egypt. 1971. Available online: http://www.palatauruscentrostudi.eu/doc/EGY_Constitution_1971_EN.pdf.

'Egypt Constitutional Changes Could Mean Sisi Rule Until 2030'. *BBC News*, April 2019. Available online: https://www.bbc.com/news/world-middle-east-47947035.

'Egypt's Morsi Declares 'State of Emergency''. *Al Jazeera*, January 2013. Available online: http://www.aljazeera.com/news/middleeast/2013/01/2013127195926600436.html.

'Egypt: New Leader Faces Rights Crisis'. *Human Rights Watch*, June 2014. Available online: http://www.hrw.org/news/2014/06/09/egypt-new-leader-faces-rights-crisis.

'Egypt Declares State of Emergency'. *Al Jazeera*, August 2013. Available online: http://www.aljazeera.com/news/middleeast/2013/08/201381413509551214.html.

'Egypt Passes Law That Could Shield Top Military Brass from Prosecution'. *Reuters*, July 2018. Available online: https://www.reuters.com/article/us-egypt-parliament-military/egypt-passes-law-shielding-senior-military-officers-from-prosecution-idUSKBN1K61L7.

'Egypt Targets Social Media with New Law'. *Reuters*, July 2018. Available online: https://www.reuters.com/article/us-egypt-politics/egypt-targets-social-media-with-new-law-idUSKBN1K722C.

Egyptian Organization for Human Rights. 'EOHR Issues Report on Impact of Emergency Law'. *IFEX*, February 2003. Available online: https://www.ifex.org/egypt/2003/02/28/eohr_issues_report_on_impact_of/.

Egyptian Organization for Human Rights. 'Egypt and the Impact of 27 Years of Emergency on Human Rights'. May 2008. Available online: http://en.eohr.org/2008/05/28/%E2%80%9Cegypt-and-the-impact-of-27-years-of-emergency-on-human-%20rights%E2%80%9D/#more-22.

El-Ghobashy, M. 'The Metamorphosis of the Egyptian Muslim Brothers'. *International Journal of Middle East Studies* 37, no. 3 (August 2005): 373–95.

Eldeen, S. 'Egypt Back under Emergency Law'. *Carnegie Endowment for International Peace*, May 2017. Available online: http://carnegieendowment.org/sada/69886.

'English Text of Morsi's Constitutional Declaration'. *Ahram Online*, November 2012. Available online: http://english.ahram.org.eg/News/58947.aspx.

Fahim, K. 'In Upheaval for Egypt, Morsi Forces Out Military Chiefs'. *The New York Times*, August 2012. Available online: http://www.nytimes.com/2012/08/13/world/middleeast/egyptian-leader-ousts-military-chiefs.html?hp.

Fawcett, L. 'States and Sovereignty in the Middle East: Myths and Realities'. *International Affairs* 93, no. 4 (2017): 789–807.

Furani, K. 'States of Exception, Ethics and New Beginnings in Middle East Politics'. *International Journal of Postcolonial Studies* 16, no. 3 (2014): 346–64.

Hendawi, H. 'Egypt's President Wins Re-Election with 97 Percent of Vote'. *AP*, April 2018. Available online: https://apnews.com/16adfce98b7d4f6b8441f52d0b2156e0.

Hosni, H. 'Egyptians Divided as Sisi Continues to Extend State of Emergency'. *Al Monitor*, July 2018. Available online: https://www.al-monitor.com/pulse/originals/2018/06/egypt-state-of-emergency-extension-terrorism.html.

Human Rights Association for the Assistance of Prisoners. 'Detention and Detainees in Egypt 2003'. Cairo, 2003.

Humphreys, S. 'Legalizing Lawlessness: On Giorgio Agamben's State of Exception'. *The European Journal of International Law* 17, no. 3 (2006): 677–87.

International Center for Not-for-Profit Law. 'Law No. (162) of the Year 1958'. Available online: http://www.icnl.org/research/library/files/Egypt/162-1958-en.pdf.

'July 2013 Egyptian Constitutional Declaration'. *Carnegie Endowment for International Peace*, Available online: http://egyptelections.carnegieendowment.org/2013/07/15/full-text-of-the-july-2013-egyptian-constitutional-declaration.

Kassem, M. *In the Guise of Democracy: Governance in Contemporary Egypt*. London: Garnet & Ithaca Press, 1999.

Mabon, S. 'Sovereignty, Bare Life and the Arab Uprisings'. *Third World Quarterly* 38, no. 8 (2017): 1782–99.

'Mada Masr: Egypt Independent News Outlet's Office "Raided"'. *BBC News*, November 2019. Available online: https://www.bbc.com/news/world-middle-east-50537578.

Magdi, A. 'Why Executions in Egypt Are Skyrocketing and Why They Should End'. *Human Rights Watch*, March 2019. Available online: https://www.hrw.org/news/2019/03/25/why-executions-egypt-are-skyrocketing-and-why-they-should-end.

Middle East Monitor. 'Egypt Extends State of Emergency for the 11th Time since 2017'. January 2020. Available online: https://www.middleeastmonitor.com/20200115-egypt-extends-state-of-emergency-for-11th-time-since-2017/.

Revkin, M. 'Egypt's Untouchable President'. *POMEPS Briefings: The Battle for Egypt's Constitution*, January 2013, 13–16.

Osman, T. *Egypt on the Brink*. London: Yale University Press, 2010.

Ozhan, T. 'What Sisi's "Victory" Means for Egypt's Future'. *Middle East Eye*, April 2018. Available online: https://www.middleeasteye.net/columns/what-sisis-victory-means-egypts-future-1166881278.

Owen, R. *State, Power and Politics in the Making of the Modern Middle East*. Abingdon: Routledge, 2004.

Ramadan, A. and S. Fregonese. 'Hybrid Sovereignty and the State of Exception in the Palestinian Refugee Camps in Lebanon'. *Annals of the International Association of Geographers* 17, no. 4 (2017): 949–63.

Stacher, J. *Adaptable Autocrats: Regime Power in Egypt and Syria*. Stanford: Stanford University Press, 2012.

'Statement from the Supreme Council of the Egyptian Armed Forces'. *The New York Times*, February 2011. Available online: http://www.nytimes.com/2011/02/11/world/middleeast/11egypt-military-statement.html?_r=0.

Stork, J. 'Egypt: Painting "Terrorism" with a Very Broad Brush'. *Human Rights Watch*, May 2014. Available online: http://www.hrw.org/news/2014/05/05/egypt-painting-terrorism-very-broad-brush.

Zsanto, E. 'Sayyida Zaynab in the State of Exception: Shiʻi Sainthood as "Qualified Life" In Contemporary Syria'. *International Journal of Middle East Studies* 44, no. 2 (2012): 285–99.

Zwitter, A. 'The Arab Uprising: State of Emergency and Constitutional Reform'. *ASPJ Africa & Francophonie* 2 (2014): 48–65.

Weber, S. 'Bare Life and Life in General'. *Grey Room* 46 (2012): 7–24.

Wickham, C. *The Muslim Brotherhood: The Evolution of an Islamist Movement*. Princeton: Princeton University Press, 2013.

Williams, D. 'Egypt Expands 25 Years Old Emergency Law'. *The Washington Post*, May 2006. Available online: http://www.washingtonpost.com/wp-dyn/content/article/2006/04/30/AR2006043001039.htm.

Chapter 5

A FORCED MARRIAGE? PALESTINE AND THE STATE OF EXCEPTION

Sanaa Alsarghali[*]

Introduction

The Covid-19 pandemic has brought to the forefront, once again, Palestine's constitutional framework and its limitations. Palestine's decision to declare a state of emergency as a response to the public health crisis, while warranted, has caused concern among many that Palestine may be consolidating what has been termed as a 'state of exception' – the situation in which democratic countries have normalized the use of emergency powers to the extent that democracy is perpetually suspended.[1] It is in this context that Giorgio Agamben's recent warning that the Covid-19 pandemic may be utilized by governments to normalize the use of anti-democratic emergency powers[2] could become prescient. This is especially pertinent to Palestine, since it currently has no functioning parliament by which to provide checks and balances on emergency power use. Indeed, Palestine had already been using exception legislative powers as a means to govern, suggesting that the state of exception condition was already emerging.[3] Arguably the Covid-19 pandemic and Palestine's subsequent state of emergency measures are consolidating further the normalization of emergency power use in Palestine, a process that has been in progression since an emergency government was formed in 2007 following the West Bank–Gaza/Fatah–Hamas split.

Historically, using emergency measures as a 'normal' means to govern is not unprecedented to Palestine. Indeed, before the creation of the Palestinian Authority (PA), it was the most used provision of governance during British rule.[4] Furthermore, the experiences of countries in the Middle East and North Africa (MENA), prior to the Arab Spring Uprisings, serve as a stark warning of the abuses that can result from a president's unrestrained use of emergency powers and their control over the security services.[5] Presidents in particular have frequently declared states of emergency in order to rule by decree, target political opposition and consolidate executive power.[6] Oftentimes, during these exceptional periods, executives are provided with additional legislative powers that can lead to human right violations, the alteration of judicial systems and significant increases in the role of internal security apparatus in regulating society.[7] Former Egyptian president

Hosni Mubarak's use of emergency powers is perhaps the most emblematic Middle Eastern example of how a president can use such powers to avoid ordinary legal constraints, consolidate state power and suppress political and social opposition to the regime.[8] Indeed, as a consequence of Mubarak's use of powers, specific constitutional amendments were made to the Egyptian constitution of 1971 that became a wider template for other constitutional drafters used in the Middle East – including Palestine.[9]

Many scholars have applied Giorgio Agamben's use of the 'state of exception' and 'bare life' in the wider context of the Israeli–Palestinian conflict,[10] including a chapter in this volume by Adel Ruished. This chapter, however, differs in its framing as it applies the concept directly to the Palestinian Authority, the self-governing body for Palestinians in the West Bank and Gaza Strip (prior to Hamas's control over Gaza), and the Basic Law (BL) – the transitional constitutional document of the PA. This move away from viewing 'Palestine' in the wider context of Israel–Palestine opens up analysis in the face of occupation and process of illegal annexation, which automatically renders Palestine as being an exceptional state with extraordinary circumstances and therefore makes it possible to justify the PA normalization of emergency powers. The danger of such a position is that it enables the PA to potentially justify its use of emergency continually. Thus, the value of applying the state of exception concept in a (strictly) Palestinian case study is that it urges scholars to consider what constitutes emergency and highlight how exceptional states are not necessarily states of exception.[11] Furthermore, this move away from a wider Israel–Palestine context potentially allows a contribution to the larger political project around the understanding of Palestinian self-determination.[12]

As such, it is from within the Palestinian context that this chapter argues that the state of exception condition in Palestine (caused by both internal and external factors) is quite unique. The Palestinian case adds an interesting layer of complexity to the state of exception concept as the PA and its president arguably do not fulfil the definition of sovereign: 'the capacity to determine conduct within the territory of a polity without external legal constraint.'[13] The PA arguably does not meet this definition due to the Israeli role as an occupying power, as well as the reliance on wider international aid for the Palestine economy to function. If, as outlined by Agamben, only the sovereign can create the state of exception, Palestinian sovereignty is therefore being conditioned by a range of other regional and international factors.

In order to conceptualize Palestine's incomplete 'sovereignty' it is useful to consider Caroline Humphrey's work that has begun to conceptualize how sovereignty can be partial.[14] She has coined the term 'nested sovereignty' to argue that 'localized sovereign domains' can be 'nested' within 'higher sovereignties' while maintaining 'a domain within which control over life and death is operational'.[15] This is in keeping with similar studies that highlight how sovereignty is 'always relational, incomplete, and partial and that we [need to] understand political landscapes as [being] shaped by multiple overlapping and shifting claims to sovereignty'.[16] It is within this vein, this chapter argues, that the state of exception may also be considered partial or incomplete. Using Palestine's relationship with its emergency power provisions as an example, this chapter highlights how the state of exception is 'entered' (or 'exited') based on contested claims of sovereignty.

State of exception

The 'state of exception' was first formalized by Carl Schmitt to describe a state's response to an emergency or crisis that could potentially threaten its existence. Central to the term 'state of exception', therefore, is the dichotomy, and distinction, between normal and exceptional. In other words, all crises will inevitably vary in threat and magnitude, and not all crises will constitute an emergency. This tipping point, therefore, of when a crisis warrants a state of exception is inevitably a judgement of when an emergency goes beyond the parameters of what constitutes normal. As argued by Alan Greene:

> If there must exist a core of settled meaning within the term 'emergency', so too must there exist a similar core of settled meaning of instances that do not equate to emergency; i.e. the identification of when an emergency has ended, or when circumstances never equated to an emergency in the first place.[17]

The decision over what constitutes normal or exceptional is key. Inevitably, however, this tipping point is not a simple dichotomy between normal and emergency; it is rather an unresolved grey area, described by Agamben as a 'zone of indistinction',[18] in which the sovereign power can declare the suspension of the rule of law. Thus, this zone of indistinction establishes an area in which contradictory things come together to create a condition where sovereign power operates with no limitation, stemming from the constitutional suspension of the rule of law to create a space governed by the force of law. As put by Anthony Downey, 'the sovereign legal prerogative is the effective prorogation of the law itself and a "state of exception" is not the rule of law as such nor is it a fact; nor is it bound to a law or to a fact.'[19]

Thus, in legal terms, this issue of indistinction is ultimately a question regarding the application of the rule of law.[20] This emphasis on the rule of law is important, as in the 'state of exception' constitutional norms are suspended and replaced by the 'force of law without law' – a process which then continues until the exception is no longer the exception but rather has become the norm within political life.[21] It is in this vein that Agamben argues that the state of exception is inexorably linked to sovereignty, as it is the sovereign who determines the state of exception and equally, the sovereign who is constructed by the state of exception.[22] Through this reciprocal relationship between the two, the sovereign's actions go beyond the legal order of the state, as the sovereign alone is able to dictate not only whether a state of exception exists but also the necessary actions required to overcome it.[23] As described by Agamben:

> The structure in which the state of exception [. . .] is realized normally. . . . The sovereign no longer limits himself [. . .] to deciding on the exception on the basis of recognizing a given factual situation (danger to public safety): laying bare the inner structure of the ban that characterizes his power, he now de facto produces the situation as a consequence of his decision on the exception.[24]

Within the condition of the state of exception, the sovereign possesses a perennial 'natural right to do anything to anyone' due to this ambiguity created by this zone of indistinction.[25] Put another way, individuals – by virtue of their existence within the state of exception – are residing in a position simultaneously beyond legal protection yet bound by legal structures.[26] Thus the state of exception infers a blurring of the distinction between citizen and outlaw, legality and illegality, law and violence, life and death. Here the subject is subjected to sovereign power over life and death, where they are exposed to 'bare life'.

This zone of indistinction tends to be only possible within the revolutionary-democratic tradition at the heart of Western democracies, inferring that the 'state of exception' can only be applied in this context. Indeed, Agamben has detailed how democratic states of the West have voluntarily created a state of emergency in order to 'create and guarantee' the situation for exception.[27] In other words, the state of exception cannot be said to apply in all authoritarian states; rather, it must occur within a particular type of state, wherein there are political structures and there is a degree of space to allow for political activity.[28] The state of exception emerges within these conditions when the sovereign uses his prerogative – the ability to decide upon the exception – to enact emergency legislation and sovereign power more broadly. In a slight departure from Agamben's position – in terms of its application – this chapter (following Simon Mabon's introduction to this edited volume) suggests that the 'state of exception' can also occur within states beyond the West.[29] Indeed, the exception is able to manifest itself in any state whereby moments of emergency can justify the need for urgent political action if there is no time for normal forms of due process. Therefore, as 'emergencies' provide the ability to release particular moments from the norm, it can also be used as a means of determining particular situations on a case-by-case basis. I argue that the mechanisms of law and politics that necessitate suspension in order for a 'state of exception' to come into existence can also be said to be operating within Palestine.

Palestine: A state of exception or an exceptional state?

To identify Palestine as a state of exception – that is in a perpetual state of emergency – it is necessary first to qualify normalcy in Palestine. This is a difficult exercise for Palestine as it is an occupied territory (that is shrinking in the face of Israeli annexation policies) and is also suffering from an internal conflict that has split the areas under the self-governing authority's control into two separate parcels of land. Furthermore, adding to this complexity is the relationship between the PA, the governing body of the Palestinian territory and the Palestinian Liberation Organization (PLO).[30] Both these bodies represent Palestinians in different ways, and the unclear constitutional relationship between them is an example of complex and partial notions of sovereignty surrounding Palestine.

The ambiguous relationship between these two bodies stems from the Oslo Accords,[31] the international 'peace' agreement that saw the PLO gave birth to the PA. Since the creation of the Palestinian territory's governing entity, the PA, the status of the PLO, the body representing Palestinian sovereignty, has been unclear. For example, if sovereignty is typically understood as being vested within the people, then the PLO would simultaneously represent both the Palestinian diaspora, those who are refugees and in exile, and those living within the Palestinian territory. However, since the creation of the PA, this body can also claim to reflect sovereignty (of those Palestinians living in the West Bank and Gaza), especially as it contains an elected Legislative Council. Crucially, the design and status of the PA have never been fully defined; for some, the PA would play the role of a 'state in waiting', replacing the PLO after it fulfilled its role in signing the Oslo Accords and creating the PA institutions.[32] However, with the PLO, the only Palestinian entity with full international recognition and the clearly assigned role as representing all Palestinians, it has not stepped aside in favour of a PA. Indeed, the PA's first president, Mr Arafat, took measures to ensure the perpetuation of the PLO by using his dual role as PLO chairman and PA president to purposely blur the distinction between the roles of these two entities.[33]

The relationship between the two bodies has since changed depending on the political climate. Initially, the institutions of the PLO were weakened in favour of developing PA equivalents when the Fatah faction's (Palestine's largest political faction) core leadership formed the backbone of both the PLO and later the PA.[34] However, the reverse occurred when a new political faction that never had any representation in the PLO, Hamas, wanted to shift from being an opposition faction into one that could run the PA.[35] When this occurred, following their surprise legislative victory in 2006, the PLO institutions were strengthened again to act as a possible counterweight to the growing Hamas influence.[36] This strengthening of the PLO became a necessity until 2007, when the PA split between the Hamas-controlled Gaza Strip and Fatah-governed West Bank. Thus, the rise and fall of these institutions, amid domestic conflict, have tended to blur the distinction between the boundaries of sovereignty in ways which are solely unique to Palestine.

Furthermore, this abnormal 'normalcy' in Palestine has only been consolidated by the international community's unwillingness to pose sanctions on Israel for violating international law and the economic agreements forced in the Oslo Accords that have effectively positioned Palestine as an 'international financial trusteeship'.[37] As emphasized by Leila Farsakh, 'international scholars, as well as Palestinian NGOs, have long argued that the Oslo process and the Intifada did not bring the Palestinians closer to statehood, but rather confirmed an Israeli "apartheid" in the West Bank and Gaza Strip.'[38] This dependence on international aid and the effects of occupation have only increased in recent years, with Donald

Trump's Middle Eastern 'deal of the century' extending the annexation practices of Israel and normalizing the relations between Israel and Palestine's former international 'allies' in the Arab world.

As identified earlier, the Palestinian case contains many exceptional circumstances that can foster a zone of indistinction – indeed, the Oslo Accords themselves are partially responsible for codifying this exceptional Palestinian context due to the legal terms used. On the other hand, many of these same circumstances prevent a totality of sovereign power from emerging and shaping the state of exception as understood by Agamben's use of the phrase. Thus, understanding the state of exception in Palestine requires an added nuance. Indeed, the value of a Palestinian case study when applying the state of exception concept is in how it forces scholars to engage with the context of emergency and explore how exceptional states are not necessarily states of exception. Put simply, while Palestine is an exceptional state in many regards and could be considered as facing an existential threat, its condition as a state of exception, *from within its own territories*, is not necessarily automatic.

Entering the state of exception

Critical to Agamben's concept of the state of exception is its emergence from within the revolutionary-democratic tradition associated with Western democracies, that is a state of exception cannot emerge from a state which, from its conception, had no space for 'normal' democratic politics.[39] In other words, the condition of exception can only exist if there is a condition of 'democratic' normalcy. To what extent, then, has the Palestinian State afforded democratic space for Agamben's concept of the state of exception to be an appropriate lens by which to explore Palestine's current political condition?

It has been argued – from as far back as 2001 – that Palestine does not meet the standards of a democratic state. Amal Jamal, for example, argues that the 'pervasiveness of informal institutions encouraged by the dominant role of a strong founding-father has had devastating consequences, not only for the future of democracy in Palestine, but also for the political stability of the Palestinian state'.[40] However, this critique, which questions the effectiveness of the separation of powers doctrine in Palestine, perhaps under-recognizes the role formal institutions have also played in creating democratic spaces in Palestine. There can be no doubt that the PA also has the necessary legislative and judicial institutions, control over the legitimate use of force, forms of coordination between the different organs of government and an active civil society – all of which indicate the PA has a democratic foundation. While these features may have been subverted in some cases by an overly dominant executive, the very existence of these formal institutions, the high levels of activism – underpinned by a highly educated population – and the ability to criticize the president in public have prompted even Israeli officials to suggest 'what they [the PA] have done in the last five years is more democratic than any Arab society. It's a limited democracy, or guided democracy, under the very firm hand of Arafat. But it has potential'.[41] Put simply, while the normalcy – in terms of a Western democratic state – is only fledgling in Palestine, its potential suggests that the 'exception' was never guaranteed and had to undergo a process of normalization.

For the normalization of exception to occur, it is typical first for a state to declare a state of emergency – the constitutional provision that allows for the legal suspension of constitutional norms as decided by the sovereign. For Agamben, there is no distinction between the state of emergency as a constitutional provision and the state of exception as a concept.[42] The Palestinian example, however, requires a certain distinction to be made due to the circumstances involved in its declaration. The crisis that warranted emergency power legislation initially began with the legitimate election of Hamas into government on 26 January 2006. Hamas won 76 of the 132 seats in parliament, winning an outright majority. The victory of Hamas in the Palestinian Legislative Council (PLC) elections, however, came as a substantial shock to Fatah faction and the wider international community, with polling consistently suggesting a Fatah majority.[43] The implications of Hamas's victory were seismic as it was considered by the international community as a terrorist organization.[44] In response to the elections, Israel, the United States, the European Union, Russia and the United Nations demanded that the new Hamas government would unconditionally maintain all past agreements, recognize Israel's right to exist and renounce violence.[45] Hamas's continued refusal of these conditions, however, led to the international community cutting off critical aid to the Palestinian Authority.[46] This was a devastating measure as aid and Israel remunerations to Palestine make up two-thirds of Palestine's income. This, in combination with lost access to global banking services, effectively destroyed the PA's economy.[47]

Despite the actions of the international community, President Abbas attempted to form a coalition government with Hamas and appointed its leader Ismail Haniyeh as prime minister on 29 March 2006. A period of political instability soon followed as intense political infighting began to occur between the two parties – accompanied by increased tensions between Gaza and Israel – and the economic sanctions began to come into effect. Continued efforts were made, however, throughout the year to develop a political system that would accommodate the two parties. Most notable, for example, was the signed agreement on 8 February 2007 between Fatah and Hamas to form a national unity government that was carried out under the auspices of the Saudi king, Abdullah. The aim of this agreement was to end the violence and the international embargo occurring in Palestine. However, the attempt ultimately failed due to continued political factionalism and the international community's refusal to end economic sanctions with Hamas in a position of influence.[48] As a result, violent conflicts began to increase, particularly in Gaza where the bedrock of Hamas's political support is located and where tensions with Israel were at their highest. The problems in power-sharing, the unchanging manner of Hamas towards Israel and ineffective governance more generally eventually reached a tipping point. This 'tip' occurred on 14 June 2007 when the Hamas leadership took control of the Gaza Strip in a violent coup, removing all Fatah officials in that region.[49] In response, President Abbas declared a state of emergency on the basis of his two titles: the chairperson of the PLO and the president of the PA, that is as a figure of sovereign power. Using the newly afforded emergency powers, the president then acted to dissolve all Hamas representatives and forces in the West Bank.[50] This attempt to save the Palestinian economy and create a working government, through using emergency powers, created a hard split between the Fatah-controlled West Bank and the Hamas-controlled Gaza – which is still in effect today.

Crucially, the move to declare a state of emergency was partly a result of an economic threat by the international community and the political conflicts between two parties, Hamas and Fatah, that were unable to compromise, and less a move by an individual sovereign intending to create and guarantee a state of exception. Indeed, attempts were made for over year to create a working coalition between Fatah and Hamas in some form. However, practising democracy in Palestine has always depended on Israel's actions, as they have the definitive power of enforcement over the Palestinian territories and their institutions. The role Israel played in imprisoning Hamas PLC members, their refusal to recognize the 2006 election results and the economic sanctions they applied were all considerable external factors that helped cause Palestine's 2007 political deadlock. In other words, even if Fatah and Hamas had reached a political compromise, it is unlikely that political stability could have been accomplished due to the influence of Israel (and the international community). Put simply, unless the democratic aspirations of the Palestinian people are matching or serving the strategic interests of Israel, its realization will be prevented.

This form of exception in Palestine is not necessarily congruent with Agamben's definition, for the sovereign is not in this case 'de facto produc[ing] the situation as a consequence of his decision on the exception'.[51] The president's decision is in fact a response to the exceptional circumstances of Palestine that is partly independent of the sovereign. In other words, sovereignty in Palestine is partial and nested in various entities; it is not wholly invested in the Palestinian head of state but rather dispersed across different entities that are contingent on both external and internal forces and not necessarily emerging from domestic insecurity. Indeed, all 'across the Middle East, regime authority – and autonomy – can be challenged by actors operating both at a sub-state and supra-state level who are often able to lay more convincing claims to authority, legitimacy or power'.[52] This is a process that is enhanced in Palestine due to its particularly unique circumstances that have established a broad zone of indistinction. In these circumstances, the concept of 'nested' or 'nestled' sovereignty is especially useful in considering how the mechanisms of governance and governmentality (i.e. emergency powers) are there to afford regimes the ability to exercise power. This exercising of power is often a necessary response to other competing groups – that is Hamas, the international community, Israel and so on – that are also laying claim to social norms, practices, economies in their own attempts to influence and contest sovereignty.[53]

The normalization of emergency powers

In the aftermath of the 2006 election when claims of sovereignty were being exercised by different entities (in a variety of different ways), the president attempted to normalize his own powers as 'sovereign'. From 2007 onwards, the executive of the PA was able to assert this sovereignty through the use of emergency powers, which began to become normalized in Palestine due to the structure of the Basic Law and the political limbo caused by a suspended PLC.

This normalization was not a result of the 'state of emergency' declaration per se. As expected with modern constitutions, the articles within the BL relating to the use of emergency powers have precise and specific stipulations aimed at preserving the principles of constitutionalism.[54] Indeed, to extend emergency powers this way requires the presidential decree to declare the emergency purpose and length and to define the territories in which it applies (Art. 110.3);[55] it also requires the approval of two-thirds of the Legislative Council if it is to be extended (see Art. 110.2).[56] The PLC is then also authorized to review some or all of the procedures implemented during the state of emergency and cannot be dissolved or suspended during states of emergency (Art. 101.4).[57] However, due to the political circumstances of the time, the PLC was de facto suspended due to the Fatah–Hamas/West Bank–Gaza split, which allowed the president to use the emergency situation without the PLC being a check on executive powers. Indeed, it was the absence of a PLC that prompted the need for using the emergency articles and lay the foundation for emergency power use to be perpetuated (as the situation regarding the PLC could not be resolved, largely due to external factors).

These political conditions gave rise to the potential of normalizing emergency powers in two core ways: first by the invoking of Art. 43 and then by the standardization (and legitimization) of Art. 43 through the government's neoliberal state-building project.

Art. 43: The 'State of Necessity'

The president was able to begin this process of normalizing legislative powers, in lieu of a functioning PLC, by extending the emergency situation from a mandated thirty days into a perpetual condition. He did this through invoking Art. 43, 'the state of necessity', which, different to the 'state of emergency', is a single article in the BL (not an emergency provision for government) that can only be used in times of crisis or need, when the PLC is absent. Crucially, it provides the president the legislative power similar to that of the PLC:

> The President of the National Authority shall have the right, in cases of necessity that cannot be delayed, and when the Legislative Council is not in session, to issue decrees that have the power of law.[58]

This article contains a crucial ambiguity. It does not define if the period 'not in session' refers only when the PLC is ordinarily not in session, that is the recess between January and February, and between July and August, or if it could also refer to possible 'extraordinary' reasons for the PLC not being in operation. This distinction is important as, in the former context, the article could only be activated in those January–February or July–August periods.[59] This ambiguity may not be an issue in ordinary circumstances as PLC members have the right to call an 'abnormal' session at any time,[60] but it remains quite relevant in light of the unique circumstances when the elected PLC members have been forcibly suspended. The president has arguably taken advantage of this article in order to perpetuate what Agamben would call a 'situation of necessity', a zone of indistinction from which the exception could emerge.

Most notably, the president has taken advantage of this article to control the appointment of the prime minister and the government more generally. During the state of emergency, the president issued presidential decree No. (11) of 2007, which suspended Arts. 65, 66 and 67 of the BL that outlined the PLC procedure in appointing the cabinet and the means by which a prime minister could form his cabinet.[61] With these articles suspended, the president has been able, through decree No. (11), to appoint all government personnel and the prime minister without reference to other offices/bodies of government since. In other words, all appointees and dismissals of government officials have become solely accountable to the executive branch. This act, which has unconstitutionally consolidated executive power, is in keeping with the features described in Agamben's state of exception.

Normalizing Art. 43

This normalization of Art. 43 developed as a by-product of the West Bank's PA attempt to standardize its rule as a means to compensate for its lack of legitimacy. To achieve this standardization, the first emergency government (following the 2007 crisis) was designed and created to be highly technocratic. As such, President Mahmoud Abbas appointed a cabinet headed by Dr Salam Fayyad, the previous finance minister who had worked for both the World Bank and the IMF. In the absence of a functioning PLC, Fayyad's PA was able to develop an ad hoc system of government (through Art. 43) in which decree-laws could be drafted if they have the full consultation of all ministries and courts were granted extended autonomy in regard to their court orders.[62] During Fayyad's tenure, the PA's focus was on revitalizing the economy, developing a security apparatus that coordinated with Israel and fixing the Palestinian institutions that had suffered following the Hamas election.[63] In this period, Fayyad was lauded by foreign international organizations and other countries due to his commitment to neoliberal policies, having a 'soft' approach towards Israel and for playing down the issue of Palestinian refugees – issues which also made him unpopular to some in Palestine.[64]

In this period of Fayyad's leadership, described by political scientist Nathan Brown as an era of 'reform without democracy', Palestine entered a period of normalcy and political stability (relative to Palestine's 'normal') due to Fayyad's policies which integrated Palestine economy with Israel's. This direction of government received popular international support and thus ensured short-term economic and financial stability for Palestine.[65] The long-term implications of this strategy, however, would make any Hamas–Fatah reconciliation less viable and future stability more vulnerable.[66] As argued by Tariq Dana, 'the notion that an intensified capitalism and economic "interdependency" between the coloniser and colonised would bring peace is unrealistic . . . rather, capitalist peace will institutionalize structural dependency characterized by manifold forms of colonial domination and subordination, which will eventually harden resistance to this form of colonial peace.'[67] In other words, this capitalist integration has only increased the nested aspect of Palestine's sovereignty, extending further the zone of indistinction.

These developments under Fayadd – that emphasized political stability, private sector-led development and the professionalization of police and paramilitary units – are important from a state of exception perspective. In commencing security reform, while under occupation and without a clear sovereign authority, tensions between the PA's security forces and those activist groups resisting Israel would inevitably increase, in ways that would increase the tendency towards authoritarianism.[68] As suggested by Alaa Tartir:

> At best, the security reform under Fayyadism's state-building project . . . resulted in better stability and more security to Israel and its occupation, but it did not result in better security conditions for the Palestinian people in the occupied West Bank. At worse . . . [it] resulted in creating authoritarian transformations and criminalising resistance against the Israeli occupation, and as such directly and indirectly sustained it.[69]

In other words, Fayyad's state-building project contained two critical elements: on the one hand, an ad hoc government dominated by an executive branch, and on the other, an increasingly centralized security force; and both processes were becoming normalized as part of a larger neo-liberalized state-building project. Importantly, this route towards neoliberalization was largely sanctioned by Israel and a US-led international community. Indeed, the moniker 'our man in Palestine' in reference to Fayyad[70] strongly hints at the conditionality of the Palestine and its president, the capacity to enact 'sovereignty' and self-determination. Indeed, since the crisis of 2007 in which the international community was able to shape Palestinian politics through the withholding aid, that threat has continued to loom large over Palestinian policymaking. So, while these developments under Fayyad were providing a perfect setting from which a state of exception could potentially emerge from, it is not a state of exception that is being defined by a single sovereign.

Redefining the 'normal'

In 2013, following the resignation of Dr Fayyad, a new government was formed and headed by Prime Minister Dr Rami Hamdallah, an academic and the president of one of Palestine's prestigious and largest universities. His government was formed in a format similar to its predecessor, meaning that the requirement to obtain the PLC confidence was replaced by a Presidential Decision (No. 8 of 2013) as facilitated by the use of Art. 43 of the BL.[71] Hamdallah kept his position as PM from May 2013 until January 2019, serving as a PM for the fifteen, sixteen and the seventeen governments with his position maintained by regularly renewed presidential approvals.[72] During this period (between May 2013 and January 2019), the president issued more than 280 presidential decrees, with the cabinet acting as an overreaching executive that prepared legislations for the president to pass.[73]

Hamdallah's seventeenth government, known as the 'Government of National Accord', was particularly significant as it was also recognized by Hamas (which had dismissed prior West Bank governments as being illegitimate) and even involved some Hamas members in its make-up.[74] While not a full reconciliation between the two parties (since the West Bank and Gaza remained split), it can nevertheless be argued that this government was formed during a period of 'normalcy' – unlike in the periods before when strife between Fatah and Hamas was particularly heightened. The 'normalcy' represented by this government, however, still retained the legislative practices of the previous era, with governance being achieved through Art. 43 and with no serious efforts to reinstate the PLC or initiate elections. In other words, this government was convened during a zone of indistinction despite it representing a degree of stability. In fact, it helped shape Palestine's 'new normal' in that the presidential use of exceptional powers was now becoming associated with periods of relative stability – and not just with crisis.

In this respect, the use of Art. 43, as normalized through the state-building efforts of Fayyad and the quasi-reconciliation between Hamas and Fatah under Hamdallah's Government of National Accord, has enabled the state of exception to become normalized within Palestine. Put differently, since 2007, Palestine has been under a process that has 'legalised lawlessness'.[75] According to Agamben, this process is what allows the state of exception to be justified, as the law is being divided into two distinct elements: constitutional norms (which Agamben terms as the 'normative element of the law') and the means that allows the law to be applied, that is the force of law without law. In this way, political actions such as 'decrees, provisions and measures that are not formally laws acquire their "force"', despite the suspension of constitutional norms.[76] This is how, in a state of exception, the law – albeit in a reduced and atomized form – continues to exist.[77]

In Palestine's context, this form of 'state of exception' has been heavily shaped by external forces due to the partial nature of the president's sovereign power. Indeed, the zone of indistinction in Palestine has been largely shaped by circumstances outside of the sovereign's control and the emergence of the state of exception has had little relationship with the constitutional declarations of the 'state of emergency' and the state of necessity (Art. 43). Arguably, the state of exception in Palestine has been seen as convenient for the international community since 2007 hence why it has been allowed to be perpetuated by Palestine's president. It is within these conditions that the state of exception has emerged in Palestine, the development of a new normal in which constitutional norms are suspended in place of force of law without law.

Consolidating the state of exception: The role of the constitutional court

The normalization of exceptional legislative power use became consolidated and further entrenched with the development of a Palestinian constitutional court on 3 April 2016. President Abbas's decision to establish the Supreme Constitutional Court (SCC) was based on an increasing need to follow up on the rules, regulations and constitutionality of laws that had been passed since 2007.[78] However, following the tendency of Arab constitutional courts to rule in favour of the executive, as opposed to maintaining the principles of constitutionalism,[79] the SCC in Palestine similarly followed suit. Indeed, despite the potential of a constitutional court to resolve Palestine's political and constitutional deadlocks, many observers have concluded that President Abbas's goal was not to resolve the deadlock per se but rather to further legalize the current format of executive rule by decree and to ensure Fatah's dominance over Hamas.[80]

The court's most significant ruling regarding the state of exception occurred in 2018 and was concerned with the current status of the PLC. On 2 December 2018, an application requesting interpretation was submitted by the minister of justice for the interpretation of Art. 47 of the BL, Art. 47 BIS and Art. 55 of the BL. The interpretation of these articles, which concern the status of the PLC (i.e. its position as the legislative authority and the length of its term), would determine if the PLC is to be considered suspended or active – and if PLC members were still eligible for their salaries despite not sitting.

In response to this enquiry, the constitutional court took a decision on 12 December 2018 to dissolve the PLC and called for legislative elections – a decision which the president endorsed and committed himself to implementing on 22 December 2012.[81] The following day, the Minister of Justice 'Ali Abu Diak explained that what the constitutional court issued was the explanatory decision (10/2018) dated 12 December 2018.[82] He explained the two points underlying the court's decision: (1) the PLC has not functioned since being elected; (2) the PLC's elections were not held in its due time in 2010. The constitutional court's explanatory decision was then published, detailing the grounds for its justification with more substance:

> 1. the legitimacy of the PLC lies when practicing its legislative and oversight duties. Considering that it has not convened since 2007, the PLC has lost its status as a legislative authority, and thus as its status as the Legislative Council . . . 5. The President of the State of Palestine shall call for holding legislative elections within six months from the date of publishing this decision in the Official Gazette.[83]

In this decision by the court, the PLC as a legislative body was completely removed from the political scene – a particularly controversial ruling as the BL does not reference the ways in which the PLC could be dissolved.[84] The court essentially argued that although the BL provides no mechanism for the dissolving of the PLC, this interpretation has constitutional validity as the BL falsely assumed the PLC would always be in session (except for scheduled vacations).[85] Therefore, when considering the spirit of the drafters meaning when they initially wrote the BL, the court argued the BL had not considered the possibility of a perpetually suspended PLC and if it had, it would have provided the means for the PLC to be dissolved (Alsarghali, 2021).

The resulting constitutional vacuum caused by this decision has severely impacted the law-making abilities of the Palestinian government, from a constitutional perspective, impotent. Previous to the court's decision, during the suspension of the PLC, laws in Palestine were enacted by a 'decision that has the power of law' via Art. 43 of the BL.[86] However, this article is valid only while the PLC is not in session; with the PLC being dissolved completely, the president can no longer make legally binding laws. Indeed, since the court's decision (regardless of the fact that the president is still using this article to issue decrees that have the power of laws), the government has now technically lost the ability to make laws legally binding due to the absence of a legislative body and the now ineligible Art. 43. In other words, rule by decree, an emergency-type power, has become fully normalized within the law without even the 'illusion' of legality, suggesting that a full severance has now occurred between constitutional norms (i.e. law) and the means by which laws are applied.

The circumstances outlined here translate into Agamben's critique of Schmitt's understanding of sovereignty and the state of exception. For Agamben, Schmitt's understanding of sovereignty expresses the state of exception as a juridical condition, with law surviving its suspension in the form of the 'force of law'.[87] Agamben, however, argues that sovereignty in this scenario is a 'fiction' concealing the obsolete ineffectual workings of the law and the illegitimacy of authority.[88] In Palestine, with the SCC rulings, law has ceased to be in operation as it is constitutionally laid out. Instead, Palestine is governed through the executive's claims of sovereignty, which without constitutional underpinnings are ultimately illusionary.

This form of governance, through the illusion of sovereignty, has continued to proceed in Palestine since the court's decision to dissolve the PLC and to begin the election process has not occurred. Despite election proceedings being 'earmarked' to follow six months after the PLC's dissolving, they have failed to materialize, thus perpetuating the absence of a functioning PLC and a constitutionally working political system. Indeed, shortly after the ruling, on 29 January 2019, Dr Hamdallah resigned from his position as prime minister. Eleven days later, President Abbas asked Dr Mohammad Shtayyeh to form the eighteenth Palestinian government as prime minister.[89]

This eighteenth government is unique, as it only contains a president and prime minister and does not have a PLC, or recognize one, in any capacity. Unlike its previous iterations, the current eighteenth government draws its legitimacy (i.e. sovereignty) predominantly from the PLO and Fatah party. Indeed, the prime minister and the president are both Fatah Central Council members, with the latter also being chairman of the PLO of which its institutions overlapped with the PA. In this respect, a government of exception that expresses a singular claim of sovereign power has become fully formed. Put simply, this verdict of the constitutional court, the means in which it was interpreted and the unique format of the eighteenth government, lends credence to the claim that Palestine lies in a condition of a perennial state of exception.[90]

Conclusion

This chapter has outlined the constitutional history of Palestine from 2006 to 2020 and has highlighted the critical moments in regard to Palestine's relationship with the state of exception. The three critical events in this timeline have been identified as the formal declaration of the state of emergency in 2007, the appointment of the Government of National Accord (with Prime Minister Dr Rami Hamdallah) in 2013 and the constitutional court's decision to dissolve the PLC in 2018. The first event can be said to have set the conditions for the state of exception to emerge, the second signified the complete normalization of exceptional power use by the president and the third marked the consolidation of the state of exception.

The perpetual use of exceptional legislative powers by President Abbas since 2007 has, therefore, successfully normalized an authoritarian form of government within a state whose initial foundations are within a democratic constitution and a democratic political system. The process that led to the state of exception in Palestine – while dictated by internal factors like the political discord between Hamas and Fatah, the increasing dominance of the executive through use of Art. 43, structural weaknesses in the BL and the neoliberal character of various state-building projects – has not been 'guaranteed' by the sovereign. Instead, the zone of indistinction that has allowed the state of exception to flourish in Palestine has largely been outside the sovereign's control. For example, Palestine's defined – and perpetuating – position as a transitioning state by international agreements, the continuing and aggressive occupation by Israel and a dependence on the international community for its critical financial and economic resources have all contributed to Palestine's particular state of exception condition that is made up of competing claims of sovereignty.

These claims of sovereignty vary greatly in providence and include self-proclaimed freedom fighters and activists, the political organization of Hamas following its election success in 2006, the authority of the PA (and its executive branch) as granted by the Oslo Accords, the PLO – the body which represents the rights of all Palestinians (those within as well as outside the occupied territories) – all of which is conditioned and influenced by the interventions made by a US-led international community. Added to this is also the military might of Israeli occupation forces, which has the power to enforce its will at any time in the West Bank and Gaza. In sum, there is no clear representation of sovereignty to enforce the state of exception. So, while it has become clear in 2018, following the court's ruling to officially dissolve the PLC, that the state of exception has become fully consolidated in Palestine, it is not one shaped by an individual figure of sovereignty as classically imagined by Agamben. Indeed, this exception within Palestine cannot be complete as it is driven by only a partial sovereign and a zone of indistinction that is being shaped by external forces. Therefore, the possibility for Palestine to exit the state of exception condition is perhaps more open than it initially seems, as the claims to sovereignty are contested, there is no total control over the polity and conditions creating the zone of indistinction are not being created by Palestine's sovereign.

It is within this 'partial' state of exception that the recent Covid-19 crisis emerged, an emergency that has helped make more visible the uniqueness of Palestine's status. On the one hand, the pandemic has added to the zone of indistinction in Palestine, allowing the president to normalize his exceptional powers further. For example, due to the prolonged nature of the pandemic, the president has repeatedly extended the state of emergency using Art. 43,[91] an act that requires approval from the PLC.[92] Previous to the Covid-19 state of emergency declarations, the use of Art. 43 was justified on the premise that the president was creating legislation in absence of the PLC. However, during Covid-19 the decision to extend the 'state of emergency' via the 'power of law decree' infers that the president is now replacing the administrative capacity of the PLC (Alsarghali, 2020: 222–26).

On the other hand, though, the PA and the president during Covid-19 have also lost aspects of its 'sovereign' power. Throughout the pandemic the PA has made repeated attempts to close its borders as a measure to curb the spread of the virus. However, the Israeli government has continued to allow Palestinian workers who travel between the crossings on a daily basis to work in Israeli factories in violation of the basic sovereign right to control its national borders.[93] Thus, Covid-19 has been apt in exposing the peculiarities of Palestine's state of exception condition, illustrating how a sovereign can simultaneously guarantee the exception while also be severely lacking in sovereign power.

So, while not an obvious candidate for a 'state of exception' analysis, the Palestine example does reveal interesting observations about how the state of exception occurs even when sovereignty is nested. It highlights how the 'zone of indistinction' is all that is required for 'law' and constitutional norms to be separated from the means in which law is applied. Although sovereignty in Palestine, as represented by the Palestinian executive, does not have the capacity to determine conduct within the West Bank and Gaza without external legal (and illegal) constraints, it nevertheless has committed to a style of governance that is underpinned by the 'force of law without law'. However, the fact that sovereignty in Palestine is contested and the zone of indistinction is being perpetuated largely by external factors also offers more opportunity for the state of exception to be subverted. For example, a new constitution redraft in synch with a realignment of international policy towards Palestine could be instrumental. This would reshape the sovereign power that is defining the state of exception and potentially reset the democratic institutions to allow for a uniquely *Palestinian* state of normality.

Notes

1. Giorgio Agamben, *State of Exception*, trans. Kevin Attell (Chicago: University of Chicago Press, 2005).
2. Giorgio Agamben, 'The Invention of an Epidemic', *Quodlibet*, 26 February 2020. Available online: https://www.quodlibet.it/giorgio-agamben-l-invenzione-di-un-epidemia.
3. Simon Mabon, *Houses Built on Sand: Violence, Sectarianism and Revolution in the Middle East* (Manchester: Manchester University Press, 2020).
4. Yousef Tayseer Jabareen, 'Emergency Regulations', in *The Palestinians in Israel Readings in History, Politics and Society*, ed. Nadim N. Rouhana and Areej Sabbagh-Khoury (Haifa: Mada al-Carmel Arab Center for Applied Social Research), 67–73.
5. Sujit Choudhry, Richard Stacey, Hannah Bloch-Wehba, Sam Chaffin, Daniel Hanna, Shingira Masanzu, Morgan Miller and Akila Ramalingam, 'Semi-Presidentialism as Power Sharing: Constitutional Reform after the Arab Spring', *Centre for Constitutional Transitions and International IDEA* (2014): 29–30. Available online: http://constitutionaltransitions.org/wp-content/uploads/2014/04/Semi-Presidentialism-as-Power-Sharing-High-Res.pdf (accessed 12 August 2015).
6. Mabon, *Houses Built on Sand*.
7. Lucia Ardovini and Simon Mabon, 'Egypt's Unbreakable Curse: Tracing the State of Exception from Mubarak to Al Sisi', *Mediterranean Politics* 25, no. 4 (2020): 456–75.
8. Sadiq Reza, 'Endless Emergency: The Case of Egypt', *New Criminal Law Review* 10, no. 4 (2007): 532–53.
9. Ibid.
10. Ronit Lentin, 'Introduction: Thinking Palestine', in *Thinking Palestine*, ed. Ronit Lentin (London: Zed Books, 2008), 1–22; Sari Hanafi and Taylor Long, 'Governance, Governmentalities, and the State of Exception in the Palestinian Refugee Camps of Lebanon', *Journal of Refugee Studies* 23, no. 2 (June 2010): 134–59; Sari Hanafi, 'Governing the Palestinian Refugee Camps in Lebanon and Syria: The Cases of Nahr el-Bared and Yarmouk Camps', in *Palestinian Refugees: Identity, Space and Place in the Levant*, ed. Are Knudsen and Sari Hanafi (New York: Routledge 2010), 43–63; Adam Ramadan, 'Destroying Nahr el-Bared: Sovereignty and Urbicide in the Space of Exception', *Political Geography* 28, no. 3 (2009): 153–63; Adam Ramadan and Sara Fregonese, 'Hybrid Sovereignty and the State of Exception in the Palestinian Refugee Camps in Lebanon', *Annals of the American Association of Geographers* 107, no. 4 (2017): 949–63.
11. Nevertheless, it is still important to recognize Palestine as an entity being under colonization, as this is restricting the agency of the PA and its institutions.
12. For example, Agamben's reading of the state of exception has been critiqued for not affording agency for those experiencing 'bare life' under the state of exception, which if applied to Israel–Palestine as a whole, potentially removes Palestinian agency. See Lentin, 'Introduction', 1–22.
13. Caroline Humphrey, 'Sovereignty', in *A Companion to the Anthropology of Politics*, ed. D. Nugent and J. Vincent (Oxford: Blackwell, 2004), 418.
14. Ibid.
15. Ibid., 420.
16. Finn Stepputat, 'Formations of Sovereignty at the Frontier of the Modern State', *Conflict and Society* 1, no. 1 (2015): 131; see also Aiwa Ong, 'Graduated Sovereignty in South-East Asia', *Theory, Culture and Society* 17, no. 4 (2000): 55–75; Jean

Comaroff and John L. Comaroff, *Law and Disorder in the Post-Colony* (Chicago: University of Chicago Press, 2006).
17. Alan Greene, 'Separating Normalcy from Emergency: The Jurisprudence of Article 15 of the European Convention on Human Rights', *German Law Journal* 12, no. 10 (2011): 1767.
18. Agamben, *State of Exception*.
19. Anthony Downey, 'Zones of Indistinction: Giorgio Agamben's "Bare Life" and the Politics of Aesthetics', *Third Text* 23, no. 2 (2009): 110.
20. Agamben, *State of Exception*, 170.
21. An important distinction emphasized by Walter Benjamin (see Agamben, *State of Exception*.)
22. Agamben's work is occupied with critiquing Schmitt's notions of sovereignty and how it closes down the conceptual possibility of non-statist forms of political action. See Daniel McLoughlin, 'The Fiction of Sovereignty and the Real State of Exception: Giorgio Agamben's Critique of Carl Schmitt', *Law, Culture and the Humanities* 12, no. 3 (2016): 509–28.
23. Carl Schmitt, *Political Theology: Four Chapters on the Concept of Sovereignty* (Chicago: University of Chicago Press, 2005), 25–7.
24. Agamben, *State of Exception*, 170.
25. Ibid., 109.
26. Ibid.
27. Agamben has highlighted how Western democracies have voluntarily created permanent states of emergencies through the extension of military authority's wartime powers into the civil sphere and by suspending constitutional norms which protect civil liberties. See Agamben, *State of Exception*.
28. Agamben, *State of Exception*.
29. As sovereign authority in Islamic states is also derived from the Quran, it poses interesting questions regarding the (increased) 'zone of indistinction' in these Middle Eastern and Gulf states.
30. The PLO is an organization founded in 1964 with the intention of liberating Palestine. It is recognized as the 'sole legitimate representative' of the Palestinian people by over 100 states with which it holds diplomatic relations.
31. The Oslo Accords refer to two mid-1990s international agreements that marked the start of the Oslo peace process. It aimed to achieve a peace treaty between Israel and Palestine and fulfil the right of the Palestinian people to self-determination.
32. Asem Khalil, 'A Constitutional Framework of a Future Palestinian State-Synthesis of Leading Palestinian Thinking and Public Perceptions', *SSRN 1559213* (2009).
33. Khalil, 'A Constitutional Framework'.
34. BBC, 'Palestine Territories Profile', *BBC*, 8 April 2019. Available online: https://www.bbc.com/news/world-middle-east-14630174; WAFA, 'The Palestinian National Liberation Movement "Fatah"'. Available online: https://info.wafa.ps/ar_page.aspx?id=3544 (accessed 1 December 2019).
35. Khaled Hroub, 'A "New Hamas" through Its New Documents', *Journal of Palestine Studies* 35, no. 4 (2006): 6–27.
36. Hamas has never been involved in the PLO or its structure.
37. Raja Khalidi, 'Reshaping Palestinian Economic Policy Discourse: Putting the Development Horse before the Governance Cart', *Journal of Palestine Studies* 34, no. 3 (2005): 77–87; Adel Samara, 'Globalization, The Palestinian Economy, and the "Peace Process"', *Social Justice* 27, no. 4 (Winter 2000): 117–31.

38 Leila Farsakh, 'Independence, Cantons, or Bantustans: Whither the Palestinian State?', *The Middle East Journal* 59, no. 2 (2005): 231.
39 Agamben, *State of Exception*.
40 Amal Jamal, 'State-Building, Institutionalization and Democracy: The Palestinian Experience', *Mediterranean Politics* 6, no. 3 (2001): 1.
41 Deborah Sontag, 'There's No Bossing a Democracy, Arafat Learns', *New York Times*, 13 December 1998. Available online: https://www.nytimes.com/1998/12/13/world/there-s-no-bossing-a-democracy-arafat-learns.html.
42 Agamben, *State of Exception*.
43 Aluf Benn, 'Polls: Fatah Leads Hamas by Up to 11%', *Ha'aretz*, 25 January 2006; see also Simon Jefferies, 'Hamas Celebrates Election Victory', The *Guardian*, 26 January 2006. Available online: https://www.theguardian.com/world/2006/jan/26/israel1.
44 Aaron Pina, 'Palestinian Elections', *Congressional Research Service*, 9 February 2006. Available online: https://fas.org/sgp/crs/mideast/RL33269.pdf.
45 Global Security, 'Hamas'. Available online: https://www.globalsecurity.org/military/world/para/hamas.htm (accessed 1 December 2020).
46 Pina, 'Palestinian Elections'.
47 Global Security, 'Hamas'. Available online: https://www.globalsecurity.org/military/world/para/hamas.htm (accessed 1 December 2020).
48 Global Security, 'Hamas'. Available online: https://www.globalsecurity.org/military/world/para/hamas.htm (accessed 1 December 2020).
49 Reuters, 'TIMELINE: Key Events since 2006 Hamas Election Victory', *Reuters*, 20 June 2007. Available online: https://www.reuters.com/article/us-palestinians-timeline/timeline-key-events-since-2006-hamas-election-victory-idUSL1752364420070620.
50 Palestinian Gazette, 'President Decree No. 8 & 9 of 2007'. Available online: http://muqtafi.birzeit.edu/en/pg/.
51 Agamben, *State of Exception*.
52 Mabon, *Houses Built on Sand*, 21.
53 Humphrey, 'Sovereignty'; Mabon, *Houses Built on Sand*.
54 Basic Law (Amended 2003) Art. 110/1 reads:
    'The President of the National Authority may declare a state of emergency by decree when there is a threat to national security caused by war, invasion, armed insurrection or in times of natural disaster, for a period not to exceed thirty (30) days.' Available online: https://www.palestinianbasiclaw.org/basic-law/2003-amended-basic-law.
55 Basic Law (Amended 2003) Art. 110/3 reads: 'The decree declaring a state of emergency shall state its purpose, the region to which it applies and its duration.' Available online: https://www.palestinianbasiclaw.org/basic-law/2003-amended-basic-law.
56 Basic Law (Amended 2003) Art. 110/2 reads: 'The state of emergency may be extended for another period of thirty (30) days if a two-thirds majority of the members of the Legislative Council vote in favor of the extension.' Available online: https://www.palestinianbasiclaw.org/basic-law/2003-amended-basic-law.
57 Basic Law (Amended 2003) Art. 110/4 reads: 'The Legislative Council shall have the right to review all or some of the procedures and measures adopted during the state of emergency, at the first session convened after the declaration of the state of emergency or in the extension session, whichever comes earlier, and to conduct the necessary interpellation in this regard.'

58 Basic Law (Amended 2003) Art. 43. Available online: https://www.palestinianbasiclaw.org/basic-law/2003-amended-basic-law.
59 PLC Bylaws 2000, Art. 16. Available online: http://muqtafi.birzeit.edu/pg/getleg.asp?id=14227.
60 PLC Bylaws 2000, Art. 16. Available online: http://muqtafi.birzeit.edu/pg/getleg.asp?id=14227.
61 Palestinian Gazette, President Decree No. 11 of 2007. Available online: http://muqtafi.birzeit.edu/en/pg/.
62 Nathan Brown, 'Palestine: The Schism Deepens', *Carnegie Endowment for International Peace*, 20 August 2009. Available online: http://carnegieendowment.org/2009/08/20/palestine-schism-deepens/3v05.
63 Brown, 'Palestine'.
64 Nathan Thrall, 'Our Man in Palestine', *The New York Review of Books*, 14 October 2010. Available online: https://www.nybooks.com/articles/2010/10/14/our-man-palestine/; Thomas Friedman, 'Let's Fight Over a Big Plan', *The New York Times*, 17 March 2010. Available online: https://www.nytimes.com/2010/03/17/opinion/17friedman.html.
65 Brown, 'Palestine'.
66 Brown, 'Palestine'.
67 Tariq Dana, 'The Symbiosis between Palestinian "Fayyadism" and Israeli "Economic Peace": The Political Economy of Capitalist Peace in the Context of Colonization', *Conflict, Security & Development* 15, no. 5 (2015): 474.
68 Alaa Tartir, 'The Evolution and Reform of Palestinian Security Forces 1993–2013', *Stability: International Journal of Security and Development* 4, no. 1 (2015): 1–20.
69 Tartir, 'Evolution and Reform', 14.
70 Thrall, 'Our Man in Palestine'.
71 Palestinian Gazette. Available online: http://muqtafi.birzeit.edu/en/pg/.
72 Palestinian Gazette, Presidential Decree No. 5 of 2013; Presidential Decree No. 8 of 2013; and Presidential Decree No. 19 of 2015. Available online: http://muqtafi.birzeit.edu/en/pg/.
73 Palestinian Gazette. Available online: http://muqtafi.birzeit.edu/en/pg/.
74 WAFA, 'The Palestinian National Liberation Movement "Fatah"'. Available online: https://info.wafa.ps/ar_page.aspx?id=3544 (accessed 1 December 2019).
75 See Stephen Humphries, 'Legalising Lawlessness: On Giorgio Agamben's *State of Exception*', *The European Journal of International Law* 17, no. 3 (2006): 677–87.
76 Agamben, *State of Exception*, 38.
77 Agamben, *State of Exception*. See also McLoughlin, 'The Fiction of Sovereignty', 6.
78 President Abbas created the Supreme Constitutional Court with Administrative Decision No. 57 of 2016, which was issued on 31 March 2016. The decision was published in the Official Gazette on issue No. One-Hundred and Twenty on 29 March 2016. Available online: https://www.lab.pna.ps/newspaper/380.html (accessed 27 July 2019).
79 Tamir Mousafa, 'Law and Resistance in Authoritarian States: The Judicialization of Politics in Egypt', in *Rule by Law: The Politics of Courts in Authoritarian Regimes*, ed. Tom Ginsburg, Tamir Moustafa (Cambridge: Cambridge University Press, 2008), 132–56.
80 Iyad Qatrawi, 'Is Abbas Tightening His Grip on Power with New Constitutional Court?', 26 April 2016. Available online: https://www.al-monitor.com/pulse/originals/2016/04/palestine-abbas-decree-constitutional-court-legality.html.
81 Alhaq, 'Position Paper by Palestinian Civil Society Organisations and the Independent Commission for Human Rights on the Decision by the Supreme Constitutional Court

to Dissolve the Palestinian Legislative Council and to Call for Legislative Elections', 27 December 2018. Available online: http://www.alhaq.org/advocacy/6120.html.
82 WAFA, 'Justice Minister: Constitutional Court Ruling on Legislative Council in Line with Basic Law', 23 December 2018. Available online: http://english.wafa.ps/page.aspx?id=1h4D54a107879299044a1h4D54.
83 PCHRGAZA, 'Position Paper: Constitutional Court's Decision to Dissolve PLC Is Political and Illegal', 21 March 2019. Available online: https://www.pchrgaza.org/en/?p=12167.
84 PNN, 'Constitutional Court Decision to Dissolve PLC Is Political and Illegal', 24 March 2019. Available online: http://english.pnn.ps/2019/03/24/pchr-constitutional-court-decision-to-dissolve-plc-is-political-and-illegal/.
85 This oversight by the drafters and Arafat – the president at the time – is perhaps due to the expectation that the president and the PLC would always be in the same political party.
86 Basic Law (Amended 2003), Art. 43 reads: 'The President of the National Authority shall have the right, in cases of necessity that cannot be delayed, and when the Legislative Council is not in session, to issue decrees that have the power of law. These decrees shall be presented to the Legislative Council in the first session convened after their issuance; otherwise they will cease to have the power of law. If these decrees are presented to the Legislative Council, as mentioned above, but are not approved by the latter, then they shall cease to have the power of law.'
87 McLoughlin, 'The Fiction of Sovereignty', 509–28.
88 Ibid.
89 WAFA, 'President Abbas Asks Mohammad Shtayeh to Form the New Government', WAFA, 10 March 2019. Available online: https://english.wafa.ps/page.aspx?id=9g2eWba108714938178a9g2eWb.
90 A condition which has no likely end date as elections, following their supposedly firm announcement for the summer of 2021, have once again been indefinitely delayed - and will be for the foreseeable future. See Daniel Estrin, 'Palestinian Authority Postpones Parliamentary Elections', npr, 29 April, 2021. Available online: https://www.npr.org/2021/04/29/992065009/palestinian-authority-postpones-parliamentary-elections?t=1652219019040
91 DCAF Palestine, *Decree No. 3 of 2020*, 4 April 2020. Available online: https://security-legislation.ps/law/100127.
92 Basic Law (Amended 2003) Art. 110/2. Available online: https://www.palestinianbasiclaw.org/basic-law/2003-amended-basic-law.
93 BBC, 'Palestinians Working in Israel Face Coronavirus Dilemma', 29 April 2020. Available online: https://www.bbc.co.uk/news/world-middle-east-52470718; Al-Jazeera, 'Palestinians Brace for a Coronavirus Outbreak as Workers Return', 6 April 2020. Available online: https://www.aljazeera.com/news/2020/4/6/palestinians-brace-for-a-coronavirus-outbreak-as-workers-return.

References

Agamben, Giorgio. *State of Exception*. Translated by Kevin Attell. Chicago: University of Chicago Press, 2005.
Agamben, Giorgio. 'The Invention of an Epidemic'. *Quodlibet*, 26 February 2020. Available online: https://www.quodlibet.it/giorgio-agamben-l-invenzione-di-un-epidemia.

Alhaq. 'Position Paper by Palestinian Civil Society Organisations and the Independent Commission for Human Rights on the Decision by the Supreme Constitutional Court to Dissolve the Palestinian Legislative Council and to Call for Legislative Elections'. Available online: http://www.alhaq.org/advocacy/6120.html (accessed 27 December 2018).

Al-Jazeera. 'Palestinians Brace for a Coronavirus Outbreak as Workers Return'. Available online: https://www.aljazeera.com/news/2020/4/6/palestinians-brace-for-a-coronavirus-outbreak-as-workers-return (accessed 6 April 2020).

Alsarghali, Sanaa. 'An (Un) Constitutional Hangover: An Analysis of the Current Palestinian Basic Law in Light of Palestine's Constitutional Heritage'. *University of Illinois Law Review* (2017): 497.

Alsarghali, Sanaa. 'The dissolution of the Palestinian Legislative Council by the Palestinian Constitutional Court: a missed opportunity for reform.' *IACL-AIDC Blog*, 1 July 2021. Available online: https://blog-iacl-aidc.org/menaregion/1-7-21the-dissolution-of-the-palestinian-legislative-council.

Alsarghali, Sanaa. 'Palestine', In *2020 Global Review of Constitutional Law*, edited by R. Albert, D. Landau, P. Faraguna, and S. Drugda, 222–26. I•CONnect and the Clough Center for the Study of Constitutional Democracy at Boston College, 2020.

Ardovini, Lucia and Simon Mabon. 'Egypt's Unbreakable Curse: Tracing the State of Exception from Mubarak to Al Sisi'. *Mediterranean Politics* 25, no. 4 (2020): 456–75.

Basic Law. Amended 2003 edition. Available online: https://www.palestinianbasiclaw.org/.

BBC. 'Palestinians Working in Israel Face Coronavirus Dilemma'. *BBC*, 29 April 2020. Available online: https://www.bbc.co.uk/news/world-middle-east-52470718.

BBC. 'Palestine Territories Profile'. *BBC*, 8 April 2019. Available online: https://www.bbc.com/news/world-middle-east-14630174.

Benn, Aluf. 'Polls: Fatah Leads Hamas by Up to 11%'. *Ha'aretz*, 25 January 2006.

Bjørnskov, Christian and Stefan Voigt. 'Why Do Governments Call a State of Emergency? On the Determinants of Using Emergency Constitutions'. *European Journal of Political Economy* 54 (2018): 110–23.

Brown, Nathan. 'Palestine: The Schism Deepens'. *Carnegie Endowment for International Peace*, 20 August 2009. Available online: http://carnegieendowment.org/2009/08/20/palestine-schism-deepens/3v05.

Choudhry, Sujit, Richard Stacey, Hannah Bloch-Wehba, Sam Chaffin, Daniel Hanna, Shingira Masanzu, Morgan Miller and Akila Ramalingam. 'Semi-Presidentialism as Power Sharing: Constitutional Reform after the Arab Spring'. *Centre for Constitutional Transitions and International IDEAs*, 2014, 29–30. Available online: http://constitutionaltransitions.org/wp-content/uploads/2014/04/Semi-Presidentialism-as-Power-Sharing-High-Res.pdf (accessed 12 August 2015).

Comaroff, Jean and John L. Comaroff. *Law and Disorder in the Post-Colony*. Chicago: University of Chicago Press, 2006.

Dana, Tariq. 'The Symbiosis between Palestinian "Fayyadism" and Israeli "Economic Peace": The Political Economy of Capitalist Peace in the Context of Colonization'. *Conflict, Security & Development* 15, no. 5 (2015): 455–77.

DCAF Palestine. 'Decree No. 3 of 2020'. 4 April 2020. Available online: https://security-legislation.ps/law/100127.

Downey, Anthony. 'Zones of Indistinction: Giorgio Agamben's "Bare Life" and the Politics of Aesthetics'. *Third Text* 23, no. 2 (2009): 109–25.

Farsakh, Leila. 'Independence, Cantons, or Bantustans: Whither the Palestinian State?'. *The Middle East Journal* 59, no. 2 (2005): 230–45.

Friedman, Thomas. 'Let's Fight over a Big Plan'. *The New York Times*, 17 March 2010. Available online: https://www.nytimes.com/2010/03/17/opinion/17friedman.html.

Global Security. 'Hamas'. Available online: https://www.globalsecurity.org/military/world/para/hamas.htm (accessed 1 December 2020).

Greene, Alan. 'Separating Normalcy from Emergency: The Jurisprudence of Article 15 of the European Convention on Human Rights'. *German Law Journal* 12, no. 10 (2011): 1764–85.

Hanafi, Sari. 'Governing the Palestinian Refugee Camps in Lebanon and Syria. The Cases of Nahr el-Bared and Yarmouk Camps'. In *Palestinian Refugees: Identity, Space and Place in the Levant*, edited by Are Knudsen and Sari Hanafi, 43–63. New York: Routledge, 2010.

Hanafi, Sari and Taylor Long, 'Governance, Governmentalities, and the State of Exception in the Palestinian Refugee Camps of Lebanon'. *Journal of Refugee Studies* 23, no. 2 (June 2010): 134–59.

Hroub, Khaled. 'A "New Hamas" through Its New Documents'. *Journal of Palestine Studies* 35, no. 4 (2006): 6–27.

Humphrey, Caroline. 'Sovereignty'. In *A Companion to the Anthropology of Politics*, edited by D. Nugent and J. Vincent, 418–36. Oxford: Blackwell, 2004.

Humphries, Stephen. 'Legalising Lawlessness: On Giorgio Agamben's *State of Exception*'. *The European Journal of International Law* 17, no. 3 (2006): 677–87.

IDEA. 'Emergency Powers'. *International IDEA Constitution-Building Primer*, 30 May 2018. Available online: www.idea.int/publications/catalogue/emergency-powers (accessed 12 September 2020).

Jabareen, Yousef Tayseer. 'Emergency Regulations'. In *The Palestinians in Israel Readings in History, Politics and Society*, edited by Nadim N. Rouhana and Areej Sabbagh-Khoury, 67–73. Haifa: Mada al-Carmel Arab Center for Applied Social Research, 2011.

Jamal, Amal. 'State-Building, Institutionalization and Democracy: The Palestinian Experience'. *Mediterranean Politics* 6, no. 3 (2001): 1–30.

Jefferies, Simon 'Hamas Celebrates Election Victory'. *The Guardian*, 26 January 2006. Available online: https://www.theguardian.com/world/2006/jan/26/israel1.

Khalidi, Raja. 'Reshaping Palestinian Economic Policy Discourse: Putting the Development Horse before the Governance Cart'. *Journal of Palestine Studies* 34, no. 3 (2005): 77–87.

Khalil, Asem. 'A Constitutional Framework of a Future Palestinian State – Synthesis of Leading Palestinian Thinking and Public Perceptions'. Available at SSRN 1559213 (2009).

Lentin, Ronit, 'Introduction: Thinking Palestine'. In *Thinking Palestine*, edited by Ronit Lentin, 1–22. London: Zed Books, 2008.

Mabon, Simon. *Houses Built on Sand: Violence, Sectarianism and Revolution in the Middle East*. Manchester: Manchester University Press, 2020.

McLoughlin, Daniel. 'The Fiction of Sovereignty and the Real State of Exception: Giorgio Agamben's Critique of Carl Schmitt'. *Law, Culture and the Humanities* 12, no. 3 (2016): 509–28.

Mousafa, Tamir. 'Law and Resistance in Authoritarian States: The Judicialization of Politics in Egypt'. In *Rule by Law: The Politics of Courts in Authoritarian Regimes*, edited by Tom Ginsburg and Tamir Moustafa, 132–56. Cambridge: Cambridge University Press, 2008.

Nice, Alex, Raphael Hogarth, Joe Marshall and Catherine Haddon. *Emergency Powers*. London, UK: Institute for Government. Available online: www.instituteforgovernment.org.uk/explainers/emergency-powers (accessed 23 October 2020).

Ong, Aiwa. 'Graduated Sovereignty in South-East Asia'. *Theory, Culture and Society* 17, no. 4 (2000): 55–75.

Palestinian Gazette. 2007–2019. Available online: http://muqtafi.birzeit.edu/en/pg/.

PCHRGAZA. 'Position Paper: Constitutional Court's Decision to Dissolve PLC Is Political and Illegal'. Available online: https://www.pchrgaza.org/en/?p=12167 (accessed 21 March 2019).

PLC Bylaws. Birzeit University. 2000. Available online: http://muqtafi.birzeit.edu/pg/getleg.asp?id=14227.

Pina, Aaron. 'Palestinian Elections'. *Congressional Research Service*, 9 February 2006. Available online: https://fas.org/sgp/crs/mideast/RL33269.pdf.

PNN. 'Constitutional Court Decision to Dissolve PLC Is Political and Illegal'. 24 March 2019. Available online: http://english.pnn.ps/2019/03/24/pchr-constitutional-court-decision-to-dissolve-plc-is-political-and-illegal/.

Qatrawi, Iyad. 'Is Abbas Tightening His Grip on Power with New Constitutional Court?'. 26 April 2016. Available online: https://www.al-monitor.com/pulse/originals/2016/04/palestine-abbas-decree-constitutional-court-legality.html.

Ramadam, Adam 'Destroying Nahr el-Bared: Sovereignty and Urbicide in the Space of Exception'. *Political Geography* 28, no. 3 (2009): 153–63.

Ramadan, Adam and Sara Fregonese. 'Hybrid Sovereignty and the State of Exception in the Palestinian Refugee Camps in Lebanon'. *Annals of the American Association of Geographers* 107, no. 4 (2017): 949–63.

Reuters. 'TIMELINE: Key Events since 2006 Hamas Election Victory'. *Reuters*, 20 June 2007. Available online: https://www.reuters.com/article/us-palestinians-timeline/timeline-key-events-since-2006-hamas-election-victory-idUSL1752364420070620.

Reza, Sadiq. 'Endless Emergency: The Case of Egypt'. *New Criminal Law Review* 10, no. 4 (2007): 532–53.

Roy, Sara. 'Reconceptualizing the Israeli-Palestinian Conflict: Key Paradigm Shifts'. *Journal for Palestine Studies* 41, no. 3 (Spring 2012): 71–91.

Samara, Adel. 'Globalization, the Palestinian Economy, and the "Peace Process"'. *Social Justice* 27, no. 4 (Winter 2000): 117–31.

Schmitt, Carl. *Political Theology: Four Chapters on the Concept of Sovereignty*. Chicago: University of Chicago Press, 2005.

Sontag, Deborah. 'There's No Bossing a Democracy, Arafat Learns'. *New York Times*, 13 December 1998. Available online: https://www.nytimes.com/1998/12/13/world/there-s-no-bossing-a-democracy-arafat-learns.html.

Stepputat, Finn. 'Formations of Sovereignty at the Frontier of the Modern State'. *Conflict and Society* 1, no. 1 (2015): 129–43.

Tartir, Alaa. 'The Evolution and Reform of Palestinian Security Forces 1993–2013'. *Stability: International Journal of Security and Development* 4, no. 1 (2015): 1–20.

Thrall, Nathen. 'Our Man in Palestine'. *The New York Review of Books*, 14 October 2010. Available online: https://www.nybooks.com/articles/2010/10/14/our-man-palestine/.

WAFA. 'Justice Minister: Constitutional Court Ruling on Legislative Council in Line with Basic Law'. Available online: http://english.wafa.ps/page.aspx?id=1h4D54a107879299044a1h4D54 (accessed 23 December 2018).

WAFA. 'The Palestinian National Liberation Movement "Fatah"'. Available online: https://info.wafa.ps/ar_page.aspx?id=3544 (accessed 1 December 2019).

WAFA. 'President Abbas Asks Mohammad Shtayeh to Form the New Government'. *WAFA*, 10 March 2019. Available online: https://english.wafa.ps/page.aspx?id=9g2eWba108714938178a9g2eWb.

Chapter 6

SOVEREIGN POWER IN AN ICY CLIMATE

AN EXPLORATION OF VIOLENCE, ENVIRONMENTAL CHALLENGES AND DISPLACEMENT IN THE BEKAA VALLEY, LEBANON

Ana Maria Kumarasamy

The Bekaa Valley in Lebanon has become a site for a demanding environment, changing demographics and various forms of violence. This includes harsh winters with heavy snow and flooding,[1] inadequate and insecure informal refugee camps,[2] and conflict spillover from the Syrian civil war.[3] These factors are some of many that contribute to political instability; however, they are essential in unpacking sociopolitical dynamics, political ordering and the regulation of life. This chapter seeks to explore the interplay between these factors through the lens of biopolitics and Giorgio Agamben's theories of *the state of exception*[4] and *bare life*.[5] A state of exception is defined as the ability of the sovereign to create exceptional laws, like states of emergencies, and integrate them into the judicial order so they appear to be 'true state law'.[6] In the Bekaa Valley this is demonstrated by hybrid actors, such as the Lebanese Armed Forces (LAF) and Hezbollah, that regulate border security and the lives of the inhabitants in the region. Bare life is simply defined as life that is exposed to death, which is moved from the political life (*bíos*) to a lesser life (*zoé*), a person who is stripped from its political status. Refugees in Lebanon have often been described as such through their regulation and limited status. Through the utilization of these concepts, this chapter seeks to analyse political instabilities and their relation to sovereign power.

The Bekaa Valley is situated between the Mount Lebanon and the Anti-Lebanon mountain ranges, to the west and east of Lebanon, respectively. The area holds the governorates of Bekaa and Baalbeck-Hermel, and it includes approximately one million inhabitants, almost 350,000 Syrian refugees[7] and a relatively small number of Palestinian refugees.[8] Since the start of the Syrian civil war, the sociopolitical conditions have deteriorated due to pressures on resources like shelter and food, but also due to concerns regarding the complex demographic and confessional balance in Lebanon which is politically sensitive as a result of the previous experience with Palestinian refugee camps during the Lebanese civil war (1975–90).[9]

Moreover, due to its location, the Bekaa Valley has been known since antiquity as the crossroad to Damascus and a vital part of the region's breadbasket.[10] Today, however, agriculture remains relatively small in scale and is susceptible to climate variations including harsh weather such as storms, floods and drought.[11] Furthermore, the region is affected by both internal politics (including factors such as religion, sect and class) and the external geopolitical climate in the Middle East and beyond (through interventions from state and non-state actors). In consequence, the Bekaa Valley includes a complex set of salient features like environmental instabilities, large numbers of refugees and political instabilities that are interlinked with questions on order-building, sovereignty and power.

As a result, this chapter will answer the following question: How does sovereign power and environmental insecurity affect Syrian refugees in the Bekaa Valley? The chapter starts by considering the theoretical implications of Giorgio Agamben's space of exception and bare life in the context of environmental insecurity,[12] refugee movements[13] and violence. The second section seeks to unpack these issues of order-building, sovereignty and power structures in the border regions of the Bekaa Valley. Finally, the chapter examines sources of instability and intersections of harsh winters and floods, the ongoing Syrian refugee crisis and spillover effects from the Syrian civil war.

Biopolitics, sovereign power and the camp

At the centre of this inquiry are ideas around order-building, sovereign power and spaces of control. However, these structures in Lebanon are often seen as weak domestically because of regional instability and external support to non-state actors.[14] This understanding of sovereignty, however, can be 'misleading and even obstructive of peace in Lebanon'.[15] Notably, Sara Fregonese argues that hybrid sovereignty in Lebanon is far more productive in addressing state and non-state actors as practices among groups resemble sovereignty.[16] Similarly, Waleed Hazbun describes sovereignty as 'an assemblage of state and non-state actors has been able to navigate between rival understandings of insecurity, producing at all times shared, but still contested, understanding which have sustained a system of plural governance over security that has been able to respond to a shifting geography of threats'.[17] Moreover, the archetypal utilization of hybrid sovereignty as Simone Tholens points out fails to capture the holistic picture of security threats and the empowerment of subnational actors in border areas.[18] Border areas, in the case of the Lebanese-Syrian border, include spaces of collaboration and even integration between different hybrid sovereigns.[19] In sum, an extensive analysis of hybrid sovereignty in Lebanon does not just address state and non-state actors, but it also includes cooperation between groups in times of crisis.

Biopolitics and sovereign power

In the development of biopolitics, Michel Foucault presented the idea as 'the growing inclusion of man's natural life in the mechanism and calculations of power',[20] thus transcending the traditional approach to power and focusing on institutional sources of power. This shift marks a broader change in the understanding of sovereign power and its relation to inhabitants. Drawing on Foucault's ideas, Agamben brings in the work of Hannah Arendt's work on totalitarian states,[21] thus merging the biopolitics with totalitarian power structures[22] – thereby explaining the inclusion of biological life as the nucleus of sovereign power, thus making the quality of life inseparable from institutions and power relations. This will later be exemplified through the analysis of border security in the Bekaa Valley, where the life of the inhabitants is closely knit to the border security provided by the Lebanese Armed Forces and Hezbollah. As such, the centre of this analysis lies within an undisclosed state of emergency, embedded in the legal framework of the sovereign[23] – or in the Lebanese case the hybrid sovereigns.

The state of exception in the Bekaa Valley is the act of self-suspension by state and non-state actors. For Zigmunt Bauman 'self-suspension means that the law confines its concern with the exempted/excluded to holding them outside the rule-governed realm which it has circumscribed. Law acts on that concern by proclaiming the exempted to be not its concern. There is no law for the excluded.'[24] In the case of refugees in Lebanon, spaces of expiation have been a tool for unpacking political exclusion and abandonment by different actors.[25] Utilizing the state of exception, Nora Stel explores the permanent temporalities of Syrian and Palestinian refugees produced by Lebanon's post-civil war hybrid political orders that facilitates 'their control, exploitation and expulsion'.[26] In the Bekaa Valley, the self-suspension of the judicial order is decided by the LAF, Hezbollah, informal networks and the municipalities of the area that have the power to suspend the judicial order to maintain control in the region.[27] This is exemplified by the illegal mass evictions of Syrian refugees by Lebanese municipalities without due process of Article 429 of the Penal Code that forbids the right to evictions without a court order or by the LAF without sufficient consultation, compensation or assistance.[28]

The suspension of the judicial order creates a zone of indistinction where fact and law do not coincide.[29] A space in which the permanent state of exception as a fundamental component of contemporary politics that unfolds structures of a 'legal civil war' 'that allows for the physical elimination not only of political advisories but entire categories of citizens who for some reasons cannot be integrated into a political system'[30] – in this case the Syrian refugees who have been abandoned as a result of their exclusion from Lebanese law.[31] Hence, sovereign power presents itself as the threshold between law and violence. As discussed further, the Bekaa Valley is situated in a zone of indistinction that is ruled by 'emergency laws' that is the result of border management responding to spillover from the Syrian civil war.

For Agamben, one of the complications of spaces of exception is the historical Roman figure of *homo sacer* – the human being who is banned from the political city and can be killed without any legal repercussions.[32] When the exception becomes the rule and integrated into law, entire sections of the population become abandoned by the law and become bare life – thus being moved from bíos to zoé, political life to a natural lesser life.[33] According to Agamben, human beings become sacred when they do not have the same rights as an ordinary citizen and are doomed *to death*.[34] Consequently, Agamben develops a link between 'life and politics – originally divided, and linked together by means of no-man's-land of the state of exception that is inhabited by bare life (. . .), all life becomes sacred and all politics becomes the exception'.[35] As such, the inhabitants are caught in the sovereign ban, in which people are abandoned by the law and yet being bound to obey it. Later, this chapter argues that the Syrian refugees in Lebanon are being abandoned by the law and yet are bound to obey it thus becoming integrated into the calculations of order-building and Lebanese biopolitics.

Sovereign power, displacement and environmental insecurity

Through his conceptualizations of the states of exception and bare life, Agamben deduces the modern political space of the *camp*. Based on Arendt's understanding on the Holocaust, Agamben argues that the camp is a political space in which the exception becomes the rule, and it is the most biopolitical space that is realized.[36] In the conceptual space of the camp, the sovereign confronts nothing but bare life forms that are stripped from its political status. As such, the framework has been utilized in order to analyse refugee movements, refugee camps and border areas; examples of these include Mediterranean migration to the Italian island Lampedusa,[37] the enclaves on the India–Bangladesh border,[38] Australian refugee camps[39] and Palestinian refugee camps in Lebanon.[40] Adam Ramadan and Fregonese explore the work of Agamben in the context of hybrid sovereignties in Palestinian refugee camps in Lebanon, arguing that the camps have reshaped Lebanon's sovereignty through fragmented security and territoriality.[41] In short, the biopolitical spaces of the camp reflect the spaces in which sovereign power deals with refugees as non-political beings – *homenis sacri*.

The expansion of sovereign power has led theorists to argue that the state of exception and the camp has become all-encompassing; however, this approach is not that helpful in unearthing local forms of sovereign power.[42] In the context of border security, Reece Jones argues that

> [a]ll-encompassing sovereign power is potentially everywhere, but at a given moment nowhere. Beyond the unique space of the camp, the places where sovereign power actually operates are indistinct and unpredictable. Without being able to locate where sovereign power is, who is carrying out, and what actions are triggering the decision of violence, it is impossible to properly analyse its practice.[43]

Consequently, international borders exemplify permanent spaces of exception through 'spillover securitization' that makes biopolitical control possible at margin.[44] The securitization of borders does in the case of Lebanon exemplify not only contesting sovereignty between countries[45] but also contesting 'hybrid sovereignties'.[46] As argued by Mark B. Slater, law is suspended at the border, thus creating a space of exception, because the 'sovereign decides the political status of the individual as they cross the frontier: national, stateless, refugee, foreigner, alien.

The decision is absolute. (. . .) There is a zone of indistinction wherein a traveller possesses not even his/her nationality unless it is confirmed by the decision of the sovereign'.[47] For instance, Palestinian refugees in Lebanon have 'no voice in the legal formulation of his or her status and no say in either Lebanese or Palestinian political processes which affect him or her'.[48]

The interest of security beyond traditional security studies developed after the publication of Barry Buzan's *People, States, and Fear*,[49] which broadened the understanding of security from the state to relating to all human collectives, thus making room for the migration and the environment as a security concern. Migration, including involuntary or voluntary migrants, as a security concern can pose 'a threat to the people and governments of both sending and receiving states, and to relations between these two countries. It can turn civil wars into international conflicts, and it can cause the spread internationally of ethnic conflict and civil unrest'.[50] Through security studies, migration is sometimes linked with environmental insecurity. Originally, environmental security has been utilized in a causal relationship with armed conflict. One example is found in the correlation between environmental scarcity, migration and violence, as presented by Thomas F. Homer-Dixon in *Environment, Scarcity and Violence*.[51] The term has also been used in cases of resource management, pollution prevention and conservation efforts.[52]

However, environmental insecurity is rarely combined with the ideas of Agamben and one reason for this is that it is 'not even clear what a claim to sovereignty over nature would entail in Agamben's terms, since nature (lacking a political dimension of its own) can't be so reduced'.[53] And yet, it is the sovereign who is the main authority over a territorial space and thus the state is the main actor that deals with climate change and extreme weather emergencies. Therefore, it is the sovereign who decides on the response to such events, making these weather events an element of sovereign power.[54] Consequently, environmental insecurity in the context of this chapter is the contributor of bare life in camp structures that in turn exemplify the state of exception. Later, this chapter demonstrates that heavy snowfall and floods contribute to bare life in informal refugee camps based on their political status.

Furthermore, this chapter considers the relationship between migration, the environment and violence as multifaceted rather than a linear one.[55] Understanding these insecurities as a cause and effect on each other encourages a broader analysis where all factors contribute. The combination of these insecurities within border regions creates complex structures that enable the creation of bare life through spaces of exception. It becomes a zone of indistinction shaped by formal and informal sovereign power structures that only confronts human life stripped from its political meaning. The next section seeks to unpack these structures further in the context of the Bekaa Valley.

Political structures and sovereign power in the Bekaa Valley

Borderlands are meant to be markers of state sovereignty and authority. The resilience of the physical power of the state is one of the dominant themes in the lives of those who live in borderlands. But borderlands and frontier zones are also places of social and political liminality; where the 'other' and the 'us' meet.[56]

The Lebanese border is a space of authority and power, and yet the Bekaa Valley is a space where a myriad of identities intersect – sectarian, national, regional and so on. The region also includes settled Bedouins, who maintain cross-border connections that transcend the state, but most of which are barred from citizenship.[57] It has also been home to a series of refugees, including Armenians and Palestinians and their descendants. As such, the Bekaa Valley has developed multilayered identities that enhance but also compete with each other. The arrival of Syrian refugees in the aftermath of 2011 has intensified the contestation of identities, creating a space for intercommunal conflict and the securitization of the border by actors like LAF and Hezbollah.[58] Unpacking the order-building strategies of Lebanon's hybrid actors towards displaced Syrians is key to unpacking and understanding the power structures in the region.

Bekaa Valley and LAF

Despite the creation of 'Grand Lebanon' in 1916,[59] the border between Lebanon and Syria was never physically formalized. As a result, the border area 'developed complex cultures of their own, and their populations have contrived multi-layered identities to bridge these zones of liminality'.[60] After Lebanon's independence from France in 1943 and during the civil war (1975–90), the border continued to be fluid and ill-defined.[61] Prior to 2005, many towns bordering Syria were economically dependent on the border, including acquiring basic needs such as household shopping and medical services, and the smuggling of tobacco and fuel.[62]

Established shortly after independence, LAF became the state institution for tackling security questions in Lebanon, but in practice LAF was unstructured and unequipped compared to informal security forces like Hezbollah in southern Lebanon. As Simone Tholens argues:

> While the LAF's self-styled image as the only truly national institution has some merit, inasmuch as it is a relatively close-knit cross-sectarian (though not non-sectarian) entity, it is driven by many of the same tensions that affect other Lebanese institutions: competition between sects for influence, dependence on complicated political horse-trading process, and restrictions stemming from the geopolitical Iran-Saudi/US competition.[63]

In post-civil war Lebanon, LAF relied on training and collaborations with Syria that had 'extended its self-appointing role as protector of Lebanon. As an authoritarian regime, the Syrian state had little interest in promoting transparency and accountability and instead pursued a policy of installing former warlords into government positions as a means of maintaining control over Lebanon.'[64] As such, Syria held a dominant role in Lebanon until 2005 and subsequently expelled all political forces that went against them thus manifesting the loose border between Lebanon and Syria.⁶⁵

After the assassination of Rafiq Hariri, however, politics polarized and people went to the streets thus triggering the Cedar Revolution. This polarization led to the formation of pro-Syrian and anti-Syrian coalitions, the March 8 and March 14 Alliances, divided between Shi'a Hezbollah and Saad Hariri's Sunni Future Movement, respectively.⁶⁶ In border towns such as Arsal, residents celebrated 'anti-Syrian' rhetoric that called for the closure of the borders with Syria; however, many remained clear that 'they could never afford to sustain themselves if the borders closed'.⁶⁷ The division within Lebanese politics has resulted in political deadlocks and economic difficulties, leading to an overall imbalance not just within institutions like the LAF but also within broader border security and the incorporation of hybrid sovereigns.

Border management, the Syrian civil war and confrontations with Da'ish

Since 2011, the prioritization of border management has been at the high on the agenda in Lebanon due to the threat of Da'ish and fears of the Syrian civil war spreading into Lebanese territory. Many actors in the Syrian civil war were deeply interlinked with sectarian and religious counterparts in Lebanon, such as Sunni, Shi'ite, Druze, Christian and Alawite.⁶⁸ Consequently, events in Syria had a knock-on effect in Lebanon, for example 'Sunni sentiments in Lebanon turned from solidarity with the rebels to active participation in the Syrian war'.⁶⁹ Equally, in 2013, Hezbollah 'officially acknowledged its military involvement in Syria, proclaiming the dual objective of backing the Assad regime and repelling radical Islamist forces'.⁷⁰ The actions taken on the border with Syria have significant effects on internal politics in Lebanon.

In the northern and eastern border with Syria, the previously fluid border was quickly transformed into a space of three main concerns: 'territorial control, counterterrorism and migration pressures',⁷¹ thus making border security multilayered and complex. Since 2011, LAF has elevated its political standing in Lebanon through foreign backing in the fight against Da'ish, mainly from the United States and the United Kingdom.⁷² However, as a result of the multi-sectarian institution, 'LAF operates within the consensus of rival political forces and sectarian communities, avoiding actions that could challenge the interest of any particular community'.⁷³ Hezbollah, on the other hand, broadened its focus on the resistance to Israel on the southern border and increasingly became a central part of Lebanese border management.⁷⁴ Hence, order-building and security cooperation between Hezbollah, LAF, the local municipalities and external backers have increased despite deeply dividing opinions on domestic politics and the civil war in Syria.⁷⁵

Increasing border management has resulted in militarization and a zone of indifference. For Agamben the zone of indifference is the result of tensions between *oikos* – the de-politicized family – and the *polis* – the political city.⁷⁶ The utilization of the *oikos* and the *polis* unpacks and underlines the political and confessional challenges in Bekaa Valley. In the Bekaa Valley, *oikos* have become the object of politicization through the manifestation of national, confessional and regional identities, while the *polis* becomes de-politicized and insignificant in the family.[77] This process has had further complications for the ability of the LAF to respond to issues related to Syrian refugees. LAF 'has not only securitized migration but *militarized* the handling of migrants',[78] thus placing oikos at the centre for politics and the creation of *stasis* – civil war – 'best seen as the collapse of the distinction between internal and external, fiend and enemy and *oikos* and *polis*'.[79] As such, the LAF is a structure of the *polis* – one of the only cross-confessional institutions in Lebanon and yet an institution where *stasis* persists due to the sensitive nature of the diverse *oikos* within the organization. Thus, the militarization of border security by the LAF becomes a complex and intrinsic factor that affects the Syrian refugees' quality of life. Adversely, Syrian refugees are confined within their *oikos*, excluded from the *polis* and participation in order-building – left for outside of the ordered space and excluded from law.

Syrian refugees and environmental insecurity in the Bekaa Valley

Syrian refugees in Lebanon have experienced a mixture of reactions and attitudes towards them since the start of the Syrian civil war in 2011. They have been treated with kindness and kinship as well as hostility and disdain due to the precarious political situation and historical context. After the initial stage of the conflict, however, Syrian refugees in Lebanon became increasingly identified as a security threat to the confessional political system like Palestinians during the Lebanese civil war.[80] Equally, increasing pressures for already poverty-stricken Lebanese communities and the lack of funds to aid refugees' needs have led to a broad shift in perceptions of refugees as a direct threat to national security, but also Lebanon's economy and politics.[81] The understanding of refugees as a security threat is reflected within governmental policies and the exclusion from the *polis*. Moreover, '[t]reating Syrians as security threats and stripping them of rights and mobility is an attempt by the Lebanese state to produce a veneer of control over migration into the country'.[82] Lebanese authorities drafted a series of new policies restricting the mobility and the legal status of the refugees on 5 January 2015, thus ending the previous open-door policy.[83] These changes mark a broader change towards securitization of refugees and the border to Syria in the Bekaa Valley and Akkar. The security measures establish the border with Syria as a permanent space of exception, where a series of emergency and last-minute decisions are in place in order to create order and 'safeguard the border'.

The authority's stance on Syrian refugees can be explained through the previous experience with encamped Palestinian refugees and the Palestinian Liberation Organization's (PLO) role during the Lebanese civil war from 1975 to 1990. The conflict 'fuelled resentment within Lebanon against Palestinians and stigmatised the entire Palestinian Community'.[84] As of January 2019, around 180,000 Palestinian refugees[85] are estimated to live in Lebanon, with about 45 per cent living in one of the country's 12 refugee camps.[86] Consequently, 'even before the Syrian Crisis, Lebanon had one of the highest ratios of refugees-to-host population in the world'.[87] As a result, Lebanese authorities has since the 1950s sought restricted mobility of their inhabitants and limit the number of Palestinian refugee camps, which were overcrowded and lacked adequate infrastructures. The permanence of Palestinian refugee camps has created a fear of Syrian refugees staying and adding pressure on the economy, security and the confessional balance in the country.

As of January 2020, Lebanon had more than 910,000 registered Syrian refugees with 37 per cent located in the Bekaa, more than any other region.[88] The number of registered refugees, however, does not reflect the actual number of displaced persons. As of 6 May 2015, UNHCR suspended all registration of refugees as a result of governmental policy.[89] The new measures only include restrictions for Syrian nationals creating a discriminatory practice.[90] As a result, the Lebanese authorities claim that more than 550,000 refugees live in Lebanon unregistered due to the difficulties in gaining and maintaining legal residency.[91]

Lebanon is not a part of the 1951 Convention relating to the Status of Refugees, nor has it had a national policy regarding refugees, even though the country has historically hosted many different groups of refugees – most notably Armenians fleeing genocide in 1915, Palestinians arriving after the 1948 Arab–Israel War, and Iraqis arriving post-2003 invasion. Instead, the country has adopted ad hoc measures towards different groups of refugees thus excluding groups of refugees from the protection of the law. Furthermore, 'Lebanese authorities allegedly insisted upon labelling the Syrians crossing the border as "our brothers and sisters from Syria who are visiting us", but later settled on the more expedient label "displaced Syrians"'.[92] However, the term 'displaced Syrians' is not an officially recognized term within Lebanese law,[93] thus de-politicizing the refugee and the *oikos*. Consequently, the Lebanese authorities have created a framework that has been integrated into the judicial order and appears as 'true state law', without actually being included in law thus creating a space of exception and a binary between inclusion and exclusion within law.

Ad hoc measures limit refugees' mobility and rights. The Lebanese authorities have a formal agreement with the UNHCR, highlighting that refugees must be resettled and cannot remain in Lebanon.[94] Moreover, the Syrian refugees registered with the UNHCR does not have the right to reside or work in Lebanon,[95] and until 2016 refugees registered had to sign a pledge not to work.[96] Syrian refugees also need adequate documentation to enter Lebanon legally, for six months only, but this can be renewed for free for six months, however, after this period all individuals over fifteen years must pay 200 dollars.[97] Although the majority of the refugees cross through official border points, some have not had that opportunity: 'In Bekaa (. . .) some entered illegally in order to avoid the Syrian Army Roadblock'.[98] But even for refugees crossing legally, with all the required documents, the final decision lies with the General Security that can deny the application without a significant cause.[99] These regulations further entrench the marginalization of Syrian refugees as the only other option is a work permit through sponsorship by a Lebanese citizen, 'sponsored refugees have reported being required to submit to exploitative conditions in order to maintain their sponsorship (and hence their legal status)'.[100] Consequently, as Maja Janmyr argues, refugees have two options: 'either they leave the country, if they at all can, or stay and accept exploitation and marginalisation.'[101] The inclusion of human life into politics demonstrates a shift from the refugee as a political being towards what Agamben explains as bare life.

The notion of bare life is further made clear through the notion of non-encampments. Based on the manifestation of Palestinian refugee camps, the Lebanese authorities ruled out the possibility of establishing any formal Syrian refugee camps. At the start of the conflict, Lebanon was praised for its open borders and non-encampments policies, however, as the numbers of refugees grew, and hundreds and thousands lived on insecure informal sights. As a result, the UNHCR expressed a clear wish to set up some formal camps, but this received no consensus by politicians.[102] Because of the lack of designated refugee encampments

> Syrian refugees have been forced to assimilate by moving into preexisting structures in the poorest neighbourhoods in Lebanon. While refugees have been welcomed in some areas, influx of competing ideologies and new ethnic makeup (mainly among Sunni and Shi'ite groups) have begun to cause sporadic infighting.[103]

Refugees tend to get shelter in the most destitute and traditionally peripheral parts of the country, where the host communities often already live in desperate conditions.[104] Therefore, the unequal treatment of Syrian refugees by the international community has created resentful host communities resulting in conflict. This pattern is illustrated in the evacuation of Dier al-Ahmar, an informal refugee camp, on 5 June 2019 when 600 Syrian refugees had to flee immediately after a group of people from the host-community set three tents on fire and bulldozed another two.[105] The displacement of Syrian refugees from Dier al-Ahmar displays the abandonment by the Lebanese authorities, where refugees are put under pressure by the host-community to return to Syria. As such, informal encampments have resulted in close contact between refugees and host-community, thus straining the relationship between them through the competition for resources.

Informal refugee camps have also led to the rise of Syrian strongmen known as 'shawishes'. As noted by Sima Ghaddar, '[t]he State Security agency provides the shawishes with the control they use to exploit camp residents and bully international aid organisations.'[106] With some exceptions, shawishes are associated with exploitation and corruption having the control over the camps and refugees' aid opportunities, but are also defenceless against state authorities by being a Syrian refugee. Moreover, Stel argues that 'while shawishes are not recognised and often denounced by Lebanese state authorities, in practice they appear to be strategically used to control Syrian communities'.[107] Informal control over camp spaces through shawishes by state security agents thus allows for further control over the refugees by limiting their opportunities and access to secure living conditions.

Syrian refugees are not just facing complications with acquiring sufficient living conditions, they are also routinely exposed to curfews and immobilization between checkpoints. After tensions in Arsal in 2014, discriminatory curfews against Syrian refugees are increasingly implemented in some Lebanese towns and villages by police and other groups.[108] In addition, during Covid-19 lockdowns several municipalities introduced discretionary restrictions of movement on Syrian refugees alone. Human Rights Watch reported that at least eighteen municipalities in Bekaa Valley have restrictions or curfews that only target the refugee population, adding that 'the restrictions on Syrians exceeded those that the government has imposed on the general population'.[109] Furthermore, the fear of arrest and detention between formal and informal checkpoints by various security forces is high in Syrian refugee communities. Data from UNHCR found that Syrian refugees in the Bekaa Valley reported to have little freedom of movement, with 67 per cent stating this was due to checkpoints.[110] The shifting policies creates detention-like conditions for refugees, and 'the fear and anxiety brought on by their undocumented status impact the social and economic presents and futures of Syrians, especially those who come from poorer segments of society'.[111] The implementation of discriminatory and irregular curfews and checkpoints further manifests the marginalization of Syrian refugees. The life of many Syrian refugees is subjected to laws and regulations that have become included in Lebanese authorities' calculations and mechanisms of power, thus establishing biopolitics as a nucleus of sovereign power in the Bekaa Valley.

In recent years Lebanon has been increasingly difficult to live in. The country has endured Covid-19, the collapse of its currency and the large Beirut port explosion. The situation has impacted all inhabitants in Lebanon, especially the vulnerable households. Some Lebanese politicians have wrongfully blamed Syrian refugees for Lebanon's economic failures and have argued that they 'steal' Lebanese jobs.[112] The scapegoating of refugees and discrimination by some of the political leadership has been used to camouflage the failures of economic policies and corruption. To make matters worse, many refugees have lost their seasonal work due to Covid-19 and the financial crisis. The increasing political and economic hardships have made it harder for refugees to live in Lebanon, with their lives heavily regulated.

Winter in the Bekaa Valley

The environment in the Bekaa Valley varies; despite the high altitude it is hot and dry in summer, and in winter it is cold, windy, rainy and sometimes below freezing. Consequently, the refugees in the Bekaa Valley have experienced considerable weather variations. In summer, 80 per cent of the inhabitants of the Bekaa Valley experience diminished water supply, although water supply is at a deficit throughout the year.[113] Furthermore, Syrian refugees are often scapegoated for the water shortages, even though water supply was low before the arrival of the refugees in 2011.[114] In winter, Syrian refugees face a cold climate with a myriad of different obstacles which this section seeks to unpack.

The Bekaa Valley experiences yearly storms that includes everything from flooding, heavy snowfall to extreme winds. Since 2011, Syrian refugees have experienced yearly storms that have further diminished their quality of life. During Storm Karim in February 2020, Arsal was experiencing temperatures of −10 Celsius, and access was blocked due to snow, leaving the inhabitants without vital supply, including fuel, drinking water and food.[115] In order to stay warm, refugees were buying faulty nappies from a diaper factory in the area in order to heat their homes, the diapers being significantly cheaper.[116] The year before, Storm Norma resulted in several days of high wind, flooding and heavy snow, directly affecting more than 11,000 refugees and displacing more than 600 refugees in the Bekaa Valley.[117] In one settlement in Arsal, refugees had to burn clothes in order to stay warm.[118] Furthermore, in the north of the Bekaa Valley an eight-year-old child passed away after falling into a river during the storm.[119]

However, snow, high winds and flooding only reflect some of the obstacles that refugees are facing during winter storms. Landslides can also be triggered by winter storms in the Bekaa Valley. Individual risk to landslides is nine to eleven times greater among refugees based at the foothills of the Anti-Lebanon mountain range, due to 'complex marginalization on economic, social, and policy levels which force refugees to live in substandard shelters'.[120]

The Vulnerability Assessment for Syrian Refugees in Lebanon (VASyR) found that 55 per cent and 44 per cent of Syrian refugees in the governorates of Bekaa and Baalbek-El Hermel live in 'non-permanent' structures including tents and prefab units.[121] In the summer of 2019 local authorities and LAF sought to demolish and remove semi-permanent structures, creating incentive for refugees to go back to Syria, using largely unenforced housing codes in order to legally demolish these structures.[122] The LAF further threatened to demolish 5,000 solid refugee shelters, possibly placing more than 250,000 people at risk of being made homeless.[123] The local authorities gave the Syrian refugees until July 2019 to demolish their own homes or face demolition and loss of their property, leading to refugees tearing down their own homes in fear of the repercussions.[124] On 1 July 2019, LAF bulldozed 20 homes in Arsal, northern Bekaa, and since then 1,968 out of 2,500 homes had been taken down.[125] The demolition of these shelters significantly diminishes the refugee household's capability to withstand the harsh winter conditions in Arsal.[126] As argued by NGOs like Human Rights Watch,[127] Amnesty International[128] and the Norwegian Refugee Council,[129] ad hoc policies are just another piece in a broader attempt to encourage refugees to move on or return to Syria.

Consequently, Lebanese authority has moved beyond abandonment and are seeking to regulate the situation by utilizing the harsh winters in order to pressure refugees back to Syria. The refugees living in Bekaa Valley have been forced to demolish their concrete homes and rebuild them with wood and plastic in order to fulfil the building requirements.[130] The demolitions have meant that many refugees did not have adequate shelter during the following winter, when some Syrian refugees faced a colder and wetter winter than previously, especially during Storm Karim.[131] As a result, Lebanese authorities are capitalizing on environmental inequalities and *bare life* is further segmented.

The demolition of homes has increased the pressure for refugees to return to Syria; however, 'the decision to cross the border is irreversible for most and the consequences can be grave. They (the Syrian refugees) carefully weigh their difficult, often desperate situation in Lebanon against the hazards that may await them on the other side. Threats of detention and conscription weigh most heavily.'[132] On the other hand, the decision to relocate within Lebanon also holds significant risk. Crossing checkpoints without valid residency can lead to harassment and temporary detention, and, therefore, some refugees are unable to leave their local area and even more unlikely the Bekaa Valley.[133] The barriers to movement between cities and across borders show the limitations of the refugees. Their agency and power ultimately weakened by the order-building and power of hybrid sovereignties.

Conclusion

In this chapter I have introduced the ideas of Agamben as a means of understanding the relationship between mass displacement, sovereign power and environmental insecurity in the Bekaa Valley. On the one hand, it has demonstrated how border management and security have affected the Syrian refugees. Through the application of ad hoc measures in order to limit refugees' rights, Lebanese authorities are regulating the movement and the status of Syrian refugees. The status as 'displayed Syrians' does not give the refugee the right to work or stay in Lebanon reinforcing the agreement that refugees must be settled and cannot remain in Lebanon. Refugees in Lebanon are subjected to laws and regulations that have become integrated into the calculations and mechanisms of power, including curfews, checkpoints and restrictions on work.

On the other hand, this chapter has explicitly determined how LAF and local authorities have utilized 'housing regulations' in order to regulate the life of the refugees. Furthermore, Lebanese authorities sought to incentivize refugees to return to 'safe areas' in Syria. However, the demolition of almost 2,000 substandard homes did not make many Syrian refugees return, but rather left a group of refugees at increased risk over the winter months. As such, Syrian refugees have been exposed to legislations that have never been enforced but have been discriminatorily used against them. The Syrian refugee does not have the same right as the ordinary inhabitant and is therefore *doomed to death* over the cold winter months, thereupon establishing biopolitics – the inclusion of man into politics – as the nucleus of sovereign power in Bekaa Valley.

This chapter calls for a better understanding on how authorities capitalize on environmental insecurities and how sovereign entities are producing bare life or *dooming life to death*. The sovereign is the main force that deals with the response and consequences of extreme weather events, and as a result environmental inequality is a factor that can contribute to bare life. In the Bekaa Valley, the rising importance of sovereign actors in border areas has created a militarization of border politics and politicization of environmental challenges that discriminate against Syrian refugees.

Notes

1. Sorin Furcoi and Farah Najjar, 'Lebanon's Syrian Refugee Camps Battered by Winter Storms', *Al Jazeera*, 15 January 2019. Available online: https://www.aljazeera.com/indepth/inpictures/lebanon-syrian-refugee-camps-battered-winter-storms-190114210329942.html; Edith Champagne and Houssam Hariri, 'Storm Flooding Brings Misery to Syrians in Lebanon', *UNHCR*, 11 January 2019. Available online: https://www.unhcr.org/uk/news/latest/2019/1/5c386d6d4/storm-flooding-brings-misery-syrian-refugees-lebanon.html.''
2. Romola Sanyal, 'Managing through Ad Hoc Measures: Syrian Refugees and the Politics of Waiting in Lebanon', *Political Geography* 66 (2018); 'Calling on Lebanese Authorities to Stop the Demolition of Refugees Homes', *Norwegian Refugee Council*, 9 August 2019. Available online: https://www.nrc.no/news/2019/august2/calling-on-lebanese-authorities-to-stop-the-demolition-of-refugees-homes/.
3. Simone Tholens, 'Border Management in an Era of "Statebuilding Lite": Security Assistance and Lebanon's Hybrid Security', *International Affairs* 93, no. 4 (2017); Tamirace Fakhoury, 'Governance Strategies and Refugee Response: Lebanon in the Face of Syrian Displacement', *International Journal of Middle East Studies* 49 (2017); Bassel F. Salloukh, 'The Syrian War: Spillover Effects on Lebanon', *Middle East Policy* XXIV, no. 1 (2017).
4. Giorgio Agamben, *State of Exception* (Chicago: Chicago University Press, 2005).
5. Giorgio Agamben, *Homo Sacer: Sovereign Power and Bare Life* (Sandford: Sandford University Press, 1998).
6. Giorgio Agamben, *Stasis: Civil War as a Paradigm* (Edinburgh: Edinburgh University Press, 2015).
7. 'Bekaa (Zahle)', *UNHCR*, 10 March 2020. Available online: https://www.unhcr.org/lb/bekaa-zahle.
8. Almost 9,460 Palestinian refugees registered in Wavel camp as of 2018, but this figure does not reflect the actual number as UNEWA does not track habitual movements. 'Wavel Camp', *UNEWA*, 10 March 2020. Available online: https://www.unrwa.org/where-we-work/lebanon/wavel-camp.
9. See Daniel Meier, 'Lebanon: The Refugee Issue and the Threat of a Sectarian Confrontation', *Oriente Moderno* 94, no. 2 (2014).
10. Stefan Winter, *The Shiites of Lebanon under Ottoman rule 1516-1788* (Cambridge: Cambridge University Press, 2010), 43.
11. Dorte Verner, David R. Lee, Maximillian Ashwill and Robert Wilby, *Increasing Resilience to Climate Change in the Agricultural Sector of the Middle East: The Case of Jordan and Lebanon* (Washington: The World Bank, 2013), xvii.
12. 'Environmental security frequently refers to the discussions about the risk of environmental change causing armed conflict, but also refers to assumptions about resource management strategies.' See Simon Dalby, 'Environmental Change', in *Security Studies: An Introduction*, ed. Paul D. Williams and Matt McDonald (Oxon, NY: Routledge, 2018), 531.
13. 'All international migration can be divided into two categories on the basis of the motivation behind the migration: involuntary and forced (. . .). Involuntary or

forced international migration refers essentially to refugee flows, where for reasons of natural disasters, war, civil war, religious or political persecution people are forced to flee their homes.' See Phil Williams, 'Migration and Refugees', in *Security Studies: An Introduction*, ed. Paul D. Williams and Matt McDonald (Oxon, NY: Routledge, 2018), 485.

14 Noemi Gal-Or, 'Suspending Sovereignty: Reassessing the Interlocking of Occupation, Failed and Fragile State, Responsibility to Protect and International Trusteeship (Lessons from Lebanon)', *Israel Law Review* 41 (2008); Boaz Atzili, 'State Weakness and "Vacuum of Power" in Lebanon', *Studies in Conflict & Terrorism* 33, no. 8 (2010); Benjamin Miller, 'Between the Revisionist and the Frontier State: Regional Variations in State War-Propensity', *Review of International Studies* 35 (2009).

15 Sara Fregonese, 'Beyond the "Weak State": Hybrid Sovereignty in Beirut', *Environment and Planning D: Society and Space* 30 (2013): 656.

16 See Fregonese, 'Beyond the "Weak State"'. This type of hybrid sovereignty is not to be confused with Gokham Bacik's idea of 'hybrid sovereignty', which is used to describe the clash of de jure and de facto sovereignty that results in the failures within Arab political system. See also Gokham Bacik, *Hybrid Sovereignty in the Arab Middle East* (New York: Palgrave Macmillan, 2008); and Najib B. Hourani, 'Post-Conflict Reconstruction and Citizenship Agendas: Lessons from Beirut', *Citizenship Studies* 19, no. 2 (2015).

17 Waleed Hazbun, 'Assembling Security in a "Weak State": The Contentious Politics of Plural Governance in Lebanon since 2005', *Third World Quarterly* 37, no. 6 (2016).

18 Tholens, 'Border Management in an Era of "Statebuilding Lite"', 866.

19 Ibid., 882.

20 Giorgio Agamben, *Homo Sacer*, 119.

21 See Hannah Arendt, *The Origins of Totalitarianism* (New York: Schocken, 1951).

22 Agamben, *Homo Sacer*, 120.

23 Agamben, *State of Exception*, 1.

24 Zygmunt Bauman, *Wasted Lives: Modernity and Its Outcasts* (Cambridge: Polity Press, 2004), 32.

25 Nora Stel, *Hybrid Political Order and the Politics of Uncertainty: Refugee Governance in Lebanon* (Oxon, NY: Routledge, 2021), chapter 4; Adam Ramadan, 'Destroying Nahr el-Bared: Sovereignty and Urbicide in the Space of Exception', *Political Geography* 28 (2009); and Sari Hanafi and Taylor Long 'Governance, Governmentalities, and the State of Exception in the Palestinian Refugee Camps of Lebanon', *Journal of Refugee Studies* (2010).

26 Stel, *Hybrid Political Order and the Politics of Uncertainty*, 145.

27 See also Ibid.

28 Human Rights Watch. *'Our Homes Are Not for Strangers': Mass Evictions of Syrian Refugees by Lebanese Municipalities* (USA: Human Rights Watch, 2018), 38, 28.

29 Agamben, *State of Exception*, 26.

30 Ibid., 6.

31 Maja Janmyr, 'UNHCR and the Syrian Refugee Response: Negotiating Status and Registration in Lebanon', *The International Journal of Human Rights* 22, no. 3 (2017): 398.

32 Agamben, *Homo Sacer*.

33 Ibid., 170.

34 Giorgio Agamben, *Means without End: Notes on Politics* (Minneapolis: Stanford University Press, 1995), 22.
35 Agamben, *Homo Sacer*, 83.
36 Agamben, *Means without End*, 39.
37 See Nick Dines, Nicola Montagna and Vincenzo Ruggiero, 'Thinking Lampedusa: Border Construction, the Spectacle of Bare Life and the Productivity of Migrants', *Ethnic and Racial Studies* 38, no. 3 (2014).
38 See Hosna J. Shewly, 'Abandoned Spaces and Bare Life in the Enclaves of the India-Bangladesh Border', *Political Geography* 32 (2012); Reece Jones, 'Agents of Exception: Border Security and the Marginalization of Muslims in India', *Environment and Planning D: Society and Space* 27, no. 5 (2009).
39 See Lana Zannettino, 'From Auschwitz to Mandatory Detention: Biopolitics, Race, and Human Rights in the Australian Refugee Camp', *The International Journal of Human Rights* 16, no. 7 (2012).
40 See E. K. Richard, 'Giorgio Agamben and the Spatiality of the Camp: An Introduction', *Geografiska Annaler: Series B* 88, no. 4 (2006); Ramadan, 'Destroying Nahr el-Bared'; Hanafi and Long, 'Governance, Governmentalities, and the State of Exception'.
41 Ramadan and Fregonese, 'Hybrid Sovereignty and the State of Exception in the Palestinian Refugee Camps in Lebanon'.
42 Jones, 'Agents of Exception', 880.
43 Ibid., 882.
44 Mark B. Salter, 'When the Exception Becomes the Rule: Borders, Sovereignty and Citizenship', *Citizenship Studies* 12, no. 4 (2008): 377.
45 See Jones, 'Agents of Exception'.
46 See Fregonese, 'Beyond the "Weak State"'.
47 Mark B. Salter, 'The Global Visa Regime and the Political Technologies of the International Self: Borders, Bodies, Biopolitics', *Alternatives: Global, Local, Political* 31, no. 2 (2006): 171.
48 Hanafi and Long, 'Governance, Governmentalities, and the State of Exception', 147.
49 Barry Buzan, *People, States and Fear: An Agenda for International Security Studies in the Post-Cold War Era* (Colchester: ECPR, 2016).
50 Phil, 'Migration and Refugee', 485.
51 Thomas F. Homer-Dixon, *Environment, Scarcity and Violence* (Princeton, NJ: Princeton University Press, 1999).
52 Dalby, 'Environmental Change', 531.
53 Mick Smith, 'Against Ecological Sovereignty: Agamben, Politics and Globalisation', *Environmental Politics* 18, no. 1 (2009): 109.
54 Ibid., 110.
55 See Thomas L. Weiss and Juan D. Reyes, 'Breaking the Cycle of Violence: Understanding the Links between Environment, Migration and Conflict in the Greater Horn of Africa', in *Horn of Africa and Peace: The Role of the Environment*, ed. Ulf Johansson Dahre (Lund: Media-tryck, 2009).
56 Dawn Chatty, Nisrine Mansour and Nasser Yassin, 'Statelessness and Tribal Identity on Lebanon's Eastern Borders', *Mediterranean Politics* 18, no. 3 (2013): 411.
57 See Chatty, Mansour and Yassin, 'Statelessness and Tribal Identity on Lebanon's Eastern Borders', 412.
58 William Young et al., *Spillover from the Conflict in Syria* (RAND Corporation, 2014).

59 Grand Lebanon defined as Mount Lebanon and the inclusion of coastal cities (Tyre, Sidon, Beirut and Tripoli) and interior-rural areas (Bekaa, Jabal Amel and Akkar), see Nasser Yassin, 'Beirut', *Cities* 29 (2012): 67.
60 Chatty, Mansour and Yassin, 'Statelessness and Tribal Identity on Lebanon's Eastern Borders', 412.
61 Fakhoury, 'Governance Strategies and Refugee Response', 683; Daniel Masterson and M. Christian Lehmann, 'Refugees, Mobilisation, and Humanitarian Aid: Evidence from the Syrian Refugee Crisis in Lebanon', *Journal of Conflict Resolution* (2019): 7.
62 Michelle Obeid, 'Searching for the "Ideal Face of the State" in a Lebanese Border Town', *Journal of the Royal Anthropological Institute* 16 (2010): 336.
63 Tholens, 'Border Management in an Era of "Statebuilding Lite"', 871.
64 John Nagle, 'The Biopolitics of Victim Construction, Elision and Contestation in Northern Ireland and Lebanon', *Peacebuilding* (2019): 11.
65 Hannes Baumann, 'Social Protest and the Political Economy of Sectarianism in Lebanon', *Global Discourse* 6, no. 4 (2016).
66 Salloukh, 'The Syrian War', 62.
67 Obeid, 'Searching for the "Ideal Face of the State"', '336.
68 William Young et al., *Spillover from the Conflict in Syria* (RAND Corporation, 2014), 31.
69 Salloukh, 'The Syrian War', 69.
70 Fakhoury, 'Governance Strategies and Refugee Response', 685.
71 Tholens, 'Border Management in an Era of "Statebuilding Lite"', 872.
72 Ibid., 873.
73 Hazbun, 'Assembling Security in a "Weak State"', 1056.
74 Ibid., 1054.
75 Ibid., 1055.
76 Agamben, *Stasis*, 12.
77 Simon Mabon and Ana Maria Kumarasamy, 'Da'ish, Stasis and Bare Life in Iraq', in *Iraq after ISIS*, ed. Jacob Eriksson and Ahmed Kahleel (Cham: Palgrave Macmillan, 2019).
78 Tholens, 'Border Management in an Era of "Statebuilding Lite"', 875.
79 Mabon and Kumarasamy', Da'ish, Stasis and Bare Life in Iraq', 11.
80 Meier, 'Lebanon', 383.
81 Tholens, 'Border Management in an Era of "Statebuilding Lite"', 675.
82 Sanyal, 'Managing through Ad Hoc Measures', 72.
83 Ibid., 67.
84 Ninette Kelley, 'Responding to a Refugee Influx: Lessons from Lebanon', *Journal on Migration and Human Security* 5, no. 1 (2017): 83.
85 This number includes 29,000 Palestinian refugees who fled from Syria to Lebanon at the start of the Syrian civil war in 2011.
86 'Lebanon', *UNRWA*, 19 January 2020. Available online: https://www.unrwa.org/where-we-work/lebanon.
87 Are, J. Knudsen, 'Camp, Getto, *Zinco*, Slum: Lebanon's Transnational Zones of Emplacement', *Humanity: An International Journal of Human Rights Humanitarianism and Development* 7, no. 3 (2016): 445.
88 'Syria Regional Refugee Response', *UNHCR*, 31 January 2020. Available online: https://data2.unhcr.org/en/situations/syria/location/71.
89 Ibid.

90   Maja Janmyr, 'Precarity in Exile: The Legal Status of Syrian Refugees in Lebanon', *Refugee Survey Quarterly* 35 (2016): 66.
91   'Lebanon: Wave of Hostility Exposes Hollowness of Claims that Syrian Refugee Returns Are Voluntary', Amnesty International, 12 June 2019. Available online: https://www.amnesty.org/en/latest/news/2019/06/lebanon-wave-of-hostility-exposes-hollowness-of-claims-that-syrian-refugee-returns-are-voluntary/.
92   Maja Janmyr, 'UNHCR and the Syrian Refugee Response', 398.
93   Hala Naufal, *Syrian Refugees in Lebanon: The Humanitarian Approach under Political Divisions*, (Migration Policy Centre, 2012), 12. Available online: https://cadmus.eui.eu/bitstream/handle/1814/24835/MPC_RR2012-13.pdf?sequence=1&isAllowed=y.
94   Sarah Bindinger et al., *Protecting Syrian Refugees: Laws, Policies, and Global Responsibility Sharing* (Boston: International Human Rights Clinic, 2015), 29. Available online: https://www.bu.edu/law/files/2015/08/syrianrefugees.pdf.
95   'Background Paper on Unregistered Syrian Refugees in Lebanon', *Lebanon Humanitarian INGO Forum*, July 2014, 2. Available online: http://lhif.org/uploaded/News/d92fe3a1b1dd46f2a281254fa551bd09LHIF%20Background%20Paper%20on%20Unregistered%20Syrian%20Refugees%20(FINAL).pdf.
96   Amy Keith and Nour Shawaf, 'When Is Return Voluntary? Conditions of Asylum in Lebanon', *Syrians in Displacement* (2018): 63.
97   'Background Paper on Unregistered Syrian Refugees in Lebanon'.
98   Naufal, *Syrian Refugees in Lebanon: The Humanitarian Approach under Political Divisions*.
99   'Background Paper on Unregistered Syrian Refugees in Lebanon'.
100 Keith and Shawaf, 'When Is Return Voluntary?' 63.
101 Maja Janmyr, 'Precarity in Exile', 78.
102 Kelley, 'Responding to a Refugee Influx', 84.
103 William Young et al., *Spillover from the Conflict in Syria*, 28.
104 *Too Close for Comfort: Syrians in Lebanon*, International Crisis Group (Brussels: May 2013), 9. Available online: http://www.operationspaix.net/DATA/DOCUMENT/7965~v~Too_Close__For_Comfort__Syrians_in_Lebanon_Middle_East_Report_N141.pdf.
105 'Lebanon' Amnesty International; Anchal Vohra, 'Lebanon's Dier al-Ahmar', '*Al Jazeera*, 9 June 2019. Available online: https://www.aljazeera.com/news/2019/06/lebanon-deir-al-ahma-incident-displaced-600-refugees-190609095940222.html.
106 Sima Ghaddar, 'Lebanon Treats Refugees as a Security Problem – and It Doesn't Work', *The Century Foundation*, 4 April 2017. Available online: https://tcf.org/content/commentary/lebanon-treats-refugees-security-problem-doesnt-work/.
107 Stel, *Hybrid Political Order and the Politics of Uncertainty*, 93.
108 'Lebanon "Imposes Curfews on Syrian Refugees"', *BBC*, 3 October 2014. Available online: https://www.bbc.co.uk/news/world-middle-east-29484662.
109 'Lebanon: Refugees at Risk in Covid-19 Response', *Human Rights Watch*, 2 April 2020. Available online: https://www.hrw.org/news/2020/04/02/lebanon-refugees-risk-covid-19-response.
110 'The Consequences of Limited Legal Status for Syrian Refugees in Lebanon', *Norwegian Refugee Council*, Lebanon, April 2014, 15. Available online: https://data2.unhcr.org/en/documents/download/40323.
111 Sanyal, 'Managing through Ad Hoc Measures', 72.
112 Kareem Chehayeb, 'Anti-Syrian Refugee Sentiment Ramps Up in Increasingly Hostile Lebanon', *Middle East Eye*, 14 June 2019. Available online: https://www

.middleeasteye.net/news/anti-syrian-refugee-sentiment-ramps-increasingly-unwelcome-lebanon.

113 Diane Machayekhi, Michele Perpaoli and Georgio Cancelliere, 'Domestic Water in Bekaa Valley, Lebanon Demand, Access and Institutional Aspects', *International Institute for Environment and Development* (2017), 20.

114 Anne Marie Baylouny and Stephen J. Klingseis, 'Water Thieves or Political Catalysts? Syrian Refugees in Jordan and Lebanon', *Middle East Policy* XXV, no. 1 (2018).

115 'Lebanon: 30,000 Syrian Refugees Affected by Snowstorm Karim', *Action Against Hunger*, 13 February 2020. Available online: https://www.actionagainsthunger.org/story/lebanon-30000-syrian-refugees-affected-snowstorm-karim.

116 'Syrian Refugees in Lebanon, Jordan Try to Stay Warm', *Al Jazeera*, 12 January 2020. Available online: https://www.aljazeera.com/news/2020/01/syrian-refugees-lebanon-jordan-stay-warm-200112152014227.html.

117 Champagne and Hariri, 'Storm Flooding Brings Misery to Syrians in Lebanon'.

118 Richard Hall, 'Eight-Year-Old Girl Dies as Devastating Storm Piles Misery on Syrian Refugees in Lebanon', *Independent*, 9 January 2019. Available online: https://www.independent.co.uk/news/world/middle-east/lebanon-storm-weather-winter-syria-refugee-girl-death-norma-a8719776.html.

119 Ibid.

120 William Pollock et al., 'Risk at the Margins: A Natural Hazards Perspective on the Syrian Refugee Crisis in Lebanon', *International Journal of Disaster Risk Reduction* 36 (2019): 9.

121 Vulnerability Assessment for Syrian Refugees in Lebanon, *(VASyR), UNICEF, UNHCR, and WFP* (2020), 43. Available online: https://reliefweb.int/sites/reliefweb.int/files/resources/VASyR%202020.pdf.

122 'Lebanon: Syrian Refugee Shelters Demolished', *Human Rights Watch*, 5 July 2019. Available online: https://www.hrw.org/news/2019/07/05/lebanon-syrian-refugee-shelters-demolished.

123 Richard Hall, 'Syrian Refugees in Lebanon Tear Down Walls to Keep Their Homes', *Independent*, 13 June 2019. Available online: https://www.independent.co.uk/news/world/middle-east/syria-refugee-crisis-lebanon-arsal-border-middle-east-war-a8956646.html.

124 Zeina Khodr, 'Lebanon Asks Syrian Refugees to Demolish Their Houses', *Al Jazeera*, 13 June 2019. Available online: https://www.aljazeera.com/news/2019/06/lebanon-asks-syrian-refugees-demolish-houses-190613120214474.html; Hall, 'Syrian Refugees in Lebanon Tear Down Walls to Keep Their Homes'.

125 'Calling on Lebanese Authorities', *Norwegian Refugee Council*.

126 'Lebanon: Syrian Refugee Shelters Demolished', *Human Rights Watch*.

127 Ibid.

128 'Lebanon: Wave of Hostility', *Amnesty International*.

129 'Calling on Lebanese Authorities', *Norwegian Refugee Council*.

130 Hall, 'Syrian Refugees in Lebanon Tear Down Walls to Keep Their Homes'.

131 Racha El Doai, 'Surviving Winter in a Tented Settlement', *Norwegian Refugee Council*, 7 February 2020. Available online: https://www.nrc.no/perspectives/2020/surviving-winter-in-a-tented-settlement/.

132 'Easing Syrian Refugees' Plight in Lebanon, *International Crisis Group*', Brussels, 13 February 2020, i. Available online: https://d2071andvip0wj.cloudfront.net/211-easing-syrian-refugees-plight-in-lebanon.pdf.

133 'The Consequences of Limited Legal Status for Syrian Refugees in Lebanon, Norwegian Refugee Council', Lebanon, April 2014, 15. Available online: https://data2.unhcr.org/en/documents/download/40323.

References

Action Against Hunger. 'Lebanon: 30,000 Syrian Refugees Affected by Snowstorm Karim'. Available online: https://www.actionagainsthunger.org/story/lebanon-30000-syrian-refugees-affected-snowstorm-karim (accessed 13 February 2020).
Agamben, Giorgio. *Homo Sacer: Sovereign Power and Bare Life*. Sandford: Sandford University Press, 1998.
Agamben, Giorgio. *Means without End: Notes on Politics*. Minneapolis: Stanford University Press, 1995.
Agamben, Giorgio. *Stasis: Civil War as a Paradigm*. Edinburgh: Edinburgh University Press, 2015.
Agamben, Giorgio *State of Exception*. Chicago: Chicago University Press, 2005.
Al Jazeera. 'Syrian Refugees in Lebanon, Jordan Try to Stay Warm'. Available online: https://www.aljazeera.com/news/2020/01/syrian-refugees-lebanon-jordan-stay-warm-200112152014227.html (accessed 12 January 2020).
Amnesty International. 'Lebanon: Wave of Hostility Exposes Hollowness of Claims That Syrian Refugee Returns Are Voluntary'. Available online: https://www.amnesty.org/en/latest/news/2019/06/lebanon-wave-of-hostility-exposes-hollowness-of-claims-that-syrian-refugee-returns-are-voluntary/ (accessed 12 June 2019).
Arendt, Hannah. *The Origins of Totalitarianism*. New York: Schocken, 1951.
Atzili, Boaz. 'State Weakness and "Vacuum of Power" in Lebanon'. *Studies in Conflict & Terrorism* 33, no. 8 (2010): 757–82.
Bacik, Gokham. *Hybrid Sovereignty in the Arab Middle East*. New York: Palgrave Macmillan, 2008.
Bauman, Zygmunt. *Wasted Lives: Modernity and Its Outcasts*. Cambridge: Polity Press, 2004.
Baumann, Hannes. 'Social Protest and the Political Economy of Sectarianism in Lebanon'. *Global Discourse* 6, no. 4 (2016): 634–49.
Baylouny, Anne Marie and Stephen J. Klingseis. 'Water Thieves or Political Catalysts? Syrian Refugees in Jordan and Lebanon'. *Middle East Policy* XXV, no. 1 (2018): 104–23.
BBC. 'Lebanon "Imposes Curfews on Syrian Refugees"'. Available online: https://www.bbc.co.uk/news/world-middle-east-29484662 (accessed 3 October 2014).
Bindinger, Sarah, Aaron Lang, Danielle Hites, Yoana Kuzova and Elena Noureddine. 'Protecting Syrian Refugees: Laws, Policies, and Global Responsibility Sharing'. International Human Rights Clinic: Boston, 2015. Available online: https://www.bu.edu/law/files/2015/08/syrianrefugees.pdf.
Buzan, Barry. *People, States and Fear: An Agenda for International Security Studies in the Post-Cold War Era*. Colchester: ECPR, 2016.
Champagne, Edith and Houssam Hariri. 'Storm Flooding Brings Misery to Syrians in Lebanon'. *UNHCR*, 11 January 2019. Available online: https://www.unhcr.org/uk/news/latest/2019/1/5c386d6d4/storm-flooding-brings-misery-syrian-refugees-lebanon.html.
Chatty, Dawn, Nisrine Mansour and Nasser Yassin. 'Statelessness and Tribal Identity on Lebanon's Eastern Borders'. *Mediterranean Politics* 18, no. 3 (2013): 411–26.

Chehayeb, Kareem 'Anti-Syrian Refugee Sentiment Ramps Up in Increasingly Hostile Lebanon'. *Middle East Eye*, 14 June 2019. Available online: https://www.middleeasteye.net/news/anti-syrian-refugee-sentiment-ramps-increasingly-unwelcome-lebanon.

Dalby, Simon. 'Environmental Change'. In *Security Studies: An Introduction*, edited by Paul D. Williams and Matt McDonald, 526–41. Oxon, NY: Routledge, 2018.

Dines, Nick, Nicola Montagna and Vincenzo Ruggiero. 'Thinking Lampedusa: Border Construction, the Spectacle of Bare Life and the Productivity of Migrants'. *Ethnic and Racial Studies* 38, no. 3 (2014): 430–45.

Doai, Racha El. 'Surviving Winter in a Tented Settlement'. *Norwegian Refugee Council*, 7 February 2020. Available online: https://www.nrc.no/perspectives/2020/surviving-winter-in-a-tented-settlement/.

Ek, Richard. 'Giorgio Agamben and the Spatiality of the Camp: An Introduction'. *Geografiska Annaler: Series B* 88, no. 4 (2006): 363–86.

Fakhoury, Tamirace. 'Governance Strategies and Refugee Response: Lebanon in the Face of Syrian Displacement'. *International Journal of Middle East Studies* 49 (2017): 681–700.

Fregonese, Sara. 'Beyond the "Weak State": Hybrid Sovereignty in Beirut'. *Environment and Planning D: Society and Space* 30 (2013): 655–74.

Furcoi, Sorin and Farah Najjar. 'Lebanon's Syrian Refugee Camps Battered by Winter Storms'. *Al Jazeera*, 15 January 2019. Available online: https://www.aljazeera.com/indepth/inpictures/lebanon-syrian-refugee-camps-battered-winter-storms-190114210329942.html.

Gal-Or, Noemi. 'Suspending Sovereignty: Reassessing the Interlocking of Occupation, Failed and Fragile State, Responsibility to Protect and International Trusteeship (Lessons from Lebanon)'. *Israel Law Review* 41 (2008): 302–30.

Ghaddar, Sima. 'Lebanon Treats Refugees as a Security Problem – and It Doesn't Work'. *The Century Foundation*, 4 April 2017. Available online: https://tcf.org/content/commentary/lebanon-treats-refugees-security-problem-doesnt-work/.

Hall, Richard. 'Syrian Refugees in Lebanon Tear Down Walls to Keep Their Homes'. *Independent*, 13 June 2019. Available online: https://www.independent.co.uk/news/world/middle-east/syria-refugee-crisis-lebanon-arsal-border-middle-east-war-a8956646.html.

Hall, Richard. 'Eight-Year-Old Girl Dies as Devastating Storm Piles Misery on Syrian Refugees in Lebanon'. *Independent*, 9 January 2019. Available online: https://www.independent.co.uk/news/world/middle-east/lebanon-storm-weather-winter-syria-refugee-girl-death-norma-a8719776.html.

Hanafi, Sari. and Taylor Long. 'Governance, Governmentalities, and the State of Exception in the Palestinian Refugee Camps of Lebanon'. *Journal of Refugee Studies* 23, Issue 2 (2010): 134–59.

Hazbun, Waleed. 'Assembling Security in a 'Weak State:' The Contentious Politics of Plural Governance in Lebanon since 2005'. *Third World Quarterly* 37, no. 6 (2016): 1053–70.

Homer-Dixon, Thomas F. *Environment, Scarcity and Violence*. Princeton, NJ: Princeton University Press, 1999.

Hourani, Najib B. 'Post-Conflict Reconstruction and Citizenship Agendas: Lessons from Beirut'. *Citizenship Studies* 19, no. 2 (2015): 184–99.

Human Rights Watch. 'Lebanon: Refugees at Risk in Covid-19 Response'. 2 April 2020. Available online: https://www.hrw.org/news/2020/04/02/lebanon-refugees-risk-covid-19-response

Human Rights Watch. 'Lebanon: Syrian Refugee Shelters Demolished'. 5 July 2019. Available online: https://www.hrw.org/news/2019/07/05/lebanon-syrian-refugee-shelters-demolished.
Human Rights Watch. *'Our Homes Are Not for Strangers': Mass Evictions of Syrian Refugees by Lebanese Municipalities*. USA: Human Rights Watch, 2018.
International Crisis Group. 'Easing Syrian Refugees' Plight in Lebanon'. *Brussels*, 13 February 2020. Available online: https://d2071andvip0wj.cloudfront.net/211-easing-syrian-refugees-plight-in-lebanon.pdf.
International Crisis Group. 'Too Close for Comfort: Syrians in Lebanon'. *Brussels*, May 2013. Available online: http://www.operationspaix.net/DATA/DOCUMENT/7965~v~Too_Close__For_Comfort__Syrians_in_Lebanon_Middle_East_Report_N141.pdf.
Keith, Amy and Nour Shawaf. 'When is Return Voluntary? Conditions of Asylum in Lebanon'. *Syrians in Displacement* 57 (2018): 62–3.
Kelley, Ninette. 'Responding to a Refugee Influx: Lessons from Lebanon'. *Journal on Migration and Human Security* 5, no. 1 (2017): 82–104.
Knudsen, Are J. 'Camp, Getto, *Zinco*, Slum: Lebanon's Transnational Zones of Emplacement'. *Humanity: An International Journal of Human Rights Humanitarianism and Development* 7, no. 3 (2016): 443–57.
Knutsson, Beniamin. 'Responsible Risk Taking: The Neoliberal Biopolitics of People Living with HIV/AIDS in Rwanda'. *Development and Change* 47, no. 4 (2016): 615–39.
Khodr, Zeina. 'Lebanon Asks Syrian Refugees to Demolish Their Houses'. *Al Jazeera*, 13 June 2019. Available online: https://www.aljazeera.com/news/2019/06/lebanon-asks-syrian-refugees-demolish-houses-190613120214474.html.
Janmyr, Maja. 'UNHCR and the Syrian Refugee Response: Negotiating Status and Registration in Lebanon'. *The International Journal of Human Rights* 22, no. 3 (2017): 393–419.
Janmyr, Maja. 'Precarity in Exile: The Legal Status of Syrian Refugees in Lebanon'. *Refugee Survey Quarterly* 35 (2016): 58–78.
Jones, Reece. 'Agents of Exception: Border Security and the Marginalization of Muslims in India'. *Environment and Planning D: Society and Space* 27, no. 5 (2009): 879–97.
Lebanon Humanitarian INGO Forum. 'Background Paper on Unregistered Syrian Refugees in Lebanon'. July 2014. Available online: http://lhif.org/uploaded/News/d92fe3a1b1dd46f2a281254fa551bd09LHIF%20Background%20Paper%20on%20Unregistered%20Syrian%20Refugees%20(FINAL).pdf.
Mabon, Simon and Ana M. Kumarasamy. 'Da'ish, Stasis and Bare Life in Iraq'. In *Iraq after ISIS: The Challenges of Post-War Recovery*, edited by Jacob Eriksson and Ahmed Khaleel, 9–29. Cham: Palgrave Pivot, 2019.
Machayekhi, Diane, Michele Perpaoli and Georgio Cancelliere. 'Domestic Water in Bekaa Valley, Lebanon Demand, Access and Institutional Aspects'. International Institute for Environment and Development, 2017.
Masterson, Daniel and Christian M. Lehmann. 'Refugees, Mobilisation, and Humanitarian Aid: Evidence from the Syrian Refugee Crisis in Lebanon'. *Journal of Conflict Resolution* 64, Issue 5 (2019): 1–27.
Meier, Daniel. 'Lebanon: The Refugee Issue and the Threat of a Sectarian Confrontation'. *Oriente Moderno* 94, no. 2 (2014): 382–401.
Miller, Benjamin 'Between the Revisionist and the Frontier State: Regional Variations in State War-Propensity'. *Review of International Studies* 35 (2009): 85–119.
Murray, Stuart. 'Thanatopolitics: Reading in Agamben a Rejoinder to Biopolitical Life'. *Communication and Critical/Cultural Studies* 5, no. 2 (2008): 203–7.

Nagle, John. 'The Biopolitics of Victim Construction, Elision and Contestation in Northern Ireland and Lebanon'. *Peacebuilding* 8, Issue 4 (2019): 1–16.

Naufal, Hala. 'Syrian Refugees in Lebanon: The Humanitarian Approach under Political Divisions'. *Migration Policy Centre*, 2012. Available online: https://cadmus.eui.eu/bitstream/handle/1814/24835/MPC_RR2012-13.pdf?sequence=1&isAllowed=y.

Norwegian Refugee Council. 'Calling on Lebanese Authorities to Stop the Demolition of Refugees Homes'. 9 August 2019. Available online: https://www.nrc.no/news/2019/august2/calling-on-lebanese-authorities-to-stop-the-demolition-of-refugees-homes/.

Norwegian Refugee Council. 'The Consequences of Limited Legal Status for Syrian Refugees in Lebanon, Lebanon'. April 2014, 15. Available online: https://data2.unhcr.org/en/documents/download/40323.

Obeid, Michelle, 'Searching for the 'Ideal Face of the State' in a Lebanese Border Town'. *Journal of the Royal Anthropological Institute* 16 (2010): 330–46.

Pollock, William, Joseph Wartman, Grace Abou-Jaude and Alex Grant. 'Risk at the Margins: A Natural Hazards Perspective on the Syrian Refugee Crisis in Lebanon'. *International Journal of Disaster Risk Reduction* 36 (2019).

Ramadan, Adam. 'Destroying Nahr el-Bared: Sovereignty and Urbacide in the Space of Exception'. *Political Geography* 28 (2009): 153–63.

Ramadan, Adam and Sarah Fregonese. 'Hybrid Sovereignty and the State of Exception in the Palestinian Refugee Camps in Lebanon'. *Annals of the Association of American Geographers* 107, no. 4 (2017): 949–63.

Salloukh, Bassel F. 'The Syrian War: Spillover Effects on Lebanon'. *Middle East Policy* XXIV, no. 1 (2017): 62–78.

Salter, Mark B. 'The Global Visa Regime and the Political Technologies of the International Self: Borders, Bodies, Biopolitics'. *Alternatives: Global, Local, Political* 31, no. 2 (2006): 167–89.

Salter, Mark B. 'When the Exception Becomes the Rule: Borders, Sovereignty and Citizenship'. *Citizenship Studies* 12, no. 4 (2008): 365–80.

Sanyal, Romola. 'Managing Through Ad Hoc Measures: Syrian Refugees and the Politics of Waiting in Lebanon'. *Political Geography* 66 (2018): 67–75.

Shewly, Hosna J. 'Abandoned Spaces and Bare Life in the Enclaves of the India-Bangladesh Border'. *Political Geography* 32 (2012): 23–31.

Smith, Mick. 'Against Ecological Sovereignty Agamben, Politics and Globalization'. *Environmental Politics* 18, no. 1 (2009): 99–116.

Stel, Nora. *Hybrid Political Order and the Politics of Uncertainty; Refugee Governance in Lebanon*. Oxon, NY: Routledge, 2021.

Tholens, Simone 'Border Management in an Era of 'Statebuilding Lite': Security Assistance and Lebanon's Hybrid Security'. *International Affairs* 93, no. 4 (2017): 865–82.

UNHCR. 'Bekaa (Zahle)'. Available online: https://www.unhcr.org/lb/bekaa-zahle (accessed 10 March 2020).

UNHCR. 'Syria Regional Refugee Response'. Available online: https://data2.unhcr.org/en/situations/syria/location/71 (accessed 31 January 2020).

UNRWA. 'Lebanon'. Available online: https://www.unrwa.org/where-we-work/lebanon (accessed 19 January 2020).

UNEWA. 'Wavel Camp'. Available online: https://www.unrwa.org/where-we-work/lebanon/wavel-camp (accessed 10 March 2020).

(VASyR), UNICEF, UNHCR, and WFP. 'Vulnerability Assessment for Syrian Refugees in Lebanon'. 2020. Available online: https://reliefweb.int/sites/reliefweb.int/files/resources/VASyR%202020.pdf.

Verner, Dorte, David R. Lee, Maximillian Ashwill and Robert Wilby. *Increasing Resilience to Climate Change in the Agricultural Sector of the Middle East: The Case of Jordan and Lebanon*. Washington: The World Bank, 2013.

Vohra, Anchal. 'Lebanon's Dier al-Ahmar'. *Al Jazeera*, 9 June 2019. Available online: https://www.aljazeera.com/news/2019/06/lebanon-deir-al-ahma-incident-displaced-600-refugees-190609095940222.html.

Weiss, Thomas L. and Juan D. Reyes 'Breaking the Cycle of Violence: Understanding the Links Between Environment, Migration and Conflict in the Greater Horn of Africa'. In *Horn of Africa and Peace: The Role of the Environment*, edited by Ulf Johansson Dahre, 97–108. Lund: Media-tryck, 2009.

Williams, Phil. 'Migration and Refugees'. In *Security Studies: An Introduction*, edited by Paul D. Williams and Matt McDonald, 482–97. Oxon, NY: Routledge, 2018.

Winter, Stefan. *The Shiites of Lebanon under Ottoman rule 1516–1788*. Cambridge: Cambridge University Press, 2010.

Yassin, Nasser. 'Beirut'. *Cities* 29 (2012): 64–73.

Young, William, David Stebbins, Bryan Fredrick and Omar Al-Shahery. *Spillover from the conflict in Syria*. Santa Monica, CA: RAND Corporation, 2014.

Zannettino, Lana, 'From Auschwitz to Mandatory Detention: Biopolitics, Race, and Human Rights in the Australian Refugee Camp'. *The International Journal of Human Rights* 16, no. 7 (2012): 1094–119.

Chapter 7

PENAL PORTENTS, PENAL PRECEDENTS AND SPECTACLES OF UNBEARABLE LIFE

Madonna Kalousian

Spectacles of power as the embodiment of a sovereign's assertion of power include the architecturing of exclusionary sites which carry a distinctly penal character. Speaking to the systematic quality of these sites is a framework of legal, penal and punitive practices which are intended to remain hidden from public discourse and excluded from any juridical debate on state, collective or individual accountability. Prisons, including indefinite detention centres, interrogation sites and undisclosed torture camps, have, in many ways, become spaces where extra-legal categories can be violently constructed, detained and excluded from the polis, the political city. This exclusion is emblematic of the fact that law can be inherently and fundamentally violent. It also raises profound questions about the regulation of social life, about the provision or withdrawal of human rights protections and about the legitimization of the suspension of law itself.

This suspension is premised upon and results in the creation of new caesuras, contradictions and interventions in legal order. It ensures the politicization of human life, thus ultimately subjecting its political-juridical categories to 'dangerous penal precedents'.[1] Warning of these acts of suspension, Giorgio Agamben predicts that

> One day humanity will play with law just as children play with disused objects, not in order to restore them to their canonical use but free them from it for good. What is found after the law is not a more proper and original use value that precedes the law, but a new use that is born only after it. And use, which has been contaminated by law, must also be freed from its own value. This liberation is the task of study, or of play. And this studious play is the passage that allows us to arrive at that justice that one of Benjamin's posthumous fragments defines as a state of the world in which the world appears as a good that absolutely cannot be appropriated or made juridical.[2]

It is precisely within the context of a new use of law – one where the end of law itself becomes a means to a sanctioned end – that extra-legal sites such as Israel's Alkhiam prison complex in southern Lebanon, for example, was constructed. On

23 May 2000, Lebanese civilians stormed into Alkhiam and freed hundreds of Palestinian and Lebanese prisoners detained illegally and indefinitely by Israeli occupation forces. Following the Israeli withdrawal from southern Lebanon, Alkhiam became an abandoned torture prison camp and, from 2001, operated as a museum 'set up so that visitors received an "experiential tour" [...] where former inmates narrated lived experience in the very walls that held them captive'.[3] During the Israeli invasion of Lebanon in 2006, Israel bombed Alkhiam and destroyed it in an attempt to render invisible twenty-two years of the arbitrary incarceration it exercised against its detainees.[4] However, Alkhiam's legacy of violence, horror and dehumanization continues to expose the contradictions in the vague practice, meaning and instrumentalization of law by a presupposed sovereign power inflicting human suffering, political exclusion and legalized punishment onto a variety of targeted settings.

Within these legalized fissures in the practice of law, Agamben identifies a logic of singularity, a concept which is crucial for understanding Agamben's critical engagement with the paradigms which define and permeate modern politics:

> Whatever singularity, which wants to appropriate belonging itself, its own being-in-language, and thus rejects all identity and every condition of belonging, is the principal enemy of the State. Wherever these singularities peacefully demonstrate their being in common, there will be a Tiananmen, and sooner or later tanks will appear.[5]

In other words, the possibility of the emergence of any singularity of being that is able to challenge dominant metrics of belonging and initiate the excluded other into a zone of co-belonging with *other* others undermines the authority of sovereign power, exemplified here in the state. It is not the distinctive identity itself but the co-belonging that undoes the paradoxical paradigm of sovereignty, which is why 'a being radically devoid of any representable identity would be absolutely irrelevant to the State'.[6] A dangerous singularity, in this case, is a category which the sovereign is not willing to recognize as a zone of legal, right-bearing citizenship. It threatens to undo the representable homogeneity against and through which a sovereign defines itself and regulates inclusion into the polis. Reflecting 'the importance for every sovereign state to ensure a homogenous inside',[7] the sovereign cannot but single out and cast this category into the realm of unrepresentable otherness. One territory where this exclusion is carried out is the prison.

In the context of the conflict in Syria, a range of sovereign powers have sought to consolidate their own order and practise their own exclusionary politics in an attempt to carve out their own zones of inclusion and exclusion of otherness. Expressions of singularity within these zones have been met with the political action of a sovereign disturbed by the possibility of these expressions exhibiting an unrepresentability which falls outside any sanctioned homogeneous identity. In this chapter, I establish a broader context in which these zones of exclusion operate in Syria and interact with ubiquitous contradictions and gaps between law and its application. Drawing on Agamben's theorization of 'the paradigm', I explore the construction of Yassin Al-Haj Saleh and the detainees of Nadi Al-Shabāb Al-Riyaḍi in Raqqa and ʿAdra Al-ʿommaliyyah near Damascus as excluded penal subjects. Theorizing the prison as an abject intrastate within the contemporary context of spectacles of power in Syria, I argue that the figure of the prisoner is most accurately grounded at the theoretical juncture of Hannah Arendt's conceptualization of 'the superfluous', Giorgio Agamben's examination of 'the camp' as a paradigm of contemporary politics and Arthur Bradley's emphasis on what he terms 'unbearable life'. The aim is not to homogenize the experience of 'the prison' in Syria or elsewhere but to arrive at an understanding of the significance of this theoretical nexus. With this in mind, I use my analysis of the components of superfluity, virtuality and 'unbearable life' in order to examine the extent to which Syria's penal subjects inhabit the centre of this nexus. The relationship between prisoners and prisons as security institutions, on the one hand, and between prisoners and the remainder of society outside of the prison, on the other hand, is governed by an alarming proliferation of a liminality of subjecthood, spatiality and citizenship, a liminality which intensifies the urgency of understanding these relationships through the analytical lens of Agamben's notion of inclusive exclusion. What remains at the end of a period of detention and incarceration is an afterlife of meaningful witnessing at the centre of which rests a political – albeit bare, bared or unbearable – body that matters or one that is still waiting to come to matter.

Superfluity, virtuality, unbearable life

Punishment rests on one fundamental principle which systematically reproduces structures of political eradication exerted onto those who are forced to recede into an abject position within the polis. Hannah Arendt identifies this principle as superfluity. Arendt theorizes the foundations which belie the interrelationship between abjection, superfluity and processes of punishment as follows:

> The totalitarian attempt to make men superfluous reflects the experience of modern masses of their superfluity on an overcrowded earth. The world of the dying, in which men are taught they are superfluous through a way of life in which punishment is meted out without connection with crime, in which exploitation is practiced without connection with crime, in which exploitation is practiced without profit, and where work is performed without product, is a place where senselessness is daily produced anew.[8]

The way in which this punishment is carried out, as Arendt explains, not only links abjection and violence through this new emphasis on superfluity but also implicates superfluity with notions of biopolitics and the intentionally arbitrary exercising of sovereign power. Those who are deemed by a ruling apparatus to be superfluous, unnecessary and irrelevant are not only subjected to a process of exclusion from political life but also violently constructed by a ruling sovereign in order to be expelled and rejected from within. They are forced to inhabit and be inhibited by 'a position of abject inhumanity',[9] a 'space devoid of all humanity', as Saleh frames it.[10] The fact that processes of superfluity are closely tied to abjection means that the relationship between those subjected to abjection and those who exercise it on a violently built other harbours within it a complex relationship whereby the former is defined through *and* against the excluded latter. This is why the relationship between exclusion and inclusion is far more complex than the perceiving of them as merely two processes taking place simultaneously. Instead, they are two interdependent processes where a sovereign's definition of itself as such requires that it excludes subjects whose inclusion poses a risk to that very presupposed sovereign position. This instrumentalized utilitarian inclusion of the excluded other is the only way in which what is defined as superfluous is pulled back from the brink of utter superfluity into the realm of what is virtually superfluous. The status of superfluity in relation to the polis, the value and the relevance of the violently abjected other is entirely dependent on and exclusively resulting from its exclusionary inclusion.

The second concept in which the relationship between the excluded superfluous, sovereign law and society within the margins of inclusion is grounded is Arthur Bradley's notion of 'unbearable life' and the way this is connected to Agamben's theorization of virtuality and the virtually 'bared' life.[11] If we are not *born* bare, but rather have the *potential* of being captivated within a state of bareness, then I believe that the term 'bared life' 'would be a better term [than 'bare life'] for the object caught up in the sovereign ban, since it would [not only] emphasise the violent aspect of being stripped of all protections and abandoned to the force of law'[12] but also bring to the fore the fact that lives, through a variety of mechanisms, are gradually *made* bare. 'Bared life' highlights the possibility of and the process by which lives are *rendered* politically and ontologically bare. With this in mind and before I proceed with an analysis of the significance of the theoretical nexus I believe the prison maintains with Bradley's unbearable life, I first outline Agamben's notion of the virtuality of bareness.

There is, arguably, one problem with critiques of Agamben in relation to his assigning of *zoé* and *bíos*, including Judith Butler's, for instance.[13] Agamben does not argue that we are *all homines sacri*. In fact, in *homo sacer* (1998), he mentions the word 'virtually' a number of times:

> If in our age all citizens can be said, in a specific but extremely real sense, to appear virtually as *homines sacri*, this is possible only because the relation of ban has constituted the essential structure of sovereign power from the beginning.[14]

> The political system no longer orders forms of life and juridical rules in a determinate space, but instead contains at its very centre a *dislocating localization* that exceeds it and into which every form of life and every rule can be virtually taken.[15]

But what does 'virtually' mean, and what role does this word play in Agamben's argument? 'Virtually' means that the production of bare life is more of a gradual, dynamic process of being, of coming into being or, to use Butler's words, of a journey towards the, albeit sometimes abject, body. We are not born bare, but we certainly are born with the capacity and the potential to be rendered bare, to be captivated in a state of bareness, by certain biopolitical conditions that determine the relationship between our lives and sovereign law.[16] This is why in theorizing the significance of the use of the word 'virtually' by Agamben, Nick Vaughan-Williams argues that 'certain populations are more likely to be produced as bare life than others'.[17] This is also a point where Arendt's superfluity overlaps with Agamben's virtuality, for the superfluous is 'something like oneself that still under no circumstances ought to be like oneself'[18] and that has the potential to be oneself tomorrow. If bareness is not the default status of a life which has been bared, then what today is made superfluous has been defined as such through a similar dynamic process of rendering forms of life which used to inhabit the polis superfluous. In other words, what makes the concept of superfluity most disturbing is that today's superfluous subject might have been at the centre of the polis yesterday.

It is within this context that I believe Bradley's notion of unbearable life attains more significance: life is politicized in order to reduce it to bare life which then undergoes an indefinite and indeterminate process of political erasure, the result of which, Bradley contends, is the consigning of the life which has been bared 'to an oblivion beneath even bare life [. . .] which confirms the perpetual impotence of what seemingly never lived in the first place'.[19] At this unique nexus of superfluity, virtuality and unbearable life, Yassin Al-Haj Saleh, for example, was, following his earlier life of political activism, framed as an individual who is both politically and socially superfluous. Positioned within narrow margins of inclusion, Saleh's 'singularity' brought to the fore the possibility of co-belonging with other 'singular' subjects, something which threatened the established homogeneity of the category of legal subjects. This resulted in the relegation of Saleh to the sphere of unbearable life, following 'the path of abandonment [. . .] whereby political detainees are made subjects of the sovereign's ban, that is, they are cast out and exposed to eradication'.[20] Despite attempts to render him 'unborn, unlived, or non-existent',[21] the prison, for Saleh, has been a place of 'rebirth'.[22] Drawing on the theorization Arendt, Agamben and Bradley propose of these concepts, Saleh escaped the state-constructed prescriptions of civility and citizenship. Describing his confinement into the liminal recesses of the institution of the prison, Saleh argues that 'what predominantly applied to the dead is now routinely performed on the living',[23] thus echoing Bradley's understanding of practices of rendering a subject 'unborn' within the confines of the prison.

Saleh was born in 1961 in Al-Jurn Al-Aswad, a small village near Raqqa. Abdallah Al-Haj Saleh, Saleh's great-grandfather, was a prominent figure within the village and its surrounding neighbourhoods, which is why the village has also become widely known as Jurn Al-Haj Saleh. In 1971, Saleh followed in the footsteps of his three older brothers and moved to Raqqa to start secondary school. This marks the beginning of Saleh's political activism. In 1973, two years later, the Syrian Communist Party Political Bureau (SCPPB) was established. A number of anti-Ba'th Party members of the Syrian Communist Party rebelled against the rule of Khaled Bakdash, protested his decision to merge the party with the political alliance of *al-Jabha al-Waṭaniyya al-Taqaddumiyya*, or the National Progressive Front (NPF), and defected to form their own new party under the leadership of Riad Al-Turk.[24] Attending some of its earliest meetings and demonstrations, Saleh's older brothers, and Saleh himself at a later stage, were among the active younger new recruits.

The rise of SCPPB in the early 1970s coincided with escalating political tensions in neighbouring Lebanon as well as with a series of assassinations, clashes and battles all of which pushed the country to its fifteen-year-long civil war.[25] At first, Syria was drawn into the conflict with the role of an intermediary between the various opposing factions. Its role, however, started to gradually evolve into direct military intervention, followed by an increasing and continued interference in Lebanese internal political affairs over the decades that followed.[26] The SCPPB not only opposed Syria's interventionist politics in Lebanon but was also strongly and especially critical of the dynastic clientelist culture it consolidated inside Syria itself, the networks of patronage and favouritism it nurtured and mobilized, the increasing militarization and securitization of everyday life, and the policing of outlets for 'legitimate' political activity.

It is against this backdrop of contentious politics that, in 1979, also under the leadership of Riad Al-Turk, who was then briefly released from prison,[27] *Al-Tajammuʿ Al-Waṭanī Al-Dīmuqrāṭī*, or the National Democratic Gathering (NDG), was founded. Four opposition groups decided to form a political coalition: Jamal Al-Atassi's *Al-Ittihad Al-Ishtiraki Al-'Arabi Al-Dimuqrati* (the Democratic Arab Socialist Union), Ibrahim Makhous's *Hizb Al-Ba'th Al-Dimuqratiy Al-'Arabi al-Ishtiraki* (the Democratic Socialist Arab Ba'th Party), Akram Al-Hawrani's *Harakat Al-Ishtirakiyeen Al-'Arab* (the Arab Socialist Movement) and Yassin Al-Hafiz's *Hizb Al-'Umal Al-Thawriy Al-'Arabi* (the Arab Revolutionary Workers' Party).[28] The criticism this coalition voiced against the ruling elite, including its crackdown on the Muslim Brotherhood following the assassination campaign it waged against prominent Alawite figures in the country,[29] had grave consequences on the group. Its members were arrested. Its political activity in the country was significantly diminished.[30] This moment has had an ineffaceable impact on Saleh's politics, specifically on his understanding of the 'organizing' of a society 'under [the] pretext of fear of *fitna*',[31] therefore homogenizing it into an Agambenian singularity and 'transforming it into a composite of "organic" communities subordinated to a unified centre of power'.[32]

Prison/camp as paradigm

Agamben wrote *The Coming Community* in 1990, in the wake of the late 1980s revolutions in the Soviet region and the successive declarations of autonomy from Moscow, which eventually led to the collapse of the Soviet Union in 1992. *The Coming Community* is, therefore, Agamben's theoretical reflection upon the political upheaval into which these events spiralled, as well as upon the national, social and religious ideologies that permeated the establishment of the Soviet-era sense of a generic universality among the various components of the Union or its national, ethnic and regional particularities, to use Sergei Prozorov's terminology. Newly emergent approaches to singularity, sovereignty, being and belonging assumed an increasingly important role in the formulation of post-Soviet politics. Replacing what Prozorov argues to be a '"universal homogeneous" state',[33] Soviet-era politics were subsequently subsumed into a new form of 'universality *immediately* attained by subtraction from all particularity and suspension of the struggle for recognition' (emphasis in original).[34] Drawing on theories of community (re)formation, citizenship and belonging advanced by George Bataille, Jean Luc Nancy and Maurice Blanchot, Agamben's conceptualization of 'the paradigm' underpins his line of query into this emergent politics. The following critical examination of Agamben's paradigm is particularly illuminating for the analysis of the prison as a framework through which belonging, citizenship and political erasure in contemporary Syrian politics can be explored, a framework which brings together the peculiar specifications I have identified in the theoretical nexus of superfluity, virtuality and unbearable life.

Following the publication of *The Coming Community*, Agamben's critique of the epistemological foundations of contemporary Western politics, along with some of the most fundamental concepts of his political thought, including statelessness, the state of exception, sovereign power, the messianic and the hidden relationship that ties this power to violence, law and paradoxes of human rights, is most evident in three of his titles: *homo sacer*, *The Remnants of Auschwitz* (1999) and *Means without End* (2000). In these three works, Agamben registers his critique of Western politics through a redeployment of his initial use of 'the paradigm' in *The Coming Community*. This redeployment signals Agamben's reconfiguration of 'the camp', arguably, one of his most revisited and most critiqued concepts, as a paradigm of Western politics. 'The camp', for Agamben, is an existent physical or material structure of legalized eliminative violence and the ultimate theoretical hallmark of exclusive juridico-political modes of inclusion.[35]

Emerging from a temporary suspension of the rule of law and in order to embody the normalization of the exception permanently becoming the rule, the camp, as Agamben describes it,

> is a piece of land placed outside the normal juridical order, but it is nevertheless not simply an external space. What is excluded in the camp is, according to the etymological sense of the term 'exception' (*ex-capere*), taken outside, included through its own exclusion. But what is first of all taken into the juridical order is the state of exception itself. Insofar as the state of exception is 'willed,' it inaugurates a new juridico-political paradigm in which the norm becomes indistinguishable from the exception. . . . Only because the camps constitute a space of exception in the sense we have examined . . . is everything in camps truly possible. . . . Whoever enter[s] the camp move[s] in a zone of indistinction

between outside and inside, exception and rule, licit and illicit, in which the very concepts of subjective right and juridical protection no longer [make] sense.[36]

Inside 'the camp', 'bare life' is indefinitely, yet perpetually, caught in a state of exception and is transformed into 'something for which we perhaps have no name',[37] a juridically empty space and something which Saleh himself describes as '*al-farāgh*',[38] meaning 'emptiness'. The complex interplay between indefiniteness and perpetuality harbours within itself a suspension of the rule of law and a curious collusion between biopolitics, legality, legitimacy and processes of legitimization of sovereign power. Agamben describes the characteristic paradigm emerging from the blurring of these concepts into one another as follows:

> The growing dissociation of birth (bare life) and the nation-state is the new fact of politics in our day, and what we call *camp* is this disjunction. To an order without localization (the state of exception, in which law is suspended) there now corresponds a localization without order (the camp as permanent space of exception). The political system no longer orders forms of life and juridical rules in a determinate space, but instead contains at its very center a *dislocating localization* that exceeds it and into which every form of life can be virtually taken. The camp as dislocating localization is the hidden matrix of the politics in which we are still living.[39]

The camp, in other words, is both a conceptual framework for modern politics and a physical construct that underpins and territorializes the initially temporary and otherwise dislocated 'state of exception'.[40] Sovereign power detains, controls and reproduces the dwellers of the camp as 'an absolute biopolitical substance'.[41] 'It is this space of the camp', Michelle Brown argues, 'that is reopened when the state of exception becomes the rule.'[42] In order to understand what it means for 'the camp' to operate as a paradigm of modern politics, I first outline what Agamben means by paradigm.

The third chapter of *The Coming Community* is, as Steven DeCaroli points out, one of Agamben's earliest attempts to introduce his conceptualization of 'the paradigm' into his theoretical programme.[43] Titled 'Example', Agamben's chapter invokes an interchangeability between 'example' and 'paradigm', and, therefore, establishes what I believe to be a decisive distinction between 'paradigm' and 'metaphor', one that is crucial for understanding what Agamben means when he uses 'the camp' as paradigm of modern politics. With this in mind, I argue that Agamben introduces this distinction by setting up an analogy between the use of the word 'tree' and the way exclusionary politics nominates and groups certain members who appear or are made to hold a common definitive enterprise into a community that grants and denies inclusion to those who do not. Similarly, the use of the word 'tree' to signify 'all trees indifferently [. . .] posts the proper universal significance in place of singular, ineffable trees'.[44] In other words, the word 'tree' homogenizes the particularities of the trees that belong to the category of 'tree'. While the word 'tree' is meant to represent what is included in the category of 'tree', it remains unable to adequately represent all the particularities of the trees that belong to this category. These particularities are *examples* of what is included in the category 'tree', rather than a metaphor of it. Yet, their heterogeneous particularities can, at any given moment in time, cast them out as excluded others. For Agamben, the categories that remain outside this generalized expression of commonality and belonging each constitute one particularity and one *example* of what is excluded from the community, rather than a metaphor, a parody or an adequate representation of it.

The understanding of Agamben's methodological approach to the relationship between 'example' and 'paradigm' provides an insight into the way in which he believes the paradoxical structure of sovereign power suspends camp dwellers within an unliveable, de-politicized and merely biological mode of being. This is because the relationship that I perceive between the singularity of the example and the universality of the group of entities it is made to represent – or sometimes, misrepresent – is one of critical complexity. The example has to belong to the group so it can sufficiently represent it, while it has to, at the same time, exhibit some markedly different criteria which are distinct enough for it to qualify to be singled out of the group as a definitive representative. In other words, for an entity to acquire the position of example within a group, it has to belong in this group; it has to be included in it, something which takes it out of the group and makes itself evident in its exclusion. Theorizing the inclusive–exclusive positioning of the example in relation to the group it exemplifies, De la Durantaye argues that 'instead of the dialectical opposition of particularity and universality, Agamben offers, via the figure of the example, a nondialectical relation in which the singularity or example is at once a member of, and excluded from, the set of things it exemplifies'.[45] In articulating his methodology of the creation of abject subjects of modernity, Agamben, as DeCaroli demonstrates, 'draws on the work he begun in *The Coming Community* to extend his analysis of politics by arguing that the logical structure of sovereignty parallels that of the example'.[46] In fact, for Agamben, language and politics implement a similar system of relationality between part and whole, member and class, singularity and generality. Language leaves the example in a lingering state, where it is 'neither particular nor universal' but is instead 'a singular object that presents itself as such'.[47] This inclusive–exclusive position is analogous to that of the figure of *homo sacer* in relation to the paradoxical nature of sovereignty, to that of what Agamben calls 'a limit-figure of life, a threshold in which life is both inside and outside the juridical order, and this threshold is the place of sovereignty'.[48] In other words, sovereign power excludes the *homo sacer* from the political with which its relationship is neither that of inclusion nor of exclusion.

A misunderstanding of the gap between 'metaphor' and 'paradigm' underpins the criticism of Agamben's theorization of 'the camp'.[49] This misunderstanding arises from the ambiguity surrounding the meaning and origin of the term 'muselmann', as admitted by Agamben himself.[50] One of Agamben's earliest uses of the term 'muselmann' appears in his *Remnants of Auschwitz*. Establishing what he means by the term and setting out its connections with 'witnessing', Agamben introduces the muselmann as 'the untestifiable, that to which no one has borne witness', as 'an event without witnesses'[51] and as one whose name, 'in the jargon of the camp [. . .] is *der Muselmann*, literally "the Muslim"'.[52] Agamben goes on to quote Jean Amery's *At the Mind's Limits* (1980):

> The so-called *Muselmann*, as the camp language termed the prisoner who was giving up ad was given up by his comrades, no longer had room in his consciousness for the contrasts good or bad, noble or base, intellectual or unintellectual. He was a staggering corpse, a bundle of physical functions in its last convulsions. As hard as it may be for us to do so, we must exclude him from our considerations.[53]

The term has, therefore, been used by Agamben to refer to the inhabitants of the Nazi concentration camps who, due to the treatment they received within the camps, were, as he argues, no longer capable of exhibiting a 'human' relationship with their surroundings, were located at the dividing border between life and death, human and inhuman, and were, as a result, excluded and ignored by their fellow prisoners.[54] The intermediary position in which Agamben places the muselmann is, I believe, partly reminiscent of Agamben's theorization of anthropocentric hierarchies of human–animal relations. Unlike the human, the animal is captivated within its environment and is unable to take a step away from its captivation to reflect upon it. However, what problematizes Agamben's positioning of the muselmann within the environment of 'the camp' is the fact that unlike 'the animal', as Agamben presents this category in *The Open* (2002), camp dwellers *are* able to reflect upon their state of captivation. 'The camp' can, therefore, be a space where the processes of the anthropological machine that perpetually reproduce politics as biopolitics have been brought to a halt and where bare life enacts itself as political life, thus registering an interruption of the political system that constitutes them as invisible and inconsequential lives inhabiting the theoretical nexus of superfluity, virtuality and unbearability.

Embodying this very theoretical nexus in Syria is, for instance, the prisons of Douma, located just outside Damascus, and the events of 'Adra Al-'ommaliyyah, Adra Industrial City. On 11 December 2013, fighters of Al-Qaeda affiliate Al-Nusra Front attacked 'Adra and committed horrifying acts of torture and indiscriminate killing against its residents.[55] The women and children they kidnapped were taken to Douma where they were put in small cages, stripped of their status as right-bearing citizens and exchanged among Al-Nusra militants as though they were assigned a 'geopolitical currency rather than recognition or grievability'.[56] One of the most notorious examples of prisons established by ISIS in Syria is the football stadium of Nadi Al-Shabāb Al-Riyaḍi in Raqqa. ISIS fighters transformed the stadium into a mass incarceration, torture and execution complex. Its locker rooms served as makeshift solitary confinement cells, its walls as bearers of last notes inmates desperately scribbled and its main grounds as a burial site.[57] In the name of a law and of a new order, ISIS and Nusra established and sought to consolidate in their *bāqiya wa tatamaddad* moto, their fighters subjected entire populations inside Syria to enduring processes of dehumanization, reducing humanity into bare life. Similarly, in the name of fighting ISIS, US coalition forces reduced the entire city of Raqqa into a necrozone of bareness, where thousands of civilians were killed 'by mistake'.[58] This resulting loss of life was cast into the realm of collateral damage seen by US forces as proportionate in relation to a desired military advantage.

Camp dwellers, as well as prison inhabitants, are able to recognize and witness their captivation as such, even if the politics that captivates them seeks to strip them of the ability to testify to their captivation, to register their captivation within the camp, to memorialize it and to grieve for it. Their political exclusion strips them of the legal right to testify to the atrocities they have witnessed. This political gap between 'to witness' and 'to testify' brings to attention a paradoxical gap Agamben identifies between two types of what he perceives as impossible narratives of the camp.[59] According to Agamben, those who 'survived' the camp cannot be held as reliable witnesses to its atrocities because they have not suffered the *full* horrors of the camp. This category, within Agamben's limited and limiting conceptualization of testimony, cannot bear witness to the experience of the camp 'from the outside [of it] – since the outsider is by definition excluded from the event'.[60] Within this understanding, it is only those who have suffered the full horrors of the camp by losing their lives within its walls who can serve as witnesses – but this is yet another impossible narrative of the camp as admitted by Agamben himself. For Agamben, 'it is impossible to bear witness to it [the camp] from the inside – since no one can bear witness from the inside of death, and there is no voice for the disappearance of voice'.[61]

The question now is who can bear witness if, for Agamben, this is neither the outsider, who has survived the camp, nor the insider, who has been reduced to the status of the captivated musselmann. At the end of *Remnants of Auschwitz*, Agamben answers this question by proposing the theory that 'the survivor and the *Muselmann*, like the tutor and the incapable person and the creator and his material, are inseparable; their unity-difference alone constitutes testimony'.[62] This conclusion leaves unanswered the question of who might deliver this testimony to the world that lies beyond the environment of the camp. Ironically, it also captivates testimony in the very inclusive–exclusive liminality of which Agamben is critical. The *homo sacer* is both inside and outside the political; the example, as I argue earlier, is both inside and outside language. Similarly, testimony, according to Agamben, remains suspended between an impossible speakability and a speakable actuality, between 'what can be said and what cannot be said, between the sayable and the unsayable of a language'.[63] Testimony, for Agamben,

> takes place where the speechless one makes the speaking one speak and where the one who speaks bears the impossibility of speaking in his own speech, such that the silent and the speaking, the inhuman and the human enter into a zone of indistinction in which it is impossible to establish the position of the subject, to identify the 'imagine substance' of the 'I' and, along with it, the true witness.[64]

The problem with Agamben's impossible relationship between the witness and the survivor, what he calls 'the impossible dialectic between the survivor and the *Muselmann*, the pseudo-witness and the "complete witness"',[65] starts with the problematic term 'muselmann' itself. As I have already stated, the fact that the muselmann is captivated within the experience of the camp does not, in any way, instantiate a parallel between this figure and the animal. Those captivated within the camp *can*, unlike the animal, distance themselves from their captivation, witness it as such and *testify* to it as such, something which renders the abjected prison as Saleh has conceived of it, as I demonstrate in the following section, into an exceptional political space in a way that Agamben's camp is not.

1980–96: The prison notebooks

On 7 December 1980, at the age of twenty, Saleh was arrested by state security from his home in Aleppo where he moved to study medicine at the University of Aleppo. It was only after twelve years of imprisonment – on 14 April 1992 precisely – that Saleh's trial at the State Security High Court in Damascus began. Two years later, having been subject to *att-awqīf al-'urfī*, or 'administrative detention', and deprived for so long of the 'right to a countdown to a definite release date',[66] Saleh received his fifteen-year sentence of which he had already spent fourteen years by this point. Saleh was transferred to the notorious Tadmur Prison,[67] then back to Damascus, before he was released on 21 December 1996. Saleh recounts his experience of imprisonment in his *Bil Khalāṣ Yā Shabāb: 16 'ām fī A-ssujūn A-ssūriya*, Arabic for *Salvation O Boys: 16 Years in Syrian Prisons*. This was completed in 2011 when Saleh found it incumbent upon himself to publish his 'prison notebooks' as the events of the 'Syrian Uprisings' broke out[68] and was published in 2012 by Beirut's Dār Al-Sāqi.

Bil Khalāṣ Yā Shabāb is focused, as Saleh states in its introduction, on the following three main aspects of his story: his experience of the prison as a political prisoner between 1980 and 1996, his conceptualization of the prison as a recollected and memorable experience, and the experience of other previous political prisoners and their post-prison existence.[69] Questions about how Saleh lived under and after the horrors of imprisonment, and more importantly, the unsettling questions about how he has lived *with* the memory of imprisonment are, therefore, central to his book. In its first chapter, titled 'A-ṭṭarīq 'ila Tadmur', or 'the Road to Tadmur', Saleh describes what the arrival of December, the month of his arrest as well as release, feels like and how it functions as a reminder of the significance of relieving himself of that which he cannot forget:

> Every year, when December looms, and with it, the memory of my arrest and release comes back to life, I feel a renewed urge to document more fragments of my story [. . .]. However, every year since my release, which took place nearly seven years ago, I run away from these unforgettable fragments and choose to delay my confrontation with them for yet another year.[70]

This inability to forget, accompanied by the awareness of the need to remember, grounds itself partly, as Saleh explains, in the curious paradoxical balance created by the state between forgetting and remembering. This is because memory, not unlike the exception or the exceptional prisoner, is simultaneously included in and excluded from post-prison consciousness. Saleh explains this paradox as follows:

> No one has helped those released prisoners to forget, especially that the authorities have not provided the thousands who have, for so long, suffered the horrors of imprisonment any reassurance [. . .]. It is as though the state wants to keep the memory of fear alive, while simultaneously ensuring that we remember enough so we continue to be afraid, but also that we forget enough not to demand anything or question any of the measures which have been arbitrarily taken against us.[71]

With the exception of the first section of *Bil Khalāṣ Yā Shabāb*, Saleh insists that this book neither falls under the category of what he calls *adab a-ssujūn*, Arabic for 'prison literature' or 'prison memoir', nor is an ethnographical study. *Bil Khalāṣ Yā Shabāb* is not a political polemic written with the aim of exposing 'the regime' either. What unites the three main focus points of the book is, according to Saleh, a problematization of the concept of 'the prison'. Saleh presents his book as a project of witnessing, testifying and memorialization which 'aims at theorising "the prison" as a culture, as well as at demystifying the institution of the prison itself by turning it from a myth or a taboo into a topic for discussion'.[72] The final notes the detainees of Raqqa's Nadi Al-Shabāb Al-Riyaḍi scribbled on the walls of their cells take up this very task but stand as a paradigm of a different culture of imprisonment, a different framework for the management of life.[73]

Prison as culture, ban as practice

For Saleh, the experience of 'the prison' under Syria's 1963 state of emergency, which was brought to an end in 2011 as the protests broke out, is no longer subject to the limitations of time and space.[74] It is a nomos which lies beyond a specific spatial and historical moment. It is a broader nomos which transcends the border zone of 'the prison'. This wilful act of the broadening of the border zone of exception parallels and is contingent on a limiting of legal order and the suspending of the jurisdiction of law. At this point, the state of emergency transforms itself into a borderless state of exception. This transformation is complete when

> the sovereign decision on the state of exception is no longer in response to any factual danger, but declares a permanent state of emergency [. . .]. Since sovereign power in totalitarianism derives its legitimacy directly from the life of the people, each sovereign decision on emergency declares at the same time what constitutes viable forms of collective life [. . .] and on what life is no longer worthy of living.[75]

Sovereign power under a state of emergency decides not only what uniform form of life constitutes 'a livable life, that is, a life that can be lived'[76] but also what lives do not conform and are, therefore, *unbearable* for this ruling sovereign to include. The prison of course is one way to punish unbearable life. Here, the prison becomes synonymous with the foundation of political life, the original condition of the modern state itself, as well as the hallmark of the management of life inhabiting the prison and the sociopolitical space beyond it. The management of life 'in the biopolitical regime [. . .] isn't so much the capacity to put to death as it is to nullify life in advance' within and outside the borders of the prison.[77] This is most evident in the way Saleh, while wondering whether 'prison can become a way of life' and a 'national experience',[78] describes how he has had to live with the horrors of the prison even *after* he was released. The instrumental balance between remembering and forgetting which Saleh describes in his *Bil Khalāṣ Yā Shabāb* has been used by the state in order to not only maintain a spectre of power, as Saleh argues, but also transform and merge the two spaces of the prison and what lies outside of the prison into one zone of indistinction, thus subjecting those within and *without* the prison to the same spectre of power which can induce inclusion and exclusion at its own will.

This is why, under these circumstances, any subject can be deprived of their legal rights and stripped of its political attributes. Saleh, however, has been able to escape this liminality through writing, which for him is synonymous with what he perceives as 'the taming of the prison beast'[79] and which perhaps is also predicated on a 'close contact with an animality that is at once intimate and extrinsic, at once the ground of our being and that which we must externalise in order to experience ourselves as human, as speaking political beings'.[80] While law can be suspended to create a state of exception only as a result of the sovereign's will, Saleh contends that 'prison is a beast with whom one cannot live unless it was tamed and put under control',[81] and it is at this point where Saleh tells us he begins to 'remember and forget by choice; at my *own* will'.[82]

The decision to abandon a penal subject in the realm of bare life, or even in that of unbearable life, is always a biopolitical decision embedded within social and legal structures. A critical lens through which to understand the violence to which this decision incessantly and unremittingly points is Foucault's *Society Must Be Defended* lectures. Foucault illuminates the features of the position in which a subject awaiting decision on life and death is placed. Here, the question whether the subject is in fact dead or alive is irrelevant; what matters is that it is the sovereign's – and only the sovereign's – decision to process, patrol and administer the frightening proximity of life and death. Foucault's fundamental argument here is that in terms of the subject's relationship with the sovereign, the subject does not make the decision

> to transfer part of their rights or their powers to someone – or to several people. They do not even decide, basically, to transfer their rights. On the contrary, they decide to grant someone – or an assembly made up of several people – the right to represent them, fully and completely. This is not a relationship in which

something belonging to individuals that is surrendered or delegated; it is the representation of those individuals that is surrendered or delegated.[83]

In Saleh's case, the decision was to consign him into the realm of unbearable life, to politically and ontologically erase him through incarceration, with the only decision left for Saleh to make is to remember or forget, at his own will, this experience of abjection, this punishment for representing a dangerous singularity. Saleh's transformation of the abject space of the prison from a state of de-politicized bareness into a space of witnessing, however, does not carry with it a sense of co-belonging with witnesses and penal subjects of other zones of exclusion in Syria. The political act of witnessing, in other words, does not evolve into an act of co-belonging with *other* others in Syria. It fails to establish a sense of co-belonging with penal subjects of non-state acts of exclusion in the country, as is evident in some of Saleh's more recent writing on Syria. For example, in an interview with Andy Heintz in 2018, Saleh is critical of 'the American pressure on Turkey and other regional countries not to efficiently arm the FSA [the Free Syria Army] since late 2011'.[84] Saleh does not explain what he would conceive of as 'efficient', despite the fact that the international military, financial and political support of the FSA is well documented[85] and so is the FSA's harrowing record of violations of human rights throughout the country.[86]

Theorizing the position of the state of exception in relation to the violence in Syria, Salwa Ismail conceives of a 'logic of the "us versus them"' which, she argues, frames the opposition as expendable population.[87] Citing the massacres committed against the Alawite population of Latakia countryside in August 2013, Ismail argues that following the outbreak of protests in 2010, opposition fighters, jihadists and others, including the FSA which she does not mention, reproduced and redeployed this very logic. She conceives of the acts of violence the opposition has carried out as a performance of 'organised mimicry',[88] a 'play of mirror images',[89] a set of 'templates and scripts in which mimicry and parody are at work'.[90] Ismail is critical of this reductive frame of analysis, contending that these acts of violence follow 'their own logic and processes'.[91] However, while condemning the government's crackdown as a 'military option early on in the confrontation',[92] Ismail proceeds to dismiss the political exclusion the Muslim Brotherhood practised not only against prominent Alawite army generals but against members of the Alawite sect in the 1970s as dissident insurgency mimicking a form of violence and articulating 'a mirror image of the regime's polarising discourse'.[93]

Each being rooted within its own political context, neither of these forms of violence is reproducing any template. Similarly, no resulting form of imprisonment and political erasure is a metaphor of an overarching prison culture. Every prison is an example and a paradigm in an Agambenian sense and in its own right. 'Template' not only parallels 'metaphor', rather than 'paradigm' and 'example' – and these, for Agamben, are not interchangeable, as I have demonstrated earlier in this chapter – but also implicitly suggests that those who follow a template are devoid of political agency and, therefore, cannot be as complicit in the violence as those who willingly choose it. In fact, there is no template, and to speak of one is itself symptomatic of an exclusionary reading of violence in Syria, when it is the very different processes of exclusion and inclusion, along with their own identifications of superfluous otherness and right-bearing humanness, which undergird the contentious politics in and for Syria. It would, of course, be naïve to suggest that it is only the overcoming of these exclusions which can bring the cycle of violence to a halt, but to perpetuate exclusionary politics is premised on and results in the suspension of an urgently needed new politics of inclusion. Within this politics, precarity is no longer selectively assigned and Syrians are recognized as equally grievable.

Notes

1. Michelle Brown, *The Culture of Punishment: Prison, Society, and Spectacle* (New York: New York University Press, 2009), 24.
2. Giorgio Agamben, *State of Exception*, trans. Kevin Attel (London: The University of Chicago Press, Ltd, 2005), 64.
3. Lucia Volk, *Memorials and Martyrs in Modern Lebanon* (Indiana: Indiana University Press, 2010), 186.
4. For an eye-witness account of the horrors of this camp prison, see *Khiam*, a documentary film created by Joana Hadjithomas and Khalil Joreige who interviewed six of its ex-prisoners, one of whom, Souha Bechara, wrote her own account of ten years of detention in Alkhiam, six of which she was made to spend in solitary confinement. See Souha Bechara, *Resistance: My Life for Lebanon* (New York: Catapult, 2003); Randa Chahal Sabbag, dir., *Souha, Surviving Hell* (2001; Beirut: Cinétévé, Leil Production, Le Comité des Détenus de Khiam), DVD.
5. Giorgio Agamben, *The Coming Community*, trans. Michael Hardt (Minneapolis: The University of Minnesota Press, 2003), 86.
6. Ibid., 87.
7. Bas Schotel, *On the Right of Exclusion: Law, Ethics and Immigration Policy* (Oxon: Routledge, 2010), 87.
8. Arendt, *The Origins of Totalitarianism* (New York: Harcourt Books, 1968), 457.
9. Emma Larkin, *Refugees and the Myth of Human Rights Life Outside the Pale of the Law* (New York: Routledge, 2014), 150.
10. Yassin Al-Haj Saleh, *Bil Khalāṣ Yā Shabāb: 16 'ām fi A-ssujūn A-ssūriya* (Beirut: Dār Al-Sāqi, 2012), 83.
11. Contra Clayton Crockett, who argues that 'virtuality' is 'another name for potentiality, a more postmodern name'. I do not propose to use the term 'virtuality' interchangeably with Agamben's concept of 'potentiality'. The distinction I perceive resonates with Quentin Meillassoux's analysis. See Quentin Meillassoux, 'Potentiality and Virtuality', trans. Robin Mackay, in *The Speculative Turn: Continental Materialism and Realism*, ed. Levi Bryant, Nick Srnicek, and Graham Harman (Melbourne: re.press, 2011), 230–2.
12. Sergei Prozorov, *Agamben and Politics: A Critical Introduction* (Edinburgh: Edinburgh University Press, 2014), 99.
13. See, for example, Judith Butler, *Frames of War: When Is Life Grievable* (London: Verso, 2010), 19; Butler, *Undoing Gender* (New York: Routledge, 2004), 11.

14 Giorgio Agamben, *Homo Sacer: Sovereign Power and Bare Life* (Stanford: Stanford University Press, 1998), 11.
15 Ibid., 175.
16 For an extensive analysis of the implication of the use of 'virtuality', see Stephen Legg and Alexander Vasudevan, 'Geographies of the Nomos', in *Spatiality, Sovereignty and Carl Schmitt: Geographies of the Nomos* (New York: Routledge, 2011), 14.
17 Nick Vaughan-William, *Border Politics: The Limits of Sovereign Power* (Edinburgh: Edinburgh University Press, 2009), 106. One example that Butler gives of the different populations to whom Vaughan-William refers is the lives of people who live in Gaza Strip, which, according to Gayatri Spivak, 'might be aptly described as an "open-air prison"'. For Butler, the exclusion of a de-politicized figure from the *polis* does not necessarily render this figure bare. The figure can be precarious but not bare. Her argument on the people of Gaza is an example of this difference: 'No simple exclusionary logic can be set up between life and politics. Or, rather, any effort to establish such an exclusionary logic depends upon the depoliticization of life and, once again, writes out the matters of gender, menial labour, and reproduction from the field of the political.' See Judith Butler and Gayatri Chakravorty Spivak, *Who Signs the Nation-State?: Language, Politics, Belonging* (London: Seagull Books, 2011), 7; 38.
18 Arendt, *Origins of Totalitarianism*, 191.
19 Arthur Bradley, *Unbearable Life: A Genealogy of Political Erasure* (New York: Colombia University Press, 2019), 2–3.
20 Salwa Ismail, *The Rule of Violence: Subjectivity, Memory and Government in Syria* (Cambridge: Cambridge University Press, 2018), 34.
21 Bradley, *Unbearable Life*, 3.
22 Saleh, *Bil Khalāṣ Yā Shabāb*, 121.
23 Ibid., 3.
24 See Bassam Haddad and Ella Wind, 'The Fragmented State of the Syrian Opposition', in *Beyond the Arab Spring: The Evolving Ruling Bargain*, ed. Mehran Kamrava (Oxford: Oxford University Press, 2014), 203–6; Alan George, *Syria: Neither Bread Nor Freedom* (New York: Zed Books, 2003), 47–52.
25 For more information on the earlier stages of the Lebanese Civil War, see Tim Llewellyn, *Spirit of the Phoenix: Beirut and the Story of Lebanon* (London: I.B. Tauris, 2010), 53–72; Rayyar Marron, *Humanitarian Rackets and Their Moral Hazards: The Case of the Palestinian Refugee Camps in Lebanon* (New York: Routledge, 2016), 64–88; Bassil A. Mardelli, *Middle East Perspectives: From Lebanon (1968-1988)* (Bloomington: iUniverse, Inc., 2012); Samir Khalaf, *Civil and Uncivil Violence in Lebanon: A History of the Internationalization of Communal Conflict* (New York: Colombia University Press, 2002), 204–31.
26 Rola El-Husseini, *Pax Syriana: Elite Politics in Postwar Lebanon* (Syracuse: Syracuse University Press, 2012), 15–17.
27 Sune Haugbolle, 'The Victim's Tale in Syria: Imprisonment, Individualism, and Liberalism', in *Policing and Prisons in the Middle East: Formations of Coercion*, ed. Laleh Khalili and Jilian Schwedler (London: C. Hurst & Co., 2010), 229–31.
28 Karim Atassi, *Syria, the Strength of an Idea: The Constitutional Architectures of Its Political Regimes* (Cambridge: Cambridge University Press, 2018), 252–337.
29 Leon T. Goldsmith, *Cycle of Fear: Syria's Alawites in War and Peace* (London: C. Hurst & Co. Publishers ltd, 2015), 93–107.

30 Najib Ghadbian, 'Contesting Authoritarianism: Opposition Activism under Bashar al-Asad, 2000-2010', in *Syria from Reform to Revolt*, ed. Raymond Hinnebusch and Tina Zintl (Syracuse: Syracuse University Press, 2015), 105–7.
31 Yassin Al-Haj Saleh, *The Impossible Revolution: Making Sense of the Syrian Tragedy* (London: C. Hurst & Co. Publishers ltd, 2017), 132.
32 Ibid.
33 Prozorov, *Agamben and Politics*, 80.
34 Ibid., 80. For an extensive analysis of Agamben's complex concept of 'universality', see Ibid., 80–6.
35 See, for example, Agamben's examination of police control areas in airports as zones of exception in *Homo Sacer*, 175, and of Guantanamo Bay in *State of Exception*, 50.
36 Agamben, *Homo Sacer*, 142.
37 Agamben, *The Open, Man and Animal*, trans. Kevin Attell (Stanford: Stanford University Press, 2002), 83.
38 Saleh, *Bil Khalāṣ Yā Shabāb*, 29.
39 Agamben, *Homo Sacer*, 144.
40 Some notable examples of the use of Agamben's paradigm of 'the camp' as a theoretical framework for investigating modern exclusionary politics include Yen Le Espiritu, *Body Counts: The Vietnam War and Militarised Refuge(es)* (California: University of California Press, 2014); and David Farrier, *Postcolonial Asylum: Seeking Refuge before the Law* (Liverpool: Liverpool University Press, 2011).
41 Giorgio Agamben, *Remnants of Auschwitz: The Witness and the Archive*, trans. Daniel Heller-Roazen (New York: Zone Books, 1999), 83.
42 Brown, *The Culture of Punishment*, 38. See also Giorgio Agamben, *Means without End: Notes on Politics*. Translated by Vicenzo Binetti and Cesare Casarino (Minneapolis: University of Minnesota Press, 2000), 37.
43 Steven DeCaroli, 'Paradigm/Example', in *The Agamben Dictionary*, ed. Alex Murray and Jessica Whyte (Edinburgh: Edinburgh University Press, 2011), 144.
44 Agamben, *The Coming Community*, 9.
45 De La Durantaye, *Giorgio Agamben*, 163.
46 DeCaroli, 'Paradigm/Example', 145.
47 Agamben, *The Coming Community*, 10.
48 Agamben, *Homo Sacer*, 26.
49 A number of critical readings of Agamben's thesis of 'the camp' as paradigm of modern politics have argued that Agamben simplifies, condenses and aestheticizes the experience of the Nazi concentration camps into a homogenizing metaphor and/or metaphor. This, as I argue previously, is because these readings have misinterpreted the meaning of paradigm and conflated it with metaphor. For examples of these misinterpretations, see John Lechte and Saul Newman, *Agamben and the Politics of Human Rights: Statelessness, Images, Violence* (Edinburgh: Edinburgh University Press, 2013), 97–100; Alejandro Baer and Natan Sznaider, *Memory and Forgetting in the Post-Holocaust Era: The Ethics of Never Again* (New York: Routledge, 2017), 49–50; Risa B. Sodi, *Narrative and Imperative: The First Fifty Years of Italian Holocaust Writing (1944-1994)* (New York: Peter Lang Publishing, 2007), 57–9. This misunderstanding of Agamben is also a result of the overlooking of the relationship between Michel Foucault's use of the 'panopticon' as a diagram of power and Agamben's use of camp as paradigm. One of the most extensive readings of this link is Catherine Mills, *The Philosophy of Agamben* (New York: Routledge, 2008), 81–106.
50 Agamben, *Remnants of Auschwitz*, 44–6.

51 Ibid., 35.
52 Ibid., 41. See Gil Anidjar's extensive analysis of the history of the development of the term 'muselmann'. Gil Anidjar, *The Jew, The Arab: A History of the Enemy* (Stanford: Stanford University Press, 2003), 113–49.
53 Ibid., 41. See also Jean Amery, *At the Mind's Limits: Contemplations by a Survivor on Auschwitz and Its Realities*, trans. Sidney Rosenfeld and Stella P. Rosenfeld (Bloomington: Indiana University Press, 1980), 9.
54 Ibid., 47.
55 For further details on the massacres of Adra Industrial City, see Mansour Al-Amri, 'mukhṭaṭafu ʿadra al-ʿommaliyya ḍaḥāya ayḍan', *Enab Baladi Online*, 9 April 2018. Available online: https://www.enabbaladi.net/archives/219798.
56 Jennifer Fluri and Rachel Lehr, *The Carpetbaggers of Kabul and Other American-Afghan Entanglements: Intimate Development, Geopolitics, and the Currency of Gender and Grief* (Georgia: Georgia University Press, 2017), 46.
57 Stewart Ramsi, 'Inside Islamic State's "Prison of Death" in Fallen Raqqa', *Sky News*, 21 October 2017. Available online: https://news.sky.com/story/inside-islamic-states-prison-of-death-in-fallen-raqqa-11090263.
58 'Syria: Unprecedented Investigation Reveals US-led Coalition Killed More Than 1,600 Civilians in Raqqa "Death Trap"', *Amnesty International*, 25 April 2019. Available online: https://www.amnesty.org/en/latest/press-release/2019/04/syria-unprecedented-investigation-reveals-us-led-coalition-killed-more-than-1600-civilians-in-raqqa-death-trap/.
59 See also Primo Levi's influence on Agamben's theorization of witnessing within the camp. Agamben, *Remnants of Auschwitz*, 51–8.
60 Ibid., 35.
61 Ibid.
62 Agamben, *Remnants of Auschwitz*, 150.
63 Ibid., 160.
64 Ibid., 120.
65 Ibid.
66 Saleh, *Bil Khalāṣ Yā Shabāb*, 42. This text is not available in English. The Arabic-to-English translations I provide in this chapter of quotes from this book are my own, unless otherwise stated.
67 Ibid., 18–20.
68 Ibid., 10.
69 Ibid., 9.
70 Ibid., 15–16.
71 Ibid., 16.
72 Ibid., 9.
73 While Saleh's project focuses on the biopolitics to which he was subjected by 'the state' up to the point of his release, if not onwards, the conflict which unfolded in Syria following the publication of his book has paved the way for a number of sovereign powers – within and *beyond* – 'the state' to exercise a variety of interpretations of the right to life and to, therefore, apply extra-juridical killings. While Saleh's diagnosis of the past decade in Syria continues to be focused on state violence, writing on the Syrian conflict by a number of other Syrian writers and activists makes a plea to analyse human rights and the human condition within the wider context of warring biopolitical governmentalities. Having emerged against a backdrop of unruly forms of death and killing, including drone strikes, public

executions and beheadings, and suicide bombings, which have irreversibly, yet not unpredictably, transformed social and political life in Syria, writing by authors such as Haidar Haidar, Maha Hassan, Khaled Khalifa, Rami Tawil and Samar Yazbek illustrates the points where Saleh's writing remains limited.

74 For an examination of the implications of Syria's 1963 emergency rule, see Ismail, *The Rule of Violence*, 32–3.
75 Rosalyn Diprose and Ewa Plonowska Ziarek, *Arendt, Natality and Biopolitics: Toward Democratic Plurality and Reproductive Justice* (Edinburgh: Edinburgh University Press, 2018), 157.
76 Judith Butler, *Notes Toward a Performative Theory of Assembly* (Cambridge: Harvard University Press, 2015), 161.
77 Roberto Esposito, *Bíos: Biopolitics and Philosophy*, trans. Timothy Campbell (London: University of Minnesota Press, 2008), 145.
78 Saleh, *Bil Khalāṣ Yā Shabāb*, 29.
79 Ibid., 30.
80 Claire Colebrook, 'Animal', in *The Agamben Dictionary*, ed. Alex Murray and Jessica Whyte (Edinburgh: Edinburgh University Press, 2001), 23.
81 Saleh, *Bil Khalāṣ Yā Shabāb*, 31.
82 Ibid., 17.
83 Michel Foucault, '*Society Must Be Defended*': *Lectures at the College de France, 1975-76*, trans. David Macey (New York: Picador, 2003), 93–4.
84 Yassin Al-Haj Saleh, 'Dissidents of the Left: In Conversation with Yassin al-Haj Saleh', interview by Andy Heintz, *Al-Jumhuriyah*, 18 August 2018. Available online: https://www.aljumhuriya.net/en/content/dissidents-left-conversation-yassin-al-haj-saleh.
85 For example, Gadi Eisenkot, former general in the Israeli army, has recently confirmed that Israel has indeed provided weapons to a number of opposition fighters in Syria, including the FSA. See 'Ex-Israel Army Chief Admits Arming Syria Opposition', *Middle East Monitor*, 3 February 2020. Available online: https://www.middleeastmonitor.com/20200203-ex-israel-army-chief-admits-arming-syria-opposition/; Kim Sengupta, 'Revealed: What the West Has Given Syria's Rebels', *The Independent*, 12 August 2013. Available online: https://www.independent.co.uk/news/world/middle-east/revealed-what-west-has-given-syria-s-rebels-8756447.html.
86 See, for example, 'You Can Still See Their Blood: Executions, Indiscriminate Shootings, and Hostage Taking by Opposition Forces in Latakia Countryside', *Human Rights Watch*, 10 October 2013. Available online: https://www.hrw.org/report/2013/10/10/you-can-still-see-their-blood/executions-indiscriminate-shootings-and-hostage.
87 Ismail, *The Rule of Violence*, 184.
88 Ibid., 184.
89 Ibid., 185.
90 Ibid., 184.
91 Ibid.
92 Ibid., 58.
93 Ibid.

References

Agamben, Giorgio. *Homo Sacer: Sovereign Power and Bare Life*. Translated by Daniel Heller-Roazen. Stanford: Stanford University Press, 1998.

Agamben, Giorgio. *Means without End: Notes on Politics*. Translated by Vicenzo Binetti and Cesare Casarino. Minneapolis: University of Minnesota Press, 2000.

Agamben, Giorgio. *Remnants of Auschwitz: The Witness and the Archive*. Translated by Daniel Heller-Roazen. New York: Zone Books, 1999.

Agamben, Giorgio. *State of Exception*. Translated by Kevin Attel. London: The University of Chicago Press, Ltd., 2005.

Agamben, Giorgio. *The Coming Community*. Translated by Michael Hardt. Minneapolis: The University of Minnesota Press, 2003.

Agamben, Giorgio. *The Open: Man and Animal*. Translated by Kevin Attell. Stanford: Stanford University Press, 2000.

Al-Amri, Mansour. 'mukhṭaṭafu ʿadra al-ʿommaliyya ḍaḥāya ayḍan'. *Enab Baladi Online*, 9 April 2018.

Al-Haj Saleh, Yassin. *Bil Khalāṣ Yā Shabāb: 16 ʿām fi A-ssujūn A-ssūriya*. Beirut: Dār Al-Sāqi, 2012.

Al-Haj Saleh, Yassin. 'Dissidents of the Left: In Conversation with Yassin al-Haj Saleh'. Interview by Andy Heintz, *Al-Jumhuriyah*, 18 August 2018. Available online: https://www.aljumhuriya.net/en/content/dissidents-left-conversation-yassin-al-haj-saleh.

Al-Haj Saleh, Yassin. *The Impossible Revolution: Making Sense of the Syrian Tragedy*. London: C. Hurst & Co. Publishers ltd, 2017.

Amery, Jean. *At the Mind's Limits: Contemplations by a Survivor on Auschwitz and Its Realities*. Translated by Sidney Rosenfeld and Stella P. Rosenfeld. Bloomington: Indiana University Press, 1980.

Anidjar, Gil. *The Jew, The Arab: A History of the Enemy*. Stanford: Stanford University Press, 2003.

Arendt, Hannah. *The Origins of Totalitarianism*. New York: Harcourt Books, 1968.

Atassi, Karim. *Syria, the Strength of an Idea: The Constitutional Architectures of Its Political Regimes*. Cambridge: Cambridge University Press, 2018.

Baer, Alejandro and Natan Sznaider. *Memory and Forgetting in the Post-Holocaust Era: The Ethics of Never Again*. New York: Routledge, 2017.

Bechara, Souha. *Resistance: My Life for Lebanon*. Translated by Gabriel Levine. New York: Catapult, 2003.

Bradley, Arthur. *Unbearable Life: A Genealogy of Political Erasure*. New York: Colombia University Press, 2019.

Brown, Michelle. *The Culture of Punishment: Prison, Society, and Spectacle*. New York: New York University Press, 2009.

Butler, Judith. *Frames of War: When Is Life Grievable*. London: Verso, 2010.

Butler, Judith. *Notes toward a Performative Theory of Assembly*. Cambridge: Harvard University Press, 2015.

Butler, Judith. *Undoing Gender*. New York: Routledge, 2004.

Butler, Judith and Gayatri Chakravarty Spivak. *Who Signs the Nation-State?: Language, Politics, Belonging*. London: Seagull Books, 2011.

Colebrook, Claire. 'Animal'. In *The Agamben Dictionary*, edited by Alex Murray and Jessica Whyte, 22–3. Edinburgh: Edinburgh University Press, 2001.

De la Durantaye, Leland. *Giorgio Agamben: A Critical Introduction*. Stanford: Stanford University Press, 2009.

DeCaroli, Steven. 'Paradigm/Example'. In *The Agamben Dictionary*, edited by Alex Murray and Jessica Whyte, 144–7. Edinburgh: Edinburgh University Press, 2011.

Diprose, Rosalyn and Ewa Plonowska Ziarek. *Arendt, Natality and Biopolitics: Toward Democratic Plurality and Reproductive Justice*. Edinburgh: Edinburgh University Press, 2018.

'Ex-Israel Army Chief Admits Arming Syria Opposition'. *Middle East Monitor*, 3 February 2020. Available online: https://www.middleeastmonitor.com/20200203-ex-israel-army-chief-admits-arming-syria-opposition/.

El-Husseini, Rola. *Pax Syriana: Elite Politics in Postwar Lebanon*. Syracuse: Syracuse University Press, 2012.

Espiritu, Yen Le. *Body Counts: The Vietnam War and Militarised Refuge(es)*. California: University of California Press, 2014.

Esposito, Roberto. *Bíos: Biopolitics and Philosophy*. Translated by Timothy Campbell. London: University of Minnesota Press, 2008.

Farrier, David. *Postcolonial Asylum: Seeking Refuge before the Law*. Liverpool: Liverpool University Press, 2011.

Fluri, Jennifer and Rachel Lehr. *The Carpetbaggers of Kabul and Other American-Afghan Entanglements: Intimate Development, Geopolitics, and the Currency of Gender and Grief*. Georgia: Georgia University Press, 2017.

Foucault, Michel. *'Society Must Be Defended': Lectures at the College de France, 1975–76*. Translated by David Macey, New York: Picador, 2003.

George, Alan. *Syria: Neither Bread Nor Freedom*. New York: Zed Books, 2003.

Ghadbian, Najib. 'Contesting Authoritarianism: Opposition Activism under Bashar al-Asad, 2000–2010'. In *Syria from Reform to Revolt*, edited by Raymond Hinnebusch and Tina Zintl, 91–112. Syracuse: Syracuse University Press, 2015.

Goldsmith, Leon T. *Cycle of Fear: Syria's Alawites in War and Peace*. London: C. Hurst & Co. Publishers ltd, 2015.

Haddad, Bassam and Ella Wind. 'The Fragmented State of the Syrian Opposition'. In *Beyond the Arab Spring: The Evolving Ruling Bargain*, edited by Mehran Kamrava, 397–436. Oxford: Oxford University Press, 2014.

Haugbolle, Sune. 'The Victim's Tale in Syria: Imprisonment, Individualism, and Liberalism'. In *Policing and Prisons in the Middle East: Formations of Coercion*, edited by Laleh Khalili and Jilian Schwedler, 223–40. London: C. Hurst & Co., 2010.

Hyde, Alan. *Bodies of Law*. Princeton: Princeton University Press, 1997.

Khalaf, Samir. *Civil and Uncivil Violence in Lebanon: A History of the Internationalization of Communal Conflict*. New York: Colombia University Press, 2002.

Hadjithomas, Joana and Khalil Joreige, dirs. *Khiam*. 2000; Beirut: Abbout Production. DVD.

Ismail, Salwa. *The Rule of Violence: Subjectivity, Memory and Government in Syria*. Cambridge: Cambridge University Press, 2018.

Larkin, Emma. *Refugees and the Myth of Human Rights Life Outside the Pale of the Law*. New York: Routledge, 2014.

Legg, Stephen and Alexander Vasudevan. 'Introduction: Geographies of the Nomos'. In *Spatiality, Sovereignty and Carl Schmitt: Geographies of the Nomos*, edited by Stephen Legg, 1–23. New York: Routledge, 2011.

Llewellyn, Tim. *Spirit of the Phoenix: Beirut and the Story of Lebanon*. London: I.B. Tauris, 2010.

Mardelli, Bassil A. *Middle East Perspectives: From Lebanon (1968–1988)*. Bloomington: iUniverse, Inc., 2012.

Marron, Rayyar. *Humanitarian Rackets and Their Moral Hazards: The Case of the Palestinian Refugee Camps in Lebanon*. New York: Routledge, 2016.

Meillassoux, Quentin. 'Potentiality and Virtuality'. Translated by Robin Mackay. In *The Speculative Turn: Continental Materialism and Realism*, edited by Levi Bryant, Nick Srnicek, and Graham Harman, 224–36. Melbourne: re.press, 2011.

Mills, Catherine. *The Philosophy of Agamben*. New York: Routledge, 2008.
Newman, Saul and John Lechte. *Agamben and the Politics of Human Rights: Statelessness, Images, Violence*. Edinburgh: Edinburgh University Press, 2013.
Prozorov, Sergei. *Agamben and Politics: A Critical Introduction*. Edinburgh: Edinburgh University Press, 2014.
Ramsi, Stewart, 'Inside Islamic State's "Prison of Death" in Fallen Raqqa'. *Sky News*, 21 October 2017.
Sabbag, Randa Chahal, dir., *Souha, Surviving Hell*. 2001; Beirut: Cinétévé, Leil Production, Le Comité des Détenus de Khiam. DVD.
Scarry, Elaine. *The Body in Pain: The Making and Unmaking of the World*. New York: Oxford University Press, 1985.
Schotel, Bas. *On the Right of Exclusion: Law, Ethics and Immigration Policy*. Oxon: Routledge, 2010.
Sengupta, Kim. 'Revealed: What the West Has Given Syria's Rebels'. *The Independent*, 12 August 2013. Available online: https://www.independent.co.uk/news/world/middle-east/revealed-what-west-has-given-syria-s-rebels-8756447.html.
Sodi, Risa B. *Narrative and Imperative: The First Fifty Years of Italian Holocaust Writing (1944–1994)*. New York: Peter Lang Publishing, 2007.
'Syria: Unprecedented Investigation Reveals US-led Coalition Killed More Than 1,600 Civilians in Raqqa "Death Trap"'. *Amnesty International*, 25 April 2019. Available online: https://www.amnesty.org/en/latest/press-release/2019/04/syria-unprecedented-investigation-reveals-us-led-coalition-killed-more-than-1600-civilians-in-raqqa-death-trap/.
Vaughan-William, Nick. *Border Politics: The Limits of Sovereign Power*. Edinburgh: Edinburgh University Press, 2009.
Volk, Lucia. *Memorials and Martyrs in Modern Lebanon*. Indiana: Indiana University Press, 2010.
'You Can Still See Their Blood: Executions, Indiscriminate Shootings, and Hostage Taking by Opposition Forces in Latakia Countryside'. *Human Rights Watch*, 10 October 2013. Available online: https://www.hrw.org/report/2013/10/10/you-can-still-see-their-blood/executions-indiscriminate-shootings-and-hostage.

Chapter 8

THE POLITICS OF SECULAR CULTURAL PROPERTY IN EAST JERUSALEM

THE CASE OF BIRKET HAMAM AL-BATRAK

Adel Ruished

Introduction

In 2019, Israeli News Channel 13 reported that the Israeli Municipality of Jerusalem and the Israeli Development Authority prepared the restoration project of 'Birket Hamam al-Batrak' historical site, which is one of the largest and oldest water pools in the Old City of East Jerusalem. In the details, the Israeli reporter alleged that there were covert and indirect cooperation with officials in the Palestinian National Authority (PNA) government, Islamic Waqf Department and al-Quds University for implementing this project. Of significance, the reporter explained that the covert cooperation meant to silence Israeli criticism, which considered proceeding in the project would erode sovereign claims of the Israeli authorities in East Jerusalem. The reporter continued saying that the indirect cooperation meant also to pacify the PNA government concerns of losing credibility in Palestinian Jerusalemite street that would interpret the cooperation as coordination with the Israeli authorities in the city.[1] Interestingly, the report condoned to mention that the al-Quds University launched the restoration project in 2012 and these same Israeli authorities obstructed its implementation since then. Absent from the report was also the fact that the PNA government showed reluctance in engaging in the university restoration project under the pretext of refusing to work under Israeli authorization in an attempt to preserve its sovereign claims in the city. While some Palestinian Jerusalemites spoke about the necessity for restoring it, others concluded that disclosing the information about such cooperation was nothing but reproducing similar mechanisms to those who earlier undermined the university initiative of restoring the pool.[2]

At all matters, disclosing the details of the restoration project of the Patriarch's Pool shed light on the political contestation, which erupted between the PNA government and the Israeli government to claim ownership of historical narrative of cultural heritage property in East Jerusalem following the Oslo Peace Accords. In this regard, the Israeli government considered such ownership vital for entrenching its political claim that considered East Jerusalem part of the unified and eternal capital of the State of Israel. On its side, the PNA government considered the ownership of cultural heritage property provided significant support for its declaration of East Jerusalem as future capital of the nascent Palestinian State. Hence, the Israeli government prevented Palestinian Jerusalemite initiatives aiming at safeguarding and revitalizing such property. On its side, the PNA government abandoned supporting independent Palestinian Jerusalemite initiatives for safeguarding and revitalizing these properties without its direct control and engagement. As such, the political contestation for claiming ownership of cultural heritage property revealed a double exclusion policy: practised by the Israeli government on one side and the PNA government on the other. Of interest, this double exclusion policy appeared to be consistent with the 'state of exception' concept of Giorgio Agamben. According to Agamben, the state of exception concept bestows wide authoritative powers to governmental bodies and enables political rulers to disrupt the functioning of normal laws and replace them with exceptional ones. Such exceptional laws bind and abandon population and urban spaces depending on political wishes and interests of the ruler(s). As such, spaces and populations lose their clear legal definition, wherein chaotic conditions prevail over urban spaces, and populations become residing in bare life without protection.[3] In the same context, Simon Mabon argues that the state of exception concept provided political power with instrumental mechanisms for regulating life and ordering space in contested urban environments.[4] As such, the report about the restoration project brought attention to the Israeli government's state of negligence and to the PNA government's state of abandonment of the Patriarch's Pool post-Oslo.

This chapter advances the concept of the 'state of exception' to understand the impact of the Israeli–Palestinian political contest on safeguarding of secular cultural property and cultural heritage in East Jerusalem after the Oslo Peace Accords. The chapter begins with the explanation of how the employment of the state of exception concept in cultural heritage can be used as policy to reinforce sovereign claims in a specific geographical area. Then, the chapter traces the imposition of the Israeli state of exception on secular cultural heritage property in East Jerusalem. It then moves to highlight the emergence of the Israeli–Palestinian cultural heritage contest to enforce political claims in East Jerusalem after Oslo. This will include explanation of the emergence of the Palestinian and Israeli double state of exception on secular cultural heritage property with clarification on how this double exception was calibrated to preserve claims of political legitimacy in the city. Finally, the impact of the double exception will be projected onto the al-Quds University restoration project of the Patriarch's Pool. This double exclusion curtailed Palestinian Jerusalemite initiatives of revitalizing the pool as well as deprived Palestinian Jerusalemites the right to conserve and reclaim the cultural heritage of the pool. This study seeks to challenge unfair deprivation of Palestinian Jerusalemites of accessing, safeguarding and revitalizing secular cultural heritage property in the city, with the hope that it would contribute to end degradation state of these sites.

Suspending legal status of cultural property

Secular cultural property has long been a valuable source for future generations, exploring and documenting the traditions of past life and the history of ancestors' civilization.[5] Thus, cultural property was considered an important part of humankind's heritage and represented a vital instrument for enhancing the preservation of social cohesion and consolidation of the identity and character of individuals, communities and cities. Hence, conservation and revitalization of cultural heritage sites in the world have been utilized to enhance the development of a peaceful and stable society, founded on respect for human rights, the rule of law and democracy.[6] Therefore, national governments acquired ownership over cultural property by virtue of their sovereignty and appropriated them to national treasure.[7] However, claims to cultural heritage excluded specific communities and created divisions between rulers and ruled. Moreover, such exclusion is exacerbated when sovereignty is contested, wherein occupying powers utilized secular cultural heritage property, its conservation plans and heritage claims to erase and obliterate those of the occupied.[8] More crucially, 'heritage claims whether based in the practice of archaeology or the preservation of cultural artifacts, have long been recognized to bolster discourses of nationalism, identity, belonging and exclusion'.[9]

In his book *homo sacer: Sovereign Power and Bare Life*, Giorgio Agamben defines the state of exception concept as an exclusionary political project, wherein it provides political rulers with extra controlling powers, which not necessarily employed for the benefit of the population, as much as it furnishes ground for entrenching political influence and economic domination.[10] According to him, political rulers could attain extraordinary powers, whereupon determining putative internal or external threat to safety and security of community necessitates suspension of the functioning of the normal rule of law and 'the ordering of space'.[11] The potentiality of suspending the normal law stemmed from the legal loophole whereby

> the specification that the sovereign is 'at the same time outside and inside the juridical order' is not insignificant: the sovereign, having the legal power to suspend the validity of the law, legally places himself outside the law . . ., or the law is outside itself.[12]

Consequently, the motive behind implementing this approach is that it equips political rulers with extrajudicial powers in times of political crisis and contest for regulating population and ordering spaces. In other words, when the ability to prevail and implement absolute power within the delimited political-territorial domain wanes, the political ruler turns to impose state of exception regulations for retaining as much as possible of his influence. Through the exclusion of part of population or urban space from the rule of normal law, the political ruler is enabled to define the exception rendering himself authorized to blur the borders between legal and illegal definitions of rights and property and situate them in a zone of indistinction and impose exceptional laws and regulations for serving his political, religious and economic interests. This resulted in severing population legal protection and strip them of civil human rights. Interestingly, this political strategy was recently apparent in many Middle Eastern states. Simon Mabon aptly argued that larger population in the region stripped of their rights, whereupon state structures relied heavily on emergency or exceptional regulations to retain political power during the recent 'Arab Spring' Uprisings.[13] Hence, population exposed to existential threat, turning them into vassal and laid into exceptional state of life. Consequently, this exceptional state of life 'is neither simple natural life nor social life but rather bare life or sacred life, is the always present and always operative presupposition of sovereignty'.[14] Moreover, as Simon Mabon argues in the introduction of this book: 'the fundamental practice of sovereign power is the creation of bare life, the stripping of political meaning from life, reducing it to its *natural* form but remaining exposed to sovereign power.'[15] Accordingly, the sovereign embarks on perpetuating the reproduction of bare life conditions for this part of population in order to entrench political power and influence in contested urban spaces. In this sense, the perpetuation of bare life conditions turned out to be one of the major roles of the sovereign power, wherein the sovereign constantly implemented exclusionary policies to justify his role and necessity in the eyes of the whole population. Agamben explained that modes of power that formed the 'governmentality' concept, which are individual disciplinary regulations and population biopower technologies, are only just an introduction for applying the state of exception. In this regard, he argued that while these elements were presented as working in the interest of, and caring for, the individual and the population, they represented at the same time a vital tool for depriving the individual and population natural human rights and freedom of expression, as well as restricting liberties.[16]

In East Jerusalem, ownership, access, conservation plans and claim of owning the cultural heritage and historical narrative of secular cultural property have been contested between the Israeli government and the PNA government post-Oslo. Indeed, these governments employed control and supervision of these properties for entrenching political claims and maximizing their economic interests in the city.[17] This resulted in situating the secular cultural properties in the city in the double state of exception. Whereas the Israeli government's state of exception neglected these cultural properties, the PNA government's state of exception abandoned them. It followed that this double exclusion led to the suspension of the legal definition of these properties as significant secular cultural heritage sites in East Jerusalem. The double exclusion also deprived Palestinian Jerusalemites of the right to safeguard and revitalize these properties. Moreover, I argue that neither the Israeli government nor the PNA government showed interest in advancing local conservation and revitalization plans for these properties, without having exclusive control and their direct intervention in such plans. Furthermore, I argue that the Israeli and the PNA governments employed various modes of power for calibrating the double exclusion, aiming at perpetuating the regulation of local and international revitalization initiatives of these properties. Certainly, such calibration resulted in exacerbating the state of degradation of these cultural properties in the city. In the following sections, I combine interviews with actors involved in the process with archival work and my previous practical experience, which I accumulated as al-Quds University's coordinator for the revitalization project of the Patriarch's Pool as one of the significant secular cultural property in East Jerusalem.

The history of the Patriarch's Pool (Birket Hamam el-Batrak)

Birket Hamam el-Batrak (the Pool of the Patriarch's Bath in English) represented an important element of the ancient water system in Jerusalem, wherein it was used to secure water for local needs of drinking, hygienic and purification requirements, in peaceful times and in times of political conflict and siege alike.[18] The Patriarch's Pool is an open water reservoir with an estimated capacity of 30,000 cubic metres and covers a land area of over 3 dunums.[19] The Patriarch's Pool is located in the Christian Quarter in the Old City of East Jerusalem and is surrounded by buildings and shops from all sides. The sole entrance to the pool is located on its northern side through the Khan of the Copts.[20] David Gurevich suggests that the Patriarch's Pool was built around the late Hellenistic or early Roman periods in Jerusalem.[21] Significantly, successive empires and powers that ruled the city showed interest in controlling and maintaining the pool and called it with names that reflected its ownership of the pool.[22] As such, the pool was known as the Patriarch's Pool due to its closeness to the Patriarch's residence during the Byzantine period (Boas 2001). As for the early Muslim rule in Jerusalem, the pool was known 'I'ad Pool' after the companion of the Prophet 'I'ad Ben Ghanam'.[23]

Interestingly, the pool acquired political significance when the Fatimid Caliph Al-Mustansir promised the Christian Patriarch to retain exclusive administrative and judicial autonomy over the Christian Quarter in return for refortifying the north-western part of the wall of Jerusalem. Accordingly, the Patriarch renamed the pool as the 'Pool of the Patriarch'. On their turn, the Crusaders maintained this exclusive control, and the pool became known as the 'Pool of the Patriarch's Bath' because the pool used to provide water to the bathhouse located across the Christian Quarter street.[24] After the liberation of Jerusalem from the Crusaders, the Ayyubid Sultan Salah el-Din (Saladin) endowed 'al-Batrik Water Pool (birka) and its adjacent bathhouse (Hamam) including its upper and lower floors'.[25] Interestingly, *Saladin* incorporated the pool to the 'Khanqah al-Salahiya' Endowment and called it 'Birket Hamam al-Batrak'. Since then, this endowment instituted ownership of the Patriarch's Pool to the Islamic Waqf Department in the city and defined its legal status as secular public Waqf property, knowing that this also continued during the Mamluke and Ottoman rule in Jerusalem.[26]

The Israeli exclusion of secular cultural property in East Jerusalem

The Israeli occupation of East Jerusalem in 1967 paved the way for the Israeli government to proceed in Judaizing secular cultural property and antiquity sites in the city, reiterating what it had previously done in West Jerusalem since 1948.[27] In effect, these properties and sites were not only vital tools for strengthening Israeli political hegemony and control over East Jerusalem but were also utilized for establishing historical Jewish ideological claims in the city.[28] In this regard, the Israeli authorities initially concentrated its efforts to Judaize the southern and the southern-western area of the Old City of East Jerusalem, which is the area surrounding al-Haram al-Sharif (the Noble Sanctuary).[29] To some extent, the Israeli authorities reaffirmed Ottoman and British status quo as well as relied on the Israeli Law for the Protection of Holy Places with regard to sacred (holy) cultural places in East Jerusalem.[30] As for secular cultural property in the city, these authorities initially relied on the British Antiquities Law of 1928 and subsequently resorted to the Israeli Antiquities Law of 1978, to regulate archaeological sites, thereby establishing ownership of the Israeli state of these property and sites, and subjecting them to scientific and archaeological inquiries only.[31] Moreover, Simone Ricca contends that the plan of the Israeli authorities sought to alter and erase the centuries-old Arab past of East Jerusalem and replace its character with an exclusively Jewish one. In this context, the demolition of the Moroccan (Mughrabi) Quarter and expelling of its Palestinian Jerusalemite inhabitants immediately after the Israeli occupation for enlarging the Wailing Wall Plaza had represented the initial step of this plan.[32]

Subsequently, these authorities expanded the plan to include the whole of the Old City of East Jerusalem and the area surrounding its walls. For this purpose, the Israeli authorities demarcated the Old City as a sacred and archaeological zone and categorized it the 'Historic and Holy Basin'.[33] Effectively, this categorization enabled the Israeli political authorities to devise a 'carefully planned double dimension' framework that allowed constant shift between archaeological (secular) and holy (sacred) symbolism of secular cultural heritage property in the city. Consequently, this framework blurred the distinction between secular and sacred cultural property.[34] As such, this double dimension framework situated secular cultural heritage property in East Jerusalem into a state of exception and suspended their legal definition. Unlike sacred sites in the city in which religious communities retained relative autonomy for administering their respective holy sites,[35] and unlike secular cultural property in the cities of the West Bank and Gaza Strip wherein responsibility was transferred to Officer of Archaeology in the Israeli military,[36] the responsibility for secular cultural property in East Jerusalem was 'uneasily shared' between the Israeli Ministry for Religious Affairs and Israeli Department of Archaeology and Museums (IDAM).[37] It is important to note that this shared responsibility frequently escalated tensions between the Israeli religious and archaeological authorities. Yet, both sides confirmed Israeli and Jewish exclusiveness of these property regardless of its sacred or archaeological nature.[38]

More importantly, this uneasily shared responsibility resulted in establishing chaotic conditions and overlapping authorities between these Israeli authorities. Interestingly, the Israeli political authorities exploited this chaotic condition for achieving its religious, economic and cultural heritage interests in East Jerusalem.

In this regard, Agamben argues that 'since there is no rule applicable to chaos, chaos must first be included in the juridical order through the creation of a zone of indistinction, ... wherein the sovereign decision on the exception is the originally juridical-political structure, on the basis of which what is included in the juridical order and what is excluded from it acquire their meaning'.[39] Hence, the Israeli political authorities exploited the established chaotic condition to manipulate legal definition of secular cultural property for serving its interests. Under pretext of arbitration in frequently escalated tension between Israeli religious and archaeological authorities, the Israeli political authorities appropriated many secular cultural properties surrounding al-Haram al-Sharif throughout the 1970s and 1990s, and adapted them into Israeli national monuments or Jewish religious sites.[40] Therefore, Katharina Galor confirms that issues pertaining to sacred and secular cultural property and heritage in East Jerusalem were governed by political authorities outside the jurisdiction of normal legal frameworks.[41] This was manifested when the Israeli occupying authorities, after demolishing the Mughrabi Quarter, exploited ostensible tension between Israeli religious and archaeological authorities with regard to legal definition and proper development and adapted the enlarged Wailing Wall Plaza. In this regard, the Israeli government designated the closer area of the Plaza to the Wailing Wall as sacred under the jurisdiction of the rabbinates of the Ministry of Religious Affairs. The farther area of the plaza, however, was allocated by the government for Israeli national ceremonies and under the jurisdiction of the Israeli Municipality of Jerusalem.[42]

It is noteworthy that the Department of Archaeology and Museums at the Hebrew University (IDAM) and Israeli National Parks Authority (INPA) represented the governmental arms of the Israeli political authorities.[43] In this context, the INPA imposed planning schemes that turned the whole area of the Old City and its surroundings into national parks imbued with exclusive narratives of Jewish cultural heritage. Indeed, such schemes intended to achieve as much as possible territorial and properties seizure for the Israeli state in East Jerusalem.[44] In its turn, the IDAM was provided with wide power for conducting massive archaeological excavations, explorations and surveys, including the issuance of archaeological publications and reports. Central to this was a practice for transforming truths about many of these secular cultural properties. Nadia Abu El-Haj mentions that Israeli archaeologists manipulated cultural property and archaeological findings and meagerly produced reports about archaeological findings that related to non-Jewish history.[45] As a result of these Israeli manipulations, the UNESCO inscribed the Old City of Jerusalem and its Surrounding Walls on the World Heritage List (WHL) in 1980 and on the WHL in Danger (WHLD) in 1982, calling the Israeli government to refrain from altering the cultural character of the city and enable competent local authorities to conduct preservation and restoration of cultural property.[46]

Yet, the Israeli government refused to concede the authority of archaeological activities to international or local Palestinian Jerusalemite organization, neglected the rest of secular Palestinian cultural property in East Jerusalem, exposing them to disappear in the context of rapid urban development and increased population density in the Old City of East Jerusalem.[47] At all events, this encouraged the emergence of local and international NGOs concerned with the preservation and maintenance of built cultural heritage in East Jerusalem.[48] Certainly, preservation efforts and archaeological activities of these NGOs were unable to meet challenges posed by the various Israeli archaeological authorities in the city.[49]

The contest for claiming cultural heritage in East Jerusalem post-Oslo

In the years following the Oslo peace agreement that was signed between the Israeli government and the Palestine Liberation Organization in 1993, political contest heightened between the Israeli government and the Palestinian National Authority to increase their political influence in the City of East Jerusalem.[50] In this regard, the Israeli government pursued its political project which considered East Jerusalem part of the united and eternal capital of the State of Israel and the Jewish people. On its part, the PNA considered the city the future capital of the nascent Palestinian State.[51] Significantly, secular cultural property and ownership of the cultural heritage in East Jerusalem became entangled amid the Palestinian-Israeli political contest, rendering efforts of their administration, protection and revitalization politicized and highly complicated.[52] This was due to the fact that the Israeli government considered protection and development of secular cultural property in East Jerusalem its sole responsibility, while the PNA insisted its sole right to protect and develop them. Michael Dumper and Gary Larkin argue that for Israel, this cultural heritage contest

> revolves around attempts to legitimize a specific Jewish historical perspective and justify the current status of Israeli control and political authority; yet for Palestinians, on the other hand, it is part of the struggle to preserve their cultural heritage and therefore is more often about recent history and the protection of living communities in the Old City. Heritage preservation in Jerusalem's Old City therefore remains not only the loci for cultural and ideological confrontation, the 'field on which the desired pasts battle for hegemony' but continues to be a pragmatic tool for securing and legitimizing physical presence, ownership and right to the land.[53]

As a result of this contest, the Israeli government neglected secular cultural properties in the city, hoping that this would result in their disappearance or facilitate their adaptation according to Jewish traditional imagination. The Israeli government also curtailed protection efforts of Palestinian Jerusalemites to preserve these properties.[54] On its side, the PNA abandoned conducting excavations and refrained initiating revitalization plans of these property under permission of Israeli authority, hoping to expose inequality of Israeli laws and de-legitimization of Israeli occupation in East Jerusalem.[55] Certainly, this political contest resulted in obliterating the Arab Islamic and Christian character of East Jerusalem. Hence, I argue that between the Israeli government's negligence and the PA government's abandonment, secular cultural property in East Jerusalem is caught in a double state of exception (exclusion) post-Oslo.[56] In fact, each government defied the other's ability to practise absolute authority in preserving and developing these properties, hoping to enhance their cultural heritage claim in the city.[57]

The state of Israeli negligence

Following the Oslo Peace Accords, the Israeli occupying authorities intensified the utilization of cultural heritage for strengthening the link between ancient Israelite history and subsequent Israeli and Jewish sovereign rights in East Jerusalem. Thus, it hastened to control secular cultural property and claim ownership of its cultural heritage.[58] For this purpose, these authorities expanded its control plans to include secular cultural property located in the Christian, Muslim and Armenian Quarters of the Old City, and in its outside surroundings and even underground.[59] Accordingly, the Israeli government resorted again to the 'Holy Basin' categorization.[60] In fact, this categorization was nothing but reproducing the (sacred–secular) double dimension framework which fluctuated the legal definition of secular cultural property between sacred Jewish sites and Israeli antiquity sites, depending on the closeness of the property to the Temple Mount.[61] Thus, loose and fluctuated legal definition emerged for these urban secular cultural property, situating them into a zone of indistinction. Unlike sacred cultural sites wherein relevant autonomy was left in the hands of related religious bodies, and secular property in the cities of the Gaza Strip and the West Bank, the agreement for establishing a joint committee of Israeli and Palestinian experts for the coordination of archaeological excavations, preservation plans and freedom of access to archaeological sites and secular cultural property in East Jerusalem has never been materialized.[62] Rather, responsibility and conservation activities of secular cultural property were intimately shared between Israeli archaeological and municipal authorities, and ideological Jewish settler movements in East Jerusalem post-Oslo.[63] This was reflected in the openly stated intention of Israeli municipal and archaeological authorities to transform secular cultural property into Israeli touristic attractions or Jewish traditional sites.[64]

More importantly, the intimate shared responsibility utilized the fluctuated and loose legal definition of these urban secular cultural spaces to reincorporate them into the sovereign ban.[65] This was asserted when the Israeli government established the Israeli Antiquities Authority (IAA) in the early 1990s and provided it wide authoritative powers. Adding to this, the Israeli government preserved ultimate decision concerning conservation or destroying secular cultural property in East Jerusalem with the office of the Israeli prime minister and the director of the Antiquities Authority, subject to the approval of the competent ministerial committee.[66] Consequently, such 'administrative framework reserves the power to decide what aspects of the heritage should be highlighted to a governmental body, in which the professional archaeological voice plays only a marginal role'.[67] Thus, the absence of clear definition in Israeli law differentiating between holiness and secularity of cultural property deepened the chaotic definition and enabled Israeli court to rule that holiness relied on the personal perspective of believer, making secular Palestinian cultural property under the mercy of political and religious motives.[68] This was reflected in the administrative composition of the IAA, which included ideological religious Jewish organizations that supported and financed a series of archaeological excavations in the Old City of East Jerusalem with the aim to highlight Jewish historical periods and reject 'other' historical periods.[69]

In effect, the IAA employed the administrative framework and composition to facilitate the control of Jewish activists of many secular cultural properties in East Jerusalem under the pretext of conducting archaeological salvage excavations.[70] This was demonstrated when the Israeli prime minister ordered in 1996 the opening of the northern end of the tunnel with its outlet end in the Muslim Quarter in the Old City, knowing that its entrance starts beneath the Islamic court next to the Wailing Wall. Interestingly, the tunnel was promoted as tangible evidence of the primacy of the Temple in Jerusalem's heritage and was adapted as an Israeli-Jewish touristic attraction managed by the Western Wall Heritage Foundation, which directed from the Israeli Prime Minister's Office.[71] It is important to mention that before the intensification of the contest over cultural heritage in East Jerusalem, the Israeli Ministry of Religious Affairs had previously adapted the entrance of the tunnel as a synagogue following tension between the religious and archaeological bodies with regard to professional restoration and its proper legal definition. Needless to mention that such promotion excluded other archaeological findings that attested to Muslim Umayyad or Christian Byzantine periods in Jerusalem and neglected warnings that the tunnel would expose the wall and gates of the al-Haram and Palestinian Jerusalemites homes above to the danger of collapse.[72]

Concurrently, the IAA curtailed the efforts of Palestinian Jerusalemite non-governmental organizations to conserve secular cultural property and heritage sites in East Jerusalem. This was demonstrated when the IAA repeatedly excluded the implementation of protection plans of the Waqf Islamic Department and the Welfare Organization, among many other NGOs, and neglected authorizing safeguarding or revitalization plans of secular cultural property in East Jerusalem.[73] In effect, the IAA calibrated the fluctuated legal definition of secular cultural property for perpetuating the state of neglect and the deterioration of the physical conditions of these property, leaving them for sabotage and destruction.

Calibrating the negligence

The calibration of the state of negligence was achieved through the employment of the Law of Protection for Holy Places, or the Israeli Law of Antiquities, municipal planning schemes or the Israeli national public parks law. In this regard, the conservation of secular Palestinian cultural property in East Jerusalem was often neglected and disallowed revitalization under the pretext of one of these laws.[74] Indeed, these laws represented invisible modes of power, wherein the Israeli occupying authorities employed to calibrate the chaotic legal definition for sustaining the state of negligence at many secular cultural properties in East Jerusalem post-Oslo. Starting with racial discrimination policies, passing through iniquitous disciplinary regulations and ending with biopolitical mode of power, the IAA impeded Palestinian Jerusalemite local NGOs conservation and development initiatives and denied them the right to access, preserve and claim archaeological and cultural heritage of many significant historical sites in the city.[75]

Prevention of conservation and development

The Israeli racial discrimination spatial infrastructural and planning policies resulted in the destruction of secular Palestinian cultural property in and around the Old City of East Jerusalem and the erection of new sites.[76] Indeed, the IAA excluded Palestinian Jerusalemites from the archaeological excavation and revitalization process and from the historical–cultural heritage narrative that accompanied it. Raphael Greenberg contends that Israeli archaeologists conducted excavations under armed cover and executed their surveys on archaeological sites in East Jerusalem among themselves rendering their work invisible to the general public. Such an approach resulted in destroying, covering over or leaving these sites undeveloped after finishing work at these sites. Moreover, he says that the Israeli Municipality of Jerusalem neglected secular Palestinian cultural property, allocated inadequate financial resources for infrastructural and conservation works and left them to decay.[77] According to a report issued by the Palestinian Jerusalemite Welfare Nongovernmental Organization in 2004, the Israeli development and municipal authorities not only neglected secular cultural property in East Jerusalem but also curtailed efforts of Palestinian Jerusalemite NGOs for restoring or developing these property. The aim was to perpetuate the deterioration of the physical conditions, with the IAA focused on finding evidence that would assert Israeli political sovereignty in East Jerusalem and Jewish ideological and cultural heritage claims.[78]

Iniquitous regulations

The disciplinary mode of power represented the imposition of iniquitous regulations that aimed at curtailing efforts of protecting and developing secular Palestinian cultural property in East Jerusalem.[79] In this regard, the IAA tended to marginalize local Palestinian Jerusalemite archaeologists and architects and rejected their participation in archaeological or preservation works concerning secular cultural property. This resulted in curtailing local Palestinian Jerusalemite efforts pertaining to cultural heritage in the city.[80] In addition, Katharina Galor mentions that due to these political stances, since 2000 minimal coordination and cooperation existed between the Waqf Department and other local NGOs on one side, and the IAA on the other side.[81] Moreover, Hamdan Taha states that the Israeli occupying authorities stipulated complicated procedures to get permission for developing secular Palestinian cultural property in the city and according to its own interests. According to him, the Israeli Ministry of Tourism also obstructed adapting many of the significant cultural property as touristic attractions that reflect the cultural heritage of the whole humankind in the city. This ministry also declined to license Palestinian Jerusalemites tourist guides, disallowed them to accompany tourists and prevented them from organizing alternative tours in the city.[82] Furthermore, the Israeli Armed Forces police invaded revitalization workshops and ordered halting of restoration work under the pretext of security reasons. As such, these laws and provisions have been applied selectively to obstruct the efforts of Palestinian Jerusalemites to protect and revitalize their secular cultural properties in East Jerusalem through reliance on the chaotic legal definition of these properties for serving the Israeli cultural heritage interests in East Jerusalem.[83]

Influencing public awareness

In the context of perpetuating the state of negligence of secular cultural property in East Jerusalem, the Israeli occupying authorities embarked on influencing public awareness of Palestinian Jerusalemites in the city. This was achieved through the biopolitical mode of power. To begin with, the Israeli Municipality of Jerusalem conditioned the provision of authorization for renovation of these property after conducting archaeological excavations by the IAA. This condition stipulated that owners must leave their property until the excavations are finished. As such, many Palestinian Jerusalemites tended to refrain from renovating their property, fearing losing them to the IAA.[84] In addition, the Welfare Organization clarifies that the Israeli Municipality of Jerusalem ignored raising awareness of Palestinian Jerusalemites regarding the significance of secular cultural properties, and neglected providing those living next to these properties proper garbage collection services. Hence, the physical condition of these properties deteriorated, paving the way for the Israeli municipality to order evicting many of them under the pretext of its invalidity for living.[85] Moreover, the Israeli Ministry of Tourism produced maps and tourist guides wherein it changed names of secular cultural property in East Jerusalem with Israeli-Jewish names, aiming to distort Palestinian Jerusalemites' awareness and influence their identity.[86] Israeli tourist guides also bypassed secular Palestinian cultural property in their touristic tours in the city, turning them invisible for visitors and tourists.[87] In tandem with this, the IAA employed sound and light in addition to computer technologies to influence public awareness of Palestinian Jerusalemites as well as tourists in the city. This was demonstrated through projecting traditional Israelite features on secular Palestinian cultural property without supportive archaeological evidence of the Jewish origins of these properties.[88] Therefore, political and ideological stances led Israeli occupying authorities to exclude attempts of Palestinian Jerusalemites to access and preserve, let alone claim and enjoy the cultural heritage of these properties.

The PNA government state of abandonment of secular cultural property

Following the Oslo peace agreement, the Palestinian National Authority established the Palestinian Ministry of Tourism and Antiquities (PMOTA) in 1994, which included the Palestinian Department of Antiquities and Cultural Heritage (PDACH), wherein the ministry administered and organized tourism activities, while the PDACH managed archaeological activities and supervised and managed secular cultural property.[89] Given the condensed and formidable built Christian and Muslim monuments attesting to the Arab character, the PNA government sought to advocate the city's cultural heritage as a way to boost its political and sovereign claims in East Jerusalem.[90] However, the PMOTA and the PDACH were disallowed to conduct archaeological excavations, preservation and development of secular Palestinian cultural property and heritage in East Jerusalem, wherein these were excluded from their jurisdiction according to the Oslo peace agreement.[91] Moreover, the Israeli government continued to see East Jerusalem as an integral part of the Israeli State and reiterated its refusal to concede protection and development efforts of cultural heritage to Palestinian or international body, fearing weakening of its sovereign claims and political physical control in East Jerusalem.[92] Hence, the PMOTA situated secular Palestinian cultural property in East Jerusalem and its preservation and development plans in state of exception.[93]

Unlike sacred cultural property in the city wherein relevant religious communities have enjoyed relative autonomy for conducting preservation activities, and secular cultural property and heritage in the cities of the West Bank and Gaza Strip wherein it launched excavations and implemented preservation and economic development activities,[94] the PMOTA opted to abandon conducting archaeological excavations and conservation plans with regard to secular cultural heritage and property in East Jerusalem.[95] Consequently, preservation and revitalization efforts of secular Palestinian cultural property in East Jerusalem were voluntarily distributed between various local independent administrative bodies, such as the Islamic Waqf Department, the Welfare Organization and the Islamic movement in Israel in addition to other Palestinian Jerusalemite local institutions. Therefore, these efforts became scattered and isolated without a comprehensive plan and unified vision and in the absence of a national regulating authority.[96]

Calibrating the abandonment

Interestingly, the PMOTA exploited this state of abandonment to maintain its contest in claiming the city's cultural heritage. This necessitated rendering Palestinian Jerusalemites to behave according to heritage interests of the ministry in the city. In this regard, Chiara De-Cesari argues that the PMOTA espoused the concept which says that 'states also govern by cultural heritage'.[97] Rather, I argue that the PMOTA governed by abandoning cultural heritage in East Jerusalem post-Oslo. This was attributed to the fact that 'the politics of heritage is not only about the inclusion or exclusion of certain narratives and identities in and out of dominant public representations; it is also about the concrete management of people's lives through the reshaping of their living environments and the spatial regulation of their daily practices'.[98] At stake were protection and development efforts of local non-governmental organizations in East Jerusalem that sought to reduce 'the divide between mobilizing heritage to defend vulnerable communities and resist the encroachment of the (Israeli) state, and using heritage to develop institutions and help build the (Palestinian) state'.[99] To effectuate this exclusion the PMOTA implemented the Foucauldian governmentality concept represented by invisible modes of power.[100] These modes of power tended to abandon including secular cultural property in East Jerusalem in enacted Palestinian laws that provided protection to similar property in the West Bank. In this context, Suad Ghazal pointed out the absence of legal protection mechanisms of secular cultural property in East Jerusalem from Palestinian national laws, regional and international cooperation agreements that the ministry developed since 1995 for protecting secular cultural property in Palestine.[101]

Indifferent disciplinary regulations

Adding to the exclusion of secular cultural property in East Jerusalem from legal protection mechanisms, the PMOTA opted to discipline individual Palestinian Jerusalemite architects and archaeologists, as well as local NGOs active in the field of conservation and development of secular cultural property in the city. In this regard, Chiara De-Cesari mentions that the PDACH debated boycotting dealing with related Israeli occupying authorities in East Jerusalem and urged Palestinian Jerusalemite architects, archaeologists and local NGOs to behave accordingly. In fact, the ministry meant to distance Palestinian Jerusalemite experts and local NGOs, despite accumulated experience they gained in the field of heritage preservation and development in the city.[102] In addition, the PDACH kept decision concerned with secular cultural property in East Jerusalem for its upper echelon officials and experts only, under the pretext that best practices of conservation and revitalization programmes subjected to expert discourses and expert practices.[103] This was manifested when the PMOTA transferred many responsibilities of local NGOs pertaining to cultural heritage and tourism sector in East Jerusalem to its departments, rendering offices of some of these organizations relocating outside the city in order to get closer to the ministry and causing others inside the city to halt totally their activities.[104]

Regulating public awareness

The calibrated mechanism of the PMOTA state of abandonment required the regulation of Palestinian Jerusalemites' public awareness concerning the secular cultural property in East Jerusalem. Such regulation tended to raise Palestinian Jerusalemites' public awareness about exclusionary Israeli policies and underpin their steadfastness, while ignoring their awareness about the importance of maintaining and developing built secular cultural property and heritage in the city.[105] In this context, the Welfare Organization study stressed on the importance of raising awareness of Palestinian Jerusalemite public about the value and significance of secular cultural property, the need for protecting it as well as economic and tourism benefits attributed to these cultural property in the city.

According to this study, the clear absence of the PMOTA role was noticed in raising public awareness and public participation in the decision-making process regarding rehabilitation and revitalization of these properties. Such absence resulted in Palestinian Jerusalemites' lack of appreciation of secular cultural property, wherein they neglected and turned many of these properties into garbage and sewage disposal containers and hideouts for drug addicts. Certainly, this resulted in deteriorating environmental and health conditions of general public living and working in this area, let alone establishing tourists and visitors negative impression about attitudes of Palestinian Jerusalemites and their behaviours towards these properties.[106]

A private sector study pointed out in 2010 the state of abandonment and negligence of secular cultural property in East Jerusalem. According to this study, such abandonment deprived many Palestinian Jerusalemites the opportunity to take advantage of these properties in tourism industry in the city, which would offer opportunity for many to improve their financial incomes and living standards. The study also alluded to the failure of the PMOTA in suggesting mechanisms to facilitate Palestinian Jerusalemite access to soft loans for developing secular cultural property and related trade, resulting in creating feelings of distrust among many Palestinian Jerusalemites and raising their depression.[107]

As such, the Israeli government and the PNA have doubly excluded secular cultural property to serve their political and economic interests in East Jerusalem. This resulted in not only neglecting and abandoning these properties but also depriving Palestinian Jerusalemites of the right to safeguard, revitalize and weaken their connection with historical and cultural heritage in the city. Accordingly, I will now turn to employ this understanding to study the case of the Patriarch's Pool as one of the significant secular cultural property in the city.

The case of the Patriarch's Pool

Immediately after occupying East Jerusalem, the Israeli authorities sought to Judaize the Patriarch's Pool, among other ancient water infrastructures in the city and own its cultural heritage and historical narrative.[108] Drawing on its earlier experience at the Mughrabi Quarter, the Israeli government utilized demarcation of the Holy Basin to classify the Patriarch's Pool according to a combination of archaeological, religious and architectural values. Hence, the pool became subordinated to conflicted jurisdictions between the INPA, IDAM and the Israeli Municipality of Jerusalem. More importantly, such classification facilitated the restoration of the pool according to Israeli archaeological and architectural perception, and ancient Jewish religious narratives.[109] Thus, the Patriarch's Pool acquired a double (sacred–secular) dimension, which fluctuated its legal classification between Israeli antiquity site and Jewish holy site. As such, the pool was situating it into a state of Israeli exception. Consequently, Arieh Sharon, the then Israeli municipality architect, suggested in 1974 rejuvenating the Patriarch's Pool according to its ancient Israelite origins during the first and the second Temple periods. In fact, such schemes aimed at developing Israeli and Jewish cultural heritage through the museumization of the Patriarch's Pool as well as restoring it according to a former pattern that prevailed in earlier generations.[110]

Though managed by 1976 to restore some secular cultural property in East Jerusalem according to its ancient Jewish and historical perception and develop them for its political, economic and tourism interest in the city, the Israeli authorities have not managed to accomplish restoration or development of the Patriarch's Pool. This was attributed to international and local controversies and criticisms against Israeli policies of conscious demolition and exclusion of significant archaeological remains of pre-existing Christian and Muslim periods at these properties, as well as unprofessional practices of Israeli municipal and archaeological authorities.[111] Nevertheless, the Israeli government utilized the Israeli Law of Antiquities of 1978, which provided IDAM with leverage over other conflicting Israeli authorities for establishing state ownership over antiquity sites as well as monopolization of archaeological excavations. In addition, IDAM manipulated the Antiquities Law to circumvent international and local criticisms. Under the pretext of conducting salvage excavations before restoration, Israeli archaeologists continued their surveys, searching for ancient Israelite antiquity, while erased Muslim and Christian traces at many historical sites in East Jerusalem, including the Patriarch's Pool.[112] Effectively, these archaeologists sought to Judaize the Patriarch's Pool and establish Israeli ownership claims over its cultural heritage and historical narrative. Hence, they tended to secretly conduct their excavations away from the public eye.[113] During my field research in East Jerusalem in 2019, a Palestinian Jerusalemite living at the Coptic Khan that overlooks the Patriarch's Pool mentioned that

> during the 1980s and early 1990s, we used to see some people coming equipped with tools, entering into the Patriarch's Pool, and taking measures and conducted diggings without knowing who are they, what they were doing and what for,. . . . I think they were Israeli archaeologists who used to disguise as foreign tourists, bribe a resident, or pay in return of teas and coffees in other times, for facilitating their sneak to the Pool. . . . They used to leave potholes after departure.[114]

In tandem with this, various Israeli authorities curtailed attempts of local Palestinian Jerusalemite NGOs to maintain the pool. Indeed, Israeli municipal architects ignored informing or consulting with Palestinian Jerusalemites living next to the pool about potential future development plans of the pool. In addition, the Israeli Municipality of Jerusalem neglected the provision of proper and adequate municipal services and garbage collection and contributed to lack of public awareness about the pool's archaeological and cultural heritage significance. This resulted in turning the Patriarch's Pool into a container for sewage and the remains of construction materials, as well as garbage for nearby shops and homes, creating environmental and health hazards of the pool on locals, visitors and tourists of the city.[115] Certainly, such exclusionary policies aimed at deteriorating the physical conditions of the Patriarch's Pool leaving it to decay on its own without accusing the Israeli occupying authorities of reordering the pool according to its political, economic and religious interests in East Jerusalem. Moreover, these policies also established inequitable and unhealthy conditions for Palestinian Jerusalemites who live and work next to the Patriarch's Pool and resided them in bare life stripped of their right to live in the city and enjoy the cultural heritage of the pool. It was hoped that such bare life conditions would push these Palestinian Jerusalemites to leave their homes and shops next to the pool, without accusing the Israeli occupying authorities of committing deportation.

Consequently, these Israeli exclusionary measures raised concern among some Palestinian Jerusalemites, who attempted to initiate development plans in cooperation with the Waqf Department for the pool. Yet, it seems that during this period ownership dispute erupted over the Patriarch's Pool and its surrounding structures between the Waqf Department and the Coptic Church, which resulted in the obstruction of the implementation of these development initiatives and contributed to perpetuating the dilapidated environmental and deteriorated physical conditions of the pool.[116] Significantly, this ownership dispute extended throughout the years following the Oslo peace agreement of 1993. This resulted in bringing the Patriarch's Pool, among other secular cultural properties in East Jerusalem, into contending the political bazaar between the Israeli government and the newly established PNA. In effect the Israeli occupying authorities and the PNA engaged in a competition over controlling the Patriarch's Pool and claiming its cultural heritage and historical narrative. Certainly, control over the Patriarch's Pool and its development initiatives represented an indispensable tool for both political powers to enhance their contending sovereign and political claims in East Jerusalem, as well as to boost their religious and historical interests and economic and tourism potentials in the city.[117]

Accordingly, the Israeli authorities hastened to regulate local conservation and developmental works at the pool. Considering the disinterest of the Waqf Department and the Coptic Church to work under its authorization, the Israeli occupying authorities not only perpetuated the state of negligence and chaotic conditions at the Patriarch's Pool but also prevented cleaning, conserving and developing it.[118] On its side, the PNA imposed its own state of exception against conducting protection initiatives and developmental projects at the Patriarch's Pool under Israeli authorization. This resulted in abandoning support and protection for local development initiatives, which contributed to the deterioration of the physical conditions of the pool. Consequently, between the state of Israeli negligence and the state of PNA abandonment, the Patriarch's Pool has been caught within a double state of exception post-Oslo. In the rest of the chapter, I will first discuss the Israeli state of exception at the pool, then will move to show the PNA state of exception, taking into consideration that the two states were implemented simultaneously.

The state of Israeli negligence of the Patriarch's Pool post-Oslo

Amid this cultural heritage contest, the Israeli Antiquities Authority, which was established in the early 1990s, in cooperation with the INPA, the Israeli

Municipality of Jerusalem, Israeli Jerusalem Development Authority as well as non-governmental Jewish religious groups, expanded excavation and restoration programmes to include the Patriarch's Pool. In effect, this new archaeological circuit intensified and accelerated its attempts to Judaize, control and own the cultural heritage and historical narrative of the Patriarch's Pool for serving its political contest in East Jerusalem.[119] This was through the reintroduction of the 'Holy Basin' demarcation, which subjected legal definition of the Patriarch's Pool in a zone of indistinction. In other words, such classification fluctuated legal definition of the pool between Jewish holy site (sacred) and ancient Israelite monument (secular) simultaneously. Thus, the responsibility of protection, conservation and development at the Patriarch's Pool became intimately overlapped between religious and secular Israeli bodies in the city. This was exemplified when the Israeli *Jerusalem Post* newspaper presented the Patriarch's Pool as a significant Jewish holy site in East Jerusalem. With a photo of the Patriarch's Pool in the background and under the title 'Drawing Deep: Many Temple Period Pools of Water Necessary for Rituals Existed in Old City; Many Can be Found Today', the newspaper pointed out that the pool was an important Jewish religious bath specified for conducting ritual purifications for worshippers on their way to pray on the Temple Mount.[120]

Subsequently, a Jewish religious group identified the Patriarch's Pool with the Jewish king Hezekiah,[121] despite lack of archaeological evidence, and embarked on lobbying the Israeli Parliament for enhancing the IAA to launch conservation project at the pool accordingly. Thus, the municipality workers broke the rear of a shop on the Christian Market Street in 2011 and bulldozed the Patriarch's Pool.[122] More importantly, the Jewish religious group called on the Israeli Municipality of Jerusalem to lift damage inflicted on the Patriarch's Pool, criticizing its neglect towards such a significant site for the Jewish people and its cultural heritage in East Jerusalem.[123] In effect, many Palestinian Jerusalemites considered the municipality action as an attempt to obliterate and ruin potential artefacts findings that would testify to non-Jewish cultural heritage in the Patriarch's Pool.[124] Also, the exceptional fluctuated legal status of the Patriarch's Pool, between significant religious Jewish site and important Israeli archaeological cultural property enabled the new Israeli archaeological circuit to combine the implementation of architectural and archaeological laws from one side and holy places law from the other side at the Patriarch's Pool. Commenting on bulldozing the pool, the Al Jazeera Satellite Channel reported that the Israeli occupying authorities' development plan of the Patriarch's Pool for tourism purposes was nothing but preparation for seizing and Judaizing it.[125] In addition, the *al-Nahar Kuwaiti* newspaper disclosed that the municipality planned to erect Israeli settlement at the pool.[126] In its turn, the Israeli *All About Jerusalem* website referred the Patriarch's Pool to the ancient Jewish cultural heritage in East Jerusalem and pointed that Israeli authorities considered turning the Patriarch's Pool into a public park, playground or commercial centre after cleaning it.[127]

Consequently, the Israeli measures provoked the Waqf Department protest and the Coptic Church condemnation against the violation of their ownership rights of the Patriarch's Pool.[128] In this regard, the two institutions explained that the cleaning work was done without coordination with them and threatened to litigate the Israeli Municipality of Jerusalem, describing the Israeli action as a devious plan for seizing and owning the cultural heritage of the Patriarch's Pool.[129] More importantly, the two institutions agreed to rent out the Patriarch's Pool to al-Quds University in late 2012.[130] In turn, the university planned to safeguard and revitalize the Patriarch's Pool as a significant secular cultural heritage property for all mankind, believing that Israeli policies of politicizing and commodifying the pool curtailed previous local development initiatives at the pool. For this purpose, an assigned university team embarked on preparing a developmental plan for the pool for submitting it for approval to the Israeli Municipality of Jerusalem.[131] Yet, this Israeli municipality opted to calibrate the state of negligence at the Patriarch's Pool and relied on various modes of power to reproduce chaotic conditions and establish bare life for Palestinian Jerusalemites living and working next to it.

Calibrating the Israeli negligence

The calibration of the state of negligence at the Patriarch's Pool was achieved through the implementation of a combination of visible and invisible modes of power. It is important to mention that while these modes of power appeared on the surface as regulating conservation plans, they were actually intended to calibrate and perpetuate a state of negligence at the pool. To begin with, the Israeli authorities insisted on reproducing the Jewish name of the Patriarch's Pool – 'Hezekiah's Pool' – in governmental reports, official documents and correspondences at the expense of using the Islamic or Christian historical names of the pool. Indeed, such a policy intended to entrench Israeli ownership and assert the Jewish cultural heritage and historical narrative of the Patriarch's Pool.[132] Moreover, it appeared that the Israeli authorities have long racially discriminated against the Waqf Department's attempts to clean and maintain the pool. On the other hand, these authorities responded and cooperated with the Jewish group in its conserving and cleaning of the pool. In this context, the Israeli police restricted access of the Waqf Department workers to implement maintenance at the pool as well as bringing in raw construction materials under the pretense of security measures.[133] In an interview with a former Jordanian diplomat, it appeared that the Jordanian government allocated 150,000 Jordanian dinars for cleaning the pool and assigned this job to a company specialized in this field, but the Israelis failed to issue the required permission. According to him, the Israeli police ostensibly justified its rejection under the pretext of preventing the provocation of an ownership dispute over the Patriarch's Pool between the Waqf Department and the Coptic Church.[134]

Apparently, the Israeli authorities exploited the ownership dispute over the Patriarch's Pool between the Waqf Department and the Coptic Church to discipline the two local institutions and regulate their activities at the pool. In effect, these authorities aimed at provoking hostility and planting distrust between the two institutions to undermine potential future cooperation between them at the pool.[135] In this context, the Israeli Municipality of Jerusalem claimed that the cleaning of the pool was coordinated with the Coptic Church. This prompted the Waqf Department to hold the church responsible for losing ownership of the pool. In fact, the Israeli municipality threatened and pressured to get the church's approval.[136] Worse than this, the Israeli Municipality of Jerusalem sought to overburden budget of the Waqf Department by sending a voucher of about three million new Israeli shekels (almost one million US dollars), in exchange of its work at the pool and requested the department payment. It is important to mention that Israeli authorities justified these policies under the pretext of the two institutions' refusal of cooperation with it over the pool. [137]

Even after both sides overcame their internal dispute and agreed to rent out the Patriarch's Pool to al-Quds University, the Israeli occupying authorities continued to impose disciplinary regulations against the university to weaken its capacity to revitalize the pool. In this context, the IAA prevented the archaeological team of the university from executing renovation of the pool's entrance. After negotiation, the IAA conditioned the provision of permission with its supervision over the work and the university payment for this supervision. The IAA also constricted the digging to 10 centimetres below the surface of the floor. Even the Israeli Water and Drainage Company associated with Israeli police invaded the pool, intimidated the university workers and stopped the pumping of the collected rainwater in the pool to municipal sewage system, under the pretext that the university had not submitted a request to the Water Company. In a letter sent by its lawyer to the mayor of the Israeli Municipality of Jerusalem and the director of the Israeli Water Company, the university administration deplored these Israeli actions and clarified that it started pumping the water after coordination with the municipality.[138] In addition, the municipality and the Israeli Jerusalem Development Authority procrastinated approving the university's suggested development plan of the Patriarch's Pool until incorporating their perception into this plan. It appeared subsequently that the perception reflected a traditional Israelite treatment of the Patriarch's Pool, which imagined it as a ritual bath used by Jewish worshippers for purifying before ascending to the Temple Mount. Moreover, the approval of the plan was conditioned with designation of the Patriarch's Pool as public park that entailed its perpetual openness to the public and subordination of the pool to the INPA jurisdiction. Interestingly, the Israeli Municipality of Jerusalem relied on such designation to prevent the university from installing a door and employment of security guard at the pool's entrance. In fact, the municipality planned to weaken the university's sovereign control over the pool through the regulation of various initiatives and activities at the site.[139]

Moreover, the rejection of fixing the door at the entrance of the Patriarch's Pool also served another goal. It appeared that the entrance was utilized as a meeting point for drug dealers and alcoholics. In an interview with Palestinian Jerusalemites living at the Khan of the Copts, it appeared that they have long been complaining to the Israeli police about gathering of these criminals at the pool's entrance, mainly during the night. One resident said, 'we felt unsecured and got worried about our kids and families . . . the Israeli police came couple of times and arrested some of these criminal[s], but many of them shortly came back. We haven't felt the imposition of rigorous and deterring measures by the police, as they do in other places'.¹⁴⁰ Through ineffective dealing with the residents' complaints, the Israeli police meant to regulate Palestinian Jerusalemite public, mainly those living and working next to the Patriarch's Pool. In this context, the Israeli police sought to exacerbate feelings of disgust among these residents, hoping that this would push them to leave their homes at the Khan. It should be noted that the Israeli Municipality of Jerusalem on its turn had long prohibited connecting sewage pipes of Palestinian Jerusalemite homes in the Khan of the Copts to the municipal sewage network, not to mention neglecting the provision of appropriate municipal services, including garbage collection.¹⁴¹ This resulted in these Palestinians directing their sewage and throwing their garbage into the pool, exacerbating environmental and health conditions in and around it. Certainly, the municipality not only hoped that this would push these Jerusalemites to leave the area but also attempted to show their disinterest in preserving it. In this sense, the municipality did not bother to highlight the historical and cultural importance of the Patriarch's Pool, which resulted in a lack of attention of these Palestinians in preserving the cultural heritage of the pool.¹⁴²

Moreover, architects of the municipality refrained from disclosing future developmental plans and consulting their plans with these residents and shop-owners. In an unpublished social study, it appeared that the Palestinian Jerusalemite public regularly expressed both their interest in seeing such plans and a desire to have their say, albeit to no avail. Unsurprisingly, Israeli tourist guides condoned mentioning existence of Palestinian Christian and Muslim historical and cultural narrative about the Patriarch's Pool and only concentrated on highlighting the Israeli and Jewish narratives. In the same interview, Palestinian Jerusalemites living at the Khan of the Copts stated that 'Israeli guides who accompanied foreign and Israeli visitors and tourists tended to highlight Jewish heritage eras at the Pool, while condoned mentioning Islamic or Christian cultural history'.¹⁴³ Indeed, the news publishing about the ownership dispute and reciprocal accusations between the Waqf Department and the Coptic Church meant to regulate and plant distrust between Palestinian Jerusalemite public and the local institutions. Moreover, the recent news leakage about cooperation between the university and the Waqf Department on one hand and the Israeli occupying authorities from the other concerning development of the Patriarch's Pool also meant to provoke questioning about the significance of the Patriarch's Pool and the right of the public to claim its cultural heritage and historical narrative. Significantly, these were nothing but Israeli population techniques that tended to turn this public into Foucauldian docile and passive bodies, which led to a limited account of its identity and agency.

The state of PNA abandonment of the Patriarch's Pool

In the aftermath of the Oslo peace agreement, subordination of the Patriarch's Pool, among other secular cultural property in East Jerusalem, to the newly established PMOTA jurisdiction proved impractical and ineffective due to the Israeli objection against the ministry's functioning in the city. Accordingly, the ministry became incapable to directly control, supervise and manage developmental projects at the pool. Hence, the PMOTA showed reluctance in providing sufficient archaeological expertise and financial support and adequate development plans.[144] More importantly, dual ownership claim of the Patriarch's Pool between the Waqf Department and the Coptic Church further made the ministry lacking genuine political will and hesitant in specifying adequate public investment, effort and time to engage in supporting local conservation and revitalization initiatives of the pool.[145] In general, the ministry showed reluctance in seeing cultural properties flourishing without having exclusive management and control.[146] Hence, the PMOTA opted to govern by refraining from supporting the implementation of conservation and development initiatives, rendering efforts for developing the Patriarch's Pool scattered and uncoordinated between several local NGOs, the Palestinian private sector and various religious endowment institutions.[147] Under the pretext of restrictions of the Oslo peace agreement against its functioning in East Jerusalem, the PMOTA excluded the Patriarch's Pool, among other secular cultural property in the city, and situated it in state of abandonment, unlike secular cultural property in the cities of the West Bank and Gaza Strip.[148]

Accordingly, this state of abandonment resulted in suspending the legal status of the Patriarch's Pool as significant Palestinian secular cultural property in East Jerusalem. Indeed, the PMOTA employed the suspension to exempt itself from the protection and development of the cultural heritage of the pool, which created a vacuum with regard to proper responsibility. As such, this vacuum resulted in increasing competition between the Waqf Department and the Coptic Church for managing and supervising developmental programmes at the pool. More importantly, this competition wasted the time and resources of the two institutions and resulted in abandoning the pool and obstructing each other's cleaning and development initiatives, while also thwarting several local Palestinian Jerusalemite initiatives. This was manifested in 2003 when the Coptic Church refused to allow the Waqf Department to clean and maintain the Patriarch's Pool. In fact, the Coptic Church threatened to litigate the Waqf Department and requested immediate withdrawal of the Waqf working crew from the pool.[149] Significantly, the PMOTA capitalized on this competition and utilized it to remotely govern restoration and development initiatives at the Patriarch's Pool, while marginalizing local Palestinian Jerusalemite initiatives. This was manifested when the PMOTA coordinated privatizing and commoditizing the Patriarch's Pool with the Palestinian private sector in return for benefiting from its economic and touristic potentials.[150] Thus, in 2010, the PNA's intimately connected Palestinian Development and Investment Company (PADICO) proposed renting the pool to the Waqf Department for a long term. Other than indicating its commercial interests and construction capabilities, PADICO showed a lack of interest of the cultural heritage and historical significance of the Patriarch's Pool and failed to offer social and cultural sustainable development vision.[151] As a result, the Waqf Department and the Coptic Church sublimated over their ownership dispute and agreed to rent out the Patriarch's Pool to the al-Quds University.

Calibrating the state of abandonment of the Patriarch's Pool

The al-Quds University plan stemmed from the notion of rendering inoperative the double state of exclusion that prevailed over the Patriarch's Pool throughout the years post-Oslo. In this context, the university sought to revitalize the pool as a significant secular cultural heritage property for all mankind. In essence, the university attempted to neutralize the ownership dispute and the PNA politicization and commercialization objectives that resulted in curtailing local development initiatives of the pool.[152] However, the university's intervention did not bring any changes in the PMOTA attitudes towards safeguarding and revitalization of the Patriarch's Pool. In fact, the PMOTA contented to urge only for resisting Israeli restoration programmes and Jewish agendas concerned with the cultural heritage and historical narrative of secular cultural property in East Jerusalem, including the Patriarch's Pool. In this regard, the ministry expressed its incapacity to work under Israeli occupation and reluctantly offered viable sustainable development alternatives.[153] This was translated into the reluctance of supporting the implementation of the university revitalization plan at the Patriarch's Pool. Ironically, the PMOTA calibrated the dilapidated conditions at the Patriarch's Pool as a result of its abandonment policy, in order to serve the political interest of the PNA in exposing Israeli discrimination policies of the cultural heritage of the site and the city. To effectuate this calibration, the ministry embarked on employing a combination of visible and invisible modes of power that curtailed the university's revitalization plan of the Patriarch's Pool.

The PMOTA's modes of power

The first mode of power that the PMOTA employed to calibrate the deteriorated conditions at the Patriarch's Pool was exemplified through discrimination against incorporating the pool in the Palestinian and international laws and mechanisms concerned with the protection of cultural heritage in East Jerusalem. In this regard, there were many Palestinian Jerusalemite experts who questioned the ministry's reluctance in employing these legal mechanisms to protect and defend the cultural heritage of the Patriarch's Pool in the face of the Israeli unilateral and exclusionary plan.[154] While others contended that involving related international organizations and agencies would provide international legal protection mechanisms for the Patriarch's Pool and minimize Israeli restrictions against the implementation of the university's revitalization plan of the pool.[155] It is important to point out that UNESCO designated in 2006 the Patriarch's Pool as a significant cultural heritage site in East Jerusalem.[156] In this regard, the university thought that the employment of such designation would definitely define the legal status of the Patriarch's Pool as a significant secular cultural property for all mankind and facilitate the implementation of its plan at the pool.

However, the PMOTA preferred the suspension of the legal definition of the pool and showed reluctance in involving the UNESCO fearing diminishing sovereign claims in the site.¹⁵⁷ Interestingly, the suspension of the legal status of the Patriarch's Pool also affected the PMOTA provision of proper archaeological expertise and scientific intervention techniques for developing the pool. In this context, archaeological and architectural experts of the DACH at the PMOTA refrained from cooperating or offering archaeological expertise and scientific intervention techniques to the university's archaeologists and architects. In an interview, a Palestinian Jerusalemite archaeologist expressed his desperation concerning the passive role of PMOTA. According to him,

> when it comes to projects in East Jerusalem, they say no. This is psychological attitude . . . it is not the Israeli occupation issue, this is irresponsibility and lack of future vision, I do not understand anything and I cannot explain, . . . they content themselves with words and slogans . . . , the ministry did not cooperate with us never in projects, and there is no correct archaeological activity in Jerusalem . . . when we spoke with them about al-Birkeh, . . . the Department of Antiquities did not want to engage . . . that's it.¹⁵⁸

As for financial support, the PMOAT lacked the genuine political will to support the university's project at the Patriarch's Pool. Despite many Palestinian presidential and ministerial commitments to allocate adequate and proper financial and training resources, few financial amounts, if any, have been invested for conserving and revitalizing East Jerusalem's cultural heritage sites, including the Patriarch's Pool.¹⁵⁹ Even when the university managed to raise $1 million for revitalizing the Patriarch's Pool from the Palestinian Economic Council for Development And Reconstruction (PECDAR), the PMOTA failed in bailing out the university's project, taking into consideration that the allocated amount from the council was inadequate for such a huge project. In addition, this amount has been withdrawn following the leakage of the news in 2019. Interestingly, there were those who admitted the PMOTA failure in dealing with the city's secular cultural property as national priority and pointed out to huge Israeli financial allocations for investing in development and revitalization programmes, warning that this would pave the way for control over and seize these sites, including the Patriarch's Pool.¹⁶⁰ Moreover, the PMOTA ignored promoting the Patriarch's Pool, among other secular cultural property in East Jerusalem, nor in its official publications and related tourism itineraries or even on its website.¹⁶¹

Furthermore, the ministry failed in raising awareness of the Palestinian Jerusalemite public concerning the historical and cultural heritage of the Patriarch's Pool, let alone consulting them concerning the commoditizing of the development project at the pool. In this regard, many pointed out that supporting a developmental project at the Patriarch's Pool would have enhanced living conditions and opened employment opportunities for this public in tourism industry in the city. Hence, they concluded that the prevalent dispersion feeling, deterioration of living conditions and distrust towards the PMOTA attitude were apparent among those living next to the pool.¹⁶² According to conclusions of the social study conducted by the university's revitalization team, it was found that raising awareness of Palestinian Jerusalemites living and working next to the pool would have enhanced their behaviours towards safeguarding the pool, reaching to stop throwing their garbage into it. The study also found that local Palestinian Jerusalemites living and working next to the pool in the Coptic Khan and the nearby Christian Quarter Market were never consulted concerning the future of the site. According to a Palestinian Jerusalemite living in the Khan, many Palestinian organizations, companies and personalities visited the pool and prepared various developmental plans, but none participated, consulted or incorporated opinions and needs of the Khan residents within their plans.[163] In effect, the state of the PMOTA abandonment calibrated the deteriorated living conditions and lack of awareness of Palestinian Jerusalemite public, aiming to regulate and push them to behave according to its political will and economic plans. Consequently, this resulted in depriving Palestinian Jerusalemites the opportunity to claim and enjoy the cultural heritage and historical significance of the Patriarch's Pool.

Conclusion

In 2006, the World Heritage Committee of the UNESCO pointed out a double state of exception that prevailed at the Patriarch's Pool 'Birkat Hammam el-Batrak' throughout the years post-Oslo. In its report, the committee attributed the devastating physical condition of the pool stemming from Israeli administrative problems in obtaining necessary renovation permits and unforeseeable changes in security measures. In addition, the report mentioned the difficulty to get through the necessary building materials and workers, due to Israeli strict access regulations. Moreover, the report also pointed out to the Palestinian ownership dispute of the entrance to the pool between the Waqf Department and the Coptic Church, contending that this resulted in curtailing the cleaning of the pool and removal of serious health hazard. Finally, the committee report called for urgent need of action plan for safeguarding Jerusalem's Old City monuments, including the Patriarch's Pool as a significant cultural heritage site for all mankind.[164] Rather than permitting the al-Quds University initiative of safeguarding and revitalizing the Patriarch's Pool, the Israeli occupying authorities opted to calibrate the state of negligence to thwart this initiative, perpetuating the deteriorated conditions at the Patriarch's Pool.

In the same token, the absence of any role of the PMOTA in the UNESCO report confirmed the state of abandonment that the ministry adopted in distancing itself from intervening to solve ownership dispute of the Patriarch's Pool, between the Waqf Department and the Coptic Church, and subsequently in calibrating the abandonment to ignore supporting al-Quds University safeguarding and revitalization initiative of the pool. According to Said Ghazal, the loss of control over Jerusalem should not justify failure of the PMOTA in fulfilling its duties regarding secular cultural property in East Jerusalem.[165] It remains to be seen whether the news leakage in 2019 concerning the al-Quds University development plan of the Patriarch's Pool was also coordinated or not between the related Israeli and Palestinian authorities.

Conclusively, the Patriarch's Pool case study showed that the creation and reproduction of a zone of indistinction (state of exception) is the main function of political power seeking to retain control in a contested urban space. Accordingly, the contest between the Israeli and Palestinian governments to control built cultural heritage in East Jerusalem and own its historical narrative perpetuated the deterioration of the physical condition of the pool and deprived Palestinian Jerusalemites the right to claim and enjoy its cultural heritage.

Notes

1. A screen recording is available with the author.
2. Ibid.
3. Giorgio Agamben, *Homo Sacer: Sovereign Power and Bare Life*, trans. Daniel Heller-Rosen (Stanford: Stanford University Press, 1998).
4. Simon Mabon, 'The World Is a Garden: Nomos, Sovereignty, and the (Contested) Ordering of Life', *Review of International Studies*, Cambridge University Press 45, special issue no. 5 (2019): 870–90.
5. Albert Glock, 'Archeology as Cultural Survival: The Future of the Palestinian Past', *Journal of Palestine Studies*, University of California Press 23, no. 3 (Spring, 1994): 70–84.
6. Magdalena Pasikowska-Schnass, 'Cultural Heritage in EU Policies', *European Parliamentary Research Service*. Available online: https://www.europarl.europa.eu/RegData/etudes/BRIE/2018/621876/EPRS_BRI(2018)621876_EN.pdf. Visited 2020.
7. Kimberly Alderman, 'The Human Right to Cultural Property', *Michigan Journal of International Law* 32 (2011): 19. Available online: http://ssrn.com/abstract=1872707.
8. Helanie Silverman and Fairchild Ruggless, 'Cultural Heritage and Human Rights', in *Cultural Heritage and Human Rights*, ed. Helanie Silverman and Fairchild Ruggless (New York: Springer, 2007), 3–22.
9. Michael Dumper and Craig Larkin, 'The Politics of Heritage and the Limitations of International Agency in Divided Cities: The Role of UNESCO in Jerusalem's Old City', *Review of International Studies*, Cambridge Journals 38 (2012): 25–52. Available online: http://journals.cambridge.org/abstract_S026021051100026X.
10. Agamben, *Homo Sacer*.
11. Ibid., 19.
12. Ibid., 17.
13. Simon Mabon, 'Sovereignty, Bare Life and the Arab Uprisings', *Third World Quarterly*, Routledge, Francis and Taylor Group 38, no. 8 (2017): 1782–99. Available online: https://doi.org/10.1080/01436597.2017.1294483.
14. Agamben, *Homo Sacer*.
15. Mabon, 'The World', 876.
16. Agamben, *Homo Sacer*.
17. Dumper and Larkin, 'The Politics', 38.
18. E. W. G. Masterman, 'The Water Supply of Jerusalem: Ancient and Modern', *The Biblical World*, The University of Chicago Press 19, no. 2 (February 1902): 87–112.
19. One dunum equals 1,000 square metres.
20. Hani Nor Eldin and Ghassan Najajreh, 'بركة حمام البطرك/ البلدةالقديمة-القدس: دراسة أثرية', 'The Pool of the Patriarch's Bath in the Old City of East Jerusalem: Archaeological

Study', *Ya Quds*, al-Quds University Newsletter 1 (2016). Available online: https://dspace.alquds.edu/bitstream/handle/20.500.12213/1829/Ya%20Quds%20Issue1-Arabic.pdf?sequence=1&isAllowed=y.
21 David Gurevich, 'The Water Pools and the Pilgrimage to Jerusalem in the Late Second Temple Period', *Palestine Exploration Quarterly* 149, no. 2 (2017): 103–34.
22 Yousef, Natsheh, 'بركة حمام البطرك في البلدة القديمة لمدينة القدس دراسة تاريخية ورؤية مستقبلية',' The Patriarch's Pool in the Old City of Jerusalem: Historical Study and Future Vision. This study was prepared for the al-Quds University renovation project of the pool (2015). A copy is available with the author.
23 Mujeer Hanbali, الأنس الجليل بتاريخ القدس والخليل (Palestine: Dandis Library, 1999).
24 Adrain Boas, *Jerusalem in the Time of the Crusades: Society, Landscape and Art in the Holy City under Frankish Rule* (London; New York: Routledge, 2001).
25 Yeshou'a Frenkel, 'Political and Social Aspects of Islamic Religious Endowments ("awqāf"): Saladin in Cairo (1169–73) and Jerusalem (1187–93)', Cambridge University Press, *Bulletin of the School of Oriental and African Studies (SOAS)*, University of London 62, no. 1 (1999): 1–20.
26 Natsheh, 'The Patriarch's Pool', 2015.
27 Elena Corbett, *Competitive Archaeology in Jordan: Narrating Identity from the Ottoman to the Hashemites* (USA: University of Texas Press, 2015).
28 Simone Ricca, 'Heritage, Nationalism and the Shifting Symbolism of the Wailing Wall', *Archives de Sciences socials des Religions*, Open Edition Journals (2010): 169–88.
29 Nadia Abu El-Haj, 'Translating Truths: Nationalism, the Practice of Archaeology, and the Remaking of Past and Present in Contemporary Jerusalem', *Wiley on Behalf American Ethnologist* 25, no. 2 (1998): 166–88.
30 Dumper and Larkin, 'The Politics', 28.
31 Katharina Galor, *Finding Jerusalem: Archaeology between Science and Ideology* (USA: University of California Press, 2017).
32 Ricca, 'Heritage', 2010.
33 Wendy Pullan and Maximilian Gwiazda, 'Jerusalem's "City of David": The Politicization of Urban Heritage', in Conflict in Cities and the Contested State, *Jerusalem Quarterly 39*, Institute for Palestine Studies (2009): 61. Available online: https://oldwebsite.palestine-studies.org/sites/default/files/jq-articles/39_Pullan_City%20of%20David.pdf.
34 Ricca, 'Heritage', 171.
35 Pullan and Gwiazda, 'Jerusalem's City', 2009.
36 David Keane and Valentina Azarov, 'UNESCO, Palestine and Archaeology in Conflict', *Denver Journal of International Law and Policy 309* 41, no. 3 (2013).
37 Neil Silberman, 'If I Forget Thee, O Jerusalem: Archaeology, Religious Commemoration and Nationalism in a Disputed City, 1801–2001', *Nations and Nationalism*, Ename Center for Public Archaeology 7, no. 4 (2001): 487–504.
38 Ricca, 'Heritage', 175.
39 Agamben, *Homo Sacer*, 19.
40 Ricca, 'Heritage', 177.
41 Galor, *Finding Jerusalem*, 35.
42 Ricca, 'Heritage', 180.
43 Galor, *Finding Jerusalem*, 43.
44 Menachem Klein, 'East Jerusalem Freed', 2010. Available online: https://www.limesonline.com/en/east-jerusalem-freed?refresh_ce.

45 Abu El-Haj, 'Translating Truths', 169.
46 Dumper and Larkin, 'The Politics', 37.
47 Ibid., 39.
48 Nazmi Jubeh, 'Cultural Heritage in Palestine: RIWAQ New Experience and Approaches', 2009. Available online: https://www.jerusalemsverein.de/downloads/Texte/Cultural_Heritage_in_Palestine.pdf.
49 Galor, *Finding Jerusalem*, 2017.
50 Menachem Klein, 'Jerusalem as an Israeli Problem: A Review of Forty Years of Israeli Rule over Arab Jerusalem', *Israel Studies*, Indiana University Press 14, no. 2 (2008): 54–72.
51 Adnan Abu Odeh, 'The Ownership of Jerusalem: A Jordanian View', in *Jerusalem Today: What Future for the Peace Process?* ed. Ghada Karmi (UK: Ithaca Press, Garnet Publishing Limited, 1996).
52 Galor, *Finding Jerusalem*, 2017.
53 Dumper and Larkin, 'The Politics', 2011.
54 Welfare Association, 'Jerusalem: Heritage and Life. The Old City Revitalization Plan', Prepared by the Technical Office Old City of Jerusalem Revitalization Programme, (2004). Available online: http://ocjrp.welfareassociation.org/sites/default/files/publications/20121203_englishjrevplanj.pdf
55 Galor, *Finding Jerusalem*, 2017.
56 Chiara De-Cesari, 'World Heritage and Mosaic Universalism: A View from Palestine', *Journal of Social Archaeology* 10, no. 3 (2010): 299–324. Available online: https://doi.org/10.1177/1469605310378336.
57 Lapidoth, 'The Historic Basin – Its Main Problems', in *The Historic Basin of Jerusalem: Problems and Possible Solutions*, ed. Amnon Ramon (The Jerusalem Institute for Israel Studies, series no. 408: The Hay Elyachar House, 2010).
58 Galor, *Finding Jerusalem*, 2017.
59 Nazmi Jubeh, 'Archaeological Excavations in Jerusalem since 1967: From Making the Biblical Narrative to Settlement Activity', *Madar Israeli Affairs 73*, Archeology and Ideology (2019).
60 Pullan and Gwiazda, 'Jerusalem's City', 2009.
61 Raphael Greenberg, 'Extreme Exposure: Archaeology in Jerusalem 1967–2007', *Conservation and Management of Archeological sites* 11, no. 3–4 (W.S. Maney & Son Ltd, 2009): 262–81.
62 Dumper and Larkin, 'The Politics', 2011.
63 Ibid., 2009.
64 Ricca, 'Heritage', 2010.
65 Agamben, *Homo Sacer*, 1998.
66 Galor, *Finding Jerusalem*, 2017.
67 Ibid., 2017.
68 Lapidoth, 'The Historic Basin', 2010.
69 Emek Shaveh, 'Archaeological Activities in Politically Sensitive Areas in Jerusalem's Historic Basin', 2014. Available online: http://alt-arch.org/en/wp-content/uploads/2015/09/Meuchad-Peilut-Eng-01.pdf.
70 Greenberg, 'Extreme Exposure', 2009.
71 Wendy Pullan, Mximilian Stenberg, Lefkos Kyriacou, Carig Larkin and Michael Dumper, 'Sacred Space' in Modern Times: Jerusalem Paradoxes', in *The Struggle for Jerusalem's Holy Places* (New York: Routledge, 2013), 37.
72 Silberman, 'If I Forget Thee', 2001.

73 Galor, *Finding Jerusalem*, 2017.
74 Welfare, 'Jerusalem: Heritage and Life', 2004.
75 Galor, *Finding Jerusalem*, 2017.
76 Khaldun Bshara, 'Jerusalem: Heritage Preservation of the Holiest, the Fairest and the Wretched', Paper presented in Preserving the Cultural and Religious Character of Jerusalem in International Conference on the Question of Jerusalem (2019).
77 Greenberg, 'Extreme Exposure', 2009.
78 Welfare, 'Jerusalem: Heritage and Life', 2004.
79 Jihad Awad, 'تجربة الحفاظ على التراث المعماري في فلسطين', *Journal of Science and Technology*, Architecture Engineering Dept 13, no. 1 (Yemen: University of Science and Technology, 2008).
80 Greenberg, 'Extreme Exposure', 2009.
81 Galor, *Finding Jerusalem*, 2017.
82 Hamadan Taha, 'السياحة في القدس المحتلة', Tourism in Occupied Jerusalem, (2013). Available online: https://www.academia.edu/22182472/السياحة_في_القدس_المحتلة.
83 Welfare, 'Jerusalem: Heritage and Life', 2004.
84 Jubeh, 'Archaeological Excavations', 2019.
85 Welfare, 'Jerusalem: Heritage and Life', 2004.
86 Ibid.
87 Evan Taylor, 'Alternate Routes: Interpretive Trails, Resistance, and the View from East Jerusalem', *Journal of Community Archaeology and Heritage* 2, no. 2 (2015): 106–20 (Routledge, Taylor &Francis Group, 2015).
88 Silberman, 'If I forget thee, O Jerusalem', 2001.
89 Jubeh, 'Cultural Heritage in Palestine', 2009.
90 Galor, *Finding Jerusalem*, 2017.
91 Jubeh, 'Cultural Heritage in Palestine', 2009.
92 Dumper and Larkin, 'The Politics', 2011.
93 De-Cesari, 'World Heritage', 2010.
94 Jubeh, 'Cultural Heritage in Palestine', 2009.
95 Galor, *Finding Jerusalem*, 2017.
96 Ibid.
97 Chiara De-Cesari, 'Heritage between Resistance and Government in Palestine', *International Journal of Middle East Studies* 49, Special issue 4 (Cambridge Core: Cambridge University Press, 2017): 747–51.
98 De Cesari, 'Heritage between Resistance', 2017.
99 Ibid.
100 Ibid.
101 Suad Ghazal, 'حماية الممتلكات الثقافية في القدس في ظل القانون الدولي', Protecting Cultural Property in Jerusalem in the Wake of International Law, unpublished Master dissertation (Nablus: An-Najaf University, 2013). Available online: https://scholar.najah.edu/sites/default/files/سعاد%20غزال.pdf.
102 De-Cesari, 'World Heritage', 2010.
103 De-Cesari, 'Heritage between Resistance', 2017.
104 Taha, 'Tourism', 2013.
105 Maryvelma O'Neil, 'One Giant House: Civil Society Mobilization and the Protection of Palestinian Cultural Heritage and Identity in Al-Quds Al-Sharif', *Journal of Holy Land and Palestine Studies* 17, no. 1 (Edinburgh: Edinburgh University Press, 2018): 87–113. Available online: https://www.euppublishing.com/doi/pdfplus/10.3366/hlps.2018.0181.
106 Welfare, 'Jerusalem: Heritage and Life', 2004.

107 Paltrade Report, 'رؤية القطاع الخاص الفلسطيني حول الاقتصاد المقدسي: حوافز التصدير', Vision of Palestinian Private Sector with Regard to Jerusalemite Economy: Export Incentives (2010). Available online: https://www.paltrade.org/upload/multimedia/admin/2014/06/53a0193ced84e.pdf.

108 Galor, *Finding Jerusalem*, 2017.

109 Jon Seligman, 'The Place of Archaeology and Heritage in the Planning of Jerusalem, 1976–1991', in *Study of Jerusalem through the Ages*, ed. Y. Ben Arieh, et al. (2015). Available online: https://www.academia.edu/41952469/The_Place_of_Archaeology_and_Heritage_in_the_Planning_of_Jerusalem_-_1917-1976_בין_ארכיאולוגיה_ומורשת_בנייה_בתכנון_ירושלים.

110 'Restoration of the Pool of Hezekiah', Arieh Sharon, *Planning Jerusalem: The Old City and Its Environs 1968–1971*. Available online: https://www.ariehsharon.org/PlanningJerusalem.

111 Seligman, 'The Place of Archaeology', 2015.

112 Galor, *Finding Jerusalem*, 2017.

113 Taha, 'Tourisim', 2013.

114 Interview with local resident at the Coptic Khan in the Christian Quarter in the Old City of Jerusalem 2019.

115 Mohammad Maher, 'نافذة المنزل المطل على بركة السلطان في حارة النصارى', *al-Yaum Daily*, 13 December 2013. Available online: https://www.alyaum.com/a/863665.

116 Jonathan Harrington, 'Birket Hammam al-Batrak (Pool of the Bath of the Patriarch)', in *Al-Quds/Jerusalem 2015 Program* (Istanbul: Research Center for Islamic History, Art and Culture (IRCICA), 2008 report).

117 Natsheh, 'The Patriarch's Pool', 2015.

118 Welfare, 'Jerusalem: Heritage and Life', 2004.

119 Emek Shaveh, 'Archaeological Activities', 2015.

120 Nitza Tanner, 'Drawing Deep: Many Temple Period Pools of Water Necessary for Rituals Existed in the Old City: Many Can be Found Today', *The Jerusalem Post Daily*, 21 October 2005. Available online: https://www.jpost.com/Local-Israel/In-Jerusalem/Drawing-deep.

121 According to the biblical narrative, Hezekiah is a Jewish king who assumed the throne of Judah at the age of twenty-five and reigned for twenty-nine years (see 2 Kings 18:2, 2 Chronicles 29:1).

122 Emek Shaveh, 'Archaeological Activities', 2015.

123 'Pool of Hezekiah Conservation Project', *Historic Jerusalem*, 23 April 2009. Available online: s://jerusalemconservation.wordpress.com.

124 Interview with Palestinian Jerusalemite Historian in East Jerusalem, 2019.

125 Juman Abu Arfeh, "محاولات مقدسية لحماية بركة البطرك من التهويد", *al-Jazeera Online*, 12 December 2016. Available online: https://www.aljazeera.net/news/alquds/2016/12/18/محاولات-مقدسية-لحماية-بركة-البطرك-من.

126 'إسرائيل تخطط لتحويل «بركة حمام البطرك» في القدس إلى مستوطنة', *al-Nahar Daily*, 17 June 2011. Available online: http://www.annaharkw.com/annahar/Article.aspx?id=278182&date=17062011.

127 Ami Mitav, 'Hezekiah's Pool in the Christian Quarter – Thorough Cleaning for Centuries', in *All About Jerusalem*, 2018. Available online: http://allaboutjerusalem.com/he/article/בריכת-חזקיהו-ברובע-הנוצרי-ניקיון-יוסדי-מזה-מאות-שנים.

128 'A Historical Pool Inside the Old City May be the Cause of a Diplomatic Crisis between Israel and Jordan and Egypt', *al-Quds Daily*, 17 June 2011. p-1 and p-5.

Available online: http://192.116.4.13/PDF/Alquds%20News%20Paper/2011/Jun-2011/17%20Jun.2011.pdf.
129 Natsheh, 'The Patriarch's Pool', 2015.
130 A copy of the lease agreement is available with the author.
131 A copy of the university's development plan is available with the author.
132 Natsheh, 'The Patriarch's Pool', 2015.
133 The Waqf Department archive, letter sent to the Israeli police in Jerusalem complaining against these restrictions.
134 Interview in London 2019.
135 'Islamic and Christian Landmarks Are Transformed into Jewish Religious Sites and the Names of Arab Neighborhoods Are Converted into Hebrew Names', *al-Byader Online*, 15 July 2017. Available online: http://al-bayader.com/readarticle.aspx?articleid=18201.
136 Natsheh, 'The Patriarch's Pool', 2015.
137 Nir Hasson, 'King Hezekiah's Inheritance: A Cesspool of Political Garbage', *Ha'artez Daily*, 16 June 2011. Available online: https://www.haaretz.com/1.5022203.
138 Al-Quds University archives. A draft copy of the letter is available with the author.
139 Based on conversation with the author during his coordination of the pool project between 2012 and 2016.
140 Interview with local resident at the Coptic Khan in 2019.
141 'The Khan of the Copts: Housing Crisis Has Transformed Shoe Workshops in It into Shelter', *The Palestinian Information Center*, 14 February 2013. Available online: https://www.palinfo.com/64996.
142 Welfare, 'Jerusalem: Heritage', 2004.
143 Interview with resident at the Coptic Khan, Jerusalem, 2019.
144 Taha, 'Tourism', 2010.
145 Interview with senior officer at the 'Welfare Association' in East Jerusalem in 2019.
146 Abdelhamid Ali and Eman Amad, 'Historical Centers and Palestinian Cultural Identity', *Janistica* 41 (An-Najah University, 2005). Available online: https://staffold.najah.edu/sites/default/files/Historical_Centres_and_Palestinian_Cultural_Identity.pdf.
147 Welfare, 'Jerusalem: Heritage', 2004.
148 Ghazal, 'Protecting Cultural Property', 2013.
149 Natsheh, 'The Patriarch's Pool', 2015.
150 Paltrade, 'Vision', 2010.
151 Natsheh, 'The Patriarch's Pool', 2015.
152 Ibid.
153 Taha, 'Tourisim', 2013.
154 Interview with Palestinian Jerusalemite archaeologist in East Jerusalem in 2019.
155 Natsheh, 'The Patriarch's Pool', 2015.
156 UNESCO, 'State of Conservation: Old City of Jerusalem and Its Walls', 2006. Available online: https://whc.unesco.org/en/soc/1128.
157 Interview with senior officer at the Welfare Association in East Jerusalem, 2019.
158 Interview with Palestinian Jerusalemite archaeologist in East Jerusalem, 2019.
159 Paltrade, 'Vision', 2010.
160 Taha, 'Tourism', 2013.
161 Interview with senior officer at al-Quds University in Jerusalem, 2019.
162 Paltrade, 'Vision', 2010.

163 Social study conducted in preparation for the University's Pool Project is available with the author.
164 UNESCO, 'State of Conservation', 13.
165 Ghazal, 'Protection', 2013.

References

Abu Arfeh, Juman. 'محاولات مقدسية لحماية بركة البطرك من التهويد'. Available online: https://www.aljazeera.net/news/alquds/2016/12/18/محاولات-مقدسية-لحماية-بركة-البطرك-من (accessed 12 December 2016).

Abu El-Haj, Nadia. 'Translating Truths: Nationalism, the Practice of Archaeology, and the Remaking of Past and Present in Contemporary Jerusalem'. *Wiley on Behalf American Ethnologist* 25, no. 2 (1998): 166–88.

Abu Odeh, Adnan. 'The Ownership of Jerusalem: A Jordanian View'. In *Jerusalem Today: What Future for the Peace Process?* edited by Ghada Karmi, 59–65. Reading: Ithaca Press, Garnet Publishing Limited, 1996.

Agamben, Giorgio. *Homo Sacer: Sovereign Power and Bare Life*. Translated by Daniel Heller-Rosen. Stanford: Stanford University Press, 1998.

al-Byader Online. 'Islamic and Christian Landmarks Are Transformed into Jewish Religious Sites and the Names of Arab Neighborhoods Are Converted into Hebrew Names'. Available online: http://al-bayader.com/readarticle.aspx?articleid=18201 (accessed 15 July 2017).

Alderman, Kimberly. 'The Human Right to Cultural Property'. *Michigan Journal of International Law* 32 (2011): 19. Available online: http://ssrn.com/abstract=1872707.

Ali, Abdelhamid and Eman Amad. 'Historical Centers and Palestinian Cultural Identity'. *Janistica* 41 (2005). Available online: https://staffold.najah.edu/sites/default/files/Historical_Centres_and_Palestinian_Cultural_Identity.pdf.

al-Nahar Daily. 'إسرائيل تخطط لتحويل «بركة حمام البطرك» في القدس إلى مستوطنة'. Available online: http://www.annaharkw.com/annahar/Article.aspx?id=278182&date=17062011 (accessed 17 June 2011).

al-Quds Daily. 'A Historical Pool Inside the Old City May be the Cause of a Diplomatic Crisis between Israel and Jordan and Egypt'. p-1 and p-5. Available online: http://192.116.4.13/PDF/Alquds%20News%20Paper/2011/Jun-2011/17%20Jun.2011.pdf (accessed 17 June 2011).

Awad, Jihad. 'تجربة الحفاظ على التراث المعماري في فلسطين'. *Journal of Science and Technology* 13, no. 1 (2008): 18–42.

Boas, Adrain. *Jerusalem in the Time of the Crusades: Society, Landscape and Art in the Holy City under Frankish Rule*. London; New York: Routledge, 2001.

Bshara, Khaldun. 'Jerusalem: Heritage Preservation of the Holiest, the Fairest and the Wretched'. Paper presented in Preserving the Cultural and Religious Character of Jerusalem in International Conference on the Question of Jerusalem, 2019.

Corbett, Elena. *Competitive Archaeology in Jordan: Narrating Identity from the Ottoman to the Hashemites*. USA: University of Texas Press, 2015.

De-Cesari, Chiara. 'World Heritage and Mosaic Universalism: A View from Palestine'. *Journal of Social Archaeology* 10, no. 3 (2010): 299–324. Available online: https://doi.org/10.1177/1469605310378336.

De-Cesari, Chiara. 'Heritage between Resistance and Government in Palestine'. *International Journal of Middle East Studies* 49, no. 4 (2017): 747–51.

Dumper, Michael and Craig Larkin. 'The Politics of Heritage and the Limitations of International Agency in Divided Cities: The role of UNESCO in Jerusalem's Old City'. *Review of International Studies, Cambridge Journals* 38 (2012): 25–52. Available online: http://journals.cambridge.org/abstract_S026021051100026X.

Emek Shaveh. 'Archaeological Activities in Politically Sensitive Areas in Jerusalem's Historic Basin'. (2014). Available online: http://alt-arch.org/en/wp-content/uploads /2015/09/Meuchad-Peilut-Eng-01.pdf.

Frenkel, Yeshou'a. 'Political and Social Aspects of Islamic Religious Endowments ('awqāf'): Saladin in Cairo (1169–73) and Jerusalem (1187–93)'. *Cambridge University Press* 62, no. 1 (1999): 1–20.

Galor, Katharina. *Finding Jerusalem: Archaeology between Science and Ideology*. USA: University of California Press, 2017.

Ghazal, Suad. 'حماية الممتلكات الثقافية في القدس في ظل القانون الدولي'. Protecting Cultural Property in Jerusalem in the Wake of International Law, unpublished Master dissertation. Nablus: An-Najaf University, 2013. Available online: https://scholar.najah.edu/sites/ default/files/سعداد%20غزال.pdf.

Glock, Albert. 'Archeology as Cultural Survival: The Future of the Palestinian Past'. *Journal of Palestine Studies* 23, no. 3 (Spring 1994): 70–84.

Greenberg, Raphael. 'Extreme Exposure: Archaeology in Jerusalem 1967–2007'. *Conservation and Management of Archeological Sites* 11, no. 3–4 (2009): 262–81.

Gurevich, David. 'The Water Pools and the Pilgrimage to Jerusalem in the Late Second Temple Period'. *Palestine Exploration Quarterly* 149, no. 2 (2017): 103–34.

Hanbali, Mujeer. الأنس الجليل بتاريخ القدس والخليل *Al-Ons al-Jalil in the History of Jerusalem and Hebron*. Palestine: Dandis Library, 1999.

Harrington, Jonathan. 'Birket Hammam al-Batrak (Pool of the Bath of the Patriarch)'. In *Al-Quds/Jerusalem 2015 Program*. Istanbul: Research Center for Islamic History, Art and Culture (IRCICA), 2008 report.

Hasson, Nir. 'King Hezekiah's Inheritance: A Cesspool of Political Garbage'. *Ha'artez Daily*, 16 June 2011. Available online: https://www.haaretz.com/1.5022203.

Historic Jerusalem. 'Pool of Hezekiah Conservation Project'. 23 April 2009. Available online: https://jerusalemconservation.wordpress.com.

Jubeh, Nazmi. 'Cultural Heritage in Palestine: RIWAQ New Experience and Approaches'. 2009. Available online: https://www.jerusalemsverein.de/downloads/Texte/Cultural _Heritage_in_Palestine.pdf.

Jubeh, Nazmi. 'Archaeological Excavations in Jerusalem since 1967: From Making the Biblical Narrative to Settlement Activity'. *Madar Israeli Affairs* 73 (2019): 52–67.

Keane, David and Valentina Azarov. 'UNESCO, Palestine and Archaeology in Conflict'. *Denver Journal of International Law and Policy, 309* 41, no. 3 (2013): 1–37.

Klein, Menachem. 'East Jerusalem Freed'. 2010. Available online: https://www.limesonline .com/en/east-jerusalem-freed?refresh_ce.

Klein, Menachem. 'Jerusalem as an Israeli Problem: A Review of Forty Years of Israeli Rule over Arab Jerusalem'. *Israel Studies* 14, no. 2 (2008): 54–72.

Lapidoth, Ruth. 'The Historic Basin – Its Main Problems'. In *The Historic Basin of Jerusalem: Problems and Possible Solutions*, edited by Amnon Ramon. The Jerusalem Institute for Israel Studies, series no. 408: The Hay Elyachar House, 2010.

Mabon, Simon. 'The World Is a Garden: Nomos, Sovereignty, and the (Contested) Ordering of Life'. *Review of International Studies* 45, no. 5 (2019): 870–90.

Mabon, Simon. 'Sovereignty, Bare Life and the Arab Uprisings'. *Third World Quarterly* 38, no. 8 (2017): 1782–99. Available online: https://doi.org/10.1080/01436597.2017 .1294483.

Maher, Mohammad. 'من نافذة المنزل المطل على بركة السلطان في حارة النصارى'. *al-Yaum Daily*, 13 December 2013. Available online: https://www.alyaum.com/a/863665.

Masterman, E. W. G. 'The Water Supply of Jerusalem: Ancient and Modern'. *The Biblical World* 19, no. 2 (February 1902): 87–112.

Mitav, Ami. 'Hezekiah's Pool in the Christian Quarter – Thorough Cleaning for Centuries'. In *All About Jerusalem*, 2018. Available online: http://allaboutjerusalem.com/he/article/ברִיכת-חזקיהו-ברובע-הנוצרי-ניקיון-יוסדי-מזה-מאות-שנים.

Natsheh, Yousef. 'بركة حمام البطرك في البلدة القديمة لمدينة القدس، دراسة تاريخية ورؤية مستقبلية [The Patriarch's Pool in the Old City of Jerusalem: Historical Study and Future Vision]'. This study was prepared for the al-Quds University renovation project of the pool (2015). A copy is available with the author.

Nor Eldin, Hani and Ghassan Najajreh. 'بركة حمام البطرك/ البلدةالقديمة-القدس: دراسة أثرية [The Pool of the Patriarch's Bath in the Old City of East Jerusalem: Archaeological Study]'. *Ya Quds, al-Quds University Newsletter* 1 (2016). Available online: https://dspace.alquds.edu/bitstream/handle/20.500.12213/1829/Ya%20Quds%20Issue1-Arabic.pdf?sequence=1&isAllowed=y.

Nitza Tanner. 'Drawing Deep: Many Temple Period Pools of Water Necessary for Rituals Existed in the Old City; Many Can be Found Today'. *The Jerusalem Post Daily*, 21 October 2005. Available online: https://www.jpost.com/Local-Israel/In-Jerusalem/Drawing-deep.

O'Neil, Maryvelma. 'One Giant House: Civil Society Mobilization and the Protection of Palestinian Cultural Heritage and Identity in Al-Quds Al-Sharif'. *Journal of Holy Land and Palestine Studies* 17, no. 1 (2018): 87–113. Available online: https://www.euppublishing.com/doi/pdfplus/10.3366/hlps.2018.0181.

Paltrade Report. 'رؤية القطاع الخاص الفلسطيني حول الاقتصاد المقدسي: حوافز التصدير'. Vision of Palestinian Private Sector with regard to Jerusalemite Economy: Export Incentives, 2010. Available online: https://www.paltrade.org/upload/multimedia/admin/2014/06/53a0193ced84e.pdf.

Pasikowska-Schnass, Magdalena. 'Cultural Heritage in EU Policies'. European Parliamentary Research Service. Available online: https://www.europarl.europa.eu/RegData/etudes/BRIE/2018/621876/EPRS_BRI(2018)621876_EN.pdf. Visited 2020.

Pullan, Wendy and Maximilian Gwiazda. 'Jerusalem's 'City of David': The Politicization of Urban Heritage'. In *Conflict in Cities and the Contested State, Jerusalem Quarterly* 39 (2009): 61. Available online: https://oldwebsite.palestine-studies.org/sites/default/files/jq-articles/39_Pullan_City%20of%20David.pdf.

Pullan, Wendy, Maximilian Stenberg, Lefkos Kyriacou, Carig Larkin and Michael Dumper. 'Sacred Space in Modern Times: Jerusalem Paradoxes'. In *The Struggle for Jerusalem's Holy Places*, 27–47. New York: Routledge, 2013.

Ricca, Simone. 'Heritage, Nationalism and the Shifting Symbolism of the Wailing Wall'. *Archives de Sciences socials des Religions* 151 (2010): 169–88.

Seligman, Jon. 'The Place of Archaeology and Heritage in the Planning of Jerusalem, 1976–1991'. *Study of Jerusalem through the Ages* (2015). Available online: https://www.academia.edu/41952469/The_Place_of_Archaeology_and_Heritage_in_the_Planning_of_Jerusalem_-_1917-1976_בין_ארכיאולוגיה_ומורשת_בנייה_בתכנון_ירושלים.

Sharon, Arieh. 'Restoration of the Pool of Hezekiah Planning Jerusalem: The Old City and Its Environs 1968–1971'. Available online: https://www.ariehsharon.org/PlanningJerusalem.

Silberman, Neil, 'If I Forget Thee, O Jerusalem: Archaeology, Religious Commemoration and Nationalism in a Disputed City, 1801–2001'. *Nations and Nationalism* 7, no. 4 (2001): 487–504.

Silverman, Helanie and Fairchild Ruggless. 'Cultural Heritage and Human Rights'. In *Cultural Heritage and Human Rights*, edited by Helanie Silverman and Fairchild Ruggless, 3–22. New York: Springer, 2007.

Taha, Hamadan. "السياحة في القدس المحتلة". *Tourism in Occupied Jerusalem*, 2013. Available online: https://www.academia.edu/22182472/السياحة_في_القدس_المحتلة.

Taylor, Evan 'Alternate Routes: Interpretive Trails, Resistance, and the View from East Jerusalem'. *Journal of Community Archaeology and Heritage* 2, no. 2 (2015): 106–20.

The Palestinian Information Center. 'The Khan of the Copts: Housing Crisis Has Transformed Shoe Workshops in It into Shelter'. 14 February 2013. Available online: https://www.palinfo.com/64996.

UNESCO. 'State of Conservation: Old City of Jerusalem and Its Walls'. 2006. Available online: https://whc.unesco.org/en/soc/1128.

Welfare Association. 'Jerusalem: Heritage and Life. The Old City Revitalization Plan'. Prepared by the Technical Office Old City of Jerusalem Revitalization Programme, 2004. Available online: http://ocjrp.welfareassociation.org/sites/default/files/publications/20121203_englishjrevplanj.pdf.

Chapter 9

BIOPOLITICS, DESTITUENT RESISTANCE AND POWER-SHARING IN POST-WAR LEBANON

John Nagle

Introduction

Lebanon's post-civil war power-sharing system (1990–) enshrines a 'covenant of coexistence' by creating a balance of power between the state's powerful sects across political and public institutions. Rather than expediting a transformation of Lebanon's sectarian cleavages, Lebanon's power-sharing has developed ossified properties rendering it practically resistant to any reform. Lebanese power-sharing has become an invasive species, increasingly inveigling itself into every 'nook and cranny' of state and society relations in the post-war era.[1]

Attempts to reform power-sharing are resisted by the sect elites – the so-called *zu'ma* – many of whom are former warlords now reinvented as political luminaries that conspire to carve up state institutions between each other while simultaneously proclaiming to act as steadfast defenders of their communities.[2] These figures invest power-sharing with almost magical qualities that make it appear essential to the maintenance of civil peace. Any attempt to change power-sharing is repelled by elites on the basis that they are the sole guarantors of *istiqrar* ('stability').[3] Thus, attempts to pass legislation for gender equality was opposed in 2015 by the minister of foreign affairs,[4] who cited sectarian demographic anxieties – what he called the need to 'save Lebanon's land' – that supposedly undergird power-sharing. When thousands of citizens took to the streets of Beirut in 2015 to demonstrate against corruption and declining public services, a sect leader accused the protesters of attempting 'to topple what is left of the institutions and the government, which would shake and endanger stability and civil peace'.[5]

These discourses, harnessed by sectarian elites to proclaim that they are protecting power-sharing and peace, are ill-disguised rhetorical flourishes designed to obscure the extent to which these figures have captured and expropriated economic and political institutions as 'bastions of privilege', especially via the extractive power of corruption. Rhetoric and acts to securitize power-sharing are inextricably bound up with attempts to perpetuate regime survival. Yet, these are powerful discursive devices that are deployed to securitize issues and actors deemed to be threats to the objective survival of power-sharing and thus the existential status of the state. Thus, through securitizing power-sharing, any actor pushing for reform, even of a minimalist type, can be repelled, if required, through exceptional, extrajudicial means.

In this chapter I turn to the work of Giorgio Agamben to address two key aspects of Lebanon's post-war power-sharing order. First, I utilize Agamben's iteration of the biopolitical to explore how particular groups and issues are securitized as threats to power-sharing.[6] Second, while Agamben's biopolitics is critiqued for presenting a totalizing framework of power that permits minimal contestation, I draw attention to Agamben's concept of destituent power to illuminate the agency and resistance used by subjects to challenge their position within biopolitical systems.[7] To lend this chapter focus, I look at two issues: rights for victims and LGBTQ rights. Victims and LGBTQ rights indicate the intertwining of bodies, life and political security in Lebanon's post-war order.[8]

The biopolitics of bare life and plural sovereignty

At the heart of Agamben's work on the biopolitical is the power of the sovereign to make distinctions with regard to forms of life through a juridico-institutional power over death.[9] Agamben here overlaps with Mbembe's articulation of 'necropolitcs', in which to 'exercise sovereignty is to exercise control over mortality and to define life as the deployment and manifestation of power'.[10]

For Agamben, biopower is a product of modernity in which biological, 'natural reproductive life' (*bíos*) and life that is politicized (*zoé*) now increasingly coincide with the political realm to form a part of sovereign power.[11] It is in this 'zone of irreducible indistinction' – which blurs the boundaries between 'zoé' and 'bíos' – where the dividing line between citizen and outlaw, legality and illegality, law and violence and ultimately life and death strategically and at times fatally overlap. It is in this in-between space where the sovereign constitutes 'bare life', an expendable form of life that exists beyond political and legal representation.[12]

In evoking the concept 'bare life', Agamben is reminding us that there is no such thing as inalienable human rights or even a basic right to life. It is the sovereign who reserves the right to decide which form of life is productive for the body politic and which is deemed a threat to its survival. It is here where Agamben summons the ancient Roman figure of *homo sacer* as a symbol of how 'bare life' becomes a life without political value. *Homo sacer* was an individual completely unprotected and reduced to mere physical existence who may be killed with impunity since he or she had been given the status of outlaw from the juridical-political community. The figure of *homo sacer* is paradigmatic of contemporary political sovereignty because we are all virtually *homines sacri*, liable to be 'set apart' from others by law and placed in the ban.

We become *homo sacer*, reducible to bare life, when the state, through the suspension of law and the decree of a 'state of exception', turns on its own citizens and produces the outlaw, who is the 'living dead', figures who have life but can be expunged without recourse to rights. Emplaced in the state of exception, the individual is deprived of civil and human rights – such as habeas corpus and systems of legality. Originally intended as an emergency procedure, the state of exception has, Agamben argues, 'tend[ed] increasingly to appear as the dominant paradigm of government in contemporary politics'.[13]

Agamben's parsing of biopolitics, however, rests on a strong relationship between a unitary form of state sovereignty and its deployment of exceptional power. Indeed, the question of sovereignty provides one point of departure from Foucault's original articulation of biopower. In distinction to Foucault's biopower, which views power as dispersed assemblages of institutions, procedures, knowledges that lack unity (*dispostif*),[14] Agamben places sovereignty at the nucleus of biopolitics. While, for Foucault, power no longer asserts itself as a deduction, as a 'right of death', sovereignty, for Agamben, equates to power over death.[15]

This vision of a homogenous sovereign is problematic in relation to Lebanon. Rather than a unitary sovereign – defined as possessing exclusive authority and a monopoly over the legitimate use of violence – Lebanon is marked by 'plural' or 'hybrid' forms of sovereignty, in which 'localized forms of sovereignty' are 'nested' within 'higher sovereignties' but nevertheless 'retain a domain within which control over life and death is operational'.[16] Thus, the state of exception in Lebanon involves state and non-state actors, in which the Lebanese state enact rule through collaboration with non/quasi-state actors. For example, Hezbollah, the militia/political party, operates as a de facto state within Lebanon with its own army but yet also remains a leading actor within power-sharing governance. This complex mode of sovereignty is further intensified by the penetration of powerful external actors – particularly Iran, Syria and Saudi Arabia – into Lebanon, thus ensuring Lebanon is 'marked by a perpetual blurring of imagined boundaries between the state and its outside'.[17]

Yet, while post-war Lebanon is characterized by plural sovereigns, each reserving the right to exercise power over death, it is the power-sharing system where sovereignty congeals into something that resembles a singular form. In other words, the various elites who act as sect and political leaders uniformly see their interests as secured by power-sharing and thus use exceptional means to protect the system under the pretence that they are the guardians of peace and security. The biopolitical and the state of exception thus correspond to each other through power-sharing to determine which forms of life are marginalized. I now turn to two issues – victims and LGBTQ rights – in order to examine the potentiality and limitations of biopolitical and destituent processes in post-war Lebanon.

Victims and the cult of amnesia

Lebanon's civil war (1975–90) ended with an estimated 170,000 deaths and a million injured. Although the civil war was never simply sectarian in nature, the violence increasingly took on a sectarian character, including assassinations, massacres and revenge killings. During the war, thousands of civilians were kidnapped or abducted, often for purely sectarian reasons by the respective militias, and their bodies have never been recovered. A police report from 1991 stated that 17,415 persons were missing, a figure subsequently revised downwards.[18]

The issue of the 'disappeared' provided a litmus test for whether Lebanon's post-war order could build accountability and intercommunal trust needed to sustain reconciliation. Yet, rather than recognize the status of the disappeared and victims, the post-war order has been founded on political amnesia. This quintessential peace versus justice trade-off in post-war societies demands that the immediate exigencies of state-building take precedence over the individual needs of victims in relation to justice.[19] In short, to secure the compliance of former warlords with the new peaceful order, these figures are granted amnesty from prosecution or even from assuming any responsibility in recognizing victims.

Instead of providing mechanisms for recognizing the rights of victims or any mechanism for dealing with the legacy of the conflict, the sectarian elites embedded political amnesia into the fabric of the peace process. The post-war political elites had a vested interest in promoting forgetting. Many of them were leading sectarian warlords responsible for the atrocities carried out during the civil war, and they subsequently used their peacetime political offices to silence investigations and formal inquiries into the war. Recognizing that they would be first to be prosecuted, in 1991 the warlords used parliament to pass a general amnesty law (Law 84), which on a selective basis pardoned political crimes committed during the civil war and which also made no mention of victims. In addition, approximately 8,000 militia fighters were integrated into the security forces and the public administration. The then Lebanese president justified the amnesty law as a necessary condition for peace.[20]

This amnesia in relation to victims and the legacy of the civil war can be understood as the product of the post-war power-sharing institutions. The conflict officially ended with the 1989 Taef Agreement, which failed to mention victims or any mechanism for dealing with the legacy of the war. 'The Lebanese state and society', Jaquemet argues, 'have favored amnesia over truth seeking.'[21] This culture of social forgetting about the civil war was shaped by the resumption of power-sharing. The motto of power-sharing – 'no victor, no vanquished' – meant that none of the groups should be held accountable for the violence and duly punished. As one activist for victims explained, the law 'erected amnesia to a state religion':

> When you know very well that all of the big projects undertaken in this country were just strengthening the rule of those former warlords who whitewashed their records. You cannot tell me that with these people who promoted the religion of amnesia you can really build peace.[22]

As part of 'clean slate' ideologies designed to protect sectarian elites from accountability, the state closes any attempt to locate and retrieve the bodies of the disappeared.[23] One leading representative of a victims' organization explained in detail how Lebanon's political elites actively work to deny any possibility of gaining justice or even knowledge of the whereabouts of the disappeared on the basis that it would undermine the civil peace: 'they are all saying that it is not the right time, that there are political instabilities, security issues and it's one of the problems because it is a way to close the file.'[24]

To return to Agamben's reading of the biopolitical. For Agamben, rather than situated at the margins of the political order, 'life exposed to death (bare life or sacred life) is the originary political element'.[25] Sovereign power is exercised by banning bare life 'from the realm of law and politics [. . .] whenever and wherever the law is suspended'.[26] This power over life represents the power to expunge certain forms of life from the political community. This expression of biopower was evident during the civil war, when state and non-state actors killed thousands of people, justified as legitimate action and exceptional means to defend their respective communities. Yet, the 'disappeared' are beyond 'bare life'; they have already been violently erased from the body politic. However, these 'dead bodies' are securitized in the post-war era – the dead continue to 'speak' from the grave, they are unsettling ghostly figures who haunt the present by threatening the authority of the sectarian elite. Biopower is thus not only the power over life; it is the power to deny the dead even exist, a power to ensure that the dead remain in their graves, devoid of agential power. Such killing without punishment thus leads to deaths that are 'not honoured, mourned or memorialised'.[27]

Making sure that victims and the disappeared remain as objects of 'bare life' is central to the post-war political order. Maintaining the disappeared as 'dead', and by disavowing their relatives and wider society from claims to justice, the sectarian elite are able to exercise control. Moreover, it may be argued that by proscribing the basic needs of justice in the aftermath of violence, the sectarian elite purposely allowed a post-war society to emerge based on a lack of accountability and trust, features that have buttressed sectarian division. Indeed, the sectarian elite have used the precedence of the amnesty law as an opportunity to protect themselves from any form of accountability. In 2019, the Lebanese government sought parliamentary approval for a blanket amnesty law to pardon public officials accused of embezzlement, corruption and misuse of public office.

Sex against the order of nature

Article 534 of Lebanon's Penal Code, which criminalizes 'sex against the order of nature', is directed at the LGBTQ population, and it carries a maximum one-year jail sentence. Lebanon's LGBTQ population are further penalized under several additional articles related to morality. In this environment a major LGBTQ movement emerged in Lebanon to challenge their status and demand rights. The first and most notable activist group is Helem, which is the first 'above-ground LGBT organization in the MENA region'.[28]

In post-war Lebanon, LGBTQ rights activism and the wider LGBTQ population have been securitized by the various arms of the state. This has various dimensions and varying degrees of coercive power. The Ministry of Interior refused to formally recognize LGBTQ advocacy groups as civil society organizations.[29] The categorization of sexuality as a security issue is evident in the fact that General Security, which is the intelligence branch of the security forces charged with protecting national security, has raided LGBTQ events and arrested participants on the basis of 'protecting society from imported vices' that 'disrupt the security and stability of society'.[30] Suspects arrested under various articles associated with homosexuality can be subjected to torture, and confession under torture is permissible as evidence in court for prosecutions advanced under Article 534. Activists and human rights groups have noted a rise in activities by state actors to harass activists and LGBTQ people. In 2018 alone, activists monitored thirty-five arrests and trials, a significant rise over a five-year period.[31] Beirut Pride was shut down in 2018 after the main organizer was arrested and detained in a police cell by the vice squad. A human rights worker and activist noted, 'the more visible LGBT rights become to the fore in the political discourse the more backlash we are receiving'.[32]

LGBTQ rights and activists are essentially securitized in post-war Lebanon: discursively rendered into objects that the state frames as existential threats to the nation, thereby legitimately necessitating violent regulation. A central discourse to legitimate the backlash is that homosexuality is a Western import designed to destroy Lebanon and that local activists are native informants complicit with imperialism. Helem, for example, has been accused of receiving funds from the US State Department. Hassan Nasrallah, a leading Lebanese politician, accused Western countries of 'exporting' homosexuality to Lebanon and that 'Homosexual relations defy logic, human nature and the human mind'.

The securitization of same-sex relations and non-normative gender has a clear biopolitical dimension. Biopolitics articulates a biological conceptualization of citizenship; in its very essence it is a question of control over the body. Differences between bodies to create a politically defined community forms the originary basis for social exclusion through the operation of the state of exception. Agamben's biopolitical conceptual framework, which works with a particular biological conception of legal citizenship, inevitably and logically proceeds to the reproductive body as a key political referent. Thus, Agamben summarizes, by 'placing biological life at the center of its calculations, the modern State [. . .] does nothing other than bring to light the secret tie uniting power and bare life'.[33] In this way, because LGBTQ populations are deemed to threaten the survival of the nation, they are rendered into pollutants to the healthy body politic that, in turn, legitimate the extrajudicial processes to ensure their removal. Indeed, 'exceptions may be enacted as a claim about inhumanity'[34] – individuals are not just given 'bare', biological life, but they are non-biological or inhuman persons to which the juridical order does not apply.

Opposition to LGBTQ rights in Lebanon is profoundly embedded in power-sharing politics. In particular, the campaign of intimidation against activists and the LGBTQ population is a key instrument of the state pursuing a broader strategy to crack down on human rights and activism as part of regime survival. A human rights worker and LGBTQ activist explained:

> There is a crackdown on organising in general, freedoms of assembly, freedoms of association, freedoms of expression. The crackdown on LGBT rights specifically

is escalating and that's because it is easily weaponized as a political strategy to maintain the nation state and whatever idea of the Lebanese nation that people may have by saying that LGBT rights are against our morals.[35]

In this sense, limiting general freedoms within the exception 'institutionalizes fear of the enemy as the constitutive principle for society'.[36] Exceptional measures conjure up a sense of national threat to unite the nation, reinforcing the particular self, and delegitimizing and dehumanizing the other by reducing the alien to 'bare life'. Thus, rather than seek to eliminate LGBTQ populations, resistant states engage in an 'incitement to discourse' – the use of public discourse about sexual minorities to legitimate forms of coercive power.

This process of targeting LGBTQ rights as a security threat as part of a wider attempt to close down the space of wider civil society movements was exposed during the Thawra protests, which erupted across Lebanon in October 2019. The Thawra ('uprising'), which began as a series of daily demonstrations against corruption and the looting of public funds, quickly drew in hundreds of thousands of Lebanese across the state. Protesters were noted for transcending sect and class divisions, and they demanded 'to bring down the sectarian regime' and to rid political institutions of the warlord sectarian elites. LGBTQ activists were able to find space within the broad networks that participated in the Thawra. Yet, while LGBTQ activism provides only one dimension of the Thawra protests, it has been seized upon by elites to dismiss the movement. One elite termed the Thawra as 'a sodomy revolution' and claimed that the goal of some protesters was to phase out sectarianism so that they could pass laws supporting homosexuality. Local TV producer Charbel Khalil warned Lebanon:

If this revolution is successful, and they implement non-sectarian laws, they'll pass laws related to their homosexuality. We know what they think. Your homosexualities and your demons will not pass.[37]

Destituent resistance

How can groups and individuals challenge their status within biopolitical configurations. Agamben's description of biopolitics has been critiqued for 'his lack of attention and space for resistance and agency'. For those individuals categorized by the sovereign as *homo sacer*, there is no possibility for the re-articulation of politics. Agamben has attempted to address this absence of agency and resistance through the framework of what he calls 'destituent power'.

Destituent power differs from those expressions of resistance, which violently oppose and seek to replace the sovereign with a new 'constitutive order'. The constitutive form of resistance is ultimately reincorporated back into the sovereign's logic of power, especially by the sovereign framing such acts as illegalities that require an intensification of the exception. The security state, argues Agamben, constitutes the 'katechon' – an immunatory political rationality in which each attempt to overthrow its order further justifies its existence.[38]

Destituent resistance does not aim to overthrow and replace existing structures of governance; it is instead 'a force that, in its very constitution, deactivates the governmental machine'.[39] Destituent resistance is the type of activities that make governmental apparatuses ineffective and inoperative by evading the regulatory grasp of authority; it is nullifying and rendering powerless the practices and techniques mobilized by sovereign power. Destituent resistance opens up new ways of turning techniques of government so that they are unable to efficiently execute what they were originally aimed to do. Through the deployment of destituent power, social movements not only ensure that dysfunctionality is caused to the 'system', but they aim to be in some way ungovernable.

Destituent resistance is not a purely reactive force but instead is creative – not in the sense of producing new institutions to replace the old 'but through its deactivation of the legal order',[40] which inaugurates a new reality. The acts of rendering governmental power inoperative are achieved by seizing those forms of life that these apparatuses try to marginalize, exclude and erase. Agamben argues that 'the capacity to deactivate something and render it inoperative – a power, a function, a human operation – without simply destroying it but by liberating the potentials that have remained inactive in it in order to allow a different use of them'.[41] Destituent power thus hints at the possibility of escaping what has been seen as the totalizing power of the exception. Yet, questions remain to the extent that it allows those individuals and groups rendered into 'bare life' are able to resist and challenge their status. These issues of the biopower and destituent resistance can be explored by returning to victims and LGBTQ rights.

The living dead

As detailed earlier, Lebanon's power-sharing elite have enacted amnesty laws to shield them from accountability for war crimes and from opening investigations into the disappeared. In response, victims' groups – often composed of family members of the disappeared – have organized to challenge the state and to demand justice. These demands have often been expressed via the politics of visibility – taking to the street to unmask the tyranny of the state, especially through provocative actions designed to entice the state to react with violence against the families of the disappeared, an act which will then illuminate to wider society and the international community the moral bankruptcy of the political elite. An evocative part of their protests is the so-called mothers of the disappeared, usually quite elderly women who are at the front line of demonstrations. These women are willingly corralled into confronting the security forces guarding government and state buildings. A leading activist explained:

> We blocked the road outside the parliament as far as I remember seven or eight times. Attacking the parliament took place two times. We attacked the government building four times. The ladies lay on the road putting on chains

and things like that. They link each other with chains to remind people of the chains of the disappeared. We had a demonstration outside the parliament where we brought pictures and banners. We clashed with the security there and we had a meeting and then we stormed the Presidential Palace with the families and the civilians that came with us, and we stormed the palace and I got to parliament. So we got there and we entered the parliament. It was number one news on the night news.[42]

Yet, to return to Agamben, the protest tactics used by victims' groups represents a form of constitutive power, an attempt to overthrow or contest the power of the sovereign. Such resistance only reaffirms the power of the security state to apply the state of exception. Agamben indicates the ineffectuality of constitutive forms of resistance, noting that 'a power that has only been knocked down with a constituent violence will resurge in another form . . . between the violence that puts the juridical in place and the violence that preserves it'.[43] Rather than forging important policy changes, protest activities generated coercive responses from the state. In April 2004, the security forces attacked 500 protesters for victims with water cannon after they gathered in the city centre to submit a petition to the UN, and then in 2006 security forces arrested and interrogated members of the movement. The capacity and willingness of victims' movements to advance protest politics have declined in line with the families' and activists' scepticism that the state is willing to address the issue of the disappeared.

While the politics of visibility and unmasking ultimately generates constitutive power, can Lebanon's victims' movements deploy 'destituent power', the ability to deactivate the effects of power so that it is inoperable in terms of enforcing 'bare life'? One way in which movements evoke destituent power is through resisting any attempt by the state to classify the disappeared as officially dead. For Agamben, those defined as *homo sacer* and assigned bare life are the 'living dead', in the threshold between life and death. In Lebanon, many of the leading activists for victims refuse to accept that their relatives are dead, a position that obstructs the state's efforts to elide their complicity in sectarian murder.

On 25 May 1995, Law 434 was introduced by the Lebanese state, which provided 'principles for declaring the missing dead'.[44] Under the auspices of Law 434, any person missing for at least four years was legally classified as deceased, and the families were permitted to undertake legal procedures to record their deaths and even claim limited financial compensation. By categorizing 'the disappeared' as legally dead, the political elites hoped to completely close down any form of state-led investigation into finding the truth about those responsible for the crimes let alone attempting to retrieve the bodies. The families of the victims refused to acquiesce with Law 434.

The refusal of victims' groups to accept the disappeared are officially dead is not only a process of deactivating and making governance inoperable; it is a form of destituent resistance that liberates those potentials that have remained inactive in biopolitical order to allow a different use of them. Agamben argues that destituent resistance must be 'the rediscovery of a form-of-life' that political life cannot cancel.⁴⁵ Thus, through maintaining the status of the disappeared as the 'living dead', destituent resistance opens 'a space of political contingency in which new and autonomous practices, discourses and relations might emerge'.⁴⁶ Through retaining the status of 'disappeared' rather than 'dead' for the missing, they maintain that the Lebanese political class and indeed wider society urgently needs to confront the legacy of the civil war and that maintaining a form of social silence keeps the wounds of history open.

'What kind of relationship can be considered contrary to nature'?

While acts of direct resistance can always be included in the sovereign's logic of control – turned into security threats, illegalities and unauthorized acts that need policing – what use might destituent resistance have in helping to understand LGBTQ activism? Agamben is vague when it comes to empirical examples of destituent resistance, but notably he provides the allegory of the Apostle Paul in the face of the law, where for Paul 'it is not a matter of destroying the law . . . but deactivating its action with respect to sin'.⁴⁷ This illustration is apt for destituent LGBTQ resistance. Activists contest and contradict their categorical status as 'bare life', as sinful people, as 'unnatural' without eradicating the law.

Same-sex relations are criminalized because, according to the state, it is 'sex against the order of nature'. The destituent activism of the LGBTQ movement thus challenges the notion of 'nature' that sustains criminalization. The deployment of destituent resistance to challenge the status of LGBTQ people as unnatural is most powerfully articulated through legal activism. This legal activism is not directly intended to achieve de jure decriminalization; the aim is to make 534 inoperative by ensuring that prosecutions under 534 cannot be applied. Activists have used their connections within Lebanon's legal profession to form working relationships with lawyers and judges, specifically in connection to dealing with cases prosecuted under 534. Helem, for example, has its own legal activist team that have developed models for legal professionals to use to protect the rights of LGBTQ activists arrested, tortured and prosecuted by the security forces. These models have been disseminated by activists to legal professionals through various fora, including workshops.

On at least six occasions since 2009, judges have decided to throw out cases brought forward by the state under 534 on the basis that the concept of nature sustaining it has no legal grounding. In the first court case in 2009, the presiding judge explained to the court that the 'law did not define the specific meaning of nature or had adopted an accepted criterion confirming to what extent the reason is contradicting nature and its laws'.⁴⁸ The judge challenged the idea that nature is fixed and unchanging, existing somehow external to social forces: 'the violation of nature is linked with the thinking and mood of a society and its traditions and its capacity to accept the new norms of nature that are not yet usual.'⁴⁹ The judge concluded his ruling: 'consensual same-sex relations are not "unnatural" and therefore shouldn't be subjected to legal penalty.'⁵⁰

In another case in 2014, the presiding judge also challenged the idea of 'nature' to protect the rights of a transperson. The transperson was arrested after the police received reports that the defendant was taking part 'in acts of sodomy and group sex'. In rejecting the case put forward by the prosecution, the judge stressed that Article 534 does not clearly specify 'unnatural' in a way that is fit for legal purpose. In his final ruling the judge went further by stating that the transwoman had not broken the law since she was not in a same-sex relationship, since the 'external appearance, disposition, and psychological state of the defendant, all of which overwhelmingly indicate a female character', sexual relationships with a woman 'would be, in the view of the court, an act "more contrary" to nature than his/her engaging in sexual relations with men'.[51] Summing up, the judge announced: 'Gender identity is not only defined by the legal papers, the evolution of the person and his/her perception of his/her gender should be taken into consideration.' The ruling thus opened the way for judges to protect trans* people from prosecution under Article 534.

In a third case in 2016, the security forces arrested a Syrian refugee, because according to the police report, he 'had been wearing women's clothing, given his feminine leanings since childhood' and that he 'had been having sex with men'.[52] In his ruling the judge argued that what constitutes our understanding of human nature is often determined by socio-legal and political factors that are constantly in flux. Definitions of nature, stated the judge, should

> include multiple meanings, according to which lens is used to interpret it, particularly when it comes to human relationships – which are constantly changing, subject to the development of concepts, customs, and beliefs, and are not necessarily connected to religious or social principles.[53]

For this reason, the judge continued, it was not possible to declare that homosexuality is an aberration of nature or a product of psychological illness.

In sum, these court rulings add up to a situation in which it is now difficult for state prosecutors to successfully win cases brought forward on the basis of Article 534. This now also applies to military as well as civilian courts. In a landmark ruling in .... 2019 a military court acquitted four military personnel accused of sodomy charges. In explaining his ruling, the presiding judge said that 'sodomy is not punishable by law' as the country's penal code did not specify what 'kind of relationship can be considered contrary to nature'. The success of this legal activism is further evident by the fact that in 2018 the State Prosecution of Appeals refused to reverse a judge's decision to throw out a prosecution of Article 534. This meant that for the first time the higher courts had made a ruling in favour of LGBTQ rights and is likely to influence subsequent attempts at prosecution.

These rulings by judges not to sentence people on the basis that 'nature' has no legal grounding for determining crime represents the application of destituent power. These rulings have not led to decriminalization or any formal legislative change. At best, the destituent resistance deployed in this context deactivates and makes inoperable some aspects of the law in respect to sexuality. 'Destituent' resistance does not necessarily aim to replace existing structures of governance or even laws; it is instead 'a force that, in its very constitution, deactivates the governmental machine'.[54] Yet, precisely because destituent power lacks permanency, it achieves revocable and unstable forms of progress, imbued with inherently impermanent qualities. In a cat and mouse game, the homophobic state is often willing to adapt to the creative tactics of LGBTQ activists in order to severely constrict the space that activists can operate within. Thus, while activists have successfully worked with judges to ensure that Law 534 is rarely applied, the sectarian state has increased the number of arrests of people on charges related to morality.

Conclusion

In this chapter I have used conceptual travelling to apply the biopolitical to examine victims and LGBTQ rights within the context of power-sharing. Agamben places sovereignty at the nucleus of biopolitics, a unilateral, unaccountable, arbitrary and extra-legal form of power in which it is the sovereign who decides when the rule of law is suspended. This form of sovereignty does not apply to Lebanon; instead, it is a state characterized by plural and/or hybrid sovereignties, in which state and non-state, internal and external, actors form a multivalent domain of governance. Yet, this hybrid sovereignty comes together, though undoubtedly only weakly, through the 'allotment state', the power-sharing system which guarantees not only government positions for the powerful ethnoreligious leaders but also a high degree of communal autonomy over their own affairs.

Lebanon's sectarian power-sharing system, designed to create a balance of power between the state's main sects in order to maintain peaceful coexistence, has been used as a tool by political elites to exercise corruption, crony capitalism and clientelism to capture public resources and state institutions. In order to protect their interests, invested in power-sharing, Lebanon's political elites deploy exceptional power to securitize groups and issues that are framed as threats to the integrity of power-sharing and thus national security. The issue of the civil war 'disappeared' and LGBTQ rights, while representing very different issues, have thus been placed into biopolitical regimes of control and security to stymie human rights and justice. The issue of the disappeared and sexuality, I argue, require new ways to consider the biopolitical. Both the 'disappeared' and LGBTQ individuals are not simply accorded the status of 'bare life' in Lebanon; they are non-biological, inhuman or simply without any form of life at all.

Yet, rather than being trapped inside the iron cage of biopolitical systems of exceptional power, victims and LGBTQ activists challenge and contest their status as actors without agency. These actors do not do this by necessarily seeking to overthrow the power-sharing system. Violent resistance by those accorded bare life is ultimately reincorporated back into the sovereign's logic of power, especially by framing such acts as security threats that require an intensification of the state of apparatus. Thus, each attempt to dispute the security state further justifies its existence. For this reason, LGBTQ activists and victims' groups in Lebanon utilize 'destituent power', a mode of resistance concerned with making governance institutions deactivate and in relation to specific modalities of biopower, and with recuperating those forms of life that have been excluded and erased. While I recognize the potentiality of destituent power as resistance to biopolitics, I also recognize its limitations, contingencies and exposure to reversal when sovereign power strikes back. Any change wrought by destituent power is essentially revocable and subject to violent backlash from sovereign power. Destituent power may not effect lasting institutional or political change.

Notes

1. Bassel F. Salloukh, Rabie Barakat, Jinan S. al-Habbal, Lara W. Khattab and Shoghig Mikaelian, *The Politics of Sectarianism in Postwar Lebanon* (London: Pluto Press, 2015), 2.
2. Examples of warlords turned into post-war political leaders include Nabih Berri, Walid Jumblatt, Michel Aoun. Some other parties are led by the sons of warlords, such as Nadim Gemmayel and Tony Frangieh.
3. Carmen Geha, 'Resilience through Learning and Adaptation: Lebanon's Power-Sharing System and the Syrian Refugee Crisis', *Middle East Law and Governance* 11, no. 1 (2019).
4. Gebran Bassil.
5. The sect leader was Walid Jumblatt.
6. Giorgio Agamben, *Homo Sacer: Sovereign Power and Bare Life* (Stanford, CA: University Press, 1998);
    Giorgio Agamben, *State of Exception* (Chicago, IL: University of Chicago Press, 2005).
7. Giorgio Agamben, 'What Is a Destituent Power?' *Environment and Planning D: Society and Space* 32, no. 1 (2014); Giorgio Agamben, *The Use of Bodies* (Stanford, CA: Stanford University Press, 2016).
8. It is important to note the rich array of resistance against sectarian politics in contemporary Lebanon, including protests against corruption, dysfunctional governance and declining public services, as well as demands for gender equality, refugees and rights for kafala migrant workers.
9. Agamben, *Homo Sacer*.
10. Achille Mbembe, *Necropolitics* (Chapel Hill, NC: Duke University Press, 2019), 11.
11. Agamben argues that biopolitics and modernity are inextricably connected in the sense that which was originally excluded from politics as the exception law now become the norm, particularly within contemporary democracies.
12. See Simon Mabon, 'Sovereignty, Bare Life and the Arab Uprisings', *Third World Quarterly* 38, no. 8 (2017); Simon Mabon, *Houses Built on Sand: Violence, Sectarianism and Revolution in the Middle East* (Manchester: Manchester University Press, 2020).
13. Agamben, *Homo Sacer*, 6.
14. Michel Foucault, *The History of Sexuality*, vol. 1 (New York: Vintage Books, 1980); Michel Foucault, 'The Subject and Power', *Critical Inquiry* 8, no. 4 (1982).
15. Agamben's notion of the biopolitical strongly overlaps with the concept of 'securitization'. Securitization theory examines how specific public issues can be constructed by the state as existential threats to the nation thus requiring emergency,

defensive countermeasures. These emergency measures make use of 'extraordinary means', breaking the normal political rules of the game. Agamben's biopolitics, however, emphasizes how exceptional power, rather than extraordinary, has become the norm in contemporary politics. See Michael P. Murphy, 'The Securitization Audience in Theologico-Political Perspective: Giorgio Agamben, Doxological Acclamations, and Paraconsistent Logic', *International Relations* 34, no. 1 (2020).

16 Adam Ramadan and Sara Fregonese, 'Hybrid Sovereignty and the State of Exception in the Palestinian Refugee Camps in Lebanon', *Annals of the American Association of Geographers* 107, no. 4 (2017).

17 Najib B. Hourani, 'Lebanon: Hybrid Sovereignties and US Foreign Policy', *Middle East Policy* 20, no. 1 (2013): 17.

18 International Center for Transitional Justice, *Failing to Deal with the Past: What Cost to Lebanon?* (New York, NY: ICTJ, 2014), 15.

19 See Claire Moon, 'Healing Past Violence: Traumatic Assumptions and Therapeutic Interventions in War and Reconciliation', *Journal of Human Rights* 8, no. 1 (2009).

20 Émile Lahoud.

21 Iolanda Jaquemet, 'Fighting Amnesia: Ways to Uncover the Truth about Lebanon's Missing', *The International Journal of Transitional Justice* 3, no. 1 (2009): 69.

22 Interview with author, June 2015.

23 It should be acknowledged that this amnesia was encouraged by Syria, which had a self-appointed role as protector of Lebanon in the post-war era. As an authoritarian regime, the Syrian state had little interest in promoting transparency and accountability and instead pursued a policy of installing former warlords into government positions as a means of maintaining control over Lebanon. Thus, under Syrian tutelage, the state enforced a culture of silence about victims and the memory of the civil war, including a media censorship law (1994).

24 Interview with author, June 2015.

25 Agamben, *Homo Sacer*, 88.

26 Nick Vaughan-Williams, 'Borders, Territory, Law', *International Political Sociology* 2, no. 4 (2008): 333.

27 Patricia Owens, 'Reclaiming "Bare Life"?: Against Agamben on Refugees', *International Relations* 23, no. 4 (2009): 572.

28 Helem, 'HELEM: A Case Study of the First Legal, Above-Ground LGBT Organization in the MENA region'. Available online: https://www.moph.gov.lb/userfiles/files/Prevention/NationalAIDSControlProgram/Helem.pdf (2008).

29 John Nagle, 'Beyond Ethnic Entrenchment and Amelioration: An Analysis of Non-Sectarian Social Movements and Lebanon's Consociationalism', *Ethnic and Racial Studies* 41, no. 7 (2018).

30 Human Rights Watch, 'Lebanon: Security Forces Try to Close LGBT Conference', HRW, October 2018. www.hrw.org/news/2018/10/04/lebanon–security–forces–try–close–lgbt–conference (accessed June 2020).

31 Arab Foundation for Freedoms and Equality, *Activism and Resilience: LGBTQ Progress in the Middle East and North Africa* (New York, NY: Outright International, 2018).

32 Interview with author, September 2019.

33 Agamben, *Homo Sacer*, 6.

34 Rob. B. J. Walker, 'Lines of Insecurity: International, Imperial, Exceptional', *Security Dialogue* 37, no. 1 (2006): 76.

35 Interview with author, September 2019.

36 Claudia Aradau and Rens Van Munster, 'Exceptionalism and the "War on Terror": Criminology Meets International Relations', *The British Journal of Criminology* 49, no. 5 (2009): 689.
37 Mehr Nadeem, 'LGBTQ, Women's Rights Part of Uprising Conversation', *The Daily Star*, 14 November 2019. Available online: https://www.dailystar.com.lb/News/Lebanon-News/2019/Nov-14/495548-lgbtq-womens-rights-part-of-uprising-conversation.ashx (accessed 6 June 2020).
38 Agamben, *The Use of Bodies*, 266.
39 Agamben, 'What Is a Destituent Power?' 65.
40 Skye Bougsty-Marshall, 'Flooding Wall Street: Echoes from the Future of Resistance around Climate Change', *Capitalism Nature Socialism* 27, no. 3 (2016): 70.
41 Agamben, *Homo Sacer*, 1274.
42 Interview with author, June 2015.
43 Agamben, *The Use of Bodies*, 266.
44 International Center for Transitional Justice, *Failing to Deal with the Past*, 15.
45 Agamben, 'What Is a Destituent Power?'
46 Saul Newman, 'What Is an Insurrection? Destituent Power and Ontological Anarchy in Agamben and Stirner', *Political Studies* 65, no. 2 (2017): 288.
47 Agamben, *Homo Sacer*, 1274.
48 International Commission of Jurists, 'Article 534, Criminal Court of Al-Bitroun', *ICJ*, 2012. Available online: https://www.icj.org/wp-content/uploads/2012/07/In-Re-Article-534-Criminal-Court-of-Al-Bitroun-English.pdf (accessed 6 June).
49 Ibid.
50 Ibid.
51 Ibid.
52 Lama Karame, 'Lebanese Article 534 Struck Down: Homosexuality No Longer "Contrary to Nature"', *Legal Agenda*, 7 November 2016. Available online: https://legal-agenda.com/en/article.php?id=3149 (accessed 6 June).
53 Ibid.
54 Agamben, 'What Is a Destituent Power?' 65.

References

Agamben, Giorgio. *Homo Sacer: Sovereign Power and Bare Life*. Stanford, CA: Stanford University Press, 1998.
Agamben, Giorgio. *State of Exception*. Chicago, IL: University of Chicago Press, 2005.
Agamben, Giorgio. *The Use of Bodies*. Stanford, CA: Stanford University Press, 2016.
Agamben, Giorgio. 'What Is a Destituent Power?'. *Environment and Planning D: Society and Space* 32, no. 1 (2014): 65–74.
Arab Foundation for Freedoms and Equality. *Activism and Resilience: LGBTQ Progress in the Middle East and North Africa*. New York, NY: Outright International, 2018.
Aradau, Claudia and Rens Van Munster. 'Exceptionalism and the "War on Terror": Criminology Meets International Relations'. *The British Journal of Criminology* 49, no. 5 (2009): 686–9.
Bougsty-Marshall, Skye. 'Flooding Wall Street: Echoes from the Future of Resistance around Climate Change'. *Capitalism Nature Socialism* 27, no. 3 (2016): 64–82.
Foucault, Michel. *The History of Sexuality*, Vol. 1. New York: Vintage Books, 1980.
Foucault, Michel. 'The Subject and Power'. *Critical Inquiry* 8, no. 4 (1982): 777–95.

Geha, Carmen. 'Resilience through Learning and Adaptation: Lebanon's Power-Sharing System and the Syrian Refugee Crisis'. *Middle East Law and Governance* 11, no. 1 (2019): 65–90.

Helem. 'HELEM: A Case Study of the First Legal, Above-Ground LGBT Organization in the MENA Region'. 2008. Available online: https://www.moph.gov.lb/userfiles/files/Prevention/NationalAIDSControlProgram/Helem.pdf.

Hourani, Najib B. 'Lebanon: Hybrid Sovereignties and US Foreign Policy'. *Middle East Policy* 20, no. 1 (2013): 39–55.

Human Rights Watch. 'Lebanon: Security Forces Try to Close LGBT Conference'. *HRW*, October 2018. Available online: www.hrw.org/news/2018/10/04/lebanon–security–forces–try–close–lgbt–conference.

International Center for Transitional Justice. *Failing to Deal with the Past: What Cost to Lebanon?* New York, NY: ICTJ, 2014.

International Commission of Jurists. 'Article 534, Criminal Court of Al-Bitroun'. *ICJ*, 2014. Available online: https://www.icj.org/wp-content/uploads/2012/07/In-Re-Article-534-Criminal-Court-of-Al-Bitroun-English.pdf.

Jaquemet, Iolanda. 'Fighting Amnesia: Ways to Uncover the Truth about Lebanon's Missing'. *The International Journal of Transitional Justice* 3, no. 1 (2009): 69–90.

Mabon, Simon. 'Sovereignty, Bare Life and the Arab Uprisings'. *Third World Quarterly* 38, no. 8 (2017): 1782–99.

Mabon, Simon. *Houses Built on Sand: Violence, Sectarianism and Revolution in the Middle East*. Manchester: Manchester University Press, 2020.

Mbembe, Achille. *Necropolitics*. Chapel Hill, NC: Duke University Press, 2019.

Moon, Claire. 'Healing Past Violence: Traumatic Assumptions and Therapeutic Interventions in War and Reconciliation'. *Journal of Human Rights* 8, no. 1 (2009): 71–91

Murphy, Michael P. 'The Securitization Audience in Theologico-Political Perspective: Giorgio Agamben, Doxological Acclamations, and Paraconsistent Logic'. *International Relations* 34, no. 1 (2020): 7–83.

Nadeem, Mehr. 'LGBTQ, Women's Rights Part of Uprising Conversation'. *The Daily Star*, 14 November. Available online: https://www.dailystar.com.lb/News/Lebanon-News/2019/Nov-14/495548-lgbtq-womens-rights-part-of-uprising-conversation.ashx (accessed 6 June 2019).

Nagle, John. 'Beyond Ethnic Entrenchment and Amelioration: An Analysis of Non-Sectarian Social Movements and Lebanon's Consociationalism'. *Ethnic and Racial Studies* 41, no. 7 (2018): 1370–89.

Newman, Saul. 'What Is an Insurrection? Destituent Power and Ontological Anarchy in Agamben and Stirner'. *Political Studies* 65, no. 2 (2017): 284–99.

Owens, Patricia. 'Reclaiming "Bare Life"?: Against Agamben on Refugees'. *International Relations* 23, no. 4 (2009): 567–82.

Ramadan, Adam and Sara Fregonese. 'Hybrid Sovereignty and the State of Exception in the Palestinian Refugee Camps in Lebanon'. *Annals of the American Association of Geographers* 107, no. 4 (2017): 949–63.

Salloukh, Bassel F., Rabie Barakat, Jinan S. al-Habbal, Lara W. Khattab and Shoghig Mikaelian. *The Politics of Sectarianism in Postwar Lebanon*. London: Pluto Press, 2015.

Vaughan-Williams, Nick. 'Borders, Territory, Law'. *International Political Sociology* 2, no. 4 (2008): 322–38.

Walker, Ron B. 'Lines of Insecurity: International, Imperial, Exceptional'. *Security Dialogue* 37, no. 1 (2006): 65–82.

CONCLUDING OBSERVATIONS

In the early months of 2020, the outbreak of the Covid-19 pandemic posed existential challenges to rulers and ruled across the world. Across the Middle East this was no different, with rulers deploying a range of different strategies in an effort to thwart the spread of the pandemic. In some cases, this resulted in the declaration of states of emergency, while in others, technology was used as a means to 'track and trace' the virus, measuring its movement across the population. Central to these strategies were efforts to regulate life, stemming from the ability of the sovereign to both decide on the exception and deploy technologies of power in pursuit of health, safety and survival. It is here, once more, where the work of Giorgio Agamben finds traction.

With a body of work that draws from – and across – a range of disciplines, there is little doubt that the ideas presented by Giorgio Agamben across his canon of work pose serious intellectual challenges to those wishing to engage with it. In spite of this, as we have endeavoured to show, there is a great deal to be gained in using Agamben's ideas in the study of the Middle East, spanning disciplines including – but not limited to – Politics, International Relations, Criminology, Constitutional Law, Sociology, Political Geography, Islamic Studies and Philosophy.

As this volume has shown, there are a number of different ways in which Agamben's ideas about the nature of sovereign power and its impact on life can be used, from an exploration of constitutional processes to the regulation of space. Moreover, different aspects of Agamben's canon have the capacity to aid forensic analysis of the regulation of life across the region, from the Persian Gulf to the Levant. Yet this breadth of analysis also plays out across conceptual and thematic issues, facilitating reflection on the broader repercussions of the operation of sovereign power.

One of the main contributions of this volume is a reflection on the ways in which sovereign power operates within – and between – states and also the repercussions of these biopolitical operations for people and space across the Middle East. In doing this, the contributors reveal a complex set of interactions that take place within and across state borders, illustrating not only the multifaceted nature of sovereign power but also the permeability of political projects. Authors have demonstrated the importance of grounding the sovereign decision in time and space which operate as context-specific contingent factors, conditioning the type of decisions that can be taken.

Perhaps the most important observation made by contributors concerns the nature of sovereign power itself. Fundamentally, as Kalousian observes, the use of Agamben's ideas helps to identify the boundaries and foundations of law. While in cases that Agamben has explored sovereign power is singular and unitary, across the Middle East it is often contested, nestled or plural. Indeed, as Nagle, Szanto and Kumarasamy show, sovereign power in Lebanon and Iraq has been contested by different actors, revealing a different form of sovereign power in operation. Furthermore, as Strobl and Mabon, and Ruished show, sovereign power can also be nested, operating within the confines of another sovereign. In the case of the Gulf States, members of the GCC retain a form of sovereignty domestically yet the creation of a standing police force will leave this nestled and subservient.

Constitutional analysis is provided by Alsarghali and Ardovini, who explore the ways in which constitutional documents, basic laws and legal processes have been used as mechanisms of control under the context of states of exception. Yet as Strobl and Mabon observe, in using an Agambenian approach one is able to see the ways in which regional and local manifestations of sovereign power coalesce, with devastating implications for life.

There is of course a great deal more to be done when furthering our awareness of not only the ways in which Agamben's ideas help us to understand the Middle East but also the ways in which the Middle East helps us to better understand Agamben's work. During the Covid-19 pandemic when states of emergency replaced the rule of law, MENA region countries susceptible to such exceptional measures – many of which were ruled by an exception that became the norm – were at an increased risk, with the distinction between repression and protection becoming particularly blurred. In this vein, the location of sovereign power has been illuminated in the Middle Eastern context, seen in the cases of Lebanon, Palestine and across the Gulf, where competing sources of sovereign power interact in a complex way.

More is certainly needed on the form properties of states and the compatibility of ideas couched in Western, Judaeo-Christian thought in a non-Western and Islamic context. Moreover, Agamben's ideas broadly speak to democratic systems of government, where the suspension of the rule of law by the sovereign creates a new paradigm of government. Yet as we have sought to show, the cultivation of new paradigms of government through suspension of the norm can apply beyond these contexts. Indeed, in using Agamben's ideas, we are better able to identify and critically reflect on both the processes and the implications of such efforts, particularly with regard to the distinction between norm and exception. Additionally, what Middle Eastern cases have shown is that the process of the exception becoming the norm is not necessarily contingent upon a formal declaration of a state of emergency, but rather can be cultivated out of the residue of this derogation. The ways in which such processes develop are something that requires more detailed exploration. As, too, does the processes through which destituent power occurs, as Nagle explores in this collection, along with other forms of resistance as alluded to by Ruished.

Of course, the application of Agamben's ideas does not always fit neatly with our case study selection. As Sana Alsarghali shows, while the concept of the state of exception can shed light on the mechanisms of sovereign power, the Palestinian case raises questions about states of exception, emergency and necessity, put in the context of the Basic Law. Yet once more, the Palestinian case demonstrates the prevalence of emergency powers across the region which has seemingly become the norm.

What is abundantly clear, however, across the various cases explored in this collection is the devastating impact of the manipulation of sovereign power on agency in the Middle East. Although offering a bleak picture of the nature of sovereign power and political life across the region – the repercussions of which continue to be felt – there is a degree of hope. Although John Nagle documents the ways in which groups seek to challenge the status quo – using ideas of destituent power – the capacity for this is curtailed by the arrangement of sovereign power and its ability to regulate life across political projects. While some have criticized Agamben for a lack of focus on human agency, as Nagle demonstrates in this volume, there remains the capacity to escape bare life, to negate sovereign power and to reassert agency in the process. At a time when democracy is under increasing pressure and political life faces existential challenges, the ability to both reflect and act upon this is of paramount importance.

INDEX

agency xv, xvi, 13, 14, 16, 21, 27, 33, 41, 53, 54, 59, 61–3, 65, 67, 75–7, 79, 128, 131, 157, 187, 204, 209, 214, 221
amnesia 205, 206
Anfal 53, 60, 65
Arab xii, 55–8, 60, 61, 65–7, 100, 107, 127, 148, 172, 174, 179
Arab Spring 2, 27, 30, 32, 37, 38, 45, 57, 63, 95, 170
Arab Uprising 5, 6, 29, 31, 32, 37, 75, 76, 80–4, 88, 95, 170, 209
Arbaeen 54, 61
Arendt, Hannah 1, 121, 122, 145, 147
asabiyyah 6
authoritarian 14, 16, 27, 36, 75–7, 79, 80, 84–7, 98, 105, 109, 124
authoritarianism xii, 66, 75–81, 83–5, 86, 87, 105

Bahrain 5, 6, 29, 31, 32, 34–8, 41, 44, 46
the ban 7, 9–11, 98, 204
bare life xii, xv, xvi, 2–6, 9–14, 27, 28, 30, 31, 33, 35–7, 40, 41, 43, 45, 46, 54, 55, 58, 63, 65, 67, 76, 79, 81, 85, 87, 96, 98, 119–23, 128, 130, 131, 145–7, 150, 152–3, 156, 168–70, 183, 184, 204, 207–12, 214, 221
Barzani 56, 60, 63, 64
Bath 171, 184, 186
Ba'th 55, 61, 62, 148
Beirut xiii, 129, 154, 203, 208
Bekaa Valley 3, 119–21, 123–4, 126, 127, 129–31
biopolitics 7–9, 11–13, 119–22, 129, 131, 145, 150, 152, 203–5, 208, 209, 214, 215
border xiv, 1, 3, 12, 19, 31, 39, 42, 43, 45, 55–7, 64, 110, 119, 131–2, 152, 155, 156, 169, 219

border management 121, 125, 131
Bradley, Arthur 145–7

camp xiv, xv, xvi, 3, 6, 11–14, 21, 37, 45, 119, 120, 122, 123, 127, 128, 143, 144–5, 149–54
Christian Quarter 171, 191
citizenship xv, 32, 45, 59, 75, 81, 124, 144, 145, 147, 149, 208
colonialism 15
constitution 17, 18, 20, 21, 30, 32, 42, 66, 75–84, 86, 87, 95, 96–7, 99, 101, 103, 104, 106–8, 109–10, 210, 213, 219, 220
Coptic Church 183–8, 191
Coptic Khan 182, 191
counterterrorism 28, 29, 39, 85, 125
Covid 95, 110, 129, 219, 220
cultural heritage 167–70, 173–85, 187–92
cultural property 167–85, 187–8

Da'ish/ISIS 53, 54, 57–64, 125
dar al harb 19
dar al Islam 19
destituent power 4, 204, 209–11, 213–15, 220, 222
  resistance xiii, xiv, 14, 21, 54, 58, 63, 64, 67, 80, 105, 125, 203, 204, 209, 210–15, 220
displacement 119, 122, 128, 131

East Jerusalem 4, 167, 168, 170–84, 187, 189–92
Egypt xiii, xiv, xvi, xvii, 13, 62, 75–7, 79–80, 90, 95
Eman Salehi 5
emergency law xiii, 5, 76, 80, 82, 85, 86, 121
Emergency Regulation 2, 12, 80

Index

environmental insecurity   120, 122, 123, 126, 131
Erbil   57, 63–5
extrajudicial power   84, 85, 169
extreme weather   123, 131

freedom of assembly   81

general elections   xiii, 32, 42, 64, 66, 84, 85, 101–4, 106–9
Gülen Movement   61
Gulf Cooperation Council (GCC)   27, 29–32, 35–7–41, 43, 45

al-Haram al-Sharif/Temple Mount   172, 173, 176
Hashd al-Sha'abi   62, 63
Helem   207, 208, 212
Hezbollah   119, 121, 124, 125, 205
homo sacer   xii, xv, 1, 5, 7, 8, 11, 13, 121, 146, 149, 151, 153, 169, 204, 209, 211
Hussein, Saddam   55–7, 60–2, 65

Ibn Khaldun   6
INTERPOL   27, 28, 39–42, 44
Islam   16–19, 29, 54, 57, 59, 61, 78
Islamic   8, 16–19, 53, 57, 58, 64, 167, 174, 176, 179, 185, 187, 219, 220
Israel   3, 12, 18, 96, 99–102, 104, 105, 109, 110, 125, 127, 143, 144, 168, 174, 179
Israeli Antiquities Authority (IAA)   175, 183
Israeli government   167, 168, 170, 171, 173–5, 179, 181–3
Israeli Ministry of Religious Affairs   176
Israeli Municipality of Jerusalem   167, 173, 177, 178, 181, 182, 184–7
Israeli occupation   12, 105, 144, 171, 172, 174, 189, 190

Judaize   172, 181, 182, 184

Karbala   54, 55, 61
Kurdish   53–7, 59, 60–7

Law No. 162/1958   81

Lebanese Armed Forces (LAF)   119
Lebanon   xiv, xv, 3, 12–14, 57, 119–22, 131, 143, 144, 148, 203–15, 220

Middle Eastern Strategic Alliance (MESA)   39
Moroccan Quarter   172
Muslim Brotherhood   31, 81, 148, 157
Muslim Quarter   176

Naif Arab University for Security Services (NAUSS)   40
nakba   12
Naqshbandi   59, 60
necropolitics   53, 54, 56, 59, 61, 62

Öcalan, Abullah   61
Old City   167, 171–7, 184, 191
Oman   29, 31, 33, 36, 39, 44
Oslo Accords   99, 100, 109, 167, 168, 170, 174, 175, 177–9, 183, 187–9, 191

Palestine   3, 13, 14, 35, 95–9, 100–10, 174, 180, 220
Palestine Liberation Organization   xv, 174
Palestinian Basic Law   2
Palestinian Constitutional Court   107
Palestinian Ministry of Tourism and Antiquities (PMOTA)   178, 179–81, 187–91
Palestinian National Authority (PNA)   167, 168, 170, 174, 178, 179, 181, 183, 187–9
paradigm   xvi, 2, 3, 7, 9, 11, 12, 20, 78, 144–5, 148–51, 155, 157, 204, 205, 220
partial sovereignty   xv, 12, 13, 110
Patriarch's Pool   3, 167, 168, 171, 181–92
police training   27, 35–8, 40, 41, 80, 124
political space   xvi, 11, 75–7, 79, 82, 83, 85–7, 122, 154, 156
power sharing   3, 14, 101, 203–6, 208, 210, 211, 213, 214

Qadiri   59, 60
al-Quds University   167, 168, 171, 185, 186, 188, 189, 191
Quran   16–18

Referendum   54, 64–7, 86
refugee camps   xiv, xv, 12, 89, 119, 122, 123, 127, 128

Salafi Movement   29
Salah el-Din   171
Saleh, Yassin Al-Haj   145, 146–8, 150, 154–7
sectarian elites   203, 206, 209
sectarianization   28
Sharia   17
Shi'a discrimination   33
singularity   144, 147–9, 151, 157
al Sisi   75, 82, 83–6
Sistani, Ayatollah Ali   62
social movements   210
sovereignty   2, 3, 7, 8, 11–19, 28–31, 33, 38, 46, 54, 65, 67, 77–9, 81, 83, 96, 97, 99, 102, 103, 105, 108–10, 120, 122, 123, 149, 151, 169, 170, 177, 204, 205, 214, 220
spacio-cide   13
stasis   126
state building   79, 103, 105, 106, 109, 206, 210
state of emergency   2, 5–7, 9, 13, 18, 36, 45, 75, 76, 78, 80–7, 95, 98, 101–4, 106, 109, 110, 121, 155, 156, 220
state of exception   xii, xiii, xiv, xv, xvi, 1–3, 5–13, 15, 20, 21, 27, 28, 30–6, 38, 43, 45–6, 53, 54–5, 57–9, 61, 63–7, 75, 76–81, 83–7, 95–9, 100–3, 104–7, 108–10, 119, 121, 122–3, 149–50, 155–7, 168–70, 172, 175, 179, 183, 191–2, 204–5, 208, 211, 221
state of necessity   103, 106
Sufism   58–61
Sulaimani   57, 59–61, 64, 65
superfluous   145–7, 158
Surah   17
Syria   124–8, 130–2, 144–5, 148, 152–5, 157–8
Syrian refugees   119–22, 124, 126–32, 138

Taef Agreement   206
Talabani, Jalal   56, 57, 60, 64, 67
transnational policing   27, 28, 41–3, 46
travelling theory   2
tribalism   6

unbearable life   143, 145, 146–7, 149, 156–7
United Arab Emirates (UAE)   29, 31–7, 39, 44

victims   xvi, 3, 36, 204–7, 210, 211, 214
virtuality   145–7, 149, 152

Waqf Department   167, 171, 177, 179, 183–8, 191
Western Wall   176

Yezidi   54, 57–9, 63, 65

Zoroastrianism   54, 59, 61

www.ingramcontent.com/pod-product-compliance
Lightning Source LLC
Chambersburg PA
CBHW062148300426
44115CB00012BA/2046